Literacy and Paideia in Ancient Greece

LITERACY AND PAIDEIA IN ANCIENT GREECE

KEVIN ROBB

New York Oxford
OXFORD UNIVERSITY PRESS
1994

Oxford University Press

Oxford New York Toronto
Delhi Bombay Calcutta Madras Karachi
Kuala Lumpur Singapore Hong Kong Tokyo
Nairobi Dar es Salaam Cape Town
Melbourne Auckland Madrid

and associated companies in
Berlin Ibadan

Published by Oxford University Press, Inc.
200 Madison Avenue, New York, New York 10016

Library of Congress Cataloging-in-Publication Data
Robb, Kevin.
Literacy and paideia in ancient Greece / Kevin Robb.
p. cm.
Includes bibliographical references and index.
ISBN 0-19-505905-0
1. Greek language—Social aspects—Greece. 2. Education—Greece.
3. Literacy—Greece. I. Title.
PA227.R63 1994 302.2′244′0938—dc20 93-24618

9 8 7 6 5 4 3 2 1

Printed in the United States of America
on acid-free paper

In memory of
Eric Alfred Havelock

τοίην γὰρ καὶ γῆρυν ἀπέπνεεν ἐννέα Μουσῶν
ὁ *πρέσβευς καθαρῶν γευσάμενος λιβάδων*

Acknowledgments

An earlier version of parts of chapter 4 appeared in the *Monist* 74 (1991) and use of it is made by the kind permission of the editor of the *Monist* and the Hegeler Foundation. An earlier version of parts of chapter 7 appeared in G. Press (ed.), *Plato's Dialogues: New Studies and Interpretations* (1993) and use of it is made by the kind permission of the editor and Rowman and Littlefield Publishers, Inc.

By their admonitions and criticisms—and sometimes by silent forbearance—more colleagues and friends than I can name here have contributed to the completion of this book. They knew that writing of any sort is a lonely affair, and they were always there to help me through it, when I would let them. That is a priceless gift and I thank them for it.

A few names, stalwart souls, must be mentioned. I recall especially the support of Wallis Annenberg, Sean Burke, Michael Critelli, Norman Fertig, Paul Gabbert, Rob Gibson, John Hospers, John Jeffery, James Kjar, Susan Rybar Michaeli, William O'Keefe, Patrick Kevin O'Toole, William Power, Ron Remsberg, Pam Panasetti Stettner, Andrew Strenk, Scott Thompson, Joanne Beil Waugh, and the late Richard Alan Fletcher. Jo Kolsum, patient "language cop" on a tough beat, also read my chapters in early typescript and caught more infelicities than I care to remember.

An earlier but powerful impetus came from some conversations with Robert Brumbaugh, Fredrick Copleston, Paul Friedländer, Martin D'Arcy, Mitchell Dahood, Alex Haley, Werner Jaeger, Adam Parry, Gerald Press, Bruno Snell, Victorino Tejera, Holger Thesleff, Eric Turner, Dallas Willard, and from Istanbul days, Robert Hardy and James Baldwin. I recall them now with pleasure and gratitude. Without their stimulating words, perhaps the research that lies behind the book would not have been begun at all.

Eric Havelock, had he lived, would have given my manuscript a final reading which, once again, would have saved me from errors and oversights. It is appropriate that I dedicate this book to his memory.

My first editor at Oxford University Press, William Sisler, believed in the importance of the book and continued to support it when a less patient editor might have lost faith. Nancy Hoagland guided a long and complex manuscript through the many production stages with patience and professionalism. I am grateful to them both.

The National Endowment for the Humanities supported some early research on the Greek inscriptions that has found its way into these pages. More remote still, but warmly remembered, was support from the Thomas and Dorthy Leavey Foundation. More recently, the Albert and Elaine Borchard Foundation has lent generous support, helping to make the book possible. Its last chapter, and some final revisions, were undertaken in the rather splendid isolation of Château de la Bretesche, the Foundation's château in Brittany, for which I shall always be grateful.

Finally, no author who delves into as many areas of scholarship as I do here can be an expert in all of them, or even many of them. He knows all too well the difference between writing in his own narrow area of professional training, where he feels certain of every word, and trespassing in foreign disciplines. Errors, small and perhaps large, are inevitable, the price of reporting on important discoveries made in fields not one's own. I trust that those more knowledgeable than I will not hesitate to offer corrections, and I hope they will communicate them directly to me.

Hermosa Beach, California K.R.
October 1993

Contents

Literacy and Paideia in Ancient Greece

Introduction

Just a few decades ago, a book on a topic of early Greek orality and literacy may not have found a major publisher. The contrast with 1988, when my writing accelerated in earnest, is stark. A dozen major books, as well as more articles than can now be easily counted, had appeared in as many years, all dealing with orality and literacy in early Greece or with some of their ramifications. Thirty years earlier, in 1958, how many historians would have considered advancing literacy an important ingredient for understanding the origins and uniqueness of Hellenism, and one with instructive applications to our own time?

It is true that recovery of the oral dimension in archaic Greek life, which had begun to come to light with the publications of Milman Parry in the 1930s, was well under way by 1958. Parry's work, nearly all of it published between 1928 and 1938, was the first real impetus. Eric Havelock's *Preface to Plato,* published in 1963, was a milestone. Some insightful articles appeared in the 1950s, and, of course, A. B. Lord's *The Singer of Tales* was published in 1960. In the late 1950s, however, the terms "oral" and "illiterate" were still words in conflict with what most scholars meant by a great culture, which—especially for Hellenists—Greek civilization preeminently was.

European chauvinism may have played a role here, as did a lingering, nineteenth-century idealization of the Greco-Roman world. How could European Greeks have been illiterate when the high civilizations around them, mainly Semitic, had made some use of writing for centuries? A.J.A. Wace could not bring himself to believe that a people as clever as the Greeks could have once known writing (Bronze Age Linear B) and then have forgotten all knowledge of it, and he said so rather defiantly in his introduction to Ventris and Chadwick's monumental *Documents in Mycenaean Greek.* No one could hold Wace's view now, but some accepted it as only obvious when it was propounded in 1953. Even so, for many today the suggestion of a residual oralism in Hellas as late as the fourth century, or even the fifth, remains unacceptable, even repugnant. The reasons are not always related to the evidence.

A glance back at the reviews that greeted Havelock's book—many relentlessly negative, some uncomprehending, a few downright sputtering in their indignation—would afford a measure of how theories once viewed as shocking or eccentric at best have become respectable and rather tame.[1] Individual proposals for which Havelock was denounced in 1963 have today gained strong and eminently respectable defenders, however controversial his general thesis may have remained. For example, the restricted character of Greek literacy even later than the fifth century (on this point, out-Havelocking even Havelock) has recently been defended in a major book, *Ancient Literacy,* by William Harris of Columbia University, a careful, traditional historian. Reviews have been restrained when not laudatory. The profession has evidently concluded that the sun will, after all, rise tomorrow.

The unique character of the Greek alphabet and its superiority over all pre-Greek syllabic scripts (including the West Semitic scripts, also taken structurally as syllabaries) for creating a secular literature has been championed by Barry Powell of the University of Wisconsin in an important new book, *Homer and the Origin of the Greek Alphabet.* Powell has also defended the premise—a view adopted in this book—that, for the dating of the introduction of alphabetic writing into Greece, the epigraphical record must remain the primary evidence, requiring painstaking examination. No amount of a priori theory about what "must have been" should be permitted to overthrow what it tells us. Following Carpenter, who had reopened the whole question of dating the Greek alphabet in the 1930s, Havelock had vigorously argued for the same approach. In treating the Phoenician script as syllabic, Powell is mainly following the distinguished Semiticist, Ignace Gelb, as I also had done, starting in 1969. Havelock had read Gelb only after his own views had been formulated, and at that point welcomed a confirming assessment from one of the world's foremost scholars on Semitic languages and scripts.[2]

That all early Greek "literature" although no doubt created or preserved with the aid of the pen at least from Hesiod onward, was communicated to its intended audience exclusively in recitation or performance has been recently defended by Cole, Detienne, Gentili, Nagy, Segal, Svenbro, Russo, Tejera, Thalmann, Vernant, and many others. Archaic Greece was a culture of hearers, not habitual readers; that is now generally recognized. This oral dimension of early Greece had, of course, been detected long before Havelock—I call attention to the remarkable F. B. Jevons (1886) in a concluding chapter—but Havelock's strenuous reassertion of it in 1963, including his appeal to the unimpeachable evidence of Plato, was widely ridiculed and angrily denied by not a few of his critics. A chord very different from that struck by the reviewers of *Preface to Plato* was recently sounded by Marcel Detienne:

> For about the last fifteen years the dogma that Greek culture was a written one has been seriously threatened. The works of E. Havelock, which extend the surveys of M. Parry on productions of the epic and signs of orality, have demonstrated decisively that the Homeric epic could no longer be considered the last remaining islet of an ancient oral culture that since the end of the ninth century was submerged under a civilization recorded by writing. When Plato, at the beginning of the fourth century deals . . . with Homer, he incriminates not only a production consolidated into a book or a text written for philologists, but attacks also the founder of a *paideia.*[3]

Detienne observes that the dominant position for Homer in Hellenic paideia had been stubbornly preserved in some of the best nineteenth-century scholarship, although in this century what the ancient reports so clearly claimed for Homer (and his epical partners, notably Hesiod) had too often been ignored or dismissed. Poetry was too familiar as an aesthetic phenomenon; as habitual literates, we were too far removed from its functional, oral roles. But the "Homer" revered by all later Greeks down to Plato's day was, continues Detienne, "a cultural system more or less conceived as an encyclopaedia of collective knowledge, handed down by mouth and by ear, performed musically and memorized by means of rhythmic phrases." Finally, the memory of epical originals—in terms of both language and even of individual episodes—that dominates the consciousness of later composers and audiences alike has now been extensively documented, affecting notably our reading of the Presocratic philosophers. Xenophanes, Parmenides, Empedocles (all poets composing in the epic meter), and Heraclitus have received a number of treatments from this perspective, constituting something of a historical backlash to the analytical approaches so prominent in much British and American scholarship since the 1950s. From many possible examples I mention only one, Mitchell Miller's "Parmenides and the Disclosure of Being," which appeared in the philosophical journal *Apeiron,*

> The opening ten lines [of the Proem: B.1] are dominated by echoes of Homer . . . by this combination of Odyssean and Achillean motifs, Parmenides masterfully appropriates Homer to introduce his project: a far-ranging quest for knowledge which will do battle with the opinion of others.[4]

As Miller observes, the density and intricacy of epical allusions assume that the sixth-century audience in Elea knew versions of Homer's and Hesiod's poems intimately, "by heart," and that an author could effectively use this knowledge to communicate his reforming vision to them. This was equally true in the same century of Heraclitus' Ephesus, and Xenophanes' Colophon.[5] We shall discover that the same widely shared knowledge of epical verse and the ability to imitate some of it must lie behind the manufacture of the first "long" inscriptions in the eighth century, at the very inception of Greek literacy. The "Homer" they knew so well was, of course—in the sixth century as well as in the eighth—not epical verse as read, a rare phenomenon before Aristotle, but as it was heard, savored, and memorized.

These proposals were bold and bitterly resisted thirty years ago. When Havelock first tried to weave them into a comprehensive theory that explored how a sophisticated society had moved out from centuries of primary orality into the uncharted waters of literacy, he met a personal hostility that is uncommon even among classicists, who are professionally trained to respect facts and distrust theories not closely and demonstrably bound to them. Resistance from those who would reduce writing history to cataloging "the pins and the pans" could be expected, but hostility ran much deeper. Perhaps the proposals touched some exposed nerves that are no longer so sensitive. Another theory is that the vigor of Havelock's prose and the sweeping manner of his exposition were felt to be intemperate.

In those early, wintry years Havelock compounded a prophesy of a favorite and deliberate mix of metaphors, and he often repeated it: "Today we may be out on a lonely limb, but tomorrow we will be in the forefront of a stampede.'' It was intended, I suspect, as encouragement for a small band of mainly younger supporters who were about to learn what it can mean, in terms of professional survival or at least advancement to go up against an entrenched establishment opinion.

Havelock thought the reversal of scholarly fortunes would take a minimum of twenty years. Moreover, a younger generation of scholars would prove more tolerant of unsettling ideas and previously unconsidered evidence than would an older one, his own. For reasons not entirely academic, this younger generation would be more accepting of theories that acknowledged the power of a sophisticated oralism over daily Hellenic life, especially when the words were poetic, rhythmical, and allied to music. This generation would be the first to have felt the full effects on society of the wireless transmission of sounds everywhere, at every moment of the day and night, through the media of radio and television.

This generation will have awakened to the orality in their midst as a contemporary fact, in ways no educated generation in Europe had known for centuries. Instinctively, they would understand orality's appeal to the human consciousness, mediated as it is by what seduces the listening ear, not by what addresses the reading eye. The monopoly of the document and the printed page over important communication in Europe would come under some serious threat for the first time since, roughly, Charlemagne, or at least so Havelock believed. He lived long enough to hear his predicted stampede rumbling in the distance, and to be able to welcome it in his final book, *The Muse Learns to Write.*[6] Appropriately, it bore the subtitle, *Reflections on Orality and Literacy from Antiquity to the Present.*

The appearance of these studies has removed all need either to tout the importance of the orality and literacy interlock in early Greece or to defend the importance of the invention of the complete alphabet to human culture. Alphabetic literacy ''and the difference it makes'' are now being explored on all sides, from both a historical and a contemporary perspective. Accusations of ''technological determinism'' or of committing the dreaded ''monocausal fallacy'' are also being widely heard as scores of anthropologists, archaeologists, folklorists, sociologists, musicologists, philosophers, and students of linguistics have in their own good time joined as laborers in a common vineyard, albeit tending rather differently set-out rows. I deliberately do not mention the biblical scholars in this group, for they are not latecomers. Some of their number, such as the remarkable Gunkel, were toiling away long before Parry.

So that my readers may know in advance where I stand on a number of controversial points raised in some of the recent literature on Greek orality and literacy, especially where its authors refer to earlier publications of mine, I touch briefly on several of them here, but without suggesting that other authors who go unmentioned are any less important. This section also serves to introduce the reader to some views I still hold, and to a few that I do not.

Ancient Literacy (1989) by W. V. Harris splashed considerable cold water, as my text notes, on those who would proclaim popular literacy immediately upon the appearance of the first inscriptions—or indeed, in Harris's view, in *any* century in antiquity. His book valuably reviews the difficulties in defining ''literacy,'' a protean term. He argues, as well, that we shall always lack the sort evidence that can be translated into statistical conclusions for Greco-Roman antiquity. "We shall obviously never know in a clear-cut numerical way how many people were literate, semi-literate, or illiterate in the Greco-Roman world in general, or even in any particular milieu within it."[7] Long ago I arrived at the same conclusion as a result of living for some years in Turkey in the 1960s. I had followed with interest the various government attempts, possessed of far better machinery for measurement than anything we now have for assessing ancient Greek literacy, to arrive at an accurate percentage figure for the country's literate population. Not even the Turks had any real confidence in the results. For one thing, there was no agreement on what constituted literacy. If a visiting Anatolian peasant could sound out "Bebek" on the Istanbul ferryboat signs and could write his name, but could not read a printed version of the Koran in Turkish or make sense of rudimentary instructions about how to replace a carburetor, was he literate? The confusion concerning degrees of literacy or even different kinds of literacy rendered the figures little better than intuitive guesses, as any statistical figures for ancient Greece would be.

These considerations, it seemed to me, gave added importance to fixing the point at which the major institutions of a society—such as law and education—have clearly grown dependent on literacy. The process is normally gradual, but at some point it is beyond dispute that dependence on memories has largely been replaced by writing; oral procedures and practices have been largely supplanted or at least supplemented by written ones. At some point we can be sure that those who control the most important social institutions must be, to the degree their daily tasks require, competent readers and often practiced writers as well. I put these issues as questions to myself concerning ancient Greece, and only in retrospect do I now realize that I had already begun to plan this book.

Harris also puts a welcome emphasis on the lack of a school system in antiquity of the sort that has been necessary in "every single early-modern or modern country which has achieved majority literacy," noting that this network of schools has normally been supported by religion or the state.[8] With the exception of some fitful private attempts on the part of wealthy and eccentric individuals in a few Hellenistic cities, no similar endeavor to render the general populace literate was known in Greco-Roman antiquity. Harris perceptively, if briefly, notes that scholars have overlooked the only gradual assimilation of legal procedures to literate practices, a lacuna that I hope has been partially rectified in the present book. Harris further reminds scholars that the needs of imperial Athens in the fifth century in dealing with overseas client cities and allies must have accelerated dependence on literacy and forcied an increase in the numbers of citizens who knew their letters. This too, oddly, has been neglected. Harris's very full bibliography is itself a contribution, freeing others from duplicating the task, for a while at least.[9] The attention to some neglected Italian scholarship is welcome and useful to English-speaking readers.

One minor objection concerns Harris's reference to "the recurrent notion that [Greek alphabetic] writing was devised specifically as a vehicle for what had been oral poetry," citing works by H. Wade-Gery and K. Robb.[10] The view is, in Harris's estimate, "suspiciously romantic," although, as I hope I make clear in the following pages, my belief is that epical poetry itself served utilitarian purposes in Greek oral life. The desire to record appropriate epical hexameters on guest gifts and votives also served directly utilitarian ends, not aesthetic or "romantic" ones.

In any case, I remain convinced that to record the hexameters of dedications was the initial motive that called the complete Greek alphabet into existence. The first uses of writing were inscriptional; the content was poetry, specifically the epical hexameter. However, it was quickly, if not immediately, followed by short proprietary notices. The early inscriptions that go beyond a name (perhaps in the genitive, sometimes with *eimi*) and so with some syntax, approaching a sentence at least, preserve verses that had been sung or declaimed on important social occasions of oral life. For convenience, and following a growing convention, these are here referred to as the "long" inscriptions, a useful but perhaps misleading designation. The complete hexameter of the Dipylon graffito is a "long" inscription, that has only six words. A "short" inscription might be no more than a floating letter or two, sometimes not certainly Greek rather than Phoenician.

The main alternative theory favored by Harris among many others is that mercantile jottings were the first use for the Greek alphabet. This view has a weakness normally fatal for historical argument: No existing evidence supports it; all the existing evidence supports an alternative theory. Behind the mercantile hypothesis lie two separate facts. The origin of the Greek alphabet is the Phoenician version of the West Semitic script, and the Phoenicians were famous as great traders. These two facts have generated two assumptions, so far without any material evidence to back them. Eighth-century Phoenician *merchants* and *traders* were literate (ignoring the scribal character of the Semitic literacy of the period, save for craftliteracy); and the Greeks borrowed their script to accomplish mercantile ends similar to those they saw being accomplished by their Phoenician counterparts.

Barry Powell, in *Homer and the Origins of the Alphabet,* rejects curtly the mercantile theory for the same reasons that had previously persuaded me, lack of evidence.[11] He also has accepted the theory that the Greek alphabet was invented to record hexameter verse. Powell observes that "H. T. Wade-Gery, in the J. H. Grey lectures for 1949, suggested in an *obiter dictum* of eight paragraphs that the Greek alphabet may have been fashioned explicitly in order to record hexametric verse."[12] Powell notes that support for this view was next advanced by Robb (1978), Heubeck (1979), Havelock (1982), and Schnapp-Gourbeillon (1982). These authors did not always advance the same evidence and argument for their conclusion, however. I had argued in 1978 (and earlier) that the meter of the hexameter, created by a sequence of syllables that are either long (heavy) or short by reason of the vowel they contained and its relationship to a consonant, suggested that the adapter was a fine phonetician who heard the vowels very precisely. Any recording system for Greek poetry, especially for the hexameter—the meter of all the "long" inscriptions—would require that the vowels be indicated. The Phoenician script lacked precisely this feature; the script required predictable adaptation to record Greek verse (see chapter 10).

Without the idea of vowel notation and signs for at least five vowel sounds, any attempt to use the Phoenician consonantal script to record Greek verse would have broken down and been abandoned. Strong motive was, thus, required behind the Greek effort, and what the motive was should be sought in the extant inscriptional evidence of the eighth century. Powell agrees that recorders of Greek verse, as opposed to Semitic recorders of their very different poetry, could not have been content to ignore the rhythm generated by the sounds of the vowels. Rather, Greek recorders "set great store by the subtle, sinewy, and complex rhythm of the hexameter, recognizable at once even in fragments, small or corrupt."[13]

The *idea* of vowel notation and the complete graphic system for it were the creation of one man, at one time, in one place. Moreover, it happened only once. Following Gelb, I had concluded that the Phoenician script was structurally syllabic or at best a "quasi-alphabet." Also, I denied that a transition inscription would one day turn up with only partial vowel notation, an idea defended by Gelb because he suspected that the *matres lectionis* ("mothers of reading") played a role in the dawning of vowel notation. I had doubted this. The Semitic script the Greeks had borrowed, the Phoenician, had never used the *matres*.

In all of this Powell fully concurs, if I read him correctly. According to Powell, the adapter's motivation was to record not a few hexameters but a text of the entirety of Homer. I find this unlikely but not impossible. Some of my reasons are given in the following chapters. Nevertheless, Powell's argument will, I am certain, receive the close attention from scholars that it richly deserves.

Alan Johnston, a leading British archaeologist, offered some remarks on the origins of the alphabet and its first uses before the International Symposium of the Royal Swedish Institute in Athens, held in June 1981. The proceedings were published in what has turned out to be a seminal book: *The Greek Renaissance of the Eighth Century* B.C.*: Tradition and Innovation,* edited by Robin Hägg. The title was a reminder that the eighth century, especially its second half, was a very long distance from the depressed conditions of the eleventh or tenth centuries that had followed the Bronze Age collapse. The people who witnessed the return of writing to Greece were certainly preliterates, but they were also highly sophisticated and culturally advanced, enjoying a rich economic and cultural renaissance. The Hellenism we have come to admire was born and had impressively developed among a people who could neither read nor write.

Johnston's contribution to the Athens symposium began too modestly: "This topic has been discussed several times of late, and in a sense I am merely embroidering the treatments of Jeffery, Guarducci, Page, Havelock, Robb and Heubeck. There are also some corrections to be made. . . . "[14] What Johnston succeeded in doing, in fact, was to make available to scholars in all fields the latest discoveries, some unpublished, from notably Lefkandi, Pithekoussai, and Eretria; to assess on the basis of the evidence the earliest probable uses of the alphabet (the distinguished author of *Trademarks on Greek Vases* favors proprietary concerns); and to reiterate some long-held views on the probable area where the invention took place. Since its publication in 1983, Johnston's work has been cited widely in professional treatments and at present is the standard source for the latest epigraphic evidence.

Here I wish only to voice again some hesitations to which Johnston has taken polite exception. The dating of especially the Lefkandi material depends on stratigraphic evidence, and time is normally required to be sure that such dating will hold up to scrutiny and debate. Also, letter comparison is notoriously subjective and often of questionable value when an inscription is very early. Initial assessments often require later adjustment as a result, usually by being lowered. The Lefkandi remains are drastically fragmentary and, as Johnston observes, "of little diagnostic value." The situation from Pithekoussai seems unclear as more material becomes available (some adjustment in dating has already occurred), and the rumors from Naxos persist. Semitic and Hellenic epigraphists recall the many cases in which dates have been lowered after reassessment or seriously questioned. Especially for inscriptions that will be first, or very early, in a series, this is understandable when the remains are generally very fragmentary. One thinks of the inscriptions from Corinth, Gordion, and Perachora, and in the Semitic cases (where dating is especially contentious), the proto-Canaanite bowl with five very old signs from Lachish (eventually lowered by David Diringer himself from the second quarter of the fourteenth century to well into the thirteenth century, in *Lachish IV*).[15] I am, of course, not questioning or even doubting any excavator's conclusions. I am merely observing that, however careful the excavator's brush has been, epigraphic dust, too, takes time to settle.

Johnston reports thirty-five "probably" Greek alphabetic inscriptions from Pithekoussai, mostly unpublished, that should be dated before 675 B.C. An earlier example, claimed to be Greek and consisting of two letters only, turned out more likely to be Phoenician. These thirty-five very early examples are mainly single letters on burial amphoras. Johnston also notes that a recent find of "perhaps" 740 B.C. confirms the reading of *eimi* on the famous Nestor Cup from Pithekoussai. In terms of place of invention, Johnston favors "the north-east corner of the Mediterranean," writing that he still holds "that the Greek alphabet was inspired from this quarter and that it was probably first set down there. I would gladly develop the theory of Robb and Heubeck that a natural catalyst existed in the eastern Mediterranean in the shape of the Cypriote syllabary."[16] Readers will discover that I still hold that Cyprus is the most probable locus of transfer and that the syllabary did, indeed, afford a stimulus in the adoption the five Greek vowels, especially the *upsilon.* At Kition, for example, eighth-century Greeks would arrive and, as Johnston writes, "see writing and be told, in Greek, of its uses; such writing would be both syllabic Greek and quasisyllabic Phoenician. . . . The evidence from Lefkandi, and more significantly Pithekoussai, shows that this adoption took place perhaps a generation before the first surviving graffito of ca. 740."[17] Perhaps it did, if the dating of 740 B.C. holds up and if the postulate of a generation for the letter forms to develop is really necessary. Again, there is a subjective element here concerning what looks decidedly "developed" and how long the process would take.

Johnston returns to the important question of the motive behind the adoption.

> I would be remiss in not turning to the needs which inspired Greeks to write once more [after the loss of Linear B]. Havelock, Robb and Heubeck have strongly contested the "commercial" aspect, that accounts and bills of lading were uppermost in the thoughts of transcribers. Rather, the last two have argued, on rather

> differing grounds, that a mnemonic need to set down oral poetry was the crucial factor. . . . We have no commercial uses in the regular sense of the term. Robb has argued that the vowels were created because of their importance to the meter. . . .[18]

Further argument and evidence in support of this view are offered in this book, including some linguistic considerations that I have relegated to the epilogue (chapter 10). However, I readily concede that the moment the *idea* of vowel notation has called the complete alphabet into existence, a natural impulse would have been to write one's own name, just to see what it looks like. This effort probably took place in the instruction phase, an early experiment, as the adapter listened to the instructing Phoenician pronounce the abecedarium. However, he was looking ahead to inscribing a dedication—not to Baal or Astarte, of course, but to Zeus or Aphrodite or Apollo. Also, imitation of the widely attested Semitic practice would encourage proprietary markings from the very start, in addition to dedications and short commemorative verses.

In my text I give reasons for thinking that very early dedications had less chance for survival than did potsherds with proprietary markings. Even so, some notable early dedications have come down to us. Of course, if in the future we find ourselves overwhelmed by masses of even earlier proprietary inscriptions—especially if some carry known Greek names, or Greek words with some syntax, and only the consonants appear, or some vowels are missing where we would expect them—then I am wrong.

Over many years the late Eric Havelock and I debated—often heatedly—the intriguing question of the motive for the adoption (and adaptation) of the Greek version of the alphabet, and our views developed in those years.[19] My earliest published speculation on the matter had been that the Greek alphabet might have been the creation of minstrels, professional *aoidoi*. I was impressed by the poetic sophistication of the earliest "long" inscriptions, beginning with the Dipylon, as, for example, have been Calvert Watkins and Barry Powell. The makers of the verses, it then seemed to me, had to have been singers, professional poets. What I had failed to appreciate was the degree to which members of oral societies absorb and make their own speech that is rhythmic and so poetic. Constant repetition in performances results in the people making at least pieces and parts of it their own in private speech, as we still do with popular songs.[20] They are great listeners, imitators, and rememberers—as, indeed, are our own children for the lyrics, often highly poetical, of popular songs. The comparison should not be disparaged, for we must live with the consequences. The sole difference is that the situation is heightened exponentially in oral and musical societies, where elders approve of and encourage the process. Before writing, the culture cannot function and survive in any other way, for its oral paideia, what sociologists and anthropologists now call "enculturation," depends on it.

As it turns out, I should have been less concerned about who made the splendid verses found in the earliest long inscriptions than about who wrote them down. Slowly I came to the conviction that the first uses of the alphabet were inscriptional, and that these uses were in direct imitation of well-established Phoenician practice that Greeks could view on a daily basis. It is doubtful that any Greek merchant visiting Sidon or Tyre—if one ever did—saw a Phoenician official archive, and so viewed a literary text.[21] If he had, and could assimilate what he saw displayed, presumably he would have followed the then Phoenician practice of writing consistently from right to left. That Greeks from the start did not do so (as L. H. Jeffery has demonstrated)[22] is evidence that Phoenician literary works, or archive literacy, were not the stimulus behind Greek imitation.

By contrast, the body of Phoenician inscriptions for the period afford us examples of the sorts of writing—normally very short, and only clearly *beginning* from the right—that a Greek would see in the bilingual centers of contact. If this is what the adopting Greek saw, and sought to imitate, then the first uses of the alphabet would be dedications and commemorations (for Greeks, appropriately in hexameters), and short proprietary notices in prose, or markings. They would be put on bowls, statuettes, jars, cups, axes, utensils, or the like. These are, in fact, what we find in the archaeological record—and nothing else. It follows that first users of the Greek alphabet would plausibly be the craftsmen who made the inscribed objects. Many assumptions—and perhaps a few prejudices—were going to be challenged by this theory, as I was quickly to discover. One of them requires exposure and challenge here.

For all modern, industrialized societies literacy is a product of schooling. As in the case of an athletic skill made automatic and effortless through constant practice, we tend to forget the long and painful apprenticeship. In general, the upper and middle classes, or those who can afford formal instruction, are more likely to be literate, or at least "more literate." Marginal literacy, and prolonged poverty, are rightly viewed as natural partners. Furthermore, a poor black of the inner city may not be, strictly speaking, illiterate, or (in Canada or Alaska) a poorly educated Indian may, indeed, be able to write down some Athabasan-English. But that does not mean that she or he is capable of producing "white essayist prose," as some Athabasans have called it, or even of reading it with comprehension. To write *that*—or, in recent decades, at least to be able to read it with comprehension—has become the measure of a minimum level of literacy that social institutions demand in societies of advanced literacy. Even surgeons, engineers, and lawyers cannot fall below this standard, for the minimum information they must acquire to function professionally is now preserved at this level of essayist literacy. It was not always so.

For the professions, and white collar occupations, advanced schooling is required, always favoring the affluent, or at least tending increasingly to close out the underprivileged. For it is a highly advanced, school-fostered skill that the upper classes—or any upwardly mobile class—in any fully literate society *must* possess. If it becomes widely unattainable—or even worse, irrelevant, and finally resented—then the most serious of social evils threaten the society grown dependent on essayist literacy in its controlling institutions. A breakdown in the effective socialization, or enculturation, of large numbers of people is inevitable, a disaster. Literacy empowers, until those closed out of its benefits use force to take power back. It is a different sort of "paideia crisis" from that which faced Athens at the turn of the fourth century, but it is a crisis nevertheless.

We accept this analysis of the situation for ourselves, living in the latter part of the twentieth century, but then refuse to transfer its lesson, and the implication that there are different sorts of literacy, back to Archaic Greece, a period without schools (except toward the end), no equivalent of colleges, and when texts of any kind were few and indifferently written. How were the advanced literate skills that we know are difficult to acquire under the best of modern conditions, which include printed books and staggered curricula, spread through an ancient populace? Obviously, they were not, but that we assume they were emerges when we read certain historians claim, without qualification, that from the earliest times Greece enjoyed "widespread literacy." They then proceed to discuss the society and its institutions on the assumption that they did not significantly differ from our own in this regard. Perversely, as part of the same literate bias—one born of familiarity, not meanness—what we *do* transfer back to ancient Greece is the assumption that if anyone could read and write to any degree in any period, it would surely have to be nobles or aristocrats, or at least the wealthy. That conclusion deserves to be challenged, and matched against the evidence.

Havelock came to adopt my view of the origins of the alphabet partially because, independently, he had been impressed with the early evidence for literacy, at levels sufficient for their needs, among Greek craftsmen—potters, vase painters, stone masons, and bronze workers. The evidence for "craft literacy" as he called it—which, again, does not equate with essayist literacy, either for producing a text or reading one—is abundant in the inscriptional record from roughly 700 to 450 B.C. Evidence exists for a similar level of craft literacy among Phoenician craftsmen in the period of alphabetic transfer—that, and no more.

For Greece, the evidence for craft literacy—so different from either scribe literacy or popular essayist literacy—comes earlier in the record and bulks larger than does any considerable body of evidence indicating that literacy had become a desirable or necessary accomplishment of the aristocratic class. As we shall discover, their educational system, or conventions, had, in fact, remained proudly athletic (for the old aristocrats, centered around their beloved horses), and dominantly oral, and musical, well into the fifth century. For Athens, the fifth-century schools will initiate some changes, eventually resulting in what approaches essayist literacy on the part of, probably, most upper class males by at least the early decades of the fourth century. It was a process occurring throughout the fifth century, but accelerating in the second half, with the rise of the Athenian democracy. Those in the populace who were craft literate remained so, as did their sons, taught their letters by their fathers or within the craft, not schools. About women and slaves we know little.

In making it his own, Havelock summarized masterfully an argument that I had spread over several publications and a dozen years. I quote his words here in full. Nothing has appeared in the past fifteen years to change this reconstruction, and much has come to light to confirm it. What, asks Havelock rhetorically, can have been the immediate motive behind the invention of the Greek alphabet?

> It may be appropriate here to mention the answer to this question that has been proposed by Professor Robb. The Greek device, he suggests, arose as a procedure of inscription carried out at places or in areas (Cyprus being the favored candidate) where bilingual Greeks, neighbors to the Phoenicians, cultivated the oral

> art of composing ritual dedications—a standard practice in all preliterate cultures. They were able to observe and, being bilingual, to understand the parallel practice of their Phoenician counterparts, but they also observed the Phoenician ability to inscribe symbols of their composition upon dedicatory offerings. This provoked emulation. The Phoenician oral composition required the manufacture only of cadences expressive of standard parallelisms and antitheses, rhythmic but not strictly metrical, so that decipherment, by using some guesswork, was possible even within the limitations of the script used. The Greek hexametric measure was much more exacting, requiring the oral enunciation of carefully measured vocalic breaths. The difference required the Greek imitator to supply five marks to symbolize these lengths and so render adequately the metrics of his own dedication. He had to learn the Phoenician abecedarium, i.e., the list of names of the Phoenician signs, in order to start applying the Phoenician consonants to his own Greek purposes. As he did so, and still obeying his epigraphical authority, he transferred some signs of "weak consonants" to function as symbols of vocalization because listening to them suggested some approximation to what he needed. Their new acoustic values came into existence as the Greek hexameter was pronounced. Such an explanation has the great advantage of asserting that principle of intimate partnership between oral and written practice which in my own view continued to operate and control the transition toward full literacy in the next three hundred years.[23]

To offer further supporting evidence for this reconstruction, including the crucially important observation expressed in its final sentence, is in no small measure the task of this book.

Notes

1. Of course, not all critical reviews were unfair, nor were all reviews critical. Havelock himself especially savored the insightful notice that appeared in *Mind* 74 (1965), pp. 147–148.

2. Gelb's work started to affect Havelock's only after he had written *Preface to Plato,* as Havelock notes in *The Muse Learns to Write* (New Haven, 1986), p. 59. Havelock's starting point had been a very different one from Gelb's, namely, raising questions about why the Greeks, using their remarkable alphabet, had created the first great secular literature. Nothing like it in richness and range, in the characterization of individuals, or in the preservation of popular speech had come down to us from any other ancient cultures of the Mediterranean despite their high material accomplishments. The Hebrews were a special case, for their contribution had been only literary. Their (eventual) devotion to written texts, aided always by oral means of preservation, had behind it religious motives, however, and from the ancient Hebrews we have no literature except what is found in the Old Testament. If Canaanite religion had shared a similar idea of divine revelation and of an ever-renewed covenant with Baal or their other gods as historical facts to be believed, and so accounts of them preserved, then the preservation of written literature may have been of greater concern to them. The unpointed script, aided by an oral tradition, could overcome the difficulties, but not easily. See chapter 10.

3. Marcel Detienne, *The Creation of Mythology* (Chicago and London, 1986), p. 22.

4. M. Miller, "Parmenides and the Disclosure of Being," *Apeiron* 13 (1978), p. 14.

5. For Xenophanes, see J. Hershbell, "The Oral-Poetic Religion of Xenophanes," in K. Robb, *Language and Thought in Early Greek Philosophy* (La Salle, Ill., 1983), pp.

125–133. For Heraclitus, see K. Robb, "Psyche and Logos in Fragments of Heraclitus," *Monist* 69 No. 3 (1986), pp. 315–351.

6. When he died, Havelock was at work on *The Preplatonic Philosophers of Greece,* a book that was to have been co-authored by Havelock, Thomas Cole, Jackson Hershbell, and me. Havelock's contribution, a substantial piece of work as he left it, was still receiving his attention until the final day. The other authors hope to see Professor Havelock's last composition published, perhaps with some of his uncollected papers.

7. W. V. Harris, *Ancient Literacy* (Cambridge, Mass., 1989), p. 7.

8. Ibid., pp. 15, 101ff., 324–325.

9. Also with ample but more narrowed bibliography, and published in the same year as *Ancient Literacy,* is R. Thomas, *Oral Tradition and Written Record in Classical Athens* (Cambridge, 1989). This useful book (especially on Greek archives) was initially a doctoral dissertation; in terms of bibliography, its origin has proved an advantage. Together, these two bibliographies afford a fairly complete listing of recent, important works, especially when supplemented by the epigraphical references in Barry Powell's new book on Homer and the alphabet (n. 11).

10. Harris, *Ancient Literacy,* p. 45.

11. B. Powell, *Homer and the Origin of the Greek Alphabet* (Cambridge, 1991), pp. 182, 185.

12. Ibid., p. 109 with n. 82.

13. Ibid., p. 118.

14. Alan Johnston, "The Extent and Use of Literacy: The Archaeological Evidence," in R. Hägg, ed., *The Greek Renaissance of the Eighth Century* B.C.: *Tradition and Innovation* (Stockholm, 1983) p. 63.

15. In O. Tufnell, et al., *Lachish IV* (*Tel ed-Duweir*): *The Bronze Age* (London, 1958), p. 129.

16. Johnston, "The Extent and Use of Literacy," p. 66.

17. Ibid.

18. Ibid., p. 67.

19. In K. Robb, "The Dipylon Prize Graffito," *Coranto* 7 (1971), I argued against the then entrenched view that mercantile motives were behind the adoption of the script, a point on which I have never wavered. We simply had no idea how Phoenician traders kept their accounts, and no reason to believe they went to the considerable trouble of becoming literate in order to do so. Nor would Greek traders be likely to discover one fine day that they needed to invent an alphabet in order to do what they already managed to do quite effectively, keep track of their goods (coinage is in the future). Two pieces of evidence converged, however: Gelb's analysis of the unique character of the alphabet and its unidirectional development culminating in the Greek invention, and the poetic character of the earliest Greek inscriptions. I therefore also suggested in 1971 that the motive behind the Greek invention was to record the hexameter, which view I also still hold, and that "probably" the adapter, as well as the composer of the Dipylon hexameter, were *aoidoi,* singers. The latter part of the suggestion I withdrew in 1978, in "Poetic Sources of the Greek Alphabet: Rhythm and Abecedarium from Phoenician to Greek," in E. A Havelock and J. P. Hershbell, eds., *Communication Arts in the Ancient World* (New York, 1978), pp. 23–36. The motive, I believe, was to imitate the widespread Near Eastern practice of inscribing dedications, but in the appropriate Greek medium, the hexameter. I also believe the adapter and first users were likely craftsmen. See n. 23. Support for some of my views on the alphabet and the early inscriptions, supplying a rich context in his chapter 2, "Poet and Painter in the Dark Age," came from Jeffrey Hurwit, *The Art and Culture of Early Greece, 1100–480* B.C., (Ithaca and London, 1985). See especially pp. 88–91, with Hurwit's notes.

20. This phenomenon has been noted many times, in many oral societies, starting with the great Rhadlov in the nineteenth century. The metrical phrasing (a complete hexameter and some pieces) on the crudely carved rock pederastic inscriptions on Thera are hard to explain on any other hypothesis. *IG* XII. 3 543, dated to about 700 B.C., is a complete hexameter: "Barbax dances splendidly and he gives pleasure too!" *IG* XII. 3 544 is in the hexametric meter, containing one dactyl and some bits: "Tharumakhas is just fine." *IG* XII. 3 540 is also metrical, complimenting another lad, and uses the same formulaic, erotic *agathos*. The inscriptions bring together agonistic dance, male eroticism, and poetry in a manner reminiscent of the Dipylon wine jug and Nestor wine cup inscriptions, as a number of scholars have noted, most recently Powell (1991). See also K. Robb in *Coronto* 7 (1971). Were these young craftsmen perhaps enjoying some playful display with both letters and verse, the latter of a less elevated sort than they were going to put on symposiastic vessels? A more elevated example of ordinary people in preliterate societies bursting into verse about mundane matters has been put into the historical record by Greek scholar and noted student of Gaelic poetry, George Thompson. He went to Ireland's more remote villages to learn the local speech and was startled by what he encountered: "The conversation of those ragged peasants, as soon as I learned to follow it, electrified me. It was as though Homer had come alive. Its vitality was inexhaustible, yet it was rhythmical, alliterative, formal, artificial, always on the point of bursting into poetry. . . . It had all the qualities noted by Radlov in the conversation of the Kirghiz." For additional examples, see my "Preliterate Ages and the Linguistic Art of Heraclitus, " in K. Robb, *Language and Thought in Early Greek Thought,* pp. 152–206, especially pp. 159ff.

21. Even the existence of eighth-century Phoenician archives, like the existence of a written Phoenician literature (none survives), is a vexed question and controversial. The closest thing to contemporary evidence may be an Egyptian source, the narrative of the many trials of the priest Wen-Amon's journey to Phoenicia ca. 1135 B.C., when Sidon was at its height. The scribal literacy of the royal households he encountered, to be found in at least one of the coastal cities, Byblos, is one thing; literacy among eighth-century traders and merchants plying the eastern Mediterranean in a few ships—often a change of the wind away from piracy—is another. See the astute remarks of Chester Starr, *The Origins of Greek Civilization: 1100–650 B.C.* (New York, 1991), p. 171, and his reference to J. Hasebroek, *Trade and Politics in Ancient Greece* (London, 1933), pp. 10–11, 89. That the newly invented (in Cyprus as I believe) alphabet traveled the established trade routes cannot be seriously doubted; it was, I am convinced, the very light baggage of the skilled craftsmen who widely traveled those very routes. For the evidence for very early contacts between Euboeans "abroad" and Cyprus, which was the natural base from which to investigate western Asia Minor, see David Ridgway, *The First Western Greeks* (Cambridge, 1992), pp. 22–26, and 147. As Ridgway observes of Cyprus, its own past history "meant that many Cypriot towns must have been able to muster at least a few inhabitants who spoke a tolerable version of the Greek language" (p. 22). It was in just this favorable environment, if I am not mistaken, that the Phoenician letters first transferred to the Greeks. Recent evidence suggests that almost immediately the alphabet was transferred "home" to Lefkandi by Euboeans who, I suggest, encountered it on Cyprus, although just when in the late-ninth or early-eighth-century Euboean Greeks first mixed peacefully with Cypriot Phoenicians is difficult to determine. Kition on the southeast coast of Cyprus was the first Phoenician colony overseas, having been founded early in the ninth century. I suspect, therefore, that in the future we will find no Greek inscriptions earlier than the foundation of Phoenician Kition. In any case, the physical evidence for a strong Cypriot-Euboean connection during the period of alphabetic transfer is now unmistakable. For the chronology and geographical progress of Euboean trading contacts see the exhaustive study of the

distribution of six types of the distinctive Euboean pendent semi-circle skyphoi by R. A. Kearsley, *The Pendent Semi-Circle Skyphos: A Study of Its Development and an Examination of It as Evidence for Euboean Activity at Al Mina* (*Bulletin of the Institute of Classical Studies*, Supp. 44 [London, 1989]). Kearsley's very full evidence (and useful maps and tables) demonstrates that Euboean maritime trade expanded first from the Greek mainland and islands to *Cyprus* (where her Type 5 is found) and the Levant (Al Mina) before spreading to the west on Ischia at Pithekousssai (where her Type 6 is found). Ridgway's valuable book, drawing deductions from the archaeological evidence, admirably casts further important light on the "invisible cultural cargo" that the eighth-century Euboeans took west to the colonies with them, notably a whole way of life grounded in the Homeric proprieties. See *The First Western Greeks*, pp. 50ff. (burials), 57ff. *(sumposia)*, 113–118 (partially literate eighth-century Semitic potters and craftsmen in contact with Greeks, and probably in residence at Pithekoussai), 138 (the eighth-century circulation of the Homeric poems in the west), 140 (travel and the importance of *xenia*). Ridgway (p. 138) quotes from a work I have been unable to obtain, J. N. Coldstream's "Cypro-Aegean Exchanges in the Ninth and Eighth Centuries B.C.," *Praktika tou protou Diethnou Kyprologikou Synedriou A I* (Nicosia, 1972): "The greatest gift to Cyprus from the Aegean . . . was the diffusion of the Homeric poems in the late eighth century, which inspired the people of Salamis and Paphos to honor their rulers with a manner of burial which recalled in detail the funeral rites already immortalized in the Homeric poems." Fundamental to my argument in this book is the now overwhelming evidence that the Homeric poems were widely and popularly diffused in the eighth century, the century of script transfer, and that "Homer" or oral epic served as the basis for a way of life that was not to be seriously eroded in Hellas until the age of Plato. Ridgway is careful to note that in the earliest period for diffusion of the Homeric poems we are unmistakably encountering "ancient listeners" (p. 140), not readers.

22. L. H. Jeffery—first in her doctoral dissertation—exposed as false the old view found in most of the standard handbooks Greek epigraphists were trained on. It asserted that the Greeks began by writing right to left, in imitation of the Phoenicians; then followed a transitional *boustrophēdon* (back and forth, as oxen plow) stage; finally the consistent left to right practice emerged. The early work became the basis of her monumental *The Local Scripts of Archaic Greece* (Oxford, 1961), indispensable for work in early Greek inscriptions. For the direction of Greek writing, see especially pp. 43ff. A revised edition of this book with a supplement added by Alan Johnston appeared after my own text was finished. It may be noted that *boustrophēdon* also appears fitfully in very early Canaanite writing, obviously a natural response when the conventions are fluid, or no scribal or school controls are in place. The element of willful, private deviation, such as rotating a letter or elongating a tail, common when writing is new (even among children), has been largely ignored and may have played havoc with some historical arguments from script comparison.

23. E. A. Havelock, *The Literate Revolution in Greece and Its Cultural Consequences* (Princeton, 1982), pp. 12–13, with n. 18.

I

The Origins of Greek Literacy

1

The Alphabet Enters Oral Greece

The history of Greek literacy commences with some scraps of alphabetic writing that are securely dated to no earlier than the eighth century before Christ. It culminates, or at least reaches a significant plateau, in mid-fourth-century Athens when the city's major cultural institutions, notably the courts and formal education, have grown dependent on alphabetic literacy for their daily functioning. At either end of the long chronological spectrum—a span of 400 years—the facts have now emerged into reasonably clear light. Something approaching scholarly consensus about them may be detected in recent publications from historians of Greek literacy.

Before 750 B.C., Greek society was not literate in any significant sense of the word even if, as many experts now believe, the Greek alphabet had been invented perhaps a few decades earlier than that date. Knowledge of the Phoenician signs would have been the possession of a restricted few, and the social uses would have been as yet undeveloped. This conclusion will remain true even if the invention of the Greek alphabet is eventually placed in the ninth century; the issue is the uses to which the letters are put. After some four centuries had passed, or by about 350 B.C., Athenian society had become fully literate, not in the statistical sense, about which we will never be adequately informed for antiquity, but in what may be termed the "institutional" sense. Major institutions of society, especially the administration of justice and the formal education of young males in their *meirakion* years (roughly 15 to 21), had grown dependent on alphabetic literacy.

No similar scholarly consensus on the progress of Greek literacy existed in any century earlier than our own. None may have been possible before the rediscovery of the oral dimension in early Hellenism initiated by the seminal studies of Milman Parry in the 1920s. The literacy and orality equation, as it has come to be known, has been cast in an entirely new light as a result of what Parry began. A new understanding of how "Homer" functioned in archaic Greek life—one more in keeping with what later Greeks themselves said about him—began to be heard in the sometimes musty corridors of Homeric scholarship:

> He is the most ancient of the European poets, which for all practical purposes means the oldest poet we have. Not only is he a Greek poet, but also in some sense a pre-Greek poet. . . . His work takes its place along with portions of the Old Testament as not just a poem but as a massive milestone in the history of human culture. It is a monument hewn in a curious shape. It is a likeness of the pattern of the human mind not as it exists today, but as it existed in those im-

> mense preliterate epochs when the common man did not read or write. Man's thoughts and his speech were different then, different from what they became in the age of Pericles, and far removed indeed from ours. Homer therefore addresses us, if at all, across a great gulf of literate experience and abstract thought.[1]

Milman Parry: The Oral Basis of Hellenism

Parry's argument was in the form of a deduction, which he drew after a fresh examination of two phenomena that scholars had previously treated independently. First was the complexity of the formulaic systems preserved in the vulgate text of Homer. Parry brought to their analysis an entirely new level of statistical precision and understanding. In scope, argued Parry, the Homeric systems of formulas covered all of the epic's essential characters and ideas in all grammatical configurations. In thrift, they tended to resist redundancy, or unnecessary duplication, suggesting they served a functional rather than aesthetic, or even strictly descriptive purpose.[2] Analogical formation based on established formulas permitted constant new elaboration of structurally related formulas, an ongoing "variation of the same" or the traditional, which is at the heart of all oral composition. As pervasive features of Homeric composition, found in every verse, they could not be, Parry concluded, fortuitous accidents. A causal explanation must be sought.[3]

Next Parry investigated the techniques of contemporary (1930s) illiterate singers, who learned from each other by ear only and who flourished in an established tradition of oral verse-making. The young scholar of Greek was drawn gradually—but not reluctantly—from academic pursuits in Paris and the scrutiny of texts to field experience in the Balkans, where he discovered contemporary singers who were illiterate and who exploited techniques and devices analogous to those he had cataloged in the Homeric text. For the Balkan singers, the scale was diminished and the formulaic systems were less complex, but undeniable similarities existed. Direct borrowing was, of course, out of the question. Rather, similar needs must have called similar devices into existence. Parry was gradually driven to the conclusion that Homeric composition, so heavily dependent on these traditional elements, was a kind of composition that oral poetry was known independently to be. It was not only in some sense "traditional," as had long been suspected, but *oral*.

The causal puzzle had been solved. The complexity of the formulaic systems could have served only the needs of preliterate singers who must improvise as the occasion demanded and who could not retreat into literate solitude in order to compose and then memorize a text for later performance. The performance "on demand" by Homer's blind Demodocus, deprived from birth of the means of producing a text even if he knew of such a thing, affords an illustration of the process, one with close parallels in oral societies in every age. Also, the sophisticated elements of oral composition—notably but not exclusively the formulas—could not have been the creation of a single singer or a single generation of singers. A long tradition of professional *aoidoi,* whose performances were designed for a pan-Hellenic audience, was a certain conclusion, one supported by all the contemporary Greek evidence. The poetry was created in the environment of orality, a rich oral culture, and it celebrated an oral way of life.

Parry's arguments, rather like those of Aquinas to the existence of God, were elegant ones that proceeded from visible effects we can now observe to an invisible, necessary, explanatory cause. And like the famous arguments of Aquinas, Parry's reasoning has not been beyond the objections of critics. In recent years various modifications of Parry's thesis, especially as it concerned the definition of the formula, or traditional epithet, have been advanced. They are now specialists' concerns and may be ignored here. Even if modification in the end is required, the essential thesis has largely been accepted, and its success continues to dominate scholarly discussion of Homer and of early Greek epic.

A further conclusion lurks in the wings. Epical speech, the creation of professional *aoidoi* over many generations, was not their private preserve; the making of it was not a professional secret. In varying degrees, epical speech belonged to all the people, who heard it, understood it, cherished it, and even, when appropriate, could rise to the occasion and competently imitate it. The oldest "long" inscriptions, or popular inscriptions, all so poetically accomplished, admit of no other explanation. Into this environment, one in which men and women at every level of society knew no writing but heard vast amounts of poetry, the alphabet silently intrudes.[4]

For the inception of European literacy, the scholarly spotlight must belong to archaeology and epigraphy. It affords the only contemporary—and the only reliable—evidence we have, or will ever have. We begin with a new examination of the very old dancer's graffito from the Dipylon cemetery in Athens, until recently believed to be the oldest of the surviving Greek inscriptions. It still remains the oldest of the long inscriptions, and the oldest alphabetic writing to come from Attica. "From Athens comes the earliest real Greek alphabetic inscription—a text with syntax—the hexameter and few other signs on the 'Dipylon oinochoe.' "[5] Unless there is a new find, its importance remains untouched by recent claims from Ischia, Lefkandi, or Naxos.

From our perspective, the verse scratched anonymously on the Dipylon wine jug succeeded in transforming an average, well-made pot for its day, one intended for daily household use, into one of the great monuments in the history of writing, arguably the technology that has proved to be the most useful for our species. We shall try, therefore, to extract as much information from the pot and the words scratched on it as the physical evidence will yield. In pursuing the task we shall discover that the Athens of the late eighth century that saw the manufacture of the pot and its inscription was, like Greece itself, still very much oral Athens.

The Oldest Attic Inscription

Scratched retrograde (right to left) in the Phoenician manner around the shoulder of a wine jug, an oinochoe, the graffito comprises one complete hexameter verse plus a few readable letters of a second line (Figures 1.1 and 1.2). Perhaps six

Figure 1.1. The Dipylon Oinochoe and its graffito, ca. 720 B.C. National Museum, Athens. Photographs DAI N.M. 4700 and 70/93. Courtesy of Deutsches Archäologisches Institut, Athens.

letters near the beginning of the second line may be regarded as certain. The *spiritus asper* is recorded by the Semitic letter that would become the Greek *eta*.[6] There are no lowercase letters, of course, and no word divisions; both of these conveniences for readers are late developments. The complete hexameter is not in doubt.

> hosnunorchestonpantonatalotatapazei
> ὅς νῦν ὀρχηστῶν πάντων ἀταλώτατα παίζει
>
> Whoso now of all the dancers most playfully sports.[7]

The writing, after a steady beginning, winds upward toward the neck of the jug (as the letters also grow larger) and then abruptly halts. Autopsy reveals greater disparity in the size of the letters and their shapes or stances (e.g., the important *alpha*s) than do some published drawings and tables.

There is no irrefutable physical evidence for a second hand at work in the second line, and expert opinion is divided on the matter. The attempt at recording

Figure 1.2. Detail of the Dipylon Oinochoe and its graffito. Note the inscriber's considerable freedom with the stance of the *alpha*s. Also, note the near V shape of the upsilon in *nun*.

a second verse (or so I presume it is) reveals several false starts, as well as what appears to be a correction, or scratching over (in the *iota* of *min*) before the inscriber abandoned the effort entirely. The reconstruction for the second line is much disputed, but that first proposed by Studniczka only three years after the inscription was published in 1880, *το(υ)το δεκαν μιν*, with all its admitted difficulties, remains a popular contender.[8]

The five Greek vowels, *a, e, i, o,* and *u,* are present as a complete system, as they are in all other early Greek inscriptions, indicating no period of development[9] away from the Semitic consonantal and quasi-syllabic scripts. From the perspective of the history of writing, this is the inscription's outstanding feature, especially if it continues to hold its place as the oldest of the long inscriptions.

Several epigraphical features of the inscription are notable. The *alpha*s are not upright as in all other Greek inscriptions but rest on their sides in what is sometimes called the Phoenician stance, although their "heads" point in the opposite direction from Phoenician practice.[10] These peculiar, horizontal *alpha*s have loomed large in—if, indeed, they did not inspire—the claim that the Dipylon jug was older than any other Greek inscription, for example, the Nestor cup from Ischia. Yet, this early, the Dipylon *alpha*s could be a private aberration, an individual indulgence of graphic independence inspired by no immediate Phoenician model. There was as yet no concept of a public of readers requiring standardization for easy recognition, and no scribal controls. As a result, the makers of the

Greek early inscriptions often felt free to take some license in the making of individual letter forms.

In addition to the *alpha*s, a second feature of the letter forms on the Dipylon jug is unique for Attic inscriptions, the crooked *iota*.[11] A third, a *lambda* with a hook at the top, is rare. These and other considerations have led some scholars (e.g., L. H. Jeffery, E. A. Havelock)[12] to speculate that the graffito may have been scratched by a visitor to a still illiterate Athens as a demonstration of virtuosity in an unfamiliar but, to locals, wondrous skill. Writing, on this view, was meant to impress some gathering of preliterate Athenians. The suggestion is attractive.[13] The Athenian vases of a later century intended for export abroad (mainly to Italy) that contain nonsense inscriptions, or what amounts to alphabetic gibberish, are a related phenomenon, but with Athenians now doing the impressing.

Two additional recording oddities of the Dipylon inscription may be mentioned. In the third word of the complete hexameter, an *a-* stem genitive plural ending is recorded as *-ōn*. This contracted genitive may be a concession to local (Attic) dialect of a sort found commonly in early inscriptions.[14] Also, in the sixth word, in the stem *paiz-*, the intervocalic *digamma* (a semivowel like *w*) is not recorded. The *digamma* is normal in the earliest inscriptions, and is, indeed, rather tenacious even in later ones, although not in Attica. These oddities are minor items, to be sure, and may be variously explained. Behind them we can perhaps detect some evidence of tension between what an ear heard, what it anticipated it should hear as required by the familiar rhythm of the hexameter, and what the recording hand, not guided as yet by writing conventions for the notation of verse, tried to get down on the pot.

What emerges from an examination of the graphics of the inscription is considerable discrepancy between the oral and poetic accomplishment of the first verse—a very competent hexameter, indeed—and the writer's hand, initially firm but then uncertain and wandering, that recorded it. A reasonable conclusion is that whoever composed the surviving verse was no stranger to the ancient art of oral verse-making, but that whoever attempted to inscribe it, whether the reciter or another, was not equally at ease with the recently introduced skill of alphabetic writing.

Dating the Dipylon Graffito

Had inscription occurred before the pot was fired, the evidence for dating the vessel would have been the best possible. It is a complete pot, total height of 22 cm, found in a Geometric setting, and of Late Geometric, or even Subgeometric, manufacture. A date of ca. 730 B.C. would not be off by more than a decade either way. However, a graffito could have been added to the surface of the pot as soon as it had cooled, or it could have been scratched months or even years later. The date of inscription must therefore be established circumstantially, normally the case with graffiti.

The jug was found in 1871 in Athens during clandestine digging, and there are now no associated materials to aid in its dating. The find spot is reported to have been a tomb in the area of the old necropolis near the Kerameikos, outside what came to be known as the Dipylon Gate; this may be accepted as certain. That the pot was found in a grave is an important clue. The vase, like so many of the grave goods found in the vicinity, was a household item of no great intrinsic value for its period. It is a well-made, pleasing vessel designed for everyday use. The wine jug must, therefore, have been a prized personal memento. It belonged, plausibly, to the dancer who won it.

Was the pot new when it was converted into a prize by the addition of the graffito? The question is less innocent than it sounds, for the dating of the oldest Attic inscription largely turns on it. If a private *sumposion* were the occasion, as I believe, then, as one noted expert[15] has suggested, the jug could have been in household use as long as a generation or so before being inscribed. That *could* (but need not) put the addition of the graffito somewhat later than 700 B.C. Only the very archaic lettering, often a subjective criterion for very early inscriptions, would then be left to argue against it. If, by contrast, the jug was a formal prize awarded at an official Attic dance contest, the jug surely was new when inscribed, and the approximate date of manufacture, or 730 B.C., is certain for the inscription as well.

The wording of the Dipylon verse is thoroughly Homeric. Our text of Homer must, therefore, be the preferred guide to establishing the occasion of inscription. It alone can now tell us what manner of social or civic gathering produced the verse, if that text affords any relevant information. It does.

The Homeric Wording of the Inscription

The noun *orchēstōn* (''of the dancers'') and the verb *paizei* (he ''dances,'' ''sports'') guarantee that the event being commemorated involved dancing of some kind. Also, some sort of competition must be the occasion. The wording commences with a familiar *protasis,* ''whoso now (*hos nun*),'' and includes a superlative, *atalōtata,* modifying ''he dances.'' Someone will come off best at dancing, and will get a jug of wine for his successful display.

Important further clues reside in the modifier *atalōtata*. Often it has been translated as ''most gracefully,'' a translation that has suggested to some commentators a formal, choric event, a stately *choreia,* an event of perhaps even civic importance.[16] But does ''most gracefully'' best convey the meaning for a superlative formed from the adjective *atalos* in early, especially *epical* Greek, or has the key word in the hexameter been mistranslated?

Atalōtata is not Attic dialect, but an exclusively epical word. The etymology of *atalos* remains uncertain, but the adjective and the words cognate with it are common enough; context affords clear evidence for their meaning in all instances. Based on these usages, I have elsewhere[17] argued for the meaning ''most playfully'' or ''energetically'' for *atalōtata* rather than ''gracefully.''[18] At *Iliad* XVIII. 567, *atalla phroneontes* describes a group of youths and maidens skipping with glee along a path as they carry fruit into a vineyard. The meaning is clearly ''lighthearted'' or ''playful.'' At *Iliad* XIII. 27, various creatures of the sea are said to gambol or leap *(atalle)* about the chariot of the god Poseidon as he speeds across the waves; the image evoked by the verb is one of a playful, leaping display, not a programmed, choreographed movement. A neglected usage, the participial form *atallōn,*[19] appears in Hesiod bearing the standard, intransitive meaning for this verb, "playing." The people of the Second Age of Man, that of Silver, live for a hundred years foolishly playing *(atallōn)* for the entire century, clinging the whole time to their mothers as would young children.

This clarifies the choice of the inscription's main verb, *paizō;* it is cognate with *pais,* child, and can mean either "to play" or "to sport" (as do wood nymphs at *Od.* VI. 106, or with a ball), or "to dance" (as clearly at *Od.* VIII. 251). Even when the verb means "dance," however, the context reveals that the verb implies a kind of dancing with the emphasis on energy and play, or even playful mime. Thus, when this particular verb for "dance" is used, the nuances of "play" or "sport" are present, as in the prominent example from Book VIII of the *Odyssey* discussed later in this chapter. It follows that the image of choreographed grace, so long associated with the wording of this famous inscription, is in need of revision. Homer must be our guide in discovering what it is. The fullest evidence can be found by following closely in our text Homer's description of the oral way of daily life on the fabulous island of the Phaeacians. There, as Greeks celebrate *xenia,* the *sumposion,* and mimetic dance, we shall get as close as is now possible to the social moment that inspired the words on the Dipylon inscription.

The Homeric Context: Receiving the *Xenos*

Book VIII of the *Odyssey,* which describes Odysseus' reception on the magical island of Scheria as a *xenos,* or guest-friend, has long been recognized as epical singers' idealized description of real social institutions of eighth-century Greece, but as projected back into a timeless fantasy land.[20] The singers did not, of course, invent the Hellenic institutions of the *sumposia,* male drinking parties after supper, or *xenia,* guest-friendship. Nor was the important role given to dance in oral Greek life—an activity that, like singing, does not fossilize and so largely escapes later notice—their invention either. They were prominent features of contemporary life that lasted as important social institutions of Hellenic life throughout the Archaic period.

At one level, Odysseus' sojourn among the Phaeacians is a singer's elaborate description of complex social behavior pretended to belong to a distant past. At another, as close attention to the syntax and vocabulary reveals, it emerges as behavioral prescription and proscription of the most powerful kind, designed to affect and to control the daily life of the generation who hears it and identifies with it. In a word, it is epical verse functioning as the Hellenic paideia, and it reflects the social realities of the eighth century, not Mycenae.

Unlike Mycenae or Pylos or Troy, the island of the Phaeacians was never a historical place, but was born of the epical imagination. It was, in epical function, a narrative device designed to permit Homer, which is to say, epical singers, to describe the proprieties that surrounded the institution of Greek guest-friendship. That is its heart and the burden of a narrative that, in total, involves several books of our *Odyssey*. Life among the Phaeacians permits a description of genuine Hellenic life, not as it was lived in a historical time and place but as transferred for paideutic purposes to a happy, perfect place that transcends time, where everything is as good as it gets, and nothing ever goes irretrievably wrong.

To this island comes the most famous of Greek travelers to be entertained as a guest-friend by the most perfect of hosts. Dance among the guests themselves was normal at *sumposia,* as we learn as early as Book I of the *Odyssey,* where even the suitors of Penelope dance after the singer's performance, but it will have a special role to play in Book VIII. In addition, wine after dinner and song by the *aoidos* followed by dance are revealed in Homer as normal ingredients of the proper entertainment of a guest-friend, but always according to the host's capacities. Athletic contests may play a role in a great house such as that of Alcinous, with its many young men in residence. The exchange of gifts is an invariable ingredient, essentially effecting the relationship and assuring its perpetuity across the generations. So is the *sumposion* or its equivalent, shared drink between men in trustful peace. Behind all the various features of Hellenic *xenia* is the assumption of *pompē,* safe passage or conveyance, which is fundamentally what the traveler seeks and what the host is expected to provide. The fullest description of Hellenic *xenia* is found in Homer's recounting of Odysseus' reception among these happy people. Nothing is left out, for in the great house of Alcinous nothing need be.

Odysseus—shipwrecked, alone, and naked—is first received as a *xenos* by Nausicaa. The formal words exchanged between them reveals much that can be lost in translation. Upon landing on the island, Odysseus wonders aloud (as he does so often in his journey) whether the inhabitants of this new place observe the Hellenic proprieties, in which case he is safe. If not, he is likely to be in mortal danger. At *Odyssey* VI. 120, the naked hero repeats the formulaic wording.

> Are they "outrageous" *(hubristai),* wild, and not "just"
> or are they lovers-of-the-stranger-guest *(philoxeinoi)?*

The word that denigrates, *hubristai,* denotes those who go beyond all proper bounds and the Hellenic proprieties. The positive, or approval, word, *dikaioi* ("just"), designates the opposite, or those who abide by the proprieties. *Dikaios* in epic is not as yet a legal term and barely a moral one. It is an "approval word" designating a man who observes the Hellenic proprieties, no more, but no less. For a Greek who is a stranger in a strange land, the answer to Odysseus' question is urgent information to have. Nausicaa's first word to to him contains his answer: *Xenie,* or "Hail, Stranger-guest." And then to her maidens she says the welcome, formulaic words repeated so often in the *Odyssey:*

> Him now it is necessary to tend. For from Zeus are all
> *xeinoi* (stranger-guests), a small gift but welcome
> *(dosis d'oligē te philē te).*

That is, it is little enough they do for the stranger now, but to him, in his extreme need, welcome indeed.

Later, with the preliminary ablutions and ceremonies required for the *xenos* behind him, Odysseus is suddenly made visible to Queen Arete in the palace of Alcinous. At once, he appeals to her as a *xenos* and a suppliant (VII. 151) and requests safe passage in this foreign land.

> But do you speed my *pompē* ("conveyance," "protected sending") that I may arrive at my native land.

Having said this, Odysseus, surprisingly, seats himself on the hearth, in the ashes, bringing an awed hush to the Phaeacians. For he is helpless and openly acknowledges it to them, thereby also becoming the protected suppliant. Zeus himself now watches over him, and a holy *aidōs* fills him. The oldest man present rises to speak first ("as is proper"), one Echeneos. He is described as very skilled in speech and knowing of all the "oldest" things *(palaia),* that is, the established ways of the Phaeacians. That such a person speaks first in council is standard in Homer. He exclaims (159):

> This is not the more proper (*kallion,* literally "more beautiful" or fine) way, nor is it seemly. . .

The descriptive word, *kalon,* "beautiful" or "proper" (and its negative, *ou kalon*) is a thinly disguised prescriptive designation for an action that is according to the established proprieties of the Hellenes. It is synonymous with other expressions, so pervasive in Homer, that function in this way, such as *dikaion* ("just") and *ou dikaion,* what is *themis* ("of precedent," or more anachronistically, "lawful") and *ou themis,* all of which mean what is "proper," "seemly," or their opposites. The cultural purpose of epic is to afford an opportunity to relate the hundreds of occasions when this speech is used, and so the proper ways of conduct are retold to the people. Scarcely a page of our text of Homer is without examples. When, in the fourth century, Plato complains that Homer educated Hellas, and that people live their entire lives according to this poet (*Republic* X; see chapter 8), this pervasive vocabulary, descriptive in form but prescriptive in intent and social effect, is what he has in mind.

Aged Echeneos, who best of the Phaeacians knows the ancient proprieties, continues:

> Come, make the stranger-guest arise . . .
> for he [Zeus] ever watches over suppliants, *aidōs*-filled *(aidoioi).*

Aidōs—but here used adjectively to describe suppliants—is perhaps the most powerful word in the moral vocabulary of early Greeks. Such men, suppliants and *xenoi,* the "*aidoioi*" of society, are persons charged with *aidōs,* as the untranslatable adjective suggests. That is, to all Hellenes, a stranger-guest and suppliants generally inspire a deep feeling of *aidōs,* awe and profound reverence. To violate them would be a thing for which a Hellene would feel a terrible *nemesis,* were he to view it. It would be a horrific offense against all that is proper, and so holy, an utter abomination.

Constant, persuasive repetition of the incidents in which such conduct is exemplified—in compliance as well as in violation—is required for the system of values to be learned and made one's own. In this way only will the proper, correct reactions be felt in the appropriate circumstances. In the oral situation, only singers were available to perform this culturally indispensable task. As a result, the syntax of Homeric suasion never departs from narrative description, the stuff of epic, but its deeper purpose is prescriptive.

Echeneos states that the *xenos* must be given what belongs properly to *xenia,* the proprieties of guest-friendship. King Alcinous, the model of hosts and hospitality—Phaeacian hospitality was to be proverbial into Roman times—acts accordingly, with magnificence.

Later, as the guest gifts are being prepared for the guest, Alcinous orders the proprieties of receiving a stranger-guest: feasting, *sumposion,* followed by the divine singer, games, and dance. Employing a favorite device of reciters of oral verse, Homer has the gracious king request that Odysseus listen to his words so that he can later recount them and recall for some other hero at a banquet that excellence and those deeds of the Phaeacians that "Zeus has established, through a long time, from the days of our fathers."

Now these are many, as the king remarks (VIII. 248–249), for the good things of life are many. The Phaeacians are not the very best in Greece in boxing, perhaps, but they are fine fishermen; and, too, on their feet, they are "very light."

> And always dear to us is the banquet and the lyre and the dance,
> fresh changes of clothes, hot baths, and the bed.

But of all these good things, remarks Alcinous, especially dear to them is the dance. Here the king's words, as he summons the young dancers to the contest, require close attention. Summoning the young men, the king orders that

> you of Phaeacian dancers who are best *(hossoi aristoi),*
> make sport *(paisate)* . . .

so that the stranger-guest may return home and tell his friends how skilled the Phaeacians were as dancers.[21] The king's own son is singled out and rewarded at the end of the performance as "best of dancers."

This wording, with *protasis* (involving a superlative) followed by *apodosis,* which summons the best of dancers to sport playfully, recalls at once the wording of the Dipylon inscription (but here, of course, in the plural). The verb *paizō,* in the imperative plural and translated "make sport," may, as in my translation of the Dipylon dancer's inscription, also be translated as "dance," but various Homeric translators in electing to render it "sport" have caught the nuances in this verse of the *Odyssey.* What is to follow is not a stately performance, or a well-choreographed *choreia,* but the sheer energy of flying feet, and some improvised, mimetic fun—activities suited to the skilled young dancers summoned by King Alcinous to a *sumposion* that follows the feast. Was this famous scene, then, and perhaps these very words or words much like them in the Dipylon composer's mind as he made his now famous verse? It is difficult to resist the conclusion that they were.[22]

The Symposiatic Occasion for Inscribing the Dipylon Oinochoe

In light of this Homeric scene, and especially the words of King Alcinous in announcing the dancers' competition, I conclude that the Dipylon wine jug was a casual prize awarded at a private *sumposion* in an ordinary Greek household. The vessel, we recall, is a symposiastic one, an oinochoe or wine jug. On occasions involving drink and song, dance similar to that among the legendary Phaeacians (that is, energetic, playful, mimetic, often sexually suggestive) was surely a prominent feature. The very old Thera erotic inscriptions, some in the rhythm of the hexameter, give us some further, graphic clues to the nature of the "dirty dancing." One reads "Eumelos best at dancing." The inspiration behind them is undoubtedly the male *sumposion*. Some dancers would always be expected to come off as more skillful and energetic (common enough in the Greek taverna to this day), as was the case among the competing young dancers at the *sumposion* of King Alcinous. The best would be the dancer who *atalōtata paizei,* "sports most playfully." On the perfect, magical island of King Alcinous, he turns out to be, naturally enough, none other than the king's own son, Prince Laodamas.

Presumably the Dipylon verse was hastily scratched—some very sharp object was used, perhaps a kitchen utensil or a pin—either by the host or by one of the guests. The inscriber did his graphic best, but he could not match the technical skill of the verse itself, which is splendid. The three heavy feet, all spondees, which set off the *protasis* in the rhythm – –/– –/ – –, suggest an oral proclamation, in imitation of a herald's solemn pronouncement, although here the rhythm is perhaps somewhat mock-serious. Possibly the words were those of the *sumposion*'s host, who announced that now the best of dancers among his guests, in the display to follow, will receive a jug of wine. If the scene is correctly identified as symposiastic, then plausibly the occasion, as so often in Homer, was also a part of *xenia,* the entertainment of some guest-friend. In another very old inscription on a wine jug, this time from Odysseus' island of Ithaca, we can be sure of this reconstruction from the wording itself, for *xenos* appears in the epical phrasing. It is discussed in the next chapter.

The Dipylon verse, as originally sung or chanted at a *sumposion,* was intended to recall and evoke a familiar Homeric scene and so assimilate the present occasion and its eighth-century participants to a timeless, epical one. It was followed by hundreds of similar inscriptions to come after it in the Greek *corpus* of metrical inscriptions. The nameless inscriber may well have been, as several scholars including L. H. Jeffery have suggested, an itinerant, and so perhaps not an Athenian at all. The wine jug, once inscribed, gains value and becomes a personal memento of a happy day. The successful dancer orders the treasured jug to be buried with him, but this (probably) many years later, for this sort of dance was a young man's activity, as King Alcinous' summons reminds us. The date of the manufacture of the graffito, then, as opposed to the firing of the pot, may have been anytime between, say, ca. 740 and ca. 700 B.C.

The Homeric Paideia

What has emerged is that ''Homer'' for Archaic Greece—or whatever name was used very early for epical verse,[23] if there was one—was a complex and surpassingly successful discourse of social education and control. The later Greek word for this phenomenon was *paideia,* a near-perfect choice.[24] The word reflects the Greeks' acknowledgment that paideia involves an unconscious, willing acceptance of ancestral models, even as a *pais,* a boy, models himself on his male elders, his father and his older brothers, and his most admired peers, normally the group's best warriors or best athletes. It is a process as old as our species and, especially for adolescent males, effective beyond telling.

Seemingly, every complex society of primary orality conveys its own paideia as, foremost, a body of approved discourse, a description of proper behavior believed to have been the way of ancestors.[25] By sharing in it and making the discourse one's own, the individual learns such matters as whom to marry and whom to shun, how to treat the accidental homicide, what proprieties are required toward the stranger at the gate, and a thousand more lessons like them. An oral paideia is, for the people who willingly absorb it, no less than their way of life. It is a form of discourse hoarded by the entire community, to be sure, but it is everywhere in oral societies discovered to be the special preserve of tribal singers and reciters.[26]

The contrast between the brilliantly civilized ways of the Phaeacians and the savage ways of the brutal Cyclopes, who are without the benefits of either singers or established custom ways—and so devoid of *themis*—must have been a favorite of Homeric singers. The blinded, one-eyed Polyphemus is, for example, among the earliest figures identifiably Homeric to appear in the pictorial artwork of early vases.[27] The Cyclopes, as Homer continually reminds us, have no established proprieties, no *agoras* or meeting places, no singers, no *sumposia,* no social decency. They are the perfect foil to the Phaeacians, and it is not an accident that Odysseus has his disastrous encounter with them just before washing up on the island of Scheria.

Above all, the Cyclopes do not know or respect *xenia.* So ''outrageous'' are they that they even *eat* stranger-travelers who have the misfortune to happen upon them. Each of the monsters sets the rules of his own habitation arbitrarily and proceeds to brutalize his wife and children within his own cave as the impulse moves him. The Cyclopes are, in a word, the very antithesis of civilized Hellenes—or, at least, of what Hellenes envisioned themselves to be when on their good behavior. The wretched Cyclopes are, preeminently *oude dikaioi,* ''not-just,'' in the Homeric and essentially preethical sense of *dikaios.* The positive term, as noted, designates a person who observes the established proprieties of all Hellenes. The forms of the word with the *alpha-privative,* such as Hesiodic *adika,* designate the opposite.

Most important, the words are not, strictly speaking, ethical terms or moral abstractions as we now deploy such linguistic counters and seek to analyze them in Western intellectualized ethics. The latter enterprise is a product of advanced literacy and of Greek philosophy. It is alien to any attempt to understand Homeric discourse in its own terms. In a fundamental sense, the discourse of preliterate moral suasion remains preethical. It is, however, far from being socially ineffective. Indeed, a case could be made that as a society moves away from it toward ever greater precision and abstract analysis in moral discourse—necessary to the literate mentality, and to "rationality" itself, now the unquestioned goal of ethical discourse—the society diminishes its ability to control or alter behavior, or, in Aristotle's charge, "to make men better in their cities." Be that as it may, ethics—or perhaps better, proper conduct—was in Archaic Greece a matter not of reason but of aspiration, conveyed in a form of moral discourse that required the constant narration of gifted singers. In just this manner, as Plato was still complaining almost four centuries later, "Homer educated Greece."

Conclusion: The Epical Singer and the Oral Way of Life ca. 700 B.C.

The remainder of Book VIII of the *Odyssey* concerns the proper completion of the *pompē*, the "conveyance" or escort of the guest-friend Odysseus, as he prepares to depart the court of gracious King Alcinous. Included are several more occasions that serve, borrowing the words of T. E. Lawrence, to "cocker up" at every opportunity the standing of the singer Demodocus, "held in high honor by the people."[28] Again installed in his high-backed chair, the singer is being given, at Odysseus' own direction, a prize cut of meat off "the chine of the white-tusked boar." Immortal singer is addressed by immortal hero:

> For among all men that walk the wide earth,
> singers win honor *(timē)* and deep reverence *(aidōs),*
> for her own paths the Muse has taught them, and she loves much the tribe of singers.[29]

Of these, we are again told, best of all was blind Demodocus who sang for great King Alcinous.

Book VIII, which tells us so much about Homer's world, ends with Alcinous gently asking Odysseus to fulfill his part of the formal requirements of *xenia.* He has questions to answer, welcome news to impart. Who is he? What is his real name? Where has he been, what has he seen of famous cities, and what does he know of what happened at Troy? For why, asks Alcinous carefully, is the stranger-guest so heavy of heart, and given to sudden weeping when he hears from the skilled singer the fate of the Argive Dannans, and of windy Ilium, and of those days so long (and yet not so long) ago? Surely these things the gods wrought,

> . . . and spun the web of destruction for men
> that there might be song for all the generations yet to be born.[30]

Did the stranger-guest himself perhaps lose a father in the fighting there at Troy, or a brother or other kin? Or was it some dear comrade, some brave, true friend with thoughts like his own?

For no less than a brother is a friend who knows your heart.[31]

These concluding words of Book VIII, and its last verses, belong appropriately to wise Alcinous.

In Book VIII of the *Odyssey* we discover that the banquet and the *sumposion,* song and dance and the games, the obligations and proprieties of *xenia*—and all their rewarding pleasures—belonged in a special way to oral Greece. They were, seemingly, at the heart of Homer's Greece, what its inhabitants found most pleasurable but also most useful in life, and so prized and celebrated above all else. Should it surprise us, then, that in the first scraps of writing to come from these Greeks we can hear distant echoes—remote now from our experience, but somehow evocative still—of just these oral activities?

What these inscriptions capture are moments of the oral way of life as Greeks of the late eighth century lived and enjoyed it, but now for the first time are also able to record in writing, thereby elevating the humble objects that bear the words into the timeless world of epic. In so doing, they resort to epical speech, Homer's discourse, which countless generations of skilled singers had taught them. The constant three—the male *sumposion* organized around wine and epical song, guest-friendship and hospitality in a society of unsettled political organization, and dance—were important institutions of contemporary oral life. All three underwent changes in the Archaic Age, as social conditions changed, but their Homeric origins, a product of the social conditions of preliteracy, are unmistakable.

As part of what Greeks would later call *mousikē,* especially the *sumposion,* which fostered both the composition and performance of sung poetry, much of it instructional and cautionary in tone, would remain at the core of Greece's paideia in the ages before it knew writing or learned fully to exploit its ways. Even as letters spread slowly in succeeding centuries, the traditional male *sumposion* was to retain its paideutic role. Only in the late fourth century would it at last become something of an anachronism, although we have reports of its continuation in the Academy, at Plato's direction.

If true, a note of regret or at least nostalgia may be detectable. The passing of the traditional *sumposion* as a primary institution of Hellenic paideia would mark as well the passing of oral Greece, the Hellas Plato remembered from his youth. The triumph of literacy over the ancient modes of Hellenic paideia, and so of its "music," would then be complete.

Notes

1. E. A. Havelock, "The Sophistication of Homer," in *I. A. Richards: Essays in His Honor* (New York, 1973), p. 259.

2. "This degree of scope and economy cannot be accidental; nor can it be the creation of a single poet. No one singer could construct a system so rich in metrical alternatives and at the same time so closely shorn of unfunctional variation. Even a pen and paper composer would be hard pressed to achieve such a system, and to do so he would have to behave not like a poet but a cryptographer. . . . " (G. S. Kirk, *Homer and the Epic* [Cambridge, 1965], p. 7).

3. The fundamental work is A. Parry (ed.), *The Making of Homeric Verse: The Collected Papers of Milman Parry* (Oxford, 1971). The introduction by Adam Parry to his father's published works was itself a major contribution to the literature on the Homeric question.

4. This point is basic to the argument of the present work. The scholar who, to the best of my knowledge, first fully appreciated that this conclusion follows inescapably from the Homeric diction found prominently in the oldest Greek epigrams was Paul Friedländer. This implication of his research, which was ahead of its time, did not initially receive the attention it deserved. See Paul Friedländer (with the collaboration of H. B. Hoffleit), *Epigrammata* (Berkeley and Los Angeles), 1948.

5. Barry Powell, *Homer and the Origin of the Greek Alphabet,* p. 16. William Harris, *Ancient Literacy,* p. vii, writes: "It is an impressive fact that in spite of all the Greek archaeological discoveries of recent generations the Dipylon Vase, found in 1871, remained until a short time ago the earliest known text, or was at least as early as any other." The early dating of this graffito stood up under the intense debate of over a century. Rival claimants came and went.

6. The Semitic *heth* was a guttural, initially used in the Greek alphabet to denote the *spiritus asper,* as here. For the vowels, a *spiritus lenis (aleph)* was adopted for the Greek vowel *a; he* for *e; ayin* (also a guttural) for *o; yod* for *iota.* Opinion has been divided concerning whether *u* is a differentiation of *waw* or a newly invented sign. Also, it has been neglected that Cyprus may well have been the inspiration for this sign. All five vowels are present in the Greek inscriptions from the start, but without indicating quantity, for example, long or short *o* or *e.* There is no evidence for a period of development or experiment. Script transmission required considerable cooperation between participating Phoenicians and Greeks, and friendly, oral instruction involving at least one or (more likely) two bilinguals. This implies contact beyond casual trading or barter. No amount of silent contemplation of Phoenician marks without accompanying oral instruction could have resulted in the transmission of the abecedarium and its phonetic values.

7. *IG* 1^2 919; *IG* 1 Suppl. 492a. See Jeffery, *LSAG,* pp. 15–16, 68, 76. This translation of *atalōtata* is defended subsequently. The conventional translation is "Who of all the dancers now most *gracefully* . . . " or, more rarely for *atalōtata* (Bowra and a few others), "*best.*" For extensive bibliography of earlier treatments of this famous vase, see G. Annibaldis and O. Vox, "La più antica iscrizione greca," *Glotta* 54 (1976), pp. 223ff; M. Marcovich, "On the Earliest Greek Verse Inscriptions," *ParPass* [*La Parola del Passato*] 126 (1969), pp. 217–218; A. Heubeck, *Schrift* [= Archeologica Homerica III. X] (Göttingen, 1979), p. 6.

8. Notably, the readings of especially the final letters (40 to 47) are in doubt. So too is the verb's dialect, which has been suspected of not being Greek. Marcovich (see n. 7) has offered a reading that is attractive for other than epigraphical reasons. He sees on the jug *totodeklemen,* which he would read *touto d' eklemen,* yielding in translation the attractive "to him do I belong." If correct, then, as on so many early inscriptions, the artifact speaks. This reading would require, however, as Marcovich notes, that the inscription contain an otherwise unattested (but not impossible) athematic root aorist. Also, Marcovich reconstructs *MEN* as first having been written as *MIN,* and then the *I* corrected to *E* with a vertical stroke. For a useful survey of the various attempts to read especially letters 40, 43, 44, 45, and 46, and a rejection of the wilder guesses, see M. Langdon, "The Dipylon Oinochoe Again," *AJA* 79 (1975); also B. Powell, "The Dipylon Oinochoe Inscription and the Spread of Literacy in 8th Century Athens," *Kadmos* 27 (1988), pp. 65–86.

9. See K. Robb, "Poetic Sources of the Greek Alphabet," in Havelock and Hershbell, *Communication Arts.* A "developmental period" has been a persistent refuge for those

reluctant to admit that the Greek alphabet may have been invented as late as the eighth century. Before the full force of Rhys Carpenter's challenge in the 1930s was felt, Semitic and Greek scholars alike had placed the invention of the Greek alphabet anywhere from the late twelfth to the early eighth centuries, which had the effect of obscuring the essential orality of the centuries preceding 700 B.C., during which the Greek epic tradition had developed to maturity, as evidenced in both the first inscriptions and the earliest literary productions. For example, Bury in the old *Cambridge Ancient History* (vol. IV, pp. 470–471) suggested a tenth century date for reception of the alphabet, and a ninth century date for Homer. Ullman, in "How Old Is the Greek Alphabet?" *AJA* 38 (1934), still argued for the "eleventh or twelfth centuries." Earlier, the 1894 edition of Pauly-Wissowa (s.v. "Alphabet") had settled authoritatively on the tenth century. Ten years before that, Ulrich von Wilamowitz-Mollendorf, in his *Homerische Untersuchungen* (Berlin, 1884) had ponderously argued that the Greek alphabet must have preceded the Dorian invasions. Today such high dates are not much in evidence, but a residual reluctance to accept a date as low as ca. 750 B.C., plus or minus, persists. In the late 1950s T.B.L. Webster, in his de Carle lectures at the University of Otago, published as *Greek Art and Literature: 700–530 B.C.* (Dunedin, 1959), p. 7, recognized the Dipylon as the oldest Greek inscription, placing it in the eighth century. But he placed with it in that century "at least" five other inscriptions, namely, those from Perachora, Ischia, Thebes, Corinth, and Ithaca (see p. 17, n. 17). That yielded six "certain" eighth-century inscriptions and fostered arguments for pushing the date of the alphabet's introduction back even further. We must allow, it was argued, for a traceless "developmental" period on perishable materials and for the fact that we are unlikely to find the first inscribed specimens, and so on. Thirty years later many Greek epigraphists would feel far less confident about an eighth-century date for at least three of Webster's inscriptions, and perhaps none would be placed before the last decades of that century.

10. The second exception has been claimed for the Lacco Ameno sherd from Pithekoussi, which bears only two letters *(pi, alpha).* Following Guarducci, McCarter dated it to the middle of the eighth century in *The Antiquity of the Greek Alphabet and the Early Phoenician Scripts* (Missoula, 1975), pp. 66, 134, and placed it in the Greek sequence ("entered with caution"). Later he argued that it is probably not Greek, but Phoenician. See McCarter, "A Phoenician *Graffito* from Pithekoussi," *AJA* 79 (1975), pp. 140–141. See also Alan Johnston, "The Extent and Use of Literacy," p. 63, n. 3.

11. The tall, crooked, three-stroked *iota* is already replaced by the straight *iota* in the Athenian series on the Acropolis slab, probably, as often supposed, to distinguish it from the Attic *sigma.* Such considerations (the odd *rho* on the Dipylon may also be noted) make any rigid argument from the "criterion of closest approach," or script comparisons, problematical for individual letters. Disregarding troublesome individual letters and then trying to mate the censored abecedaria becomes increasingly subjective and arbitrary, a point stressed at last in the course of the long "alphabet wars" by J. Penrose Harland in his "The Date of the Hellenic Alphabet," *Studies in Philology* 42 (1945), pp. 413ff. This leaves as evidence mainly the dating of the artifacts that bear the inscriptions. No amount of argument from script comparisons, it seems to me, especially when based on isolated letters, can overcome a total silence in the inscriptional record, as would be required by some of the controversial but stimulating suggestions of Joseph Naveh. See J. Naveh, *Early History of the Alphabet* (Jerusalem and Leiden, 1982), and, "Some Semitic Epigraphical Considerations on the Antiquity of the Greek Alphabet," *AJA* 77 (1973), pp. 1–8.

12. Jeffery, *LSAG,* pp. 16, 68; E. A. Havelock, *Literate Revolution,* p. 206, n. 14.

13. Borrowing from my own experiences of living and traveling extensively in Anatolia in the 1960s, in some early articles I suggested that writing, when added to the surface of

an artifact, increases its value in societies newly literate, or only partially so. Critics strongly questioned whether this experience could be transferred to early Greece, but I note the suggestion has gained a supporter in Powell, in *Homer and the Origin of the Greek Alphabet.*

14. In other dialects the uncontracted form would be found, *orchēstaōn, orchēsteōn* (both *a*-stem endings *-aōn* and *eōn* are possible in Homer) and also the contraction *orchēstan.* The *a*-stem ending *-an* is not found in Homer but found once each in the *Theogony* and *Works and Days.* See G. P. Edwards on the endings of the genitive plural of *a*-stems in Homer and Hesiod; the ending in *-aōn* is far more common in Homer than in Hesiod. G. P. Edwards, *The Language of Hesiod in Its Traditional Context* (Oxford, 1971), pp. 26–27.

15. Jean M. Davison, in private conversation (1979) as reported in Havelock, *Literate Revolution,* p. 5. Davison's publication on Attic Geometric workshops in *Yale Classical Studies,* 1961, especially pp. 32–33 and 73–75, proved to be seminal for the understanding of this jug. Epigraphists are reminded of the ordinary (for its time) character of the pot itself by its position in J. N. Coldstream's monumental *Greek Geometric Pottery* (London, 1968), p. 32. It is placed with the rest of the undistinguished *oinochoai* under "Minor Vases" of the period. It was a pot intended for household use, well-made, suitable for symposiastic occasions to be sure, and durable. For its day, however, it was hardly expensive or "fine." What gave it value to its owner, so that he ordered it to be part of his grave goods, surely was that it was a memento of his early victory in a young man's dance exhibition and that it bore writing, rare if not unique for the time. Barry Powell took exception to my description of the vase as a "cheap pot," in his "The Dipylon Oinochoe Inscription," p. 66. This disagreement may be a matter of semantics. Dunbabin in the 1940s, who correctly dated the pot to the second half of the eighth century, and arguing against a date then claimed by various authorities to be as early as 760 B.C., described it as "typical poor Late Geometric" (quoted in Jeffery, *LSAG,* p. 68, n. 4). That seems right to me. In any case, the pot is ceramically of little significance, either now or when it was manufactured. Perhaps "ordinary for its day" or "not expensive for its time, having been manufactured for daily use" would result in less disagreement between Powell and me. On a related matter there may yet be real disagreement. What I had sought to exclude was the automatic deduction, found in some histories, that the grave in which the pot was found belonged to an aristocrat. We do not know that. *Sumposia* were never exclusively an aristocratic practice, although the richer one was, the more elaborate they could be. Our dancer could easily have been a participant in a *sumposion* hosted by a prosperous merchant or trader emulating aristocratic (epical) practice.

16. An early attempt to pin down the religious festival was that of Lillian Lawler (*Classical Weekly* 41 (1947), pp. 50ff., who postulated a local Athenian festival in honor of Artemis, a sheer guess. (I owe this reference to Paul Friedländer.) I have come to question the festival theory and favor a private *sumposion* as the occasion for inscription. By the final Christmas before his death, Eric Havelock was similarly persuaded, as he conceded in a vigorous discussion in his home at Vassar College, made all the more memorable for me because it was to be our last of so many exchanges concerning this troublesome pot. In order to describe these ritualized ceremonies after supper, involving wine, song and dance, I shall, as has become customary, use the later term *sumposion.* The definitive history of the Greek *sumposion* and its relation to paideia—and to the production of much of what we now call lyric poetry—has as yet to be written (it is a *desideratum* of Hellenic scholarship). Oswyn Murray's recent article is a perceptive beginning. See Murray, "The *Sumposion* as Social Organization," in Robin Hägg (ed.), *The Greek Renaissance of the Eighth Century B.C.,* pp. 195–199 (with the discussion), and the contributions

in Murray (ed.), *Sympotica: A Symposium on the Symposium* (Oxford, 1990). The publications of Bruno Gentili—many available only in Italian, a situation that deserves early remedy—are also of considerable relevance and value. See now B. Gentili, *Poetry and Its Public in Ancient Greece* (Baltimore and London, 1988), with an insightful introduction by the translator, A. T. Cole. There are some useful remarks on the *sumposion* as the locus for performing archaic poetry (where we tend to suppose a text being written to be read) in J. Trumpf, "Uber das Trinken in der Poesie des Alkaios," *ZPE* 12 (1973), pp. 139–160. A useful translation of much of surviving early Greek so-called lyric poetry, with awareness of the role of ancient audiences, is D. Mulroy, *Early Greek Lyric Poetry* (Ann Arbor, 1992), especially pp. 9–11 and 15–16.

17. See K. Robb, "The Dipylon Prize Graffito," *Coranto* 7 (1971), pp. 12ff. Even Friedländer adopted the traditional translation "most gracefully," adding: "This unpretentious jug apparently served as the reward for the most graceful dancer in an Attic dancing competition" (P. Friedländer, *Epigrammata,* pp. 54–55). Friedländer, perceptive as ever, noted that the character of the verse and the language chosen by the composer gave to this modest pot and its owner an epical dimension, taking both it and him into Homer's world (see *Epigrammata* pp. 8, 55). Here I suggest that the surviving text of Homer may permit narrower identification. The dominating Homeric diction, with an emphasis on associated Homeric vocabulary and formulas, was first detailed by the oralist pioneer, James Notopoulos, in "Homer, Hesiod, and the Achaean Heritage of Oral Poety," *Hesperia* 29 (1960), pp. 195ff. The Homeric character of the diction, placing an emphasis on metrics, was also argued by Calvert Watkins in *Indo-European Studies* 2 (1975), pp. 444–446, a valuable work privately printed by the Department of Linguistics at Harvard. His argument is now more accessible in C. Watkins, "Syntax and Metrics in the Dipylon Vase Inscription," in A. Morpurgo Davies and W. Meid (eds.), *Studies in Greek, Italic, and IndoEuropean Linguistics Offered to L. R. Palmer* (Innsbruck, 1976), pp. 435–441. Also, as noted previously, the three archaic dancer inscriptions cut on some rocks near the old gymnasium at Thera are relevant, involving as they do both overt male eroticism, poetry, and competitive dancing. The dancing here is clearly of the vigorous, wild, even "riotously satyric" type (the happy designation of Rufus Bellamy). The wording of *IG*. XII. 3. 540 seems to suggest some private competition among the dancers: *Eumelos aristos orchestas.*

18. See also E. A. Havelock, *Literate Revolution,* p. 193. See M. Leuman, "ἀταλός" *Glotta* 15 (1927), pp. 153–155, for an interesting theory of the word's derivation, which, even if not correct, reveals why the etymology is puzzling.

19. *Works and Days* 131. See also *Theog*. 989 (with West's note). The word was surely in common use in eighth-century bardic vocabulary and already with the developed meaning that context uniformly reveals for it.

20. See, for example, the stimulating discussion of C. P. Segal, "The Phaeacians and the Symbolism of Odysseus," in *Arion* 1 (1962), pp. 17–74. For a pioneering work on the importance of the institution of *xenia* in Archaic Greek society, and of the role of the land of the Phaeacians as a kind of *prescribing* utopia (with the land of the Cyclopes a *proscribing* never-never land), see M. I. Finley, *The World of Odysseus* (New York, 1980), pp. 100–101. Finley's brief discussion has been taken up and expanded in Gabriel Herman, *Ritualized Friendship and the Greek City* (Cambridge, 1987). H. Hommell, in his "Tanzen und Spielen," *Gymnasium* 56 (1949), pp. 201–205, may have been the first to detect the relevance of the description of the *sumposion* and the dance in Book VIII to the wording of the Dipylon inscription. I know of no thorough treatment, however.

21. *Od.* VIII. 250–251. See a similar construction at VII. 327–328. Very close in structure (not vocabulary) is VIII. 382.

22. Several scholars have recognized that the supposition of mimetic dance, whereas

neglected in much Homeric scholarship, is almost unavoidable in the Demodocus scene as the singer describes in some hundred verses the punishment of Ares and Aphrodite by lame Hephasteus, the cuckold. This had led to the plausible speculation that dancers were regularly a part of the entourage of at least some *aoidoi* in the epical period. Albin Lesky, *A History of Greek Literature* (New York, 1966), p. 5, writes: "As he [Demodocus] sings youths dance around him. Was this a representation in mime of the story?" Certainty is not afforded in our text, of course. J. A. Davison considered epical recitations to be of two sorts: less formal, where the singer is seated and there is no chorus; and more formal, as in the Demodocus scene described here, where he stands and there is an accompanying "chorus." Presumably only the latter would readily lend itself to mimetic dance. See J. A. Davison, "The Homeric Question," in Wace and Stubbings (eds.), *A Companion to Homer* (London and New York, 1963), p. 217. The intimate relationship of mimetic dance to oral recitations in such diverse places as contemporary Africa and the Australian bush suggests that scholars' attention needs to be redirected to the evidence in archaic Greece. An *aoidos* sings a dirge, presumably also in hexameters, in a well-known passage describing Hector's funeral at *Iliad* XXIV. 720–722; in another, Achilles in his tent sings epical verse to himself and Patroclus. At a minimum, a citizen of eighth-century Hellas would expect to hear epical song *(aoidē)* at such occasions as weddings and funerals, praise songs for great men (and dead *basileis*), theogonic and other hymns, temple dedications, *sumposia,* and, of course, festival recitations, probably already agonistic. The list could be expanded. Epical and theogonic material in hexameters may not (are we certain?) have remained fashionable at the fourth-century *sumposia,* but Xenophanes (B.1, *passim*) makes it undeniable that it was still part of the evening's performance in the sixth. As with persons who hear song continually in our or any other culture, some of it—favorite snatches or even sequences of verses—become embedded in the popular memory. So do certain basic rhythms and patterns, in which other words than those originally composed can be partially substituted. Perceptively, William Thalmann writes: "For those who composed it, poetry was a profession, and for those who listened to it, a means of enjoyment. But at the same time, it was a way of knowing the world, for it told of the physical arrangement of the cosmos, of the divine powers that influenced events, and of man's place in the whole scheme. . . . By embodying the forms of thought habitual to poet and audience, the poem evolved in the course of performance as a model or mental image of the world that it sought to elucidate" (*Conventions of Form and Thought in Early Greek Epic Poetry* [Baltimore and London, 1984], p. 32). This valuable book emphasizes throughout, as I have sought to do in discussing the early inscriptions, that epic poetry was addressed to every level of society, high and low, and its content was accepted and absorbed by all, for it constituted what I term the Hellenic paideia. This is, of course, the opposite position from that held by those scholars who still accept a view of "Homer" or epical verse as aristocratic court poetry.

23. The name Homer, as is well known, appears sparsely in the earliest Greek literature. Also, what some Greek authors (e.g., Pindar) meant by Homer seems to have included the author of works not known to us or else not now considered Homeric. Even Aristotle, writing well into the fourth century, still regarded epical material other than the *Iliad* and *Odyssey* as Homeric. Clearly the attribution of Homeric authorship was initially fluid, and stabilized only gradually. One may speculate that as the epical material came to be known increasingly as written texts—at least in part—the need for a particular author for it came to be more strongly felt, a phenomenon paralleled in the case of Moses and the Pentateuch. Great *books,* in any case, are normally required to have great authors. A body of oral verse—even an authoritative one—seemingly does not, at least if other oral societies are any sort of guide.

24. There are many recent, influential, and insightful works dealing with Homeric "ethics" or values, including those by Adkins, MacIntyre and Irwin. For an analysis of how the Homeric "moral" or approval vocabulary functioned both syntactically and emotively, I have found helpful some works from an older generation of scholars, such as Lionel Pearson, T. A. Sinclair, and the historian of Greek law, George Calhoun. My debts to them emerge in later chapters. The early chapters of Werner Jaeger's long-influential *Paideia,* vol. 1, performed a great service by calling the attention of scholars to the essentially paideutic character of much of early Greek literature, especially epic. The book is out of date, but Jaeger's remarks are still pertinent.

25. The term *paideia* is normally translated "education," which conjures up images of schools, texts, curricula, and the like that can be misleading for the Archaic period. The term "enculturation," now commonly used by sociologists and some anthropologists and accepted by recent English dictionaries (as is paideia), comes closer to the Greek connotations. A related term often used by historians is "oral law" or "oral custom law," but I have grown uneasy with it. Some such term is useful, but the term "law" does not readily translate back into the vocabulary of oral or Homeric Greece. *Themis,* "precedent" or "right" (the plural is used to designate established precedents, the norms of approved behavior), does not really mean "law," and *nomos* is brought into its "ethical" use, as "custom," by Hesiod. It does not mean "written law" before Cleisthenes. A body of precedents conveyed mainly in narrative form, and so as paradigmatic actions, combined with sayings, admonitions, and the like, is one thing; an oral body of casuistic law, memorized and passed across generations, and presumably used by magistrates, is quite another. For the latter we have no Greek evidence, despite much speculation. Oral societies (to generalize precariously) have practices and procedures with similar societal functions as modern laws, but they do not really have "law" as we understand the term. At least this is true of Greek Homeric society, and of oral societies I have personally been able to observe in Africa and Australia. Loren McIntyre writes of the Xavantes in Mato Grosso on the Amazon: "Except when gathered into a mission and taught by priests and nuns to obey . . . Indian boys never need to fear punishment. Fathers [and other male initiators] chat with sons and teach them to fish and shoot and dance and fight and how to behave in a free society that knows neither please nor thank you nor headmen who command." Left to themselves, the Xavantes would have no concept that corresponds to what we mean by "law" (and so no word for it). See L. McIntyre, *Amazonia* (San Francisco, 1991), p. 101. Of course, they have established ways, ancestral precedents, and constant, instructing association (what Greeks would call *sunousia*) with male elders, together with mechanisms, allied to music, of more formally transmitting what amounts to a way of life, or paideia. Again McIntyre's report is instructive (p. 91): "I once told Orlando that I wished for the gift of perceiving the world as Indians do. 'Oh Loren, you can't get inside their heads,' he replied, 'but give it a try.' He turned me over to a Waura who was returning to his village . . . men gathered at their lodge, the flute house in the middle of the village clearing. In its dim interior three painted men stomped back and forth playing low notes on giant magic flutes that women are forbidden to behold. Then warriors finger painted each other with erucú, getting ready to exchange presents [with some visiting tribesmen], dance and wrestle with the visiting Yawalapiti. . . . " This is not Homer's Greece, of course, and yet in some oral practices may be closer to it than the later Greek institutions created by full alphabetic literacy. The Xavantes seem to be, in Michael Gagarin's useful terminology, "pre-legal," whereas epical Greece is, in his designation, "proto-legal"; that is, it possesses no legal rules recognized as such, but does have established, formal procedures for resolving disputes. See M. Gagarin, *Early Greek Law* (Berkeley and Los Angeles, 1986), pp. 8ff.

26. Alex Haley, who identified himself as an oralist in his last years, discovered this phenomenon among the *griots* of his ancestral Gambia. He described the experience movingly in the final chapters of *Roots.* A Belgian scholar, Jan Vansina, a noted oralist and Africanist, and author of *La Tradition Orale,* had been his early academic guide to African oral traditions. See Alex Haley, *Roots* (Garden City, 1976), pp. 662–688. Reciters of "historical poetry" are also found in Rwanda with a strong distinction between the gesticulating, participating audience and the professional performer. See R. Finnegan, *Oral Literature in Africa* (Oxford, 1970), pp. 6ff., citing the observations of Coupez and Kamanzei. Also, among the Nyanga, an isolated tribe in the African rainforest, the singers and performers are generally professionals, but the audience, which is totally familiar with the material, freely joins in, anticipating the responses, and so on. See Daniel Biebuyck's introduction, where further bibliography is cited, in D. Biebuyck and Kahombo Mateene, *The Mwindo Epic* (Berkeley and Los Angeles, 1971). Isidore Okepwho's moving and instructive account in *The Epic in Africa* (New York, 1976) draws on both early personal tribal experience and a thorough knowledge of Parry. The contemporary philosopher and historian of ethics Alasdair MacIntyre, whereas hardly coming at the material from an oralist perspective, is faithful to the Homeric facts in his influential *After Virtue* (Notre Dame, Ind., 1984) when he writes (p. 120): "the chief means of moral education is the telling of stories . . . such narratives did provide the historical memory, adequate or inadequate, of the societies in which they were finally written down. More than that they provided a moral background to contemporary debate [in classical Greece] . . . . " Professor MacIntyre regards this assessment as "relatively indisputable historical fact," which, of course, it should be. There is from some quarters, nevertheless, an almost passionate opposition to any suggestion that epic functioned as moral paideia for Greeks at least down to Plato.

27. See J. M. Hurwit, *The Art and Culture of Early Greece, 1100–480 B.C.* (Ithaca and London, 1985), pp. 168–169.

28. *Od.* VIII. 472. Lawrence was the author of a notable translation of the *Odyssey* under the assumed name of T. E. Shaw. The insightful introduction reveals his wide experience among preliterates, mainly Bedouin, and of the restricted literacy of Arab societies early in this century. When the famous typographer Bruce Rogers wrote to Lawrence proposing a translation of the *Odyssey,* he accepted, claiming that "it [the Greek text] goes with me, always, to every camp, for I love it . . . " (quoted from Jeremy Wilson, *Lawrence of Arabia* [New York, 1990], p. 814. Adam Parry often observed that his father found Lawrence to be a sympathetic figure and perhaps something of a fellow romantic. Lawrence had, Milman Parry believed, a good sense of what he himself called "the oral way of life," one gained from direct experience of it. He brought it to his translation of Homer. See now the perceptive introduction of Bernard Knox in T. E. Lawrence, *The Odyssey of Homer* (Oxford and New York, 1991). Also see the relevant observations in T. E. Lawrence, *Seven Pillars of Wisdom* (New York, 1935), pp. 125, 278–279, *passim.*

29. *Od.* VIII. 479–481. The range of uses for the important epical word *aidōs* deserves further attention from social historians and historians of ethics. Sophocles (*Ajax* 1073ff.) can make the Spartan Menelaus preach the supreme importance of (Spartan) *aidōs,* catching its fundamental sense of a personal, willing, deeply felt deference to the group mores. He contrasts it favorably with wayward freedom on the part of an individual. Euripides (*Hipp.* 385ff.) knows the fundamental meaning of *aidōs* but hints that unquestioning deference to group behavior can also be dangerous, a postepical sentiment.

30. *Od.* VIII. 579–580. Future fame, and so undying glory, depends on the activity of singers in oral cultures. Hesiod, addressing the Muses, observes that through Zeus mortal men are "famed or unfamed, sung or unsung, as great Zeus wishes it." See *Works and*

Days 3–4. The philosopher Xenophanes (B.6) observes that all future glory depends on a person's deeds being taken up in the family of Hellenic singers (or song). Such observations are neglected evidence that, in the society for which these men composed, the preserving book as the condition for posthumous glory, so important to later heroes both military and political, was as yet unknown. (In contrast, Alexander the Great traveled with his personal historian.) Noting the philosopher Xenophanes' references to Homer and Hesiod, Martin West has observed (rightly, it seems to me): "As Hesiod's name attracted genealogical and didactic poems, Homer's attracted heroic epics (at least nine besides *Iliad* and *Odyssey*). Thus by the fifth century B.C., if not earlier, Hesiod and Homer had come to stand, as a sort of shorthand, for the whole body of archaic hexameter poetry." So, too, had these two names come preeminently to stand for the authority of epic. See M. L. West (ed. and tr.), *Hesiod: Theogony and Works and Days* (Oxford and New York, 1988), p. xx.

31. *Od.* VIII. 585–586.

2

The Oral Way of Life at the Inception of Greek Literacy: The Lesson of the Old Inscriptions

By the turn of the seventh century, the Greeks were using the Phoenician letters to do what Phoenicians had done with them for many generations. On diverse personal possessions, such as bowls, cups and the like, Greeks inscribed some proprietary marks, or possibly a name, a single word in the genitive of possession. At times they were moved to inscribe a somewhat longer notice, running perhaps to a few lines, no more. These early "long" inscriptions are, without exception, poetic and epical.

Stray letters would be mainly potter's or owner's marks or similar identifications. Some may be trial pieces or experimental doodling. The name identifications, such as a very early one from Rhodes, could be a single word in Greek, such as "of Korakos." Possibly *eimi,* "I am," would be added, for normally the object is envisioned as speaking. A similar use of letters among both Hebrews and Phoenicians, the peoples whose scripts most closely resembled the Greek, can be demonstrated from artifacts going back some centuries earlier than the first Greek imitations. A green jasper scarab showing Egyptian influence has been in the possession of the British Museum since before the turn of this century. Beneath the now familiar *ānch* or "life" sign is an inscription in Phoenician letters: "Belonging to Hōdō the scribe." A bronze axe head from Ugarit and now in the Louvre is inscribed in alphabetic cuneiform: "HRSM, chief priest." A recent find that has caused some excitement is a large bulla inscribed, "Belonging to Berechiah, son of Neriah, the scribe." Hebrew scholars have identified the owner as Baruch, son of Neriah, the famous scribe from the Book of Jeremiah. As a practice arguably originating in the use of cylinder seals, the Near Eastern origins of personal identifications are older still and seem to have been known even to Bronze Age Greeks. They occasionally used their clumsy syllabic scripts, especially the undeciphered Linear A, to inscribe a few signs on stirrup jars and (perhaps) similar items, including at least one libation table.

In addition to proprietary identifications, Greeks of the late eighth century also inscribed various objects—cups, bowls, plaques, statuettes—with evocative hexameters that owe their origin to the Greek epical tradition. Some were intended as mementos and gifts, and others as dedications to deities. This practice, too, has direct parallels from older Semitic artifacts—more are coming to light yearly—

inscribed in the Old Phoenician or Old Hebrew script. These early hexameters normally permit the artifacts that bear them to speak, as on the Nestor Cup discussed later, and perhaps even on the Dipylon wine jug, if Marcovich's attractive restoration of the second hexameter is accepted. There is therefore hard, indisputable evidence for these early Greek uses of writing. It should not be ignored, or its implications concerning the motive behind the Greek invention swept aside, in favor of some speculative theory for which no evidence survives.

If Greeks also used the Phoenician letters before 700 B.C. to send messages between persons or cities, keep commercial accounts, preserve some laws or poems or religious tracts, make lists of kings or priest-magistrates, compose historical chronicles, or even record a monumental *Iliad*, then such uses of writing, even if they occurred, must be designated a historical "unknown." They are theoretical. Admittedly, they would not have been impossible once the alphabet was introduced, and their presence would conform to literate expectations of how minimal literacy might first have been employed. However, there is no evidence for them, either. The reconstruction of the earliest stage of Greek literacy must, in my view, begin elsewhere, in the extant evidence of the inscriptional record.

The evidence afforded by the graffito on the Dipylon wine jug, in conjunction with the Homeric episode that inspired its wording, told us much that was valuable about daily Greek life in the late eighth century. Were the Dipylon an isolated piece of evidence, the conclusions drawn might be only hesitantly accepted or even dismissed as based on an isolated instance, an eloquent aberration in the historical record. The Dipylon vase does not stand alone, however, either as archaeological fact or as testament to the control of oral epic over late eighth-century Hellenic life. Other scraps of writing—amounting now to about half a dozen—that are more than names or identifications (or stray letters) and that belong to nearly the same date as the Dipylon graffito (plus or minus a few decades) have survived for historians to read.

Important early inscriptions come to us from Pithekoussai, Ithaca, Aegina, Greek Thebes, and, if the early dating of the great temple of Hera stands up, from Perachora near Corinth. When added to the Dipylon inscription from Athens, these six very old inscriptions collectively form a body of evidence—very much a "known"—proving that the Greece into which the alphabet entered so innocuously was dominated by the oral recitation of epical verse. We turn in this chapter to a survey of the extant long inscriptions that are older than, roughly, 675 B.C., as well as a few others of similar types that are a bit younger. Like the Dipylon graffito, they reflect the rich oral society of the eighth century. The poetic eloquence and wide distribution of these popular inscriptions would be inexplicable on any other theory.

The Nestor Cup from Pithekoussai: Assuming the Persona of the Homeric Hero

From Pithekoussai (or "Monkey Island" to the Greeks, which is modern Ischia) has come a smashed skyphos, a drinking cup that, like the Dipylon jug, bears a

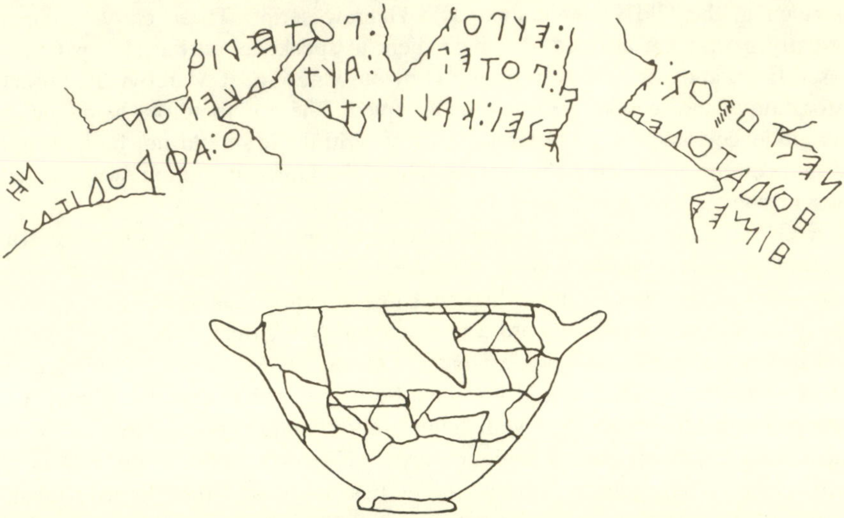

Figure 2.1. The Nestor Cup from Pithekoussai (Ischia), ca. 700 B.C. Drawing by Leonardo A. d'Ancomia after K. Ruter and K. Matthiessen in "Zum Nestorbecher von Pithekussi," *ZPE* 2 (1968), fig. 1, and J. Boardman in *The Greek Overseas,* fig. 205.

graffito that was added to the pot's surface at some point after cooling. The cup is now in the Ischia Museum. The graffito consists of two hexameters, both written retrograde, a unique avoidance of *boustrophēdon* among early inscriptions, plus a curious initial line that, if metrical, may constitute an iambic preface. (See Figure 2.1)

> *Nestoros* : *e*[*im*]*i* : *eupot*[*on*] : *poterio*[*n*]
> *hos d'a* <*n*> *tode p*[*ie*]*si* : *poteri*[*o*] : *autika kenon*
> *himer*[*os hair*]*esei* : *kalliste*[*pha*]*no* : *Aphrodites*
>
> Of Nestor I am the cup, a delight to drink from.
> He who drinks of *this* cup straightway him
> Desire shall grip even of the fair garlanded Aphrodite.[1]

Initially, the reading of the verb in the first line on this badly damaged cup was problematical, although the common formula *tou deina eimi* made *eimi* probable from the start.[2] A more recent publication (1978) of perhaps an even earlier piece, also with the genitive plus *eimi,* confirms that *eimi* must be the correct reading.[3] The Nestor Cup inscription has been dated by some scholars (Jeffery, Meiggs and Lewis) to the late eighth century and by others to the early seventh. The fabric is considered by most experts to be Late Geometric,[4] as are the associated materials found with the cup. Like the Dipylon oinochoe, the item was ordinary for its time, an object in daily use; and like it, the skyphos is a symposiastic vessel. The contrast between the sophistication of the verse and the artistic poverty of the cup, a contrast encountered often when the Archaic inscriptions are matched against the objects that bear them, has often been noted. The votive bronze statuette from Thebes will prove to be another conspicuous example. Even so, the humble clay cup was prized by the owner or a relative, or it would not have been included among the objects buried with him. The find-spot was a tomb in the old necropolis in the San Montano Valley.

Some scholars have detected in the wording elements of wordplay of the sort favored in all oral societies. Deliberate polysemy, a prominent device in, for example, the sayings of the philosopher Heraclitus, is probable. Similar wording is found in an inscription on a mid sixth-century Attic cup now in Paris.[5] Again it is the cup that speaks: "I (cup) am beautiful *(kalon eimi);* the delicious drink/cup is beautiful."[6]

Oral cleverness aside, what commands immediate attention is that the composer of the verses assumes the persona of a famous epical figure, great Nestor of Pylos, who would be thoroughly familiar to contemporary Greek audiences of epical verse. A specific scene, a version of which survives in our text of Homer, is being evoked, as many scholars have detected.[7] Even if the owner of the cup happened to be named Nestor, which is unlikely but not out of the question, the phrasing still requires that this Pithekoussan Nestor become, in his moment of epical identification, Homer's garrulous old warrior from Pylos.

The overall Homeric context in our version of the poems is a long episode in Book XI, lines 601 to 805. The plot of the *Iliad* requires such an episode because in it Nestor makes the suggestion to Patroclus that the young hero assume the armor of Achilles, thereby setting in motion events that both cost Patroclus his life and reverse the course of the war. Versions of the episode, no doubt with minor differences of treatment and wording, must have been popular among singers. The Nestor Cup inscription is our earliest evidence that, indeed, they were.

Patroclus arrives at the entrance of Nestor's tent as the elderly hero and his companions have ended a hard day's fighting. A certain lovely-haired Hekamede, a king's daughter reduced by the fortunes of war to being a servant in a conqueror's tent, is at work preparing a potion, a brew of wine mixed with other exotic ingredients. The point is that the girl is exceptional, as is the drink, as is the cup that holds it. This fabulous cup, we are told, King Nestor had brought with him to the plains of Troy from Pylos itself. Duly exaggerated in epical manner for six verses (631ff.) are its metallurgical richness, its size, and its great weight.[8]

> Another man only with great effort could lift it full from the table, but Nestor, aged as he was, lifted it with ease.

So detailed is the description of the cup that it has been claimed by archaeologists as one of the Mycenaean historical *realia* in Homer's text. That thorny issue may be ignored here. It was enough for the Pithekoussan composer that the cup was already legendary. His wording reveals that his far more modest cup has been transformed into the fabulous, epical one. The guests at a *sumposion* on Ischia could, by its evocation, momentarily become epic heroes joining great Nestor in his tent for the refreshment of drink after a hard day of fighting.

Homer stresses the swift effects that the contents of the cup had on Nestor and his exhausted companions. This especially interested the Ischian composer.

> Straightway when they had drunk of it they were rid of parching thirst, and seized by desire for the pleasures of talk, words flowed freely between them.[9]

Pithekoussan Nestor, while manifestly recalling these or very similar epical verses, proceeds to manipulate them to suit his own present purposes, which were more erotic than loquacious. He who now shall drink from *his* Nestor cup will straightway be seized not by the pleasures of flowing speech but by those that flow from Aphrodite. What will be loosed by the wine is not free flowing talk, but *erōs,* sexual desire, hence the inscribed words:

> He who drinks . . .
> Desire (him) shall grip even of the fair garlanded Aphrodite.

What these cleverly grandiloquent (for the occasion) verses[10] prove is that on Ischia ca. 700 B.C. the fabulous cup of Nestor, its contents, and the swift effects of the wine on its imbibers were already well known. Only Homeric singers could have made them so.

A late-eighth-century *sumposion* was surely what occasioned the inscription. Grammatical genders and the identification of ''Nestor'' indicate that the cup's owner and the intended imbiber were males. The owner identifies with the aged but vigorous Nestor and so sees himself as assuming the role of the *erastēs,* the older man; the person addressed is the *erōmenos.* About the inscriber, who may or may not also have been the owner-composer, the evidence permits no further speculation, except to add that he had a fine ear for the metrical articulations of the hexameter.

Oswyn Murray has recently called welcome attention to the *sumposion* as a fundamental social institution of archaic Greek life. The progress of literacy would serve gradually to render it culturally more marginal and eventually trivial. By the middle of the fourth century, other institutions more closely allied with literacy and so to schools would take over much of its paideutic function, but its importance earlier cannot be stressed enough. As Murray writes:

> It is increasingly recognized that the rituals and practices of the *sumposion* lie behind many of the most characteristic features of Archaic poetry and art. The modern emphasis [in recent scholarship] on the occasion of performance and the intended audience has led to the conclusion that much, perhaps most, of Archaic poetry was specifically intended to be performed at *sumposia,* or can at least be related to the symposiastic situation more or less directly. . . .[11]

Finally, the appearance of so old an inscription in the Chalcidian version of the Greek alphabet on the island of Ischia, situated near the Bay of Naples, may be relevant to the pathway along which letters were first diffused among the Greeks and beyond. It clearly followed the regular trade routes; Ischia at the time of inscription was occupied by Euboeans from Cyme. Feasibly, it was from Ischia that the alphabet spread over the few miles of water and land to the Etruscans, who, as their script reveals, in fact borrowed a Chalcidian-influenced version of the alphabet in the early seventh century. From the Etruscans the alphabet spread to the Romans, from Rome to medieval Europe, and thence to ourselves.

The *Xenos* Oinochoe from Ithaca: The Homeric Proprieties of Xenia

A tall, smashed Geometric oinochoe of local manufacture found at Aetos on Ithaca once bore perhaps six hexameters. They were painted left to right in a spiral around surface of the jug.[12] Only one verse is now readable with intelligibility. What survives is an almost complete hexameter:

> [––*x*]*enwos te philos* [*kai pisto*]*s etairos*[–––]
>
> guest-friend dear and trusted comrade.

The first foot is unreadable but probably scanned as a dactyl. The second foot is a spondee; the third a dactyl with the *caesura;* the fifth foot is the normal dactyl. A conventional hexameter is the result, in the meter: –u u / – – / –u u / – – / –u u / –x.

The phrasing, in all its parts, is thoroughly epical. For example, Thetis refers to Patroclus as having been the trusted comrade *(pistos hetairos)* of her son Achilles, where the phrase also completes the hexameter (*Iliad* XVIII. 460). At *Iliad* VI. 233, when Glaukos and Diomedes discover they are *xenoi,* they leap from their chariots, clasp hands, *kai pistōsanta.* The ritualistic exchange of *pista*—the pledges being expressed concretely—means that hostilities cease at once for the two heroes. Others can continue the war; these heroes will not fight each other, although only a moment before death was certain for one of them. In this incident the code of heroic friendship already reveals seeds of future tensions with the new loyalties that will be demanded by the developing polis, a conflict that has recently (1987) been made the subject of a valuable book by Gabriel Herman of the Hebrew University in Jerusalem, *Ritualized Friendship and the Greek City.* By means of the ritualized language exchanged between Glaukos and Diomedes, they had become *pistoi,* and now they reaffirm it upon mutual recognition; fidelity, the deepest personal loyalty *(pistis),* could be assumed. As Herman reminds us, as late as Euripides' *Electra* (82), Orestes can say to Pylades: "I regard you as foremost in loyalty *(piston)* and loving guest-friendship to me *(philon xenon t'emoi).*" A Greek audience heard those words and brought associations to them that can all too easily elude the modern reader.

The Ithaca *xenos* inscription was dated by its excavator, mainly on the basis of the vase itself, to "not much, if at all, later than 700 B.C." Accepting this early dating, L. H. Jeffery added evidence from several letter forms that, in her estimate, indicates the inscription's "extreme archaism."[13] Elsewhere, in discussing the Attic series, she refers to the Ithaca oinochoe as "Orientalizing."[14] A date of ca. 700 B.C., plus or minus, seems to be the safest estimate. The vase is now in the Vathy Museum on Ithaca. The distinctive word in the surviving verse, for which there exists no single English equivalent, is, of course, the epical *xenos* (recorded with the *digamma),* the "guest-friend." The letters -*ενϝος* are among the most legible.

In Homer, and for many centuries after, *xenia* remained a relationship charged with an aura of sanctity and divine protection under the watchful eye of Zeus *xeinios,* Zeus the protector of stranger-guests.[15] It should be recalled that the action, and so the entire plot, of both poems commences with a violation of the proprieties of guest-friendship. Young Paris, while a *xenos* at the court of Sparta, makes off with the wife of his *xenos*-host, Menelaus, thereby initiating the Trojan war. It is this offense, the violation of *xenia,* that the Spartan king first throws at Paris when, much later in the *Iliad,* he sees him again. Herodotus has mythical Proteus, the Egyptian king, understand the primary offense of Alexander in just these terms (Herod. II. 114–115). The *Odyssey* opens with a grievance on the part of Telemachus. While acting like *xenoi,* which initially they were, his mother's suitors, exhibiting great hubris, outrageously violate all the proprieties of guests receiving *xenia.* They seize the cattle of Odysseus, and they themselves slaughter them for endless feasts; similarly, they seize wine from the storehouse for nightly *sumposia.* In neither case do they await the host's offer, as was *dikaion* (proper). They are squandering the substance of this once great and wealthy house. The offenses to proper *xenia* multiply. The suitors force aged Phemius, the singer, to provide *aoidē,* nightly epical recital. They stay on at the *oikos* of Odysseus and plunder the estate, without reciprocation of entertainment that the institution required, either among themselves or to Telemachus. Such behavior, in violation of the proprieties of *xenia,* arouses a strong *nemesis* in Athena herself (*Od.* I. 227), who is in disguise, first as the hereditary guest-friend *(patrōios xenos)* to Telemachus, Mentis, and then as yet another hereditary guest-friend, Mentor.

So common are scenes involving the proprieties of guest-friendship in the *Odyssey* that perhaps no single passage in our text can be isolated as the specific source of the Ithaca inscription's brief wording. The epical wording does, however, closely recall the elaborate descriptions of the welcome and departure of Telemachus and his loyal traveling companion, Pisistratos, at the court of Menelaus, king of Sparta. The kingly host repeatedly salutes Telemachus as "guest-friend" and "dear," and references are made to the "comrade faithful." Commentators on the Ithaca *xenos* inscription have assumed that the "guest-friend" and the "comrade faithful" are the same person. Possibly that is correct, but grammatically it need not be so. If two persons are being referred to, the first person would evoke epical Telemachus, who discovers that he was the "guest-friend dear" to King Menelaus by heredity, through his father, King Odysseus. The second person would then evoke Telemachus' loyal traveling companion, Pisistratos, who is the young prince's "comrade faithful." He, too, discovers that he is the hereditary guest-friend to Menelaus by reason of a bond forged between the Spartan king and his father, King Nestor.

Gifts were duly exchanged between Menelaus and Telemachus, as the oral proprieties required. Foremost among them from the host was a splendid krater, a vessel for holding wine or mixing water and wine, hence a symposiastic vessel. Like the drinking cup of Nestor, the Menelaus krater also takes on epical or exaggerated dimensions.[16] Made entirely of silver except for edges of purest gold, the krater was the most esteemed of all the gifts stored in the king's house for bestowing the gifts of guest-friendship. Fashioned by none other than the god Hephaestus, it had originally been a *xenos*-gift to Menelaus from Phaidimos, king of the Sidonians. Epic exaggeration and fantasy are in full swing, although an allusion to craftsmanship in metals on the part of the Sidonians (the Homeric designation for Phoenicians) was accurate enough for the eighth century. The element of fantasy returns in the king's name. Obviously the singer did not expect his hearers to anticipate a Semitic name and so a Greek one would do just as well. In such manner, "history" and fantasy always are blurred in living oral traditions.

When the two travelers are about to depart, Telemachus, now in haste, is in danger of acting impulsively and forgetting the proprieties. Pisistratos remonstrates with him. They are guest-friends of Menelaus, and the proprieties of *xenia* mandate that, however urgent their departure, Telemachus must wait until Menelaus (*Od.* XV. 51–55),

> brings you his gifts to put in the chariot
> and speaks to us, and with kind words . . .
> A guest remembers always the man who received him,
> as a host receives a guest-friend,
> and who gave him the gifts of friendship.

With the exchange of gifts accompanied by the proper words, the bonds were both effected and solemnized, and the stage was set for one's son and son's son to become hereditary guest-friends (*patrōioi xeinoi*, e.g., *Od.* I. 175–176, 187, 417, and *passim*) of the person and his descendants "forever." These relationships among families lasted for centuries and could play important political roles in the alliances of Greek cities—or in the apparent treason of aristocrats against the *dēmos* of their own cities—well into the fourth century. Gabriel Herman persuasively traces the power and tenacity of this institution, a kind of fictionalized kinship that has been compared to traditional godparenthood, from its foundations in Homer to the political alliances among powerful individuals and cities in the Hellenistic period.[17]

The evidence is compelling that the Ithaca wine jug was a *xenos*-gift exchanged between host and traveling guest-friend(s), probably at a *sumposion*, as part of the proprieties for entertaining the *xenos*. The symposiastic vessel was not as splendid as that given by Menelaus to Telemachus when he departed from Sparta, of course, but the Ithacan host's ceremonious reenactment of the epical moment would enhance the status of the humble jug, as would the writing placed on it. The Ithacan host, in recalling the epical scene, would be elevating his guest-friend(s) to epical status. By the same wording he transforms himself into a legendary and conspicuously generous Spartan host-king.

Ithaca itself was, of course, the island of Odysseus, the hero who was so often forced to depend on the protections and hospitality of Hellenic *xenia*. What the *xenos* inscription makes indisputable is that, on the island in the closing years of the eighth century, Greeks regularly received other Greeks from afar; they did so graciously, with ritualized assurances of safety and hospitality. In those moments, we may be certain, they exchanged gifts of guest-friendship, according to the proprieties and in the specialized language of "Homer." Only contemporary oral singers could have taught them how to behave in this way.

Their motivation was not nostalgia or romantic attachment to a Mycenaean past, of which they had no clear memory, but a utilitarian concern for present dangers. Without the institution of *xenia*—before the rise of written law and before institutionalized protections for those who are not kin or members of the clan—extensive travel would have been impossible. The epical texts themselves, as well as the earliest law codes, make that abundantly clear. During the Dark Ages, we may speculate, singers increasingly came to stress the proprieties of *xenia* because the social conditions of expanding trade and travel demanded it. The protections of *xenia* may well not have been a concern of closely allied Mycenaean cities in the least, but the institution, of course, must be transferred by eighth-century singers back to distant, epical ancestors in order to secure present compliance to the custom ways.[18]

The Importance of *Xenia* before the Rise of Written Law

In oral Greece, the stranger at the gate stood outside the normal, *local* protections against assault on his person or property. As a stranger and outsider, in that place he had no clan or family relationships to furnish the threat of private vengeance, the sole external deterrent to homicide available in early Greek society. Apart from the perpetrator's internal feelings about the action—something that the culture was, therefore, especially urgent to instill—the anticipated revenge of the victim's kin on the killer long remained the sole external reason not to kill or otherwise violate the stranger.

Homicides, both accidental and deliberate, were matters to be settled between families privately, often resulting in blood feuds that lasted for generations. A mediator could, of course, be called in if both sides agreed to it (the Shield scene in the *Iliad* is the famous, early example), and blood money *(poinē)* might be accepted by the victim's kin, but there was no compulsion for such a settlement.[19] More often than not the blood money was refused by the family of a victim, and so enforced exile was common in all early periods of Greek history.

The figure of the exiled homicide appears frequently in literature from Homer to Euripides, reflecting daily life. Should a stranger's person be violated, especially if he were to be killed, his kin may never hear of it, or else would hear long after the fact. Only rumors would remain of how, or at whose hand, their relative met his death. No written records, of course, existed, and any means of long-distance communication were oral and so always delayed and unpredictable. The early evidence, both literary and in the early law codes, is consistent. In cases where no relatives retaliated, no external sanction was imposed. No public, organized body took cognizance of the act of homicide with an eye to punishment; the remedy, if any, was private or familial.

A brief episode in the *Odyssey,* no more than a few lines long, makes this clear, although the lesson is not the episode's intention. Homer briefly interrupts his tale to explain how Odysseus came by the famous bow that Penelope will require her successful suitor to string. As it happens, it was a *xenos*-gift from one Iphitos. We learn, also incidentally, that Heracles murdered Iphitos when he was his *xenos*-guest, and did so for material gain. Heracles slew him, "stranger-guest *(xeinos)* though he was, in his own house." It was a terrible violation of what is *themis.* Powerful words may be hurled at Heracles and his action by the singer, but no human agency ever punishes him (*Od.* XXI. 26ff.).

In sharp contrast to Heracles and Iphitos, the proprieties were maintained between Odysseus and Iphitos. The famous bow of Odysseus was a *xenos*-gift from Iphitos, and so greatly did he prize it that he kept it stored among his treasures at home (where Penelope now goes to fetch it), "a memorial of a guest-friend dear *(mnēma xeinoio philoio).*" The act of fetching a bow from the cellar, aided by Homer's paratactic style, becomes yet another occasion for the singer to extoll how things are done properly, and how they are not.

Hesiod, a singer who reluctantly was forced to travel over water for professional reasons, reflects the Greek attitude when he lists the violation of *xenia* with the offenses that cry to Zeus for vengeance (*Works and Days,* 327ff.). He seeks to link his brother's offense—stealing their inheritance—with the most deeply felt violations. What is common to them is that, in each case, the victim is helpless should the aggressor decide to offend the Hellenic proprieties. The offenses are (in this order): the man who violates the suppliant or the *xenos;* the man who violates his brother's marriage bed (for the brother uniquely trusted him); the man who violates the orphan (he has no family); the son who violates his aged father (he is violated by his family). At such a man (333–334),

> truly Zeus *himself* is angry, and in the end lays a heavy requital on him for the deeds that are "not-just" *(adika).*

These sins especially cry to heaven for retribution. The concluding remark that "in the end *(teleutēn)*" punishment comes from Zeus *himself* (the *autos,* is striking), suggests that no immediate punishment comes from any public authority. For that very reason, then, the society must somehow invest just these actions with as much internally felt horror or shame as it can muster. How else can one induce a human being, in a position of power over another and also enjoying invulnerability to respect the helpless person? Before written law and institutionalized sanctions there is only one way. These helpless persons must be invested with an *aidōs* that those who confront them must be induced to feel powerfully, as part of what they themselves are as Hellenes and as "just" men. No decent man would violate these persons, for that would be an abomination, an infamy. The collapse in self-esteem would be unendurable. A man of sense would feel a terrible *nemesis,* were he to witness such a violation; the gods would feel it too. Zeus watches over these helpless ones, and he always sees them. It is the best, the impressive best, that an oral society can do before written laws and regularized, civil sanctions backed by an enforcement arm. Much of the time it worked, and rather well.

At some point in reading the *Odyssey,* the suspicion may intrude on the modern reader that guest-friendship suspiciously resembles what a modern novelist would regard as the motor of the plot itself or what the work is designed to illustrate, either by elaborate examples of compliance (Nestor at Pylos, Menelaus at Sparta, above all Alcinous among the Phaeacians) or violation (the Cyclopes, the suitors on Ithaca). The illustrations and allusions to *xenia* run into the hundreds. As a result, the modern suspicion should not be dismissed lightly. No small part of the function of the *Odyssey* as paideia in oral Greece was to inculcate a respect, pan-Hellenic and deeply felt, for the institution of *xenia*. If this is true, it also follows that the *Odyssey,* although magnificent poetry, is not merely ''literature'' as that phenomenon has been known in Europe in its literate centuries. To read it as literature alone, at least from the standpoint of the culture that produced it, is in a significant sense to misread it.

A final example is especially instructive. In Book XIV of the *Odyssey,* in words with implications for the history of Greek law, the proper actions toward a stranger-guest are yet again invoked. The participants are a traveling beggar man (Odysseus in disguise) and a swineherd, the poorest of the society's poor. The words they exchange, before Eumaeus recognizes Odysseus, decisively refute the contention, sometimes maintained in scholarly literature, that what is recorded in Homer is the value system not of an entire society but only of a small elite. The episode in Eumaeus' tent proves that this was not so—as, in their differing way, the popular inscriptions also prove.

Eumaeus, the faithful swineherd of Ithaca, has received Odysseus properly, as befits a stranger-guest, but according to the swineherd's means. The best of his pigs, humble beasts as they are, shall be the night's feast. It is all that he has. The point of the epical instruction is that the proprieties remain the same; only the physical conditions vary. Not knowing that it is his own king whom he addresses, Eumaeus, feeling a proper *aidōs* for the suppliant, adds:

> Nay, stranger-guest, it is for me not ''lawful'' *(ou themis),* not even if one worse off than you should come, to slight a stranger-guest. For from Zeus are all stranger-guests and beggar men. A small gift but welcome, even from one such as me.[20]

His action and feelings are, of course, not a matter of written law but of established custom or precedent, what is simply *themis,* proper or ''right.''

The Ithaca wine jug was a small *(oligē)* gift for its time, but also welcome or dear *(philē),* coming from the guest-friend, as the wording on the jug tells us. The memory of some such Homeric occasion, or perhaps a blend of them, offers the best explanation of how the Ithaca oinochoe came to be inscribed with its beautiful, Homeric words.

The Early Dedications

The inscriptions from Athens, Ischia, and Ithaca afford the modern reader unique access into important moments of late-eighth-century oral life as it was lived in widely separated parts of Hellas. Certain common features emerged. Plausibly, all three were symposiastic in inspiration; all seemingly reflect aspects of ceremonies surrounding *xenia*; and all were phrased in epical verse, the discourse of ''Homer,'' not local dialects.

Dedicatory inscriptions also commemorate an important feature of Greek oral life, one with notable parallels in the lives of oral peoples everywhere. Ritual incantations involving bespoken dedicatory offerings of various objects are as old as any formalized verbal action of our species, and go back to time out of mind. Dedicated objects, whether inscribed or not, are well known from the ancient Near East and have Greek counterparts from the earliest periods. It may be significant to note that inscribed dedications also dominate the Phoenician series for the relevant period of script transfer. What at present is perhaps the oldest of the Greek dedicatory inscriptions, from the island of Aegina, always in close contact with Athens, has a claim to be as old as any of the inscriptions discussed in this chapter. It should not be surprising that, along with other old Greek dedications, it turns out to be thoroughly epical. It is the first of three representative examples of early dedications that we examine in this chapter.

The Votive Plaque from Aegina Dedicated to Apollo

From the island of Aegina has come a badly damaged painted plaque that bore an inscription of which only a few letters survive.[21] The letters were painted on the outer surface over a pale cream slip and until recently were thought to be the oldest painted letters on Greek pottery to survive. The plaque, after being discarded in a balk, was accidentally washed into view by a heavy rain and was fortuitously rescued by John Boardman. The find-spot was in the vicinity of the east end of the temple of Apollo, confirming the supposition that the object was dedicatory, as does its similarity to many early dedicatory plaques that are not inscribed. The original pottery, badly damaged, contained a warrior frieze of a sort common in the Late Geometric Age, indicating that the object belonged "to the years shortly before 700."[22] A date between 720 and 710 B.C. is probably about right.

Ten letters—broken off at each end—are certain and two others probable. They are painted on the plaque in what Boardman describes as clear, bold letters.[23] The initial *sigma* is virtually certain, and the final *tau* probable. The remaining letters are, as Boardman comments, not in doubt.

[– – –*lu?*]*sonosepist*[– – –]

The letters were probably put on the plaque by the painter himself. He was more accomplished at making his letters than was the person who scratched the Dipylon jug, a clumsier job. As Boardman notes, "the letters have none of the archaic crudeness of the inscription on the Dipylon oinochoe." This is, it should be noted, the correct designation for the hand that scratched the Dipylon graffito, although its graphic crudeness has often been denied.

Was the original wording also metrical and epical? Several scholars, including Boardman, have noted that the surviving letters could form words that fit into the third and fourth feet of a not unworthy hexameter. The postulated restoration would involve some syllables of a lost first foot, which was probably a dactyl. A postulated *lu* fits what follows, part of a personal name, Lusonos. Filling out the remainder of the verse after the surviving letters would be some postulated letters based on a familiar formula.

amonanetheke

This would yield a hexameter in standard meter.

[– – –*Lu?*]*sonos Epist*[*amon anetheke*]

The dedication thus would read: "Epistamon, son of Luson, dedicated. . . ." The meter would turn out to be: – u u / – u u / – u u / – – / – u u / – x.

On this reconstruction the plaque is dedicatory, following a familiar pattern. The donor's name and patronymic conform to the pattern of "X, son of Y, dedicated me," or this object. This plausible and ingenious restoration also has, as John Boardman noted, the persuasive advantage that the surviving letters would "in common with most early inscriptions form part of a hexameter verse."[24] A votive plaque (many similar uninscribed ones have been found) offered to Apollo recording a familiar dedicatory formula in epical verse is, for the period, very attractive, and the reconstruction may be accepted as certain.

The practice of speaking such dedications in epical verse may be as old as epic itself. What the newly arrived alphabet permitted was a recording of the oral practice. The inscribed words became an enduring, nonfleeting plea that remained "speaking" in the presence of the god, in his holy place, in fitting words known to please and impress him. The dedicated object speaks in epical verse, not the local vernacular, as the dedicator's tireless surrogate. Votive candles in cathedrals and written petitions placed in crevices of the Wailing Wall in Jerusalem are distantly related responses to the same human emotion.

Lost Iron Spits from Perachora Dedicated to Hera

Close in type and inspiration to the Aegina dedication is the dedicatory verse to Hera found on an inscribed limestone block. It once held a handful of iron spits that, being valuable metal, had small chance for survival. The now lost spits are imagined as speaking Homerically to the wife of Zeus. I adapt Wade-Gery's text:

Drachma ego, Hera leuk[*olene, keimai en au*]*lai.*

Drachma (handful, measure) am I, O white-armed Hera, laid up in your hall.[25]

The "hall," a certain restoration for epical *en auli,* would in this case be the temple of Hera Limenia at Peiraia, near Corinth. The Perachora inscription was once dated to ca. 700 B.C. or earlier (the excavators claimed that it was as early as 750 B.C.), but now, following a revised dating of the temple, the inscription is generally regarded as later than 700 B.C., although not by more than a few decades at most. It belongs, on any account, among the early important dedicatory epigrams in single hexameters. The missing spits alone were of an economic nature. The inscription is not economic, but of standard dedicatory type.

The emphatic "I am" at the beginning of the inscription is repeated in later dedicatory inscriptions. It puts the strongest possible emphasis on the fact that the object is thought to be speaking in place of the dedicator. The construction was already known from the more personal, proprietary inscriptions, as in the peculiar first line on the Nestor Cup. To the examples cited previously could be added the somewhat later skyphos from the Agora inscribed metrically (three dactyls): *Thario eimi potērion,* "Of Tharios I am the drinking cup." It has been dated to about a half century later than the Nestor Cup, confirming again that this phrasing was common for symposiastic cups. The guess may be hazarded, then, that the Perachora inscription and others like it were modeled on such phrasing but succeeded in incorporating the proprietary formula into the more rigid metrical demands of the hexameters and elegiacs of dedications.

The Bronze Statuette from Thebes Dedicated to Apollo

The most important of the early dedicatory inscriptions, because it is the most impressive verbally, is the famous bronze "Apollo" (so called) from Thebes, which is now in Boston (Figure 2.2). Specialists in Greek bronzes have argued that the statuette, the only secure guide to the dating, should perhaps be placed in the first quarter of the seventh century. The verses are inscribed *boustrophēdon* and the statuette speaks:

> *Mantiklos m' anetheke wekaboloi argurotochsoi*
> *tas dekatas. Tu de Phoibe didoi chariwettan amoib*[*an*].

> Mantiklos dedicated me to the far-darter [god] of the silver bow from the tithe.
> Do you, Phoebus [Apollo], give something gracious back.[26]

The composer of these elegant hexameters manages to incorporate two of Apollo's Homeric epithets into his inscription in addition to his own unusual name, which was not part of inherited epic nomenclature. As Friedländer observed, the statuette shows Greek sculpture in its infancy, but the verse is highly accomplished. "The solemn word still dominates over every other art."[27]

The first traditional epithet (e.g., *hekēbolō Apollōni* at *Iliad* I. 438, *passim*) became the more common one in dedications, no doubt following the practice of orally declaimed prayers, hymns, and dedications—always the basis of what finally got recorded. The concluding phrase "give gracious requital," or, in less elevated phrasing, "give something nice in return," is found in Mentor's prayer in the *Odyssey,* where it also completes the hexameter. Old Mentor (actually here Athena in disguise) is, in part, instructing Telemachus in the proper ways of guest-friendship. Pisistratos, representing his father as host, greets the visitors formally and then offers wine first to elderly Mentor, in deference to his age, noting that he and Telemachus are the same age. Mentor rejoices that the young man is "just" *(dikaios),* that is, behaves properly for his social position and age, and has profited from instruction. In the course of a thankful prayer to Poseidon for the proper rearing of the lad by Nestor, Mentor exclaims:

> To Nestor first of all and to his sons grant renown;
> then to the others do thou give gracious requital *(didou chariessan amoibēn).*[28]

Marks of attachment can still be made out on the Mantiklos statuette for what were a helmet or cap, a spear, and a shield, all now lost. Also missing are the

Figure 2.2. The Mantiklos "Apollo" from Boeotia (probably Thebes), ca. 700 B.C. Francis Bartlett Collection. Courtesy of the Museum of Fine Arts, Boston.

lower extremities and the right arm. The statuette depicts a *kouros* who is also a Boiotian foot soldier, not the god Apollo. The composer of the verses was the otherwise unknown Mantiklos, but it is unlikely that he was also the inscriber, who was a professional craftsman in metals, a bronze worker. Examination of the grooves of the inscribed letters reveals that the inscriber used professional tools, a set of chisels and a ring punch for the exactly duplicated letter *o,* the most difficult letter to make on a hard surface with a blunt instrument.[29] A professional craftsman was, it would seem, readily available to many customers who desired such a service at the place of dedication, which probably was the great Ismenion in

Thebes, a temple sacred to Apollo. The statuette, now part of a collection in the Boston Museum of Fine Arts, is reported to have come from Thebes. The lettering is, in any case, certainly Boiotian.[30]

The writing moves up the outer side of the right thigh, across the groin, down the left thigh, then is skewed around so as to move up the inner side of the left thigh, while also switching from left to right to right to left. No concession is made to the needs of a potential reader. A similar indifference to any readers is found on the famous Nicandra Archaic female statue[31] from Delos, and in many other inscribed dedications. This is also true of the nearly contemporary great Karatepe inscription (Phoenician, in Cilesia, but also a dedication), whose letters are similarly arranged in total indifference to a reader's needs.[32] It seems that early dedications, as in the case of the words on the Mantiklos statuette, were never intended to be *read* by humans. Rather, they permitted the object, as surrogate for donor, to *speak* continuously before the god when the dedicator had to depart from the temple. Uninscribed dedications were, of course, also surrogate reminders placed before the god, but the great advantage of the inscribed ones was that now they could ''speak'' the same words the donor had first prayerfully uttered in the god's presence.

Presumably, the words on the Mantiklos statuette were bespoken first by Mantiklos to a metalsmith when arranging for the offering to be inscribed. It was bespoken a second time, but now chanted or sung, in solemn circumstances in the temple by Mantiklos. From that point on, the bronze figure is understood to be speaking to the god and is left in the temple for that purpose. Even Mantiklos himself may not have been able to read, incidentally; only the inscriber, a craftsman, was required to know his letters. Mantiklos, however, like another foot soldier of the early seventh century, Archilochus, had thoroughly absorbed epical speech and had made it his own.

The Priority of Dedications?

At present writing, dedications seem to appear in the archaeological record just a bit later than do the ''short'' proprietary inscriptions—some only a few letters—found on the Lefkandi sherds, or the recent finds from Pithekoussai and Naxos. To reiterate what was said earlier, there are some caveats to be noted before drawing any firm conclusions from this. First, the early dating of the recent finds must hold up. The issue, I suggest, may not be if the earliest finds *could* be as early as ca. 760 B.C. or 740 B.C. Rather, could they just possibly be as late as 730 B.C., or even a bit later. An excavator, understandably, will prefer the earlier date, whenever it is defensible.

One example of revision has already been mentioned. For some time a *graffito* from Pithekoussai was thought to be dated to ca. 750 B.C., and the oldest alphabetic writing found thus far. It aroused considerable interest for this reason. Subsequent close examination and scholarly discussion have resulted in two revisions: The letters are more likely Phoenician than Greek, and, significantly, the date has been lowered to ca. 710 B.C.

There is, in addition, a question concerning the accidents of survival. Dedicated objects would not normally be converted to grave goods, but rather would often be deposited in the temple or shrine of the deity to whom they are being offered. These objects share, then, in the above-ground fate of such buildings, from earthquake and fire to looting by foreign enemies. They are also in danger from domestic theft, impious as that would be; anything made of metal would be in special danger. Religious artifacts that have survived from an earlier period but that remained in conspicuous places can also be in danger from the rise of rival religions and fanaticisms.

Assuming that we are unlikely ever to find the first inscribed objects of any given type, many more dedicatory objects would therefore be required from the earliest period for a few of them to survive. What may require comment is that we have as many early dedications as we do. Plausibly the oldest of them, from Aegina, has a good claim to be as old as any of the "long" inscriptions discussed in this chapter. It may be also significant that the object itself was of no intrinsic value, a ceramic plaque. In the somewhat later Perachora dedicatory curbs, the iron spits dedicated to Hera vanished in antiquity, but the inscribed curb holding them was of no economic worth (limestone, not metal), and survived.

Finally, there is an a priori reason for suspecting that dedications may have preceded proprietary inscriptions or at least are as old as any of them. The simple marking of an object with a few letters or even a name could be accomplished without the invention of the complete alphabet, a very ambitious undertaking, indeed. Often, as in the Semitic cases, readers who were not the original writers would be unsure about the vocalization, but the basic purpose behind personal marking would be accomplished. If rudimentary proprietary marking were the purpose for adopting the Phoenician script, I suspect it would have been adopted "as is," with vowel development later, when the more ambitious recording of verse would make it mandatory. If the initial motive were to record the hexameter, however, then a complete vowel system would be present from the start. The existence of the long inscriptions indicates that recording hexameters was well under way before 700 B.C. When the issue of motive is permitted to enter the argument, the suspicion grows that dedications in verse—now lost—must therefore have been as old as the first proprietary markings. Then again, if recording dedicatory hexameters did call the alphabet into existence, experimenting with personal names would surely appear right from the start.

The Aegina dedicatory plaque from ca. 710 B.C. or earlier, is not the only evidence for inscribed dedications that are or could be eighth century. For example, there are the very old graffiti at Thera with the names of deities; the Hymettos sherds (some may be very early indeed, and dedicatory); the very old (some inscribed) bronze caldrons dedicated at Thebes; and the very old *THEO* recently found at Pithekoussai (part of a personal name, or the dative of *theos,* "to the god"?). Evidence for dedications is thus not entirely absent from the early record. Can we, with unwavering assurance, place all of it later than the newfound proprietary inscriptions from Lefkandi and Pithekoussai, if that indeed is their nature (some are so fragmentary that any conclusion is risky)? Even if the early dating for these finds more or less holds up, are they so much earlier (a few decades, not centuries) that, given the uncertainty of so much early dating, we can conclude with finality that proprietary letters preceded dedications?[33]

What I doubt—unless overwhelming future evidence forces re-evaluation—is that the making of "short" inscriptions, dominantly proprietary of one of kind or another, was of itself sufficient motive to result in the invention of the complete alphabet. Therefore, I doubt that, historically, these inscriptions as a type preceded the first hexametric inscriptions. What is not feasible, at least to me, is that the adapter invented the complete alphabet in order merely to write a name—his own or any other—or tag some pots, or make a list of goods.

The Lesson of the Very Old Inscriptions

Let us now draw the threads together. The oldest long inscriptions, upon close examination, take us into intimate moments of Greek oral life. Three of them—those from Athens, Ischia, and Ithaca—are symposiastic in origin; the wording involves the drinking of wine (the Nestor inscription) or is preserved on the vessels that hold it, cups and wine jugs. The Dipylon graffito evokes vigorous dancing at a *sumposion.* These inscribed vessels were plausibly gifts exchanged between guest-friends, which would have most often been presented at *sumposia.* The *xenos* wording on the Ithaca wine jug, at least, commemorates such an exchange beyond a doubt. When we recall that *sumposia* were part of the celebration of Homeric *xenia,* it follows that guest-friendship may play a larger role in the making of the early inscriptions than heretofore has been suspected. Not only is *xenia* more pervasive in Homer than has often been appreciated, but also it is more pervasive in the oldest Greek inscriptions.

Only the dedicatory epigrams are certainly free of some association with either guest-friendship or *sumposia.* They are, instead, expressions of another ancient oral practice. Their wording affords glimpses, now reduced to a few verses left on stone, or clay, or metal, of one of the oldest of oral practices on the part of humans, the formalized performance of ritual incantations. Only imagination can now supply what the epical words leave out: the great temples, priests and attendants, vestments and incense, sacrifice, hymns, choral performance, instruments both wind and percussion, dance, and ritual.

The early dedicatory epigrams—notably, those on a plaque from Aegina, a curbstone from Perachora, and a statuette from Thebes—permit votive objects to speak solemnly to appropriate deities, or to statues in their temples as surrogates for their donors. They are the earliest of thousands of later Greek votive objects that also "speak" formally, ritualistically, Homerically. The objects are, of course, imitating how their donors spoke in first presenting them to the god in his temple.

These oral activities, conducted in epical speech, must have been the very stuff of Hellenic life, happening 10,000 times a day in every part of oral Greece. Only the archaeological record, once it commences, has permitted us to enter into them in such an intimate way. What we discover is ordinary Greeks of the late eighth century participating "Homerically" in *sumposia* and mimetic dance, resorting to epical speech in order to celebrate the pleasures and protections of guest-friendship, or mounting steps to a temple to honor Apollo (or Hera or Zeus) in ritual incantations and dedications.

Over and again in the very old verse inscriptions, an ordinary citizen, male or female, known to us only from a name if at all, assumes a recognizable Homeric persona and reenacts an epical moment. In so doing, he or she briefly becomes, in effect, great Nestor, the aged mentor of heroes; mighty Achilles, the young warrior supreme; Odysseus, the wary traveler who somehow always manages to survive (usually as a lucky *xenos*); Telemachus, the good son; athletic Prince Laodamos, best of dancers; ravishing Helen of the divided heart; or Penelope, the ever faithful wife.

If we had only the literary sources as evidence, we might suspect that such activities and their poetical speech were not typical of average Greeks at all but were exclusively the imaginative inventions of inspired and eminently gifted poets, the authors of the literary masterpieces we now can read, as some Homeric critics maintained as early as the eighteenth century. Even the Homeric gods themselves have been suspected of being mere literary invention, a cross between poetic convenience and cosmic joke. Only the surviving artifacts with their poetically eloquent dedications have swept away all doubts on these issues.

The Inscriptional Record after 675 B.C.

The oldest verse inscriptions not only appeared at the end of centuries of a sophisticated oral tradition, but they also are—as Parry demonstrated for the Homeric poems—a product of that mature, oral tradition. They are, no less than Homer's poems, inexplicable without a long history of sophisticated oral discourse preceding them, one that was shared by all Hellenes. Their poetic accomplishment and wide dispersion can be explained on no other hypothesis. Here they have been called "popular inscriptions" because no civic or religious official commissioned them, and no professional scribes formulated or transcribed them—and too, because they are found from one end of Greece to the other, fossilized expressions of aspects of daily life. They are, paradoxically, written evidence, the first we have, for the dominance of oralism in Greek life. That is their clear lesson. The local dialects of their makers were diverse and sometimes intrude in the wording in small ways, but the language and diction of "Homer," not a vernacular, dominates them all.

For the next century, or the period from 700 to 600 B.C., the surviving inscriptions of any length remain dominantly epical, hexameters and elegiacs. For the period from 600 to 500 B.C., epic has major role to play in the inscriptional record, but so increasingly does prose, notably in the movement toward the codification of at least some laws in a scattering of Greek cities. The first written laws appear in the archaeological record on the island of Crete, and the first experiments on the part of Hellenes with written law may well have originated on that famous southern island. The complex story of the marriage of oralism and alphabetic literacy in the area of the administration of justice is the subject of later chapters.

The same linguistic and poetic features discovered in the oldest inscriptions are also displayed prominently in the extant inscriptional record for its first 200 years, or until the turn of the fifth century, when its contents no longer concern the argument of this book. In addition to a heavy proportion of poetic inscriptions in the corpus, especially when name identifications are discounted, we find that hexameters or elegiacs dominate, especially before 600 B.C., and that these contain a great deal of epical language or strive to imitate it. Homeric formulas or variations on them gravitate to their traditional slots in the hexameter. Even individual words tend to behave formulaically, gravitating to their accustomed place in the verse, thereby governing the linguistic choices for the remainder of the verse.

Above all else, however, what we witness is that the composers seek at every point to clothe themselves in a heroic *persona* by resorting to Homeric speech, in the process effectively becoming Hector, Achilles, Agamemnon, or Helen or Penelope.[34] This feature, more powerfully than any other, emerges from a systematic scrutiny of the early verse inscriptions and their language. In general, these features begin to go into decline as the sixth century yields to the fifth, but they are still impressively displayed in many fifth-century inscriptions.

Finally, but also on a diminishing scale, the verse can be impressive indeed while the artifact, the writing, or both can be rather crude. The situation slowly (but not uniformly) improves, notably among painters such as Nearchos as early as ca. 650 B.C. For the seventh and sixth centuries, one expects the verse generally to be rather good if not splendid; about the quality of the writing that records it, one anticipates only considerable variance from case to case.

Paul Friedländer, in publishing a selection of the earliest hexametric and elegiac epigrams from the corpus of extant Greek inscriptions, never failed to stress the dominating influence of Homeric speech in their composition. In so doing, he put all Greek scholarship—and not the least the history of philosophy—in his debt. What we discover in them was not, he rightly observed, literary imitation of a sort one encounters in a later (and literate) age, with one author consciously echoing the style or phrasing of a predecessor. Rather, it was the spontaneous expression of a way of life preserved and transmitted in speech shared by all Hellenic peoples at every level of society. Greeks throughout the period (ca. 700 to 500 B.C.) are rightly said to have "delighted in giving a sepulchral inscription or a dedication to a god in the meter and style of Homer or of the elegiac or of the iambic poets. Such was the power of poetry in Greek life."[35]

Some initial examples, chosen more or less at random, are mentioned first; they are typical specimens of hundreds like them. They reveal the tone of the entire corpus. Also, I borrow comments from Friedländer where noted if the inscription was included in his collection. From Corcyra has come a late-seventh-century funerary column that "speaks" (as so many early inscribed artifacts do) with "epic stateliness," permitting the dead man to assume "the dignity, and receive the 'indistinguishable fame' of a Homeric hero buried in a Homeric sepulcher."[36] From Corinth there is a stone slab that, ca. 600 B.C., had marked a grave of one Dveinias. The Homeric speech recorded on it raises the occupant "to epic stature'' and his death to a Homeric ''hero's fate.''[37] What Friedländer considers the masterpiece of the epic funerary inscriptions is composed of three hexameters inscribed *boustrophēdon* on a limestone slab from Corcyra. One Arnidos fell in some battle or other near the river Aratthos. In the inscription, transformed by Homeric speech (nine epically based phrases appear in three lines), ''the fight assumed the epical dimension of the Battle of the Ships in the *Iliad,* Aratthos another Xanthus.'' This, for Friedländer, is the prime example of how in this period epical speech ''shaped the conception of life.''[38] Since the list could be expanded to include every verse inscription that is considered to be very old from among the more than 450 verse inscriptions that survive from the Archaic period, a more parsimonious selection is called for.

For present purposes I limit myself to four additional examples from the hundreds of possibilities that are typical of early verse inscriptions; none is an exception or a masterpiece. A closer examination of them will, I suggest, facilitate an appreciation of the control of Homeric speech over life and thought in early Greece, its degree of popular absorption, and its wide diffusion. All are funerary, in part because grieving for one's dead may well be the oldest activity of *Homo sapiens* as *sapiens* that can be detected in the anthropological record. It is also universal and so can take us into the most obscure of daily lives as ordinary men and women reach for words they feel are appropriate for expressing the deepest human emotions. Also, the funeral use of letters to commemorate the dead in epic verse (as opposed to a simple name), although thus far not instanced *very* early among the Greek inscriptions, may in fact be as early as any use of the alphabet. It would follow Phoenician practices. All of the next four examples are earlier than 500 B.C.

First, from Boiotian Tanagra, is a front relief of two young boys who are identical in appearance and have their arms around each other's shoulders.[39] Friedländer dates the relief to ca. 600 B.C., citing also Gisela Richter and F. R. Grace, whose dating falls within a decade of his, plus or minus. It seems certain that the boys were twin brothers and that the person who caused the monument to be made and was responsible for the inscription was their father, one Amphalkes, a name that, as Friedländer observes, belongs to the epic stratum of Hellenic onomatology. The mother is not mentioned, and I suspect that she was born a slave. The names of her twin boys suggest that she had some influence in the choice, however, and so a place in the affections of Amphalkes. Typically for a Greek, his sons were what mattered to Amphalkes. The father's name is placed first in the inscription, a very confident hexameter, metrically linking his name to that of his sons while also permitting it to be followed by the verb *[e]stese* in its normal position in epic verse, as at *Iliad* V. 368 and *Odyssey* XVII. 29. The names of the boys, which also appear separately under the figure of each, are recognizably epichoric and, being of local derivation, would be more difficult to fit into the hexameter. However, filling in the second part of the hexameter with two names is standard Homeric practice (e.g., at *Iliad* II. 732, *Podaleirios ede Machaōn*), and the father, in imitating Homeric versification, neatly completes the hexameter. This rather elegant verse, from an otherwise unknown Greek who sought in Homeric speech to express his grief at the premature death of his sons, becomes in English translation the deceptively simple:

> Amphalkes erected this monument over the graves of Cittylus and Dermys.

Friedländer observes that in this instance we encounter a common feature of the earliest verse inscriptions when measured against their physical artifacts: "The workmanship of the verse is superior to that of the sculpture." That is also often true even of the lettering for our other examples, as well as of the often erratic spelling, for which, however, conventions have not as yet been firmly established.

Second, on the thigh of a female dedicatory statue from Delos (ca. 650 B.C.) is an inscription of three hexameters written *boustrophēdon*. In it a certain Nicandra, "maiden beyond compare" (*Iliad* XIII. 499), by means of slight variations of three Homeric formulas, aligns herself with her father, husband, and sister in dedicating the statue to Apollo, who in turn is identified Homerically as the "Far Darter who delights in arrows." Friedländer notes the easy flow of the verses compared to the rigidity of the extremely archaic statue and comments on Nicandra's personal and familial pride that "the example of Homer enabled her to express."[40] Once again the artifact, in this case the large statue, speaks:

> Nicandra dedicated me to the Far Darter, Delighter in Arrows.
> Daughter of Deinodikes of Naxos, maiden beyond compare;
> Of Deinomenes the sister, of Phraxus the wife.

Third, from Troezen is a sepulchral column (ca. 550 B.C.) inscribed with three hexameters, the last word in a *boustrophēdon* turn.[41] Friedländer surmises that the grave was built by a father for his son. The inscription, as carved by the mason, consisted of two long vertical lines, with a short third line—one word only—in the *boustrophēdon* turn, following a common pattern. No attempt is made here to reproduce either the sequence of the hexameters or the written form of the inscription. The composer's name records, as is noted, the digamma.

> To Praxiteles V[W]ison built this monument, and groaning heavily his comrades heaped up the tomb, as a return for worthy deeds. In a day they finished it.

Only one phrase (three words) is without an exact Homeric analogy, of which Friedländer cites four examples from the *Iliad* and two from the *Odyssey*. He also notes that, beyond the obvious dominance of Homeric speech, these austere lines also capture and convey "something of Homeric life" as it was lived daily by Greeks who enjoyed, celebrated, prayed, and died "Homerically" in the society that produced such epigrams. That society, of course, belonged not to Mycenae or Pylos, but to sixth-century Hellas. It was also the Greece in which the first philosophers lived and to which they addressed their words. Like all these inscriptions, so richly and intricately Homeric, this one comes from an ordinary citizen and carries the unmistakable stamp of daily life. A father and his friends are burying his son, and the father reaches for Homeric speech to find words adequate for his grief. The composer is clearly the father, Vison. The inscriber of the stone column was likely a local stonemason from among his friends.

Fourth, from Troezen, has come another funerary column that is perhaps the latest of our examples (ca. 500 B.C.). A similar distinction between the composer and the actual inscriber of the epical words is surely also the case in this instance. The composer is a grieving mother; the inscriber is a stonemason. The inscription consists of two hexameter couplets on separate faces of the column and is inscribed *boustrophēdon*. I somewhat alter Friedländer's translation in order to display the succession of verses:

> In memory of Damotimus his loving mother wrought this tomb,
> Amphidama; for no children were born in his house.
> And here is the tripod he bore off from the footrace at Thebes
> [approximately ten syllables cannot be restored]
> . . . unharmed, and she set it up over her son.[42]

In verse 2, a certain Amphidama expresses Homerically that her son was childless by evoking the image of a heroic but barren dynasty; this mattered to her deeply and she mentions it first. In verse 3, the language for winning the footrace, an event no doubt important to the lad if perhaps less so to her, has close epic precedents. (Homeric references for all verses are given in Friedländer.) In the conclusion of verse 4, she gives her own action of burying her boy a Homeric dimension by saying with an epic flourish that she erected *(epethēke)* his treasured victory tripod over his grave. Obviously, Amphidama finds consolation in remembering her dead son as a fallen Homeric hero, and she mourns him as one. The sincerity of her grief cuts through all suggestion of posturing. Just as clearly, her son in life must have seen himself as a young Achilles, hero and athlete, and his mother will bury him in no other way. Only her own quite evident absorption of Homeric speech—and the mentality and way of life it conveyed—would have enabled her to do this and so permit this son to be memorialized as he would have wished.

However, the beginning of verse 3 *(kai tripos)* is awkward for a Homeric verse, and the two long names in verses 1 and 2 had to be forced to fit the hexameter. This inscription is an example of how the sure control over the hexameter, more evident earlier, is gradually fading away as the sixth century yields to the fifth. "The influence of epic is waning."[43] Yet the sentiments of the inscription, Homerically expressed, remain those of the mother from her heart, and she is clearly responsible for the verses whoever may have carved them for her. In addition to being so personal, they are just clumsy enough to rule out consultation with a professional singer. Only her own absorption of "Homer" permits her to speak, and so to think and feel, in ways that would not otherwise have been possible.

In these funerary inscriptions the verse comes through as expressing Homerically, or epically, the personal feelings of those who erected the tomb or artifact, and there is every reason to conclude that they personally composed the verses. As in the case of Amphidama, it is far more doubtful that many, if any, of the composers personally carved the letters. That task on stone normally fell to masons, as noted; in metals to smiths; and on pottery inscribed before painting to painter or potter. The lettering is of widely varying quality, indicating varying degrees of literate accomplishment among individual craftsmen. Such inscriptions are therefore, considered as evidence, far more silent about the literate skills of their composers than about their poetic skills. Especially with dedicatory inscriptions, the ability of the dedicator himself to read the inscription is always at question; the object remains in the temple to "speak" before the god as surrogate for the petitioner who must depart, the same impulse that leads to votive candles before statues of Christian saints. A dedicator bespeaks the verses that normally another person, the appropriate craftsman, then records.

Among the oldest inscriptions only the famous Mantiklos Apollo is a clear example of the composer, the soldier Mantiklos, and whoever incised the bronze for him, being *certainly* different persons. Statuette and lettering are, relative to what follows in Hellas, crude indeed; the verse is splendid and thoroughly Homeric. The example of Archilochus, incidentally, who was probably alive in the year the statuette was made and inscribed, serves as a warning for us to suppress our literate doubts that such accomplished Homeric verse could have come from a fighting foot soldier in seventh-century Boiotia. The lettering in none of these cases has the appearance of being the work of a professional scribe, and a reasonable conclusion is that local craftsmen normally transcribed an orally dictated text, just as they did for the later inscriptions.

Conclusion: The Lesson of the Epigraphical Record

What deserves comment as we review the corpus of early Greek inscriptions is that, as soon as a recording device—which initially is what the alphabet was—is made available to Greeks, we find unmistakable and overwhelming evidence of "Homer" as a pan-Hellenic linguistic phenomenon firmly established from the Ionian cities on the edges of the Anatolian plain to Italian Eretria, and from Boiotia to Rhodes. The clear implication, when added to the literary evidence (mainly, after Hesiod, the fragments of Archilochus and the other early poets, followed in the sixth century by the fragments of the philosophers Xenophanes, Parmenides, and Heraclitus) is that Homer had been absorbed in every part of Greece, and in every social class, to a degree we find almost impossible to comprehend. Yet happen it unmistakably did, as the first literary texts, which followed upon an earlier inscriptional practice, and even the first words from philosophers whose *ipsissima verba* we can read, unmistakably confirm.

The first of the Greek philosophers whom we can read in his own words, Xenophanes of Colophon (ca. 550 B.C.), reports indirectly on the Hellenic social situation as he had discovered it in his seven decades of travels across "Hellas land." He proclaimed (in epic verse: hence my translation):

> Since from the beginning from Homer all have learned proper conduct (μεμαθήκασι, from μανθάνειν) . . ."[44]

The quotation breaks off abruptly. Bruno Snell, followed now by James Lesher, has rightly observed that, without exception, early and especially epical uses of *manthanō* do not designate acts of learning in a broad sense, but rather something like moral enculturaltion, for example *Il.* VI. 444, "to learn to be *esthlos* always."

We possess this incomplete verse from Xenophanes only because a late grammarian (Herodian, *On Doubtful Syllables*) wants to make a point about versification. By happy chance, he chooses Xenophanes as his example, quoting only as much from the poet as serves his narrow purpose. If Xenophanes, however, had not himself produced, or had produced, a text of some length, and had he not seen to the making of at least a few copies, his words would not have survived for Herodian or us to read.

This incomplete verse from Xenophanes also marks one of the earliest identifications of the epic oral inheritance as it is being subsumed under the name of "Homer." It is fitting that, even as truncated, the verse records his (or epic's) role as the Great Enculturator or, in Plato's words, educator of Hellas.

Notes

1. See Jeffery, *LSAG,* pp. 235ff. and Pl. 47 (1), where the inscription leads the Pithekoussan series. For the history of often mistaken early restorations, see Heubeck, *Schrift,* pp. 110ff. Two dots resembling a colon separate the words in the first line, which I take to be prose. In the hexameters they mark off phrases at points that indicate formidable awareness of epical diction and metrics. This surely is the oldest known attempt to indicate graphically (and accurately) the caesurae of a hexameter. The inscriber, as well as the composer (if not the same person) had an epically trained ear. The inscription was first published in 1955 by G. Buchner and C. F. Russo in *Rendiconti Lincei* (pp. 215ff). Giorgio Buchner, who has known the site since childhood, supervised the excavation of the tombs (many hundreds of them as it would turn out) at the Valle San Montano cemetery between 1952 and 1961. Three distinct layers emerged: an upper level of burials, fifth century through Roman, mainly poor; a second level from the eighth century, all cremations under stone tumuli; under them, a third layer of eighth-century burials, all inhumations. The earliest tombs (LG I), when they contained pottery, often contained two vessels, both symposiastic: an oinochoe and a skyphos. Exceptions might be a decorated amphora, a lekythos, or, significantly, Lyre-Player-Group scarabs and seals, the latter being frequent in the early tombs. See G. Buchner, in *Archaeological Reports* 1970–1971 (with illustrations). Further report on the contents of the grave in which the Nestor Cup was found is given by P. A. Hansen, reporting personal communication from Buchner, in P. A. Hansen, "Pithecusan Humor. The Interpretation of 'Nestor Cup' Reconsidered," *Glotta* 54 (1976), pp. 27–28. The excavator believes the date of the burial was ca. 725 to 720 B.C., and that ca. 720 B.C. is the latest possible date for the manufacture of the cup. Also found in the grave were some aryballoi dated to perhaps 730 B.C. or a bit later. For oddities concerning the grave in which the cup was found and a discussion of the burial practices on the island generally, see D. Ridgway, *The First Western Greeks* (Cambridge, 1992), pp. 46–57 and 116–118. Possibly a father buried a prized object of his own with a son who had died young (age about ten) as a memento, breaking with normal practice for the graves of adolescents, a suggestion that must be pursued at a later time. For instructive remarks on the very early uses of commercial marks—Mycenaean, on Cyprus, *and* at Pithekoussai—as they relate to the earliest alphabetic markings, see A. W. Johnston, *Trademarks on Greek Vases* (Warminster, 1979), pp. 1–3.

2. For the second word in line 1 some scholars, concerned about the wide lacuna the original letters filled, have resisted the obvious *eimi,* proposing, for example, en ti or even (Calvert Watkins) *esti.* (The normal Old Attic spelling would have only one letter in the space, *M,* = *EMI.*) Many examples of *eimi* in similar inscriptions survive (some 30 examples have been adduced), but the first person, with which the inscription begins, is retained in all cases. *Only* in the Nestor Cup inscription (line 2) is there a later change to the third person. The point is notable, but I think answerable. At this period no conventions for inscribing items had as yet been firmly established. It was understood, however, that if an epical moment were being celebrated, or being evoked and recreated, as was common, then the object would speak Homerically, or epically. The first line of the Nestor inscription is not, I think, iambic trimeter—a meter which is, in any case, closer to the vernacular than the hexameter—or indeed metrical at all. I suggest the wording is modeled on personal identifications, normally in prose, and sometimes of the simplest sort, "of *X*" or "I belong to *Y.*" Then the composer wishes to evoke the Homeric moment, a different undertaking entirely. Only hexameters will do, and so they follow, well set off from the first line. The inscriber probably saw a smattering of both types of inscriptions (now lost) around him and had no good reason not to combine them on his ambitious cup. Finally, for readers who may wish to know how I read the inscription grammatically, a few quick comments. Nestoros, here in the genitive, commonly begins the hexameter in Homer, both in this and other grammatical cases. In line 1 *eimi* may now, I think, be regarded as certain. The *e* of *potērion* has been written over a mistake by the inscriber; the letter was first written as *o.* The partitive genitive, *potēriō,* in line 2 is no real problem. In epic the verb "to drink" can take either the accusative or a partitive genitive, here extended (the composer was a man of original poetic imagination) from the liquid to its container. The verb *piēsi* is an unusual but possible long-vowel subjunctive. It is not necessary, therefore, to restore *pieisi.* The relative clause with an only *seemingly* superfluous *an* is, in fact, a not uncommon example of a relative clause with *an* and the subjunctive, giving the clause the force of a conditional clause, as here, essentially a *protasis.* The verb of the main clause, the *apodosis,* of line 3 is consequently in the future. The *tōde* of line 2 is, admittedly, less usual than would be a personal pronoun, but is possible as well as poetically effective. The demonstrative "this" reinforces the contrast between two cups (as I interpret the verses), the legendary one of Nestor that loosened the tongues of heroes and the one designed for *sumposia* on Ischia bearing the wine that loosens desire. For discussions of the inscription and differences of opinion, see Page, "Greek Vases from the Eighth Century B.C." in *CR* 6 n. s. (1956), p. 95ff.; A. Dihle, "Die Inschrift vom Nestor-Becher aus Ischia" in *Hermes* 97 (1969), pp. 257–261, and especially K. Rüter and K. Matthiessen, "Zum Nestorbecher von Pithcussai" in *ZPE* 2 (1968), pp. 231–255.

3. In *ParPass* 33 (1978), pp. 135ff. Alan Johnston, to whom I owe this reference, suggests that a date as early as 740 B.C. may be possible for this recently recovered use of the genitive with *eimi.* See Johnston in "The Extent and Use of Literacy," in Hägg (ed.), *The Greek Renaissance of the Eighth Century* B.C., p. 63 (with Fig. 1). In l. 3 the epical epithet applied to Aphrodite belongs to Demeter in the later *Hymn to Demeter.*

4. Jeffery in *LSAG,* p. 235, "of late Geometric type," but allowing for the possibility that it may verge on Subgeometric. See Heubeck, *Schrift,* pp. 106ff., with very full bibliography. By 1971, early phases of excavations on Ischia had revealed local, flourishing Geometric manufacture as an extension or local version of Euboean Late Geometric. (This confirmed what had long been suspected about the Cesnola krater, illustrated in J. N. Coldstream, *Greek Geometric Pottery,* Pl. 35). Pithekoussai was evidently the thriving outpost in the far western waters of a very wide network of Euboean trade. The alphabet, in my view, did not originate in the Euboean network (I still favor Cyprus), but there now

seems little doubt that the mercantile activity of those cities afforded the new letters their first major diffusion. It may be significant that eastern influences have been discerned in a number of local crafts in the Euboean cities, but adapted as the locals preferred. The role of craftsmen in the actual transmission of letters from Phoenicians to Greeks needs further exploration. The milieu of the early symposiastic inscriptions and of early literacy seems clearly to be that of prosperous merchants and traders, who often were adventurous colonists, not the old landed aristocratic nobles. Among this group, living on an equal social basis, traveling to the colonies with them, and indispensable to the quality of life, were the many skilled, prosperous craftsmen. As Hellenes, not as old landed aristocrats, these people—merchants, traders and craftsmen—celebrated the good life, identified with Homeric heroes, and perpetuated the institutions of oral life. They were also Greece's first literates.

5. In the Louvre (F 66). Also from Pithekoussai is a fragmentary sherd perhaps a bit older than the Nestor Cup. See Johnston, "The Extent and Use of Literacy," in Hägg (ed.), *The Greek Renaissance of the Eighth Century* B.C., p. 67. *Eupota* is certain, indicating the original was poetic, although the word is not Homeric.

6. See Beazley, "Hymn to Hermes," *JHS* 52 (1932), p. 178.

7. For example, O. Murray, *Early Greece* (Stanford, 1983), p. 94, and many others. See Barry Powell, *Homer and the Origin of the Greek Alphabet,* pp. 163ff., and his references.

8. This is a favorite device of epic exaggeration even, as here, for aging heroes. Most often the hero is lifting not a famed cup but "a boulder/no two men now alive. . . . " The common formula appears at *Iliad* V. 119; XII. 449, *passim.*

9. *Od.* XI. 641–642.

10. On this see P. A. Hansen (n. 1), among others.

11. O. Murray, "The *Sumposion* as Social Organization," in Hägg (ed.), *The Greek Renaissance of the Eighth Century* B.C., pp. 196–197.

12. See Jeffery, *LSAG,* p. 230 and Pl. 45 (1), where the inscription leads the Ithakesian series. Also see M. Robertson, in *BSA* 43 (1948), pp. 82ff. Some editors would put brackets around three or four more letters, which would not affect the restoration of the verse. Because the wording on the vessel consisted of several lines, all plausibly hexameters, the Ithaca inscription belongs among the oldest "long" inscriptions and is not the least important of them. It may also, I suggest, provide a most important clue. Do all the very early long inscriptions that are not dedications commemorate, in some way, *xenia? Sumposia,* dance, *aoidē* (oral epical song), and gift-exchange are part of the ritual of entertainment required from the prosperous host for the *xenos.* Even the suitors, who are portrayed as violating the institution with much hubris, keep up the appearances. Thus at the end of Book I (*Od.* 1. 421): "Now the wooers turned to dance *(orchēstun)* and [oral, hexametric] song *(aoidē).*" The night's primary session of *aoidē* may have been provided by the reluctant Phemius, but here the clear implication is that the wooers themselves also sang. No mention is made of Phemius. Also, Achilles in his tent is described as being capable of such composition in singing to himself. The degree to which at least some competence in composing and singing hexameters is presumed to be possible for persons who are not professional *aoidoi* deserves attention.

13. Jeffery, *LSAG,* p. 230.

14. Ibid., p. 69.

15. *Iliad* XIII. 625; *Od.* IX. 271, *passim.*

16. *Od.* IV. 612ff. Telemachus, about to depart, asks about his gifts of guest-friendship, the normal expectation. He will accept anything except horses, the latter being excluded because his home island of Ithaca has no wide plains or meadowlands, as does that of Sparta. Homer, or epic singers—who need not have exact geographical information

unless the refutation of hearers would be embarrassing—seemingly knew more about Archaic Sparta than did the fourth-century literary sources, who had ideological grounds for finding early Sparta the "rude, austere and narrow barrack depicted in the written sources." See L. F. Fizhardinge, *The Spartans* (London, 1980), p. 12.

17. See G. Herman, *Ritualized Friendship and the Greek City,* (Cambridge, 1987) for literary and later inscriptional references.

18. Thucydides, at the outset of his history, remarks that remote antiquity—by which he means prior to the Trojan War—was an obscure period that cannot now be known with any certainty, but conditions were not good then. The worst of them was that "there was no commerce, and they [Hellenes] could not safely hold intercourse with one another by land or sea" (Thucd. I. 2). Private travel beyond one's own territory was unknown. Travel was only in groups and even then was rare, driven by dire necessity. Either the group had been forced to migrate from its plot of land or else badly needed to conquer more land. The historian is likely guessing in some of this, but they are shrewd guesses, based presumably on some information he possessed. If a historical period may be hazarded, it was the turbulent eleventh and tenth centuries, following the Mycenaean collapse. The quoted words are especially revealing. Commerce and even private travel were once hazardous in the extreme for all Hellenes even in their own territory. At one point in its remote history, then, Greece apparently did not know the protections of Hellenic *xenia;* they had to be fostered. This may explain the extraordinary emphasis on instruction in *xenia* in Homer, and especially in the *Odyssey.* No opportunity is missed—and many are created—to reinforce its proprieties.

19. The famous passage describing the trial scene portrayed on the shield of Achilles in the *Iliad* (XVIII. 497–508) has been the subject of a vast literature, in part because the history of Western law can be taken back to no earlier text. Gagarin's bibliography points the way to important discussions, which in turn lead to others. See his "The Settlement of Disputes in Early Greek Literature," in *Early Greek Law,* pp. 9–50. For Gagarin (p. 26) the trial scene is the strongest evidence for "the existence of public legal procedure in preliterate Greece," which it probably is. Also important is the proem to Hesiod's *Theogony,* which Gagarin also discusses.

20. *Od.* XIV. 56–59.

21. See Jeffery, *LSAG,* p. 110 and Pl. 16 (1), where the inscription leads the Aeginetan series.

22. Ibid., p. 110; elsewhere (p. 17) placed by Jeffery between ca. 720 and 700 B.C., with a question mark.

23. John Boardman, "Painted Votive Plaques and an Inscription from Aegina," *BSA* 49 (1954), p. 184.

24. Ibid., p. 185.

25. First published with plates by H. T. Wade-Gery in H. G. Payne, *Perachora* (1940), pp. 257ff. For the shrine and its date, see J. Salmon, "The Heraeum at Perachora and the Early History of Corinth and Megara," *BSA* 67, pp. 159–204. Friedländer noted that "Hera's Homeric epithet λευκώλενος must have often been heard in this and other sanctuaries," and "the 'handful' echoes the language of a singer of Homeric Hymns" in *Epigrammata,* p. 18. Hera's epithet is written *leu*[*olene,* a restored vocative, in the inscription. There is an excellent short discussion of votive offerings in the narrow sense, a gift from one's own hands given to a deity as the result of a vow, in Walter Burkert, *Greek Religion* (Cambridge, Mass., 1985): "It pervades all ancient civilizations and plays an essential part in defining the relationship between men and gods in the exchange of gifts." The inscription, when an alphabet is available to Greeks, records a vow that was, as Burkert observes, "made aloud, ceremonially, and before as many witnesses as possible—

the Greek [and Homeric] word *euchē* means simultaneously a loud cry, a prayer, and a vow'' (pp. 68–69). Burkert's influential book also has an insightful treatment of the role of oaths in preliterate societies (see pp. 250ff.), and of Homer as the Hellenic oral paideia (see ''The Spell of Homer,'' pp. 119ff.).

26. Jeffery in *LSAG*, pp. 90ff., and Pl. 7 (1), where the inscription leads the Boiotian series. First published by Froehner, *Monuments Piot*, vol. II, pp. 137ff. The statuette is presently in the Boston Museum of Fine Arts (MFA 03.997). It is often discussed in works on Greek bronzes, on bronzes in American museums, on archaic *kouroi* and in specialists' works on Boiotian art, such as by Lamb, Grace, Richter, Hampe. Based on artifacts of a similar type, and on the lettering, Jeffery favors a date of ''c. 700–675,'' but followed by a question mark. The rounded shape of the buttocks suggests a date somewhat after 700.

27. P. Friedländer, *Epigrammata*, p. 38.

28. *Od*. III. 57–58.

29. First noted and discussed by A. Casson, ''Early Greek Inscriptions on Metals: Some Notes,'' *AJA* 39 (1935), pp. 511ff. Casson also would put the statuette later than 700 B.C., by perhaps a quarter century.

30. See Jeffery's discussion in *LSAG*, p. 91. Another inscribed statuette with clumsy Boiotian lettering (''Ganyaridas, to Apollo'') currently can be seen in the British Museum. Interpreters have claimed the figure is of the god, not a hunter, but curiously the figure holds goat's horns. The inscription runs up the thigh and over the buttock, although the statue, with one foot forward in the archaic manner, is meant to face forward. It is later (ca. 550 B.C.) than the Mantiklos votive and fairly large (12.4 cm high). Somewhat later yet is a smallish (8 cm high) bronze votive statuette of a lyre player, the instrument sacred to Apollo, presently in New York's Metropolitan Museum of Art. There is an inscription on the back of the tunic, around the buttocks, ''Dolichos dedicated me.'' It is evident that even on the later votive objects the inscriber often took no thought for any future readers.

31. *IG* XII.5 1425b. The dedication is inscribed *boustrophēdon* on the right thigh of an archaic female statue dated to ca. 650–625 B.C.

32. *KAI* 25 (ca. 725 B.C.). This unique (primarily because of its length) bilingual inscription (Phoenician and Hittite) was found at Karatepe in remote Anatolia. A point often overlooked is the fact that this long inscription, in two languages and scripts and laid out in total indifference to the needs of any contemporary human reader, is itself a *dedication* to a god by a (doomed) king of his city. It is neither a political nor a mercantile ''document'' and hardly a literary text. For Karatepe, the field reports of Bahadir Alkim through the eighth campaign were published in *Belleten* (Ankara), Nos. 12 (1948), 13 (1949), 14 (1950), and 16 (1952). For expert discussion of the inscription, see R. T. O'Callaghan S.J., ''The Great Phoenician Portal Inscription from Karatepe,'' *Orientalia* 18 (1949); R. Marcus and I. J. Gelb, ''The Phoenician Stele Inscription from Cilicia,'' *Journal of Near Eastern Studies* VIII (1949). Its date, ca. 725 B.C., should make it of considerable interest to historians of the Greek alphabet—not the least for the occasionally willful *alpha*. That the inscribers were indifferent to any human readers is evident from the way the blocks and the lettering are displayed (and skewed around), an unmistakable feature when the huge inscription is viewed in situ. This was pointed out to me by the distinguished Hittite scholar, Robert Hardy, in 1962 at Karatepe. It was noted—first as far as I know—by the indefatigable Father O'Callaghan, on site.

33. The identifications of the names of deities from a large number of old rock inscriptions near offering hollows are not always certain, but Zeus and the North Wind (*Boreaios*) seem clear enough (*IG* XIII.3 357; *IG* XIII.3 360). At least two possible dedications can be found among those from Hymettus published by Carl Blegen, the excavator, in ''Inscriptions on Geometric Pottery from Hymettos,'' *AJA* 38 (1934), pp. 10–28. See Blegen's No.

12, fig. 6 (12); No. 16, fig. 8 (16). On the dating of the Boiotian *lebētes* (eighth century?) and the *theo* reported from Pithekoussai by Johnston, see Powell's remarks in *Homer and the Origin of the Greek Alphabet,* p. 146 and n. 60. An argument from theory should not be permitted to overcome hard archaeological evidence, of course, so future findings may decide the matter decisively and against me.

34. Epical names were generally avoided in Archaic Greece, rather like "Jesus" in some European countries; Nestor is unlikely as a name for a contemporary person. But the assimilation of ordinary Greeks to epical figures, revealed in the inscriptions' wording to be paradigmatic heroes, runs through the early inscriptional record, as Friedländer demonstrated.

35. Paul Friedländer, *Epigrammata,* p. 1.

36. Ibid., pp. 9–10.

37. Ibid., p. 11.

38. Ibid., p. 30.

39. Ibid,, pp. 13–14.

40. Ibid., p. 49.

41. Ibid., p. 33. *Boustrophēdon* inscriptions become more rare as the sixth century gives way to the fifth, but linger.

42. Ibid., p. 34.

43. Ibid., p. 34.

44. Xenophanes, B.10. On *manthanein* in *Homeric* Greek ("to be accustomed," always to acquire a habit or way of conduct), see J. Lesher, *Xenophanes of Colophon: Fragments* (Toronto, 1992), pp. 81–82. Lescher, rightly it seems to me, puts the Xenophonic polemic with Homer and Hesiod—a prominent feature of his fragments, as it is for Heraclitus—in the context of the still powerful paideutic role of epic in sixth century Hellas.

3

Of Muses and Magistrates: From the *Exemplum* of Epic to the First Written Laws in Europe

Michael Gagarin has suggested that the famous shield of Achilles scene from the *Iliad* is our strongest single text proving that there were established procedures for settling disputes in oral Greece.[1] He designates this period—so consistently portrayed in Homer and Hesiod—as "protolegal" because, whereas legal procedures are manifestly in place, a body of oral "law" is not. In this, it seems to me, he is correct.

This terminology, distinguishing among "prelegal," "protolegal," and "fully legal" stages in the dispensing of justice, owes debts to the positivist legal philosopher H.L.A. Hart, who also argued that writing plays a key role in the transition from "the prelegal to the legal."[2] The ideological roots can, in fact, be traced to Jeremy Bentham and John Austin. These two noted philosophers would restrict "law" properly speaking to a command of a lawgiver, which prescribes or proscribes not single acts by individuals but all actions of a similar kind for all citizens, and which attaches the threat of a sanction for an offense. As Henry Sumner Maine himself observed critically as long ago as 1861: "The results of this separation of ingredients tally exactly with the facts of mature [written] jurisprudence. . . ."[3]

They do not tally well, however, with the experience of oral societies or with what we find in the Greek epical sources. That they also do not fit well philosophically with a natural law position in ethics is another matter and beyond our concern. It is not a positivist view of law that I wish to defend—or, for that matter, any other view. Rather, what I hope to get at is a proper understanding of the Greek historical facts.

At least since the time of Maine, who addressed the issue perceptively, it has been a commonplace among some legal historians that preliterate peoples are governed by "customary law" that is not essentially different or structurally different, from written law, save that it was not written down. Literate common sense accedes readily to this view, as though we need look no further into the historical facts. It is so obvious as to be absolved of argument or proof, requiring only a clear statement to be seen as true.

> The epoch of Customary Law, and of its custody by a privileged order, is a very remarkable one. . . . The law, thus known exclusively to a privileged minority,

> whether a caste, an aristocracy, a priestly tribe or a sacerdotal college, is true unwritten law. . . . From the period of Customary Law we come to another sharply defined epoch in the history of jurisprudence. We arrive at the era of Codes . . . the codes were certainly in the main a direct result of the invention of writing. Inscribed tablets were seen to be a better depository of law, and a better security for its accurate preservation, than the memory of a number of persons however strengthened by habitual exercise.''[4]

The idea that, in preliterate societies, unwritten law existed among a privileged group who were its oral repository has not been, as Gagarin remarks dryly, ''diminished by the scarcity of actual examples of oral codes.'' Ireland and especially Iceland have the best historical claims, as Gagarin acknowledges, but even these, as also he well observes, have problems in the evidence upon closer examination. Other scholars, some of them mentioned later in this chapter, have argued for the existence of a body of oral law in the Greek epical period. Their arguments, in my opinion, have not proved convincing (as I note later), but full discussion of this interesting debate must await another occasion.

Two epical texts have played prominent roles in recent attempts by legal historians to recover the manner in which justice was administered in oral Greece. They are the Shield of Achilles scene in Book XVIII of the *Iliad* and the proem to Hesiod's *Theogony*. A brief examination of each will help take us into the manner legal disputes were settled in Greece before the rise of written law.

The Shield of Achilles

Thetis comes to the house of Hephaestus as a guest-friend (normally a relationship between males, but then she is a goddess) with a request of armor for her son, Achilles, to replace the armor lost by Patroclus at Troy. Hephaestus readily agrees to provide it, guest-friend that he is, and in splendid fashion. Included is elaborate decoration on both sides of the great shield. Because the singer's medium is verbal, the scenes must, of course, be drawn in words for his hearers. One side, the town at war, need not concern us. The other side portrays activities in a typical Greek town at peace. Hephaestus depicts a wedding, involving song, dance, and music, and also a trial underway, revealing some of the procedures surrounding a homicide. The issue at trial does not concern the act of murder, a private matter between families, but a dispute about the blood price or compensation.

Two parties are vigorously arguing in the *agora* before the town's elders. One contends that he paid all, specifically, the *poinē,* or blood price, for a man slain; the other, that he received nothing.[5] Because we are plunged into the middle of the proceedings, we do not know if the homicide was deliberate or accidental, or how this dispute over a fact (as I interpret it) arose. Perhaps the complaining man was not part of the immediate family of the slain man but feels that, as a member of the clan, he deserves to share in the compensation, a procedural matter finally settled in Athens by Draco's Law of Homicide. The other man, if he has settled with the family, claims understandably enough to have paid up in full. Alternatively, perhaps the dispute turns on a matter of formal eyewitnessing, or *marturia.*

Perhaps a person who had witnessed the paying of the *poinē*—for such matters would not go unwitnessed in oral Greece—has died or has been "bought" and now will not testify to the payment. Perhaps, as sometimes happened between two procedural witnesses, the testimony is at odds; again, one of them may have been bought. It does not matter to the poet's immediate purpose what the background facts were, for he is not a legal historian. His point is that disputes of this kind are a daily occurrence in the civilized cities of Hellas when they are at peace, no less than is a wedding. His audience would respond with the pleasure of recognition to a scene that was all too familiar to them. By accident, the poet affords us a sharp, memorable picture of well-established procedures for settling legal disputes in a typical Greek town.

Aided by other contexts in Homer, we may assume that the litigants have come voluntarily to seek a settlement of their dispute; one was not under compulsion to relinquish self-help. Further, the dispute is over a matter of fact only, that is, was the blood-price paid or not? For there was no compulsion to accept the *poinē,* and no fixed amount for payment (in goods, of course). The killer or his family could offer compensation if they wished, and the family of the deceased could accept it or not, as they saw fit. Alternatively, the killer goes into exile—or is killed. We are told that the elder who speaks the straightest *dikē* will be rewarded with the two gold talents, probably put up by the two litigants. We may perhaps assume that the reward goes to the elder who speaks the solution (they speak their *dikai* in turn) that both sides find the most acceptable. We may also fairly assume that this solution would be based on established usages and precedent that are being adapted or applied to the case at hand.

On all these matters there has been fierce scholarly disagreement.[6] Even so, the scene of a trial in the *agora,* conducted according to well-established and publicly recognized oral procedures, is vigorous and realistic; it is hardly a flight of pure bardic invention. Indeed, the legal language is semitechnical for delivering a *dikē* and is encountered elsewhere in Homer and Hesiod. Although intended only as a general impression of a typical event when the town is at peace, not as a court record, "the Shield" is our best and earliest evidence for the origins of legal procedure in Europe.

Translations of *Iliad* XVIII. 497–508 are not free of the theoretical commitments of scholars, especially for verse 500. That is also true of mine, which has been influenced by the legal historian George Calhoun.

> The folk were gathered in the speaking place *(agora).* A strife had erupted. Two men were striving about a blood-price for a man slain. One [man] claimed that he had paid all, declaiming it to the folk; the other, that he received nothing. Both pressed for a referee to bring the matter to closure.
>
> The folk were cheering each on, favoring one, then the other. The heralds constrained the folk. And the elders *(gerontes)* were sitting on seats of polished stone in the sacred circle, holding in their hands the scepters from heralds, loud-voiced, with which each would spring up, in turn giving judgment. In the center of them were set two golden talents [measures] a gift for the one among them who spoke the straightest *dikē.*

Of Muses and Magistrates

Almost as famous as the shield scene—and equally as controversial in its legal detail—is the description found in the proem of Hesiod's *Theogony* of the role that the Muses, and so poetry, play in the daily decisions of magistrates. The problematical verses from Hesiod form part of an introductory celebration of the Muses themselves, as the formidable daughters of Zeus and Memory, before the poet turns to the family of the gods and the origins of the cosmos, the subject matter of the body of the *Theogony*. The role of poetry in the singer's society (Boiotia at the turn of the seventh century) and so the function of the singer himself are also being commemorated in the persons of their patron goddesses, which is what makes the verses so valuable as contemporary evidence. The important verses (75 ff.) are:

> She [Kalliopē] is most pre-eminent of them all.
> For she attends on worshipful barons [magistrates].[7]
> For whomsoever the daughters of great Zeus do honor,
> And mark him at his birth, scion of Zeus-nurtured barons,
> On him do they pour sweet utterance, even upon his tongue
> And from his lips do honeyed *epē* [speech? verses?] flow, and the ordinary people (*laoi*)
> All look to him as he disposes the precedents *(themistas)*
> With judgments *(dikai)* that are straight. And speaking surely
> Soon he would skillfully put an end even to a great dispute.

For five additional verses, Hesiod stresses the conciliatory role of Muse-aided magistrates when the people are confused in *agora*. Then he moves toward the summary and conclusion of his extraordinary hymn within a hymn:

> Such, indeed, is the holy gift of Muses to men.
> For from the Muses and far shooting Apollo
> There are singers on the earth and lyre-players;
> From Zeus are *basileis*. . . .

Modern readers—and not a few scholars—are to be forgiven if they remain puzzled over what Hesiod has just said about the relationship of Muses (or epic poetry, whose muse is Calliope) to sitting magistrates. The issue is the precise nature of the clearly asserted dependence of aristocratic magistrates on epical singers—or, alternatively, on the content of epical poetry. How are we to imagine this working on a daily basis in the courts? Does a magistrate have, perhaps, an *aoidos,* a singer, at his side, a kind of *Mnēmōn* (official rememberer), as is found later in the early legal documents from Crete? If so, is the *aoidos* a professional versifier in the legal sphere? Are decisions put by him into verse for easy memory? Do these decisions collectively constitute a body of oral, versified, precedent law, essentially local in nature and lasting perhaps only a few generations? That solution, which has been proposed, is not out of the question for this period, but there is no direct support for it in Hesiod's text, either. Moreover, Hesiod's words strongly suggest that what the *basileus* accomplishes for the community is wrought by his own utterance as he speaks straight *dikai,* not by someone speaking for him, or whispering into his ear. It is his *epē* (words, speech, or perhaps "verses"?) that are intelligent or skillful, persuasive, and soothing.

Several solutions have, in fact, been proposed for a difficult text; four may be mentioned briefly here. They are not in all ways mutually exclusive. Hesiod's words are to be explained on the hypothesis that they assert: (1) that singers flattered princes, *basileis,* who in this period would also be magistrates; (2) that poetry aided magistrates with eloquence (but no more than that) so that they may persuade reluctant litigants; (3) that magistrates created an ever-expanding body of versified oral law passed across generations; (4) that magistrates delivered short-term legal directives given in memorable verse form, perhaps aided by a professional *aoidos.* Noted scholars, respectively, Martin West (1), Michael Gagarin (2), Catherine Roth (3), and Eric Havelock (4),[8] have defended these views. I do not think any of these solutions will do, or that any of them by itself will explain all parts of Hesiod's text, but a full defense of this belief is best reserved for another occasion. Instead, I offer here an alternative solution, one more in conformity, I suggest, with the discoveries of the previous chapters.

The *Exemplum* of Epic

A formidable body of inscriptional evidence has demonstrated that the speech of ordinary Greeks was—or could on demand be—remarkably poetized. On those occasions it was closely controlled by epical originals. Knowledge of "Homer," even including knowledge of incidents and phrasing with surprisingly close parallels to what survives in our texts, was widely dispersed and popularly absorbed in Greek society. This cultural phenomenon has been termed the Hellenic oral paideia, which grew to maturity in a period when the distinction between ethics and law—arguably the result of literacy—was unknown.

It should not surprise us, then, that epical incidents, and epical narrative of established customs, along with the thousands of maxims and sayings embedded in the narrative, were used to settle daily disputes of all sorts in all periods. This was accomplished by resorting to analogy, more natural by far to oral peoples than the syllogistic deduction that Aristotle proclaimed was his discovery. It also requires a certain elasticity in the meaning of the society's key moral terms that defies fixity in definitions of the sort that answer the Socratic "what is X?" question. This oral practice continued well into Plato's century, when it can be documented from the daily speech of the characters in his dialogues.

We have no similar record, of course, for the daily speech of Greeks of the eighth century; we have only what is contained in epic, Homer and Hesiod, and oldest inscriptions to guide us. Should the possibility be entertained that "the *exemplum* of epic," as it has happily been called, was also used to resolve disputes of a legal sort in the early period? Did magistrates, too, resort to epical precedent when it was useful or appropriate to do so? What does the only evidence we have tell us? Do we have any evidence from epic itself that epic or heroic precedent—what Hesiod in the passage under discussion (*Theog.* 100) calls the *kleea andrōn* chanted by the singer—was used to help settle disputes that were moral and especially legal in character?

The most famous dispute in Homer is that between Agamemnon and Achilles over the slave-girl Briseis and Achilles' subsequent refusal to go to war. On its resolution turns the outcome of the Trojan War itself, for only if Achilles fights will Troy be defeated. But Achilles is adamant in his famous wrath, and so broods in his tent. In Book IX of the *Iliad,* in what amounts to an appeal of last resort, an embassy of the closest comrades of Achilles, led by Phoenix, his old mentor and teacher, makes its way to the stubborn warrior's tent. The inducements offered by Agamemnon are generous: rich reparations, gifts and promises of even more booty, the girl to be returned untouched, and more promises of additional women from Lesbos, "very beautiful." The list of compensations is recounted by Odysseus, acting as the mediator, who repeats to Achilles the words and oaths of Agamemnon, but to no avail. Achilles will not relent.

At last aged Phoenix, who reminds Achilles that he taught him both the words and deeds of a Greek hero and was like a father to the boy as he grew to manhood without a father, makes his appeal. Although Phoenix is speaking within epic, he adds as his final plea the *exemplum* of epic itself, the precedent of Meleager.[9] The situations are reasonably alike, although the *exemplum* was from long ago, part of the remembered *kleea andrōn.* In an extended account, Phoenix relates how Meleager had withdrawn from battle with disastrous results for his side, and was implored by his closest comrades, and even his wife (which Achilles does not have, but the rest fits), to return to the fighting. Unlike Achilles, he listened to the pleas and relented, thereby saving his friends and family. Phoenix begs Achilles to heed the example. There is good reason to relent, for "Thus we hear the high deeds of men *(kleea andrōn)* from those who went before. . . . "

The relevant verses are perhaps best given in Lattimore's neutral translation (524ff.) to avoid any suspicion of special pleading:

> Thus it was in the old days also, the deeds we hear of from the great men, when the swelling anger descended upon them.
> The heroes would take gifts; they would listen, and be persuaded
> For I remember this action of old, it is not a new thing, and how it went; you are all my friends, I will tell it among you . . . .

The point of a long tale is that, after such an appeal from his friends and comrades, Meleager relents and fights. Achilles should now do likewise. Phoenix admonishes Achilles to heed the epical *exemplum* (600ff.):

> Listen then; do not have such thoughts in your mind; let not the spirit within you
> turn you that way, dear friend. . . .

In this case the appeal to the epical *exemplum* is not effective, although it was the final, best argument offered to Achilles.

When Ajax sees that more words will be useless, he addresses Odysseus:

> He is hard, and does not remember his friends' affection . . .
> And yet a man takes from his brother's slayer the blood-price, or the price for a

> child who was killed, and the guilty one, when he has largely repaid, remains in the country.

The point is that here are many *exempla* (quasi-legal precedents are cited) of men more wronged than he who think of the consequence to comrades of being obdurate after a fair indemnity is offered. They relent. Achilles should now relent. Yet he will not. So, at last, the comrades retire from Achilles' tent, defeated in their purpose. In this case, the *exemplum* of epic failed to persuade, but it was the last, best hope.

It may be objected that the basis of this dispute is not precisely legal, even if the crucial argument was to the precedent of epic and to *exempla* that are legal in character. However, we should recall that persuasion was part of a magistrate's task—as Gagarin, following Hesiod's text, has well emphasized—and the most persuasive appeal this culture knew was to the way of ancestors, *klea andrōn,* as analogically applied to present situations. When a *basileus* or elder in Homer, or a magistrate in Hesiod, "disposes the precedents *(themistas)* with *dikai* that are straight," which is the common formula, we do not know precisely what forms of persuasion or arguments he used. However, *themistas* is the plural of *themis,* and the regular use of the singular in Homer and Hesiod is found in the formular phrase "as is *themis.*" It is used constantly to designate established custom, and so to describe and indirectly prescribe an action regarded as right, proper, according to precedent. *Themis,* for all practical purposes, equates with precedent, and when personified is best so translated. It becomes hard to believe that appeal was not made to the *exempla* of epic by magistrates both in deciding a case, if a relevant analogy could be found—and for this maneuver oral minds were well prepared—and in persuading the litigants to accept that decision.

Appealing to Themis and the *Exempla* of Epic

An example more obviously legal in character may reinforce the argument. In Book II of the *Odyssey,* Telemachus is at his wit's end over the suitors' behavior and the plundering of his father's household, his *oikos.* Recently arrived at his maturity, Telemachus exercises his right to summon the elders and leading men of Ithaca to *agora,* the assembly of a Greek township, the first they have known in the twenty years that Odysseus has been away. The point is that the procedure was in place, an established propriety, but had been allowed to lapse during Odysseus' absence. The elders discover it will be a private grievance they are summoned to hear and attempt to resolve, in essence a tort, and not a public matter, such as an impending invasion. Telemachus has recourse, therefore, to an established procedure for redressing a private wrong, although there is no evidence that some statute of casuistic law has been violated. His appeal is not made to "the law" in the later sense of the word familiar to literate cultures. The grounds of his appeal, especially its language, designed to persuade contemporary Hellenes, are instructive.

Both the suitors and the leading men of the island, many of the latter sympathetic to Telemachus, are in attendance. The young man pleads his case; the suitors are in violation of the proprieties of *xenia* and are ruining his *oikos*; they behave outrageously. His appeal is to the sense of *nemesis* Hellenes should feel in witnessing such acts, violations of what is proper and established, and to the *aidōs* shed over the persons of true *xenoi* and their hosts, and, finally, to Themis herself. The appeal is, thus, in effect to the *exemplum* of epic. In epic recitations this behavior was described in great detail, and thus was conveyed to the people in the performances of singers. Books are, of course, out of the question.

Telemachus seeks to resolve a dispute in the proper way, following the established procedures. He speaks to the assembly formally, with the *skēptron* in hand, placed there, as custom required, by the herald. His major appeal is delivered to those already sympathetic to his plight. First, he reminds the men of Ithaca that he has just entered into manhood, is inexperienced as yet in battle, and is one against many; otherwise, self-help would have been his remedy long ago. Earlier, Telemachus had claimed that this solution would surely be Odysseus' swift and terrible remedy, were his father to return and see this abomination. Then the suitors of his mother would know terror in their hearts, for the few moments they had left to live. This presages the closing, bloody scene of the whole work. It is also a reminder that, although procedures were in place for resolving disputes, resort to them was not as yet compulsory.

Telemachus now reminds those assembled in *agora* that the violation is one against the established Hellenic proprieties, what is proper or seemly. *Nemesis* and *aidōs* are the anticipated feelings of all Hellenes. What has gone wrong? Where have they, true Hellenes, been for twenty years? Could they not see what was happening in the house of Odysseus? Zeus still watches over the Hellenic proprieties. The gods in their anger turn away from men who ignore an outrage such as this. Telemachus finally appeals to Themis herself, the personification of precedent, established usage, because that is what he wants to prevail here. The role of *themis,* custom and precedent, in the legal disputes argued in Greek assemblies is being strongly asserted, and we are pointedly reminded that Themis herself summons civilized Hellenes to their *agoras,* where their disputes are settled.

Telemachus stands before the men of Ithaca in their *agora* as their suppliant and admits he is helpless. We now scarcely can hear his words in all their implications and powerful epical associations as Greeks heard them from singers who were describing familiar, poignant incidents of eighth-century life. His crucial appeal is:

> I would defend *myself,* if I had the physical power.
> For deeds past all enduring have been done to me,
> past all that is decent *(kalōs)* has my house been plundered.
> Feel *nemesis* in yourselves, and have *aidōs* in the presence of your neighbors dwelling here about. . . .
> Fear the wrath of the gods lest they turn against you. . . .
> I pray you by Olympian Zeus, and by Themis who looses and gathers the *agoras* of men. . . . [10]

It is the most powerful appeal his culture affords him, and he makes it eloquently, although to no avail.

The appeal to *nemesis* and the *taunt* of an *aidōs* that should have been felt—both conveyed in verbs of command and supplication—defy translation into the terminology of our culture. Only Greeks who themselves were then living the epical way of life could feel their full force. That words close to these were never spoken in Archaic courts is beyond belief. Passages similar to this one are, in any case, the only evidence we now have for what, on a daily basis, may have been spoken in Archaic legal proceedings and ethical disputes before the rise of written law.

In the shield scene, the magistrate who could best speak the acceptable solution was the one who spoke a straight *dikē,* one based on the *themistes*—that is, on the traditional body of custom and proprieties conveyed primarily, but not exclusively, in epic recitals. Might he not, then, be regarded as the one whom Calliope, Fair-Utterance, and the Muses, daughters of Memory, favored? Is this not the most natural way to take Hesiod's admittedly enigmatic words—for he trusted that his contemporaries would understand him—when we consider what we now know of Greek life at the turn of the seventh century.

In Hesiod's *Works and Days,* we also learn that more than one *basileus* was available in an area, and litigants could exercise some choice in selecting them. Hesiod's magistrates are "gift-loving," ("*bribe*-loving" overtranslates), and Hesiod claims they relished deciding an inheritance dispute such as the one between him and his brother Perses. No doubt the reason was the "gift." The epical texts themselves suggest that Archaic magistrates, like other *demiourgoi,* were constantly proving their usefulness to the community and were rewarded for this service. What, then, made one magistrate superior to another? Could it be that, like the village *imam* in illiterate Arab and Turkish villages (at least as late as the 1960s), the more successful magistrate may be simply the one who knows "the Book" (in the Greek case, oral *themistes*) a bit better—or applies it more shrewdly and (Gagarin's point) persuasively? In fact, the Koran, which displaces all positive law in strict, orthodox Islam, affords an interesting comparison, for it has been so used for centuries by millions of people, more of them illiterate than literate. The claim is constantly heard that there is no human dispute or problem that does not find its solution—by artful analogy, of course—in its inspired verses. When a dispute proves seemingly intractable, litigants can seek a resolution from an especially skillful imam in a neighboring village, if both agree.

The judgment of T. A. Sinclair, in his still useful edition of *Works and Days* (first published in 1932), is pertinent. He links the magistrate's knowledge of socially approved precedents with his experience and perception of a legal situation. Noting the many references in Homer to judicial decisions given by scepter-bearing kings, Sinclair writes:

> But these decisions depended first on various usages, δίκαι, as we should say, precedents, which the arbitrator might recall, and secondly his own view of the matter. There was nothing that could be called a system of law, and apparently there was nothing to compel a man to go to law. . . . The body of law still consisted only in the [nonsystematic] recollection of previous verdicts in the minds of princes.[11]

This lack of a system or an organized body of previous decisions forming a legal corpus passed across generations to all magistrates was also clear to Sinclair as he reviewed the evidence found in Hesiod's *Works and Days*. In this assessment he seems to have been right. Sinclair's emphasis on previous verdicts guiding present ones, as an individual magistrate might remember them (mainly his own decisions and those of other magistrates in the area) *may* be right, as I suspect it partially is, but cannot be verified. It would be local decisions, in any case, that they remembered, and there would be nothing systematic or binding about the practice. Moreover, such previous verdicts as a magistrate may remember cannot be the whole story. Appeal to the *exempla* of epic and to "moral" language made persuasive to Greek ears by generations of singers must be assumed, and would, in contrast to local verdicts, be pan-Hellenic.

If we can explain Hesiod's reference to the reliance of magistrates on Muses and poets as, in part, referring to the magistrates' common appeals to the *exempla* of epic, then we can add the supportive evidence of Plato many centuries later. His dialogues are full of Socrates' contemporaries who still appeal to epical precedents and to the vocabulary of Homeric moral suasion in order to resolve contemporary moral dilemmas. This requires that they resort often to highly questionable analogical arguments, something that seems not only natural to them, but eminently reasonable or logical. Evidently, the historical Socrates balked at this. The Platonic Socrates certainly does. One such analogy, used in the attempt to solve a complex legal dispute, is justly famous. One Euthyphro has been castigated for seeking to indict his own father in a court, a violation of Athenian usage or custom, an established *nomos*. Euthyphro bemoans his legal dilemma as he and Socrates wait for the court to open for business:

> And, Socrates, see what a formidable proof *(tekmērion)* I offer you—one that I have given to others—namely, that it is the established right thing to prosecute [a father]. . . . [12]

Euthyphro has a rival *nomos* to the Athenian "established right thing," one that is ancient and impressive *(mega)*, he claims, and which he thinks should prevail. It is based on the authority of epic (Hesiod) and, in terms of logical form, is an argument from analogy to an epical *exemplum*. This case, a Platonic *reductio ad absurdum* of contemporary moral and legal debate, is discussed more fully in chapter 6.

In the absence of written law, did Greeks of the Archaic period behave so differently from Euthyphro, who in enlightened late fifth-century Athens waxes indignant over the fact that his brothers will not accept his legal reasoning based on analogy with epical precedent, an argument he fully intends to make to the Archon Basileus himself and to the court? Literates, it hardly needs saying, have often underestimated the degree to which traditional narratives, essentially the tribal stories, can function as ethical and legal exemplars in oral cultures, for the reason that they do not wear the dress of "ethics" and "law" as we now know them. For doubting literates, a careful study of the oral transmission of tribal tradition as dominantly preserved in narratives and of tribal members' daily resort to them among the Native Americans, insofar as these can now be studied, would tell an instructive story. So, too, would the experience of contemporary tribal life in parts of Africa and Australia, although this, too, is fading away in the wake of advancing literacy.

For us, this untidy mess—what E. R. Dodds called the Greek ''inherited conglomerate''—is simply not what we mean by ''law.'' It does not tell us which of so many rules or admonitions are specifically legal rules, how they are to be recognized as such, or how they are to be consistently and fairly applied in society. They are preserved in concrete language; the typical syntax is narrative, not propositional or abstract. They carry no sanctions; no authority explicitly commanded them. They simply do not constitute ''law'' or ''ethics'' as we know them. They are what they seem to be, ''stories,'' mere tales, not compendiums of how to behave.

Of course, on one level, literates are half-right. What we find in epic represents a stage of legal (and ethical) development best regarded as either prelegal or protolegal. The ''law'' as we have come to recognize it and have long known it is a product of extensive experience with alphabetic literacy, a gift to Europe from literate Greece and Rome.

Literacy and the Law: First Encounters on Crete

We turn now to the ways that a slowly spreading literacy and the administration of justice first interact on European soil. The transition from reliance on the *exempla* of epic and on remembered oral usages to exclusive reliance on written laws in the courts is not a single, discontinuous leap. There were stages along the way, and some of the early compromises between oral and written procedures are difficult yet for us to fathom. We must look first to the island of Crete.

In the literary tradition of the fourth century, two Dorian settlements, Sparta and Crete, are consistently portrayed as being famous for their laws and for *eunomia,* ''lawfulness'' or even ''law and order.''[13] The ''Spartan legend'' has clearly been born, destined to become a commonplace of fourth-century political propaganda, often in the works of Athenian writers who have philosophical interests and conservative politics.[14] To the modern historian, this coupling of Dorian settlements by reason of their citizens' superior laws presents something of a paradox. Sparta became notorious for the the ban of Lycurgus, her famous first lawgiver, against committing laws to writing, a prohibition that later Greeks believed had been observed for centuries.[15] Crete, by contrast, has yielded our earliest inscriptional evidence for the existence of written laws anywhere on Greek soil, as well as far and away the most abundant evidence, literary and inscriptional, for the adoption of written laws for the entire Archaic period. This southern island has the best claim—and the only one based on inscriptional evidence—for being the place in Europe where the practice of controlling some human behavior by means of written laws began.

At the present writing, early legal inscriptions or pieces of them survive from nearly a dozen of Crete's fabled ''ninety cities.''[16] All are short and fragmentary, with the fullest evidence also by chance being the earliest, from Dreros. On Crete the inscriptional recording of laws began early, perhaps commencing within half a century of the alphabet's introduction to the island, which was no later than ca. 700 B.C.[17] and recent finds suggest a date a bit earlier. The city of Dreros led the way, at least on the basis of present evidence; her first enactments seem to have been written down starting perhaps as early as ca. 650 B.C.

A recent find from the area of Afrati on Crete yields an important civil enactment establishing the new office of remembrancer *and* scribe, the second part of the title adding a new function to that memorialized in the more ancient title of the city's remembrancer. This inscription also receives additional brief examination in this chapter because of its unique place in the body of surviving evidence for a slowly developing alliance between literacy and the law.

The most famous of all Greek law codes, often called the Queen of Inscriptions or simply the Great Code, also comes from another of the Cretan cities, Gortyn. It is the only Archaic Greek law code that is complete, permitting us to read it from start to finish as the lawmakers intended. That, in itself, would make it invaluable evidence in the history of Greek law. It is also of considerable but neglected importance to the history of Greek literacy. The contents of the Great Code afford important evidence for the residual oralism of Greek legal practices even after some important matters were being governed by written law. What it has to tell of the pervasive role of the oral eyewitness—an important feature of residual legal oralism, although by no means the only one—even when a written law code is in place is the focus of next chapter. In this chapter we turn to Dreros and then to the new find from Afrati.

The Legal Enactments of Dreros: Europe's First Written Laws

Apart from its early laws, the city of Dreros is of historical interest to archaeologists because it was the site of an early temple known to have existed in Iron Age Greece. Of the stone version of the temple, originally built in the Late Geometric period and dedicated to Apollo Delphinios, only pieces of the walls now survive. Fortuitously, these have yielded eight fragments of the city's early enactments or "laws." If the earliest is correctly dated (on the basis of epigraphy) to 650 B.C., no city on the continent of Europe resorted to written law any earlier. What appears to be the oldest and longest of the fragments is complete, giving it a chronological pride of place in the history of European law. Because it is short, consisting of three lines written *boustrophēdon* with a fourth line cut retrograde, it will be quoted in full.

> May God be kind (?). The city has thus decided; when a man has been *kosmos,* the same man shall not be *kosmos* again for ten years.
> If he does act as *kosmos,* whatever judgments he gives, he shall owe double,
> and he shall lose his rights to the office as long as he lives, and whatever he does as *kosmos* shall be nothing.
> The swearers shall be the *kosmos* and the *damioi* and the twenty of the city.[18]

The statute forbids a person who has been *kosmos* (magistrate) again to occupy the office until ten years have elapsed and fixes some harsh penalties for violators. The thrust of the enactment is obviously not a matter of sweeping substantive law; it concerns a matter of more humble procedure. That is the pattern for the earliest use of writing to record laws.

The reason behind the enactment is obscure, but some speculation is possible. The institution of the *kosmos* was not ancient if the evidence of Aristotle may be believed, and so prohibiting iteration of office would not have been a matter of ancient tribal custom. Hence the issue invites being addressed in new, written law. Also behind the law may have been the intention to prevent the office from serving as a stepping stone to tyranny (so argue the first editors, as well as Meiggs and Lewis).[19]

The eight blocks of gray schist bearing the early civil enactments were plundered at an unknown time from a temple that was in continual use from the late Geometric period to the third century B.C. Because of the fragmentary state of the evidence and the manner of its preservation, the dating depends on the lettering. Each enactment begins with the formula *ade ewade poli* ("The City has thus decided") or with *ewade* alone. No name is attached to any of them. This was paralleled at Gortyn. That they were were official civic enactments is, however, clear.

The word *kosmos,* used to designate a ruling magistrate, was always, as noted by Aristotle, associated with Crete and probably originated there. Because the etymology implies "order" (as in the Homeric verb *kosmeō* and later in the Heraclitean noun *kosmos,* "world order"),[20] it is a reasonable conclusion, drawn by Willetts and others, that the *kosmoi* were viewed as those who brought order, and so *eunomia,* to the city. They must have done so by knowing and administering the governing customs, if "law" is to be put in scare quotes and restricted to written ordinances, as well as by administrating the new, written enactments. At least a few of them were literate.

In addition to *kosmos,* there is a second word of interest in the enactment, *polis,* here in its first epigraphical appearance. As Meiggs and Lewis[21] observe, this inscription is evidence that the concept of the Hellenic *polis* was in existence by the middle of the seventh century, if, indeed, that could have been plausibly doubted. The inscription assures us that by ca. 650 B.C. the most distinctive of Greek political institutions is in existence and flourishing on Crete, with a legal apparatus consisting at the minimum of a legislative authority (of some sort) acting in the name of the *polis.* Moreover, it assures us that there are ruler-magistrates, called *kosmoi,* who presumably deliver *dikai,* judgments, bringing order to the city. Moreover, there exists a developing body of procedural rules and fixed penalties relating to the office of a *kosmos.* We can also be sure that at least some of these rules were being committed to written form by the middle of the seventh century, as this enactment itself proves. Further, in that such promulgations are not made and recorded in a vacuum, seemingly there is some sort of an enforcement arm—some policing force—in place. Reliance for enforcement in this case is unlikely to be on self-help or communal social pressure. Given that the Homeric and Hesiodic poems have been taken by most scholars as evidence for how justice was administered under the legal conditions of Greek primary orality, there can be little doubt that partially literate Cretan Dreros has gone far beyond what is found in the epical sources.

There is a final and, for some, less palatable conclusion. Plausibly, written laws did not initially address the deepest moral concerns or the most deeply felt prohibitions of the community; these were still left to the workings of traditional, oral ways, on which the community had long successfully depended. Thus, from a practical, civil point of view, the tenure of a magistrate, a recent office, may well be more important initially to fix in writing and so be placed beyond oral manipulation than, let us say, a community's regulations concerning deliberate homicide, which were never in serious doubt. Written law, so it seems, first addressed matters not felt to be at the core of communal concern or accepted practice, however alien that suggestion may now be to our literate intuition. Those matters were left under the control of established oral usages. It follows that written law emerged only gradually. It did not spring forth whole, in the form of sweeping, comprehensive codes of "all the laws."

Rememberer and Scribe: The New *Poinikastas* Inscription

The early Cretan legal material has now been supplemented by the important "scribe" inscription from yet another Cretan city, probably Afrati or at least from the Lyttos-Afrati general area. The *editio princeps* was published in 1970.[22] It is evidence for the civil appointment of a high official whose special duty, clearly a new one, is in some manner to be responsible for *writing*, as well as remembering, the city's important affairs. For these dual tasks he is to be handsomely rewarded and made the civil and social equal of a magistrate.

As a mark of esteem for the civil importance of his new duties, the city is prepared to grant a certain Spensithios, among other exalted privileges, a hereditary title, a substantial annual income, immunity from legal prosecution (presumably in his official capacity), and an assured place of honor in the performance of sacred rites. Taken as a whole, these privileges are designed to make his office, in dignity and privilege, the equal of that of a *kosmos*, a ruling magistrate and member of the hereditary aristocracy. The inscription indicates that the *Mnēmōn* or rememberer, an official known from the Gortyn code and elsewhere in Greece, will henceforth function as both *mnēmōn* and *poinikastas*, rememberer *and* scribe. This office combined some well-established, exalted responsibilities concerning the city's affairs, carried in his ancient title "rememberer," with some new ones, carried in his title "scribe," translating a word not elsewhere instanced in the Greek language. Orality and literacy are entering into a new phase of their mutual development.

The inscription was found after the publication of Jeffery's *Local Scripts of Archaic Greece* but has been dated by her in other publications to ca. 500 B.C. That date puts it somewhat later than the Great Code from Gortyn which comprises the redaction of recent written laws and older oral customs, but perhaps not very much later. The appointment was recorded on what appears to be a bronze *mitra* (a kind of metal stomach guard for soldiers) that was converted to use as a *pinax*. It was stored in the precinct of the city, as was customary for such an item.

The inscription is cut with bronzeworker tools (the inscriber thus being a professional craftsman who is also literate) on both sides of the *mitra*, side A consisting of 22 lines and side B of 17 lines. Not all are legible, but several important lines on both sides are perfectly intelligible. Side A begins with the standard opening "Gods" followed by *ewade*, in this case the *Dataleis* (otherwise unknown to us) being named as the enacting body. The resolution is supported by the city's pledge to Spensithios of

> subsistence and immunity from all taxes to him and to his descendants, so that he be for the city its Rememberer and Scribe in public affairs both sacred and secular.

What is striking in this wording is that the office to which Spensithios was elevated was that of *mnamōn* and *poinikastas*, "rememberer *and* scribe." In the Gortyn code the office of rememberer is designated by a noun. In the present text both aspects of the office are described by infinitives, *mnamoneuwēn* and *poinikazen*, which mean "to serve as *mnamōn*, Rememberer," and "to do Phoenician things *(Phoinikēia)*," or to write. The latter term evidently preserves the Cretan awareness of the Phoenician source of the letters of the Greek alphabet. *Poinikazen* is found only here, and so is a *hapax legomenon*. This gave rise to some early controversy surrounding its meaning, which has been adequately dispelled.

The exalted public scribe is, of course, a familiar figure from the Near East, where ambiguities in reading the vowelless scripts made his office a necessity in all periods. That we also encounter such a figure—a high public figure, not a street scribe—in late Archaic Greece is intriguing, making the inscription of considerable relevance to understanding the conditions of, at best, restricted literacy found everywhere in sixth-century Greece.

The importance attached to his office is guaranteed by its appurtenances, which, like the office itself, are new, and so must be set out with some care in writing. The office shall belong exclusively to him and his sons and heirs, presumably in perpetuity, unless he or they otherwise determine. Next, the annual payment is fixed, which despite some undecipherable phrases in the text, is clearly substantial. The final legible line of side A suggests that the scribe is to have "equal portion." Judging from context, this means equality with a *kosmos* and refers to receiving some sort of goods or land tenure. Side B begins legibly enough:

> The scribe *(poinikastas)* is to have equal share in sacred and secular affairs in all cases wherever the *kosmos* [board of *kosmoi?*] may be, the scribe [is to be] also. . . .

The text now becomes garbled, but the subject matter is not in doubt. The religious privilege of the scribe to conduct public rites and sacrifices is established, but *not* so as to impinge on any already established family priesthoods,[23] and some further immunities are also established. Finally, the amount of his contribution to the important institution of the *sussitia*[24] (the public sharing of meals in the men's house) is also set out. The wording reminds us that this city is a traditional Dorian community.

> As proper dues[25] to the *andreion* (men's house) he shall give ten axes [weights] of dressed meat . . . [some garbled items and conditions follow], but nothing else is to be compulsory if he does not wish to give it.

Two final lines that are not decipherable seem to refer the reservation of certain religious matters to an elder or senior member of some body or priesthood.

This high public figure and the impressive emoluments of his office resemble most closely the exalted court scribes of the ancient Near East (Hebrew, Babylonian, Egyptian), not the street scribe or humble public scribe of Hellenistic Greece or the recent Near East. Only in a culture of restricted literacy is a scribe so honored and rewarded. When many possess his skills, his uniqueness and so his value diminish rapidly. It may in part have been the failure to appreciate the value placed on literate skills when they are as yet not widely disseminated that induced some scholars to attempt to convert this figure to a "reeve" or judge, not the city's scribe.[26] Literacy is relatively new or at least highly restricted, and so its value and importance receive high official recognition as its advantages are incorporated into civil life.

Within a century or so of the Afrati inscription, the official scribe as a figure of high respect would become to Greeks themselves a curious anachronism at best, especially in Athens. In that city, by at least early in the fourth century, public clerks or court recorders had sunk to the status of menial functionaries.[27] One readily thinks of those faceless individuals—literate clerks of the court—who so routinely were commanded to read out sections of the law in the speeches of fourth-century orators. Not so much as a name survives for any of them. That clearly is a distant cry from the exalted status, at the turn of the fifth century on Crete, of a certain Spensithios, the high *mnamōn* and *poinikastas* of his seemingly flourishing city.

Conclusion

An obvious question presents itself. Did the cities of Crete first adopt the alphabet with the intention of writing down laws? Was that their motive? If the argument from analogy with other preliterate cultures carries conviction, the answer must be no.[28] The recording of law is never the first use to which a society emerging from primary orality puts newfound literate skills. The reason is that the control of human behavior has long been a matter adequately handled by oral means in the community, or that society would not have survived and prospered, as the advanced communities of Archaic Crete so obviously had. The established oral means of social control are steeped in traditions that are at the core of the people's way of life. Orality as the mechanism of social control is woven into the fabric of religion and cult and so is shrouded in their protections. Oral ways are thus not easily abandoned when there is no immediately perceived need to do so. Rather, the pattern seems to be one of gradual realization that writing is a better—or at least a supplemental—way to accomplish some things that previously oral procedures had accomplished.

The early legal inscriptions from Crete, however, do confirm that the island was one of the first places, if not (as I believe) the first, where Greeks realized the utility of the Phoenician letters for recording (some) laws. Only the late literary sources suggest the possibility of other parts of the Greek world—mainly to the west—as the place for the legal innovation and nominate various legendary figures for the honor of first Greek lawgiver. Because these sources are late, many centuries after the event, as well as contradictory and overgrown with fantastic legend, such kernels of truth as they may contain (e.g., pointing toward the colonies as likely places to need written laws) are hopelessly contaminated. They are more safely disregarded, at least for tracing the new alliance between literacy and the law. It is with the experiments on Crete and the surviving legal records from the island that a confident history of Western written law—and therefore of Europe's fusion of literacy with law—must begin.

The new *poinikastas* inscription from Afrati is an early indication that, in matters civil and public, "doing the Phoenician thing" was to be the technology of the future, especially for the law. Before turning to Athens, where the European marriage of literacy and the law was to be completed, however, we shall examine first, in some detail, the legal situation at Gortyn and the residual oralism of the legal procedures of the city that the surviving Great Code itself makes so evident. The instructive role of the oral eyewitness, the *maiturs,* in the daily legal practice of Gortyn especially deserves close attention. Like such terms as *xenia* ("guest-friendship"), *sumposion* ("drinking party"), or *sunousia* ("association"), no modern translation does justice to the legal *maiturs,* the oral eyewitness or procedural witness, so pervasive a figure in Archaic law courts. *Marturia,* the formal act of eyewitnessing, is yet another institution of Greek oral life that advancing literacy slowly transformed into something very distant from the oral original, but more familiar to us. As in the similar cases, where terms that carry special meanings and associations for oral societies are assimilated to modern ones, exegetical havoc can result. We shall discover in the next chapter that the ancient oral eyewitness, a feature of all oral cultures, and the modern accidental witness must be carefully distinguished.

From the standpoint of the progress of legal literacy in Hellas, no document surviving from the Archaic period is of comparable importance to the Great Code of Gortyn. Because of its completeness, it has no rival as evidence for transitional stages between, on the one hand, exclusive reliance on oral custom and procedures in dispensing justice, and, on the other, a gradually increasing reliance on writing and written law in the courts.

Notes

1. M. Gagarin, *Early Greek Law,* p. 26: "The clearest and strongest evidence for the existence of a formal, public legal procedure in preliterate Greece is the trial scene on Achilles' shield . . . . "

2. H.L.A. Hart, *The Concept of Law* (Oxford, 1961), pp. 89ff.; M. Gagarin, *Early Greek Law,* p. 2.

3. Henry Maine, *Ancient Law* (London, 1861), p. 7. I quote, however, from the twelfth edition of 1888, a magnificent leather-bound volume published by John Murray, Albemarle Street, London, and printed on acid-free paper. It is still in perfect condition, an example of books as they once were, intended to be handed down to children and grandchildren, and to be read by each generation, as, indeed, this one was. The pagination remains the same as in the 1861 edition, although the author's comments about subsequent discoveries concerning "law" in uncivilized regions, especially in the prefaces to the fifth and tenth editions, are worthy of note.

4. Ibid., pp. 14–15.

5. The translation of *Iliad* XVIII. 500 is disputed. Fitzgerald is representative of the alternative version: "one claimed that all was paid . . . his opponent turned the reparation down."

6. For references that will in turn lead to other sources, see Gagarin, *Early Greek Law,* p. 25, n. 25.

7. The term *basileis* in Hesiod refers to local rulers, normally several of them in one place (hence not as in Homer "kings") who also function as local magistrates. The term "baron" may be the closest English equivalent, especially since in the baronial courts of England and especially Scotland the owners of great estates also functioned as local magistrates. Several scholars have suggested that by Hesiod's time possibly the term *basileus* could, in some contexts, mean only "magistrate," as seemingly happened for *kosmos* on Crete. This is an attractive suggestion.

8. Martin West's view is expressed in *Hesiod: Theogony,* p. 172, reflecting his speculation that the *Theogony* was the hymn performed for an *agōn* or contest at the funeral of a dead *basileus* and, importantly, before his sons, who would also be *basileis.* Hesiod on this reconstruction sang at Chalcis in Euboea, at the funeral of Amphidamas, and flattered the royal sons and patrons, as singers must do (based on *Works and Days* 651ff.). Hesiod, or the received text, also tells us that he won first prize, was awarded a tripod, and dedicated it to the Muses of Helicon. (It is intriguing to speculate that, if all of this is free of later interpolation, Hesiod may also have had his many-handled tripod inscribed, adding to the very early inscribed dedications of this type from Boiotia.) West's interesting (as always) observations do not really explain, however, Hesiod's very precise words about Muses and their contributions to magistrates. A large step in the right direction, it seems to me, is found in Gagarin, who summarizes Hesiod's assertions under what amounts to four headings: (1) The Muses and especially Calliope benefit a *basileus* in, specifically, deciding a *dikē,* a legal case; (2) the *dikē* is pronounced orally; (3) the settlement is intelligent (thus acknowledging the force of the adverb *epistamenōs*); (4) the *basileus* persuades the litigants to accept his decision. But then Gagarin, who wants no doors open to a theory involving a body of Greek oral law, restricts the influence of Muses (or poetry) to (4): "The last function alone requires the help of Muses," that is, by helping the magistrate to "speak well" and persuasively. See *Early Greek Law,* p. 25. As I view it, Hesiod's words imply that epical poetry clearly made *some* contribution to a magistrate's delivering a "straight *dikē*" that involved an application of the Hellenic proprieties and precedents to a specific case. Catherine Roth's view, that at least part of the phrasing of *Theog.* 86–90 goes beyond claiming that epical verse provides (somehow) only enhanced verbal eloquence, is in my view correct; there is also a contribution from epical poetry to the content of a *dikē* delivered by a magistrate as he "disposes the precedents." Then she goes too far (again, as I see it) in arguing that a magistrate's function included remembering and handing down a body of versified oral law and rules. We have no evidence for that, and Hes-

iod's text does not claim it. See C. Roth, "The Kings and Muses in Hesiod's *Theogony,*" *TAPA* 106 (1976), pp. 331–338. Havelock's chapter 7, "Hesiod's Hymn to the Muses," in *Preface to Plato* was brilliant, the first critical treatment to do full justice to what Hesiod's text clearly says about the function of poets and poetry in early seventh-century Hellenic society. Singers gave pleasure—indeed, intense pleasure—but epical *aoidoi* were far more than entertaining troubadours. Havelock's further position, held adamantly until he died, that *aoidoi* could and did function as local versifiers, aiding in formulating short-term legal directives, goes beyond the evidence, a point on which we often differed heatedly. Havelock thought these were, essentially, specific decisions necessary for a period in the life of the local community, and so were put into verse, but were not fundamental to the Hellenic ethos, and so need not be incorporated in the repertoire of *aoidoi*. He also thought that the early inscriptions were strong evidence that epical verse could be put to uses other than a bard's performance, which observation, by itself, is true and important.

9. This long incident dominates *Iliad,* Book IX. The embassy to Achilles commences at IX. 179, when Nestor instructs the others about how to go about persuading Achilles: "And the Gerenian Nestor gave them much instruction/looking eagerly at each and most of all at Odysseus/to try hard so that they might win over the blameless Peleion" (Lattimore translation). The embassy extends over some 500 verses, to IX. 669, where Odysseus and the others retire from the tent of Achilles in defeat.

10. *Odyssey* II. 40ff.

11. T. A. Sinclair, *Hesiod: Works and Days* (London, 1932), p. xix. In his note on *themistas* at verse 9, Sinclair remarks that a king proclaims these judgments in Homer, which, according to the *Theogony* 81–90, "were suggested to him by Muses." We may fairly interpret this to mean that Hesiod takes a somewhat more detached view and begins to try to explain and rationalize what in Homer is merely reported as the community's oral experience. That spirit runs through Hesiod. Could it have been aided by the fact that he could spend hours reflecting quietly on a text, among the first Europeans who could do so, and Europe's first author who has left us anything to read?

12. *Euthyphro* 5 E.

13. Plato, *Laws* 624Aff.; Aristotle, *Pol.* 1271B20ff.; Plutarch, *Lyc.* 6.7. The dramatic setting of Plato's *Laws* is placed on the island of Crete transparently because of the island's fame for matters legal, even if that reputation is already blurred into a mythical past. The interlocutors are a Cretan (a certain Clinias, otherwise unknown), a Spartan (a certain Megillus, otherwise unknown), and an individual who is never named but is referred to as the "Athenian Stranger." Early in the dialogue (625 B), the Athenian Stranger exhorts his Cretan and Spartan companions to converse with him concerning laws *(nomoi)* and government *(politeia),* because both had been reared in cities of ancient and noble legal institutions and customs. The Athenian Stranger asks the Cretan if, indeed, he concurs with Homer that Minos had conversed with Zeus himself (*Od.* 19.178) *before laying down the laws for the Cretan cities*. Clinias happily affirms it: "So our people now say." Moreover, they believe that the brother of Minos, Rhadamanthys, won his fame for being "most just" because of his righteous administration of *dikai* in those ancient days (625 A). This is, of course, later and fantastic elaboration on a passing reference in Homer to the fact that Minos conversed with Zeus. No subject matter, legal or otherwise, is specified in Homer. In this manner the legends surrounding the early Greek lawgivers grew and became "history" in the Hellenistic accounts.

14. The very full evidence mustered by F. Ollier in *Le Mirage spartiate,* vols. I and 2 (Paris, 1933–1945; reprint New York, 1974), is persuasive that all literary treatments of Sparta later than 400 B.C., and above all Plutarch, are part of the *"mirage spartiate,"* another instance of the process whereby myth once again is transformed into history. Further references, and a survey of theories "bad, good, even brilliant" can be found in T.

Boring, *Literacy in Ancient Sparta* (Leiden, 1979), pp. 21ff. See also the ever perceptive E. N. Tigerstedt, *The Legend of Sparta in Classical Antiquity* (Stockholm, 1965). We are on different ground altogether with the fragments that survive in respectable numbers from the poems of the seventh-century poets Tyrtaeus and Alcman, both associated with Sparta (whatever their cities of birth may have been). The Alexandrians had five "books" (scrolls) of poems that they thought belonged to Tyrtaeus, including a *Eunomia* from which later literary sources quote a total of twelve lines. There is a close dependence of especially Tyrtaeus' elegiacs (the meter of most of his composition) on epical speech. See especially Bruno Snell, *Tyrtaios und die Sprache des Epos* (Göttingen, 1969), a work of importance for appreciating the popular diffusion of epical speech in the early Archaic period. Alcman's language, which is closer to the vernacular, reveals in subject matter and vocabulary that he was demonstrably familiar both with "Homer" (e.g., the meeting of Nausicaa and Odysseus) and Hesiod, especially the *Theogony* (in some form or other). The subtle allusions require that the audiences were totally familiar with a vast body of epical verse—not necessarily our texts of Homer and Hesiod—and confirm the abundance of evidence of the rich tradition of sung poetry in early Sparta. All of this poetry was, of course, intended for performance, either in *choreia* and rituals, or else at *sumposia,* and the like. None of it was intended for readers. In the case of Alcman, we can be certain of female choruses for his Maiden Songs, and hymns for male choirs and for single male voices. Also likely, if not certain, as noted by a number of scholars, are preludes for Homeric performances, related to what we now know as the Homeric Hymns, and compositions for *sumposia.* There are two references in Alcman to the Spartan *sussition,* one of which (Alcman 98; Page) takes us directly into the dining hall itself: "At feasts and ceremonies in the *andreion* it is proper to raise the paean." See D. L. Page (ed.), *Poetae Melici Graeci* (Oxford, 1962). Once again, we encounter the exclusively male mess or meal, the *sumposion,* hymns to Apollo and other gods, poetic dedications, and chorus and dance, all under the pervasive presence of epic. We move in the unmistakable atmosphere of oral and aural Greece. This strongly confirms, of course, the evidence found in the popular inscriptions as reviewed in earlier chapters. Also from Sparta are the thousands of small lead votives found in Spartan sanctuaries (100,000 from Orthia alone). The dominant human figure is the foot soldier, reminding us of the Mantiklos "Apollo" and that the locations is, after all, Sparta. But next come musicians of all kinds, male and female, including lyre-players with single or double pipes, percussionists, cymbal-players, and many dancers. See the full treatment of the lead figurines in the standard work on Orthia, R. M. Dawkins (ed.), *The Sanctuary of Artemis Orthia at Sparta* (London, 1929), especially pp. 249ff. A Late Geometric pottery fragment from Amyclae—not much, if at all, later than the Dipylon pot—contains the figure of a lyre-player accompanying a group of dancers. These two pieces of contemporary evidence alone should cast some doubt on the portrayal of early Sparta in the literary sources, as should have the recovery from Egypt in 1855 (published in 1863) of a papyrus containing some hundred lines of a chorus for maidens by Alcman. Indeed, all the physical evidence seems to put Sparta squarely "in the main stream of archaic Greek culture" (Fitzhardinge, *The Spartans,* p. 11), especially musically. Fitzhardinge's book happily reverses the usual scholarly approach of accepting as primary the late, literary evidence and then attempting to accommodate the physical and epigraphical evidence to what the literary sources say. Fitzhardinge accepts the contemporary material evidence as primary and then asks to what extent the late, literary sources are consistent with it, a procedure adopted in this book. The Amyclae musician and dancers are on a fragment from a trinket box now in Athens, NM 234. For Alcman's chorus song, see Denys Page (ed.), *The Partheneion* (Oxford, 1951). As late as 405 B.C., in an epigram celebrating its victory over Athens, Sparta could still be hailed as "the land of lovely choirs" (Ion of Samos, in Page, *Epigrammata Graeca* [Oxford, 1975], 509). In this case the written word alone survives to tell of the vanished sounds. To the surviving fragments of these early Spartan poets should be added the fragments of Archilochus of Paros, among the oldest of the poets now called lyrical, whose heavy epical debts have been delineated by Denys Page, "Archilochus and the Oral Tradition," *Entretiens sur l'antiquité (Fondation Hardt)* 10 (Geneva, 1964), pp. 117–179. Also see James Notopolous, "Archilochus, the *Aoidos,*" *TAPA* 97 (1969), pp. 311–315. Great Pindar of Thebes has been brought solidly into the picture by Gregory Nagy's recent monumental *Pindar's Homer: The Lyric Possession of an Epic Past* (Baltimore and London, 1990). The close dependence of Xenophanes' *ipsissima verba* on epic would be a reasonable conclusion from the full evidence presented in the recent book-length treatment of the first Greek philosopher we can read in his own words by James Lesher in *Xenophanes of Colophon. Fragments* (Toronto, 1992). See Lesher's index of passages cited for the extensive entries for both Homer and Hesiod. Also, see my forthcoming review in the *Journal of the History of Philosophy.*

15. Plutarch, *Lyc.* 13.1–3. Plutarch claims, first, that Lycurgus did not establish written laws *(nomoi gegrammenoi)* and that indeed one of his "so-called rhetras" forbade them. Plutarch then turns expansive, offering detailed information concerning daily life in preliterate Sparta. This includes information on oral commercial contracts (even small money matters, *mikra chrēmatika*), *and* on Lycurgus' educational theory as it related to the deliberate avoidance of written laws, *and* of unchanging customs (suspiciously, an Aristotelian technical term is used for "unchanging"). How, after the turn of the Christian era, Plutarch could have known such detail—in deliberate absence of written legal records on his own admission—is, of course, intriguing. Sometimes neglected is that Plutarch himself observes: "Of the lawgiver Lycurgus absolutely nothing can be said that is not controversial, either about his birth, his travels or his death. Every writer gives a different version of his laws and social system. Least of all is there any agreement as to his date." On this passage Fitzhardinge astutely adds: "We are no wiser now, and it is well to admit there is no good evidence for Lycurgus as a real person; he is a product of the Greek propensity to explain history in personal terms" (*The Spartans,* p. 160). For obvious reasons, I have ignored the issue of Spartan literacy (or claimed illiteracy), but the treatment of Fitzhardinge (to whom I owe debts), when added to those of Boring and Cartledge, will afford the reader some excellent guidance. See T. Boring, *Literacy in Ancient Sparta* and P. Cartledge, "Literacy in the Spartan Oligarchy," *JHS* 98 (1978), pp. 25–37, where the inscriptions are treated. The earliest evidence of writing from Sparta is seventh century and, it may be noted, dedicatory. The oldest inscription is now thought to be a dedication to "Helen, the wife of Menelaus" inscribed on a bronze oil flask found at the Menelaeum in 1975 and dated to between 675 and 650 B.C. See H. Catling and H. Cavanagh, "Two Inscribed Bronzes from the Menelaion," *Kadmos* 15 (1976), pp. 145–157; and also Fitzhardinge, *The Spartans,* p. 130. Note, too, Fitzhardinge's references to craftsman inscriptions (also dedicatory) from Orthia; these are associated with the rebuilding of the shrine ca. 575 B.C. Partially literate craftsmen turn up in all parts of Hellas in the Archaic period, a fact that deserves both notice and explanation.

16. The ninety cities are already mentioned in Homer at *Od.* XIX. 174. Crete's claim to be the locus for alphabetic transfer has notable defenders. Some considerations have been: All the early Cretan legal inscriptions begin from right to left, in the Phoenician manner; some share a form of punctuation common in the North Semitic inscriptions but not common elsewhere in Greece; and there is independent archaeological evidence of a close eighth-century relationship with Cyprus and Rhodes, as we would expect given Crete's geographical position. For example, the Late Geometric small flasks found in family chamber tombs near Knossos were either Cypriot imports or close local imitations of Cypriot originals. Crete, if not the place of origin for the Greek alphabet, must at least have been one of its earliest receivers. The fact that Crete, unlike the other two large

islands, was not on the direct trade routes, especially those involving the Syrian coast, and indeed is rather out of the way, makes it less likely as the birthplace *and* source of wide dissemination than Cyprus. Recent finds point in the direction of a birthplace that had established trade routes with Euboea and its colony Pithekoussai, as Cyprus did at all times, a fact guaranteed by the imperative need for metals. Perhaps the strongest argument favoring Crete has been that the Cretan version of the alphabet seems to be the closest to the Phoenician because its has only eighteen letters, including the *digamma,* but not the supplemental letters placed at the end of the Greek alphabet. This argument may be less compelling than at first it seems. As late as the Gortyn code (middle fifth century), Cretans continued to write without the additional letters, long after they could have adopted them from elsewhere if any strong need was felt for them. This may suggest that the dialect as pronounced and then recorded could get along without them handily, with no real trouble or ambiguity. Some examples from Gortyn: ΠΣ could make do for Ψ; ΔΔ for Z, and so on. I do not see how we can exclude the possibility that the Cretans did not adopt the additional letters because they did not need them.

17. The epigraphical evidence places the origins of written laws in Greece on Crete. The literary evidence, such as it is, suggests that written law began in the western colonies (Locris) in the person of one Zaleucus. According to the research of the Lyceum in the fourth century (Arist. *Frag.* 548 Rose [= scholion to Pindar *Ol.* II.17]), the Locrians consulted the oracle concerning some internal turmoils and were told that they should have laws enacted for themselves. As good fortune would have it, a certain shepherd (or perhaps a slave) named Zaleucus responded with some excellent laws (*nomoi*) and, when asked whence he got them, attributed them to Athena, disclosed in a dream. He was promptly freed and appointed lawgiver for the Locrians. Such was the state of the legend when the first Greeks to be interested in a systematic way in the history of Greek law, the research scholars in Aristotle's Lyceum, tried to sort out the transmitted tales. Whatever may be the kernels of truth in this and similar accounts, the Locrian laws of Zaleucus (if any) from the seventh century are not available for examination. The serious investigation of the history of European written law must turn for its origins to Dreros and Gortyn on Crete, and to what survives of Draco's Law of Homicide in Athens, that is, to texts that we can examine. It may be noted that the legislation attributed in a late source (Diodorus 12:21–21) to Charondas and Zaleucus is contaminated by Pythagorizing, not unlike the Stoic treatments of Heraclitus. Attempts to rescue something original and uncontaminated have failed, involving as they must an arbitrary sorting of what is early from what is later accretion. A suggestion from the literary accounts does ring true, however, or at least seems plausible. From several accounts comes the suggestion (or at least hints) that some of the early written laws were the work of members of the emerging middle or merchant class, not of aristocrats. Aristotle himself (*Pol.* 1296A18–22) records this as a fact, mentioning Solon and Charondas.

18. The text is given in R. Meiggs and D. Lewis, *A Selection of Greek Historical Inscriptions* (Oxford, 1969), p. 2 (their no. 2). Hereafter this work is cited as Meiggs-Lewis. The stone block bearing the inscription can now be viewed *in situ* at Dreros. In dating the Cretan legal inscriptions, I follow Jeffery in *LSAG*. Noting the concluding reference to swearing, Gagarin has usefully called attention to the importance of oaths in Archaic Greece, citing diverse evidence both epigraphical and literary: ". . . oaths played a part in the preliterate judicial process and the swearing of true oaths is of particular concern to Hesiod in the *Works and Days.*" See Gagarin, *Early Greek Law,* p. 83, n. 10; see also n. 9. Gagarin accepts (p. 81) Jeffery's dating for the Dreros enactment (based as it is on epigraphical consideration): "tentatively dated to the middle or second half of the seventh century."

19. Meiggs-Lewis, p. 3.

20. See on Heraclitus B30, K. Robb, ''Preliterate Ages and the Linguistic Art of Heraclitus,'' p. 194.

21. Meiggs-Lewis, p. 3.

22. L. H. Jeffery and A. Morpurgo Davis, ''POINIKASTAS and POINIKAZEN: BM 1969.4–2.1, a New Archaic Inscription from Crete,'' *Kadmos* 9 (1970), pp. 118–154.

23. As clearly suggested by the root in *idialo*] at the end of line B.4, however the word is to be restored.

24. The casual reference to the important Dorian institution of common meals, held in the *andreion,* or the ''men's house,'' reminds us again of its importance in Archaic Greek life. The practice was followed in Athens among groups of prominent families but conducted in private homes, as we learn, for example, in Plato's *Laches.* As in the Dorian communities, the practice, as very regularly observed, helped meet the need of educating young men in the absence of texts and formal higher education. It was, therefore, an important part of regular *sunousia,* or ''association,'' of the younger men with an older generation in the interest of paideia.

25. ''Lawful'' dues translates *dikaia.* That is certainly the sense. Perhaps: ''as is fitting and right,'' or ''proper'' dues.

26. See the persuasive case made by G. P. Edwards and R. B. Edwards, ''The Meaning and Etymology of *poinakistes,*'' *Kadmos* 16 (1977), pp. 131–140.

27. That Athens knew a period when the scribe was a more revered figure, one closer to Spensithios in social and civic standing than to the humble street scribe, is suggested by three stately statues, partially damaged, of scribes preserved in the Acropolis Museum in Athens. Standing almost three feet tall, they are dedicatory, representing seated scribes poised with very straight backs over wax tablets; they have raised diptyches balanced on their laps. Even damaged, the figures manage to look very professional and rather grand—so much so that an Egyptian imitation has been suspected. See H. Payne, *Archaic Marble Sculpture from the Acropolis,* (New York, 1951), pp. 24, 74 (bibliography) and Plate 118. See also E. A. Havelock, *Literate Revolution,* pp. 200–210. Havelock first called my attention to these statues and to Payne's discussion.

28. As long as legal inscriptions were the earliest writing found on Crete, this view had some plausibility based on the evidence, even if historians of oral cultures may have doubted that recording law would be the first use of writing. Then in 1969 at Phaistos a fairly large storage jar was found bearing a metrical inscription (three dactyls and a spondee): ''This [jar is] of Erpetidamos, the son of Paidophilia.'' It was published by D. Levi, ''Un pithos inscritto da Festos,'' *Kritika Khronika* 21 (1969), pp. 153–176. Also see Heubeck, *Schrift,* p. 125 (10); O. Masson, ''La Plus ancienne inscription crétoise,'' in Morpurgo Davies and Meid (eds.), *Studies,* pp. 169–172. The jar is securely dated to the eighth century, and the inscription was scratched before firing. The epical meter and a proprietary inscription bring Crete into line with what is found elsewhere in Greece at the very inception of literacy.

II

The Alliance between Literacy and the Law

4

Literacy and Residual Oralism in the "Great Code" of Gortyn: The Evidence of a Transitional Document

We now possess fragmentary evidence from the Archaic period for some written laws in some Greek cities, starting with Dreros in the middle of the seventh century, but only the Great Code from Gortyn is a complete document. Only it, for all practical purposes, can provide us with evidence for the daily functioning of Archaic Greek law courts, especially where *marturia,* the formal act of witnessing, is concerned. Fortunately, that evidence is abundant indeed, although it was not always correctly understood by legal historians.[1] It is confirmed by incidental references to witnesses and the oral act of witnessing in the literary evidence, such as in the poems of Homer, Hesiod, and Solon.

The laws of Gortyn reflect an earlier stage of development than our next significant body of evidence for legal witnessing, which is the fourth-century courtroom speeches of the orators. In this, as in so many respects, the Great Code is a transitional document between the oral usages and procedures and a developing new reliance on writing and written law. As such, it is not only the key document in the history of Greek law, as has long been recognized, but also key to understanding advancing literacy in Hellas. In this latter capacity, it has not received the attention it well deserves from historians of Greek literacy.

What was to become the Queen of Inscriptions for Hellenists began to come to light with a chance discovery by Thenon in 1857. Almost from the start, scholars recognized that the Gortyn find was a legal document, that the period of lettering was Archaic, and that its great columns, as they were recovered in stages, bore the single most important find in the history of Greek law. To date, no subsequent find in any part of Hellas has altered that early assessment. As R. W. Willetts has written: "The Great Code—more accurately to be defined as a tabulation of statutory enactments amending prior written law on various topics or modifying even earlier [oral] customs—is the first European law code and the only complete code to have survived from ancient Greece."[2] This statement aptly describes the massive document—finally to number some 600 lines divided into twelve columns—that was found in pieces in the decades following initial discovery. It is not a code in the same sense as would be a highly organized and systematic collection of *all* the laws of Gortyn, collating them as a complete, written collection and so codifying "the law." A complete codification of substantive criminal law together with the more important civil and procedural enactments would be the accomplishment only of a society of advanced literacy, and there is abundant evidence that the Gortynians were not there yet. Even Athens was not to undertake such a legal endeavor or something approximating it—the first Greek city to do so—until the great revision and reinscription of law that took place under the supervision of Nichomachus at very end of the fifth century.

In his seminal article published in 1893, the English classicist and student of early law codes J. W. Headlam sought to correct some mistakes and oversights in the earlier German commentary on the Gortyn code published by Zitelmann, an able legal scholar. All relate to what now can best be understood as the unappreciated fact that many oral practices and customs remained in place in Gortyn's legal life even though literacy, in the form of written law, was making some headway. The code, although a written document, could not be correctly understood apart from also appreciating a residual oral dimension, both in the code's technical vocabulary and in certain traditional oral institutions that it left in place. Headlam, writing at the turn of this century, could not, of course, be expected to address the issue of the degrees of literacy and orality and their peculiar Hellenic symbiosis with the same nomenclature now regularly employed by oralists and historians of literacy. The recovery of the oral dimension in Greek life, as was noted earlier, was pioneered by Milman Parry, starting in the 1920s and not fully appreciated and only partially accepted by historians until perhaps the early 1960s. Several places in Headlam's text reveal, however, that he was aware that the interpretation and correction he was offering to the German legal historians turned on an understanding by habitual literates of a period in Cretan history when primary orality[3] was in the recent past. Writing was known, but along with a surviving written code as evidence for some uses of writing there were bizarre omissions, for which the code is also irrefutable evidence. The omissions can only be explained as a reflection of a sophisticated society's lingering preference for oral memories and oral procedures, what elsewhere I have termed the "residual oralism" characteristic of the Archaic period. Headlam did not use precisely this language or belabor the issue, but at the outset of his article he remarks that in Greece "alone of all European races the highest political and literary achievements came at a time when the introduction of writing was so recent that [written] law had not had time completely to supersede primitive custom. Greek states in their highest prosperity still retained many of the [oral] usages peculiar to the tribal communities from which they had grown."[4] The failure to appreciate this cultural situation had led some earlier legal commentators astray at more than one place in the code, but nowhere more fatefully than in the many references to witnessing.

The first legal commentators had understandably assumed that "witness" meant what in most instances it would in the German and other civilized law codes of the nineteenth century (and today): a person who had been a chance spectator of an event, normally but not always a crime, who might then be summoned to give testimony concerning the facts of which he had been the accidental spectator. For example, *X*, a reputable citizen, by chance happens to be at a certain corner when *A* assaults *B*. Later, as a disinterested party of good reputation, *X* is called upon in court to recount what he had seen and heard. He is an "accidental witness," and his testimony is regularly accepted into evidence in modern systems of jurisprudence; the assumption was made that the same circumstance stands behind the terminology of witnessing in early Greek law. Instead, argued Headlam, "witnesses" in the code designates—without a single exception, according to Headlam—persons who had been summoned to be present at a procedure as formal, oral eyewitnesses. Their presence was necessary to the legal character of the procedure, part of the total "performative" action (what Willetts in one place happily terms an "oral act")[5] that rendered the action legal or valid. The almost ritualized act of eyewitnessing, like the exact pronunciation of oaths of fealty in the medieval period, had to take place in the prescribed manner or the action was rendered legally null. In addition, as part of the same function, witnesses were summoned because only their future testimony, should a dispute arise, could serve as the official record that an act had occurred, that the court's order had been duly executed, or the like. Written records, if any were kept (and none is mentioned in the code), were inadmissible as evidence, as one place in the code involving the role of the *mnamōn,* "the rememberer," indirectly tells us.[6] A similar distrust of writing, as opposed to confidence in the sworn or remembered word, the witnessed word, was still a characteristic of fourth-century Athenian juries, although the situation was gradually changing in the courts in the early decades of that century.

The earlier Gortyn code reveals that procedural eyewitnesses were required in Archaic Greece to validate a formal proceeding while they also became its only "record" in the event of a future challenge by a litigant or his descendants. We have every reason to believe—and none to doubt—that this was another of the uniform features (save in details) of all Archaic Greek courts. Such actions as paying a debt, returning a runaway slave, adopting a son, appointing a relative as guardian for an heiress without close male relatives, and a thousand more like them—no aspect of life with potential consequences for the future was, it seems, left unwitnessed—required that witnesses, in varying numbers depending on the consequences of the event, be summoned. *Marturia,* the formal act of oral or procedural eyewitnessing, was far more pervasive in early Hellenic life than we, without effort and a strong dose of historical empathy, can now imagine. Perceptively, Headlam observes of the act of witnessing as a procedural act in Archaic Gortyn: "The procedure belongs of course chiefly to the period before the introduction of writing. It was soon superseded [but not in Archaic Greece] by written records and written contracts."[7]

The Distinction *in jure* and *in judicio* in the Gortyn Code

What initially caught Headlam's sharp and informed eye was that all the cases mentioned in the Gortyn inscriptions were tried before a single judge *(dikastēs)* and that all aspects were heard before *only* him. In addition, two verbs, *dikazein* and *krinein,* are systematically used to describe separate aspects of this single magistrate's duties. When one is used (*dikazei,* "he gives judgment"), the magistrate is never required to take an oath. When the other is used (*krinei,* "he decides"), he is always required to do so. Headlam realized that the distinction was too consistently maintained in the code not to be of major significance.

Zitelmann, the earliest legal scholar to write an extensive commentary on the code, had also noted the consistent difference in usage between the two verbs, commented on the connection with oath-taking, and then abandoned the matter as intractable. In a discussion devoted to another issue, Zitelmann also stated flatly that there was "no visible trace" in the Gortyn code corresponding to the division *in jure* and *in judicio* familiar to legal historians from both Attic and Roman law.[8] Headlam disagreed. Precisely that division is present in Gortyn legal procedure, which he connected with the puzzle about the verbs *dikazein* and *krinein.* What had disguised the legal facts from previous historians was a crucial difference between the situations at Gortyn, on the one hand, and at Athens (and Rome) on the other. At Gortyn both the preliminary hearing (in Attic law termed *anakrisis;* at Rome, the proceeding *in jure*) and the actual trial itself (in Attic law, termed *krisis;* at Rome, the proceeding *in judicio*) take place before the *same magistrate.* Wearing one hat, so to speak, the Gortynian magistrate undertakes *dikazein,* "to give judgment." This he does according to a strict construction of the *written* law, with no personal discretion permitted. Procedurally, this corresponds to the Attic phase of *anakrisis* and the Roman procedure *in jure.* In function, the magistrate's role in this stage approximates that of Athenian *archon* or the Roman *praetor.* As later in Athens, some matters can be settled (or dismissed) at this stage, meaning that a suit may never go to what amounts to a trial. (In what follows, for convenience I retain the Attic names for these two stages of Gortynian trials.)

If, at Gortyn, the case cannot be decided at this stage, either because (I suggest) no written law as yet exists that applies to the issue or for some other reason, the case must then go to the next, or *krisis,* stage. However, the case is not, as later at Athens, handed over to a *distastērion* for trial by jury. At Gortyn the same magistrate, but wearing his other hat and acting in a different capacity, "takes the oath and he decides *(omnunta krinei)*" the case on the pleadings. The essential point is that the magistrate cannot resolve the case "according to what is written" and "as it is written." Yet the case requires resolution for the sake of the tranquility of the community. The magistrate is then, so to speak, on his own, but he is not for that reason free to become an arbitrary tyrant. That must be the purpose of the standard oath he takes, to assure that he acts as fairly as he can, sizing up the litigants and their claims as governed by his innate sense of fairness. The wording of his oath, alas, is not given, but we may presume it was a "fairness" oath, and so we shall designate it to distinguish it from other types of oaths mentioned in the code. Presumably, then, his basis for decision would be what he knows of oral custom or remembers of precedents and previous cases; perhaps he even cites orally formulated legal rules (if any)[9] accepted by all magistrates. Unfortunately, the grounds for decision when "he [the magistrate] decides" are nowhere specified in the code, although they were, of course, well known to the citizens of Gortyn. As Headlam observed, "The important point to notice is that in the first stage [*anakrisis* in Attic terminology] the magistrate is bound strictly by the letter of the law."[10]

The crucial passage in the Gortyn code describing this procedure is inserted between some regulations concerning the renouncing of the adoption of a son and some provisions for paying a deceased man's debts. As a result, before Headlam, its importance went unnoticed. Its placement is a reminder that the code, which is an ordered document to a large extent, records written law that had developed only gradually. Consistent logic in placing individual enactments, even important ones, was not always possible and was not achieved. Chronology of formulation may have played a role, for logically this enactment should have preceded any other enactment that fell under its rule. That it is a separate enactment is not in question. *Asyndeton* and spacing gaps are regularly used in the code to set off the separate enactments and provisions, with only occasional doubts about the lawmakers' intentions. This enactment was plausibly formulated on a different occasion from what precedes or follows it and is placed here by the stonemason (or those directing him) as seeming logically to fit in this general section of the code. Despite its placement, which obscures its central importance, there can be no doubt, as Headlam was the first to appreciate, that the enactment is a most important, independent decree. It is a milestone in the history of the control of written law over human societies. Europe knew nothing like it earlier. It points ahead to the fourth-century Athenian achievement and to the great Western tradition of the rule of written law.

The important enactment, for convenience here termed the "magistrate's instruction," reads:

> Whatever is written, he [the judge] shall give judgment on; the judge shall give judgment *(dikazei)* as it is written, according to witnesses [procedural] or oaths [of, e.g., denial]; but in other matters he shall himself take an oath [of fairness] and decide *(omnunta krinei)* according to the pleas.[11]

Behind the need at last to formulate this rule so precisely, we may perhaps detect some tension in the community over what was to be governed by developing written law and what could be left to ancient, oral custom. Neither homicide nor impiety is provided for in the written code, for example, and there are other puzzling omissions. One controversial explanation is that what ought to be done in those areas was so well known and established that the need to write it down was not immediately felt. By contrast, procedural matters, always susceptible to alterations, would figure prominently in early written regulations, as would any departures or modifications from customary usage.[12]

The magistrate at Gortyn first, in what amounts to the *anakrisis,* gives judgment according to written law in such matters as are written, being bound strictly by the wording of the law, by the testimony of witnesses (in the oralist sense, procedural witnesses), and by oaths (also in the oralist sense, mainly of denial). The magistrate himself takes no oath because the resolution is viewed as automatic or mechanical. If matters between the litigants cannot be resolved in this phase for whatever reason, however, the magistrate himself then must take the oath (of fairness), and decide the case as best he can. As noted, we do not know on what basis. Whether in the *krisis* stage he considered or invited the testimony of what amounted to accidental "witnesses" (but perhaps this early called by some other name) is therefore also unknown. The important point, if Headlam is correct, is that in *all* cases mentioned in the code, covering every spectrum of social life, there are no examples of accidental witnesses. Without exception,

> "μαίτυρες" refers to the witnesses of formalities. The form or act they have to prove is sometimes proceedings in court, sometimes those parts of a process which are essential but take place out of court, sometimes contracts or agreements. In all cases, the witnesses are official, they must have been summoned beforehand for the purposes of witnessing the act; it does not include the evidence of accidental spectators.[13]

The Range of Procedural Witnessing in Early Greece

The Great Code, disappointingly for some, does not commence with a ringing statement of general principles or even a weighty matter of substantive or criminal law. Instead, as is true in several Near Eastern law codes, including the Hebrew, the code begins with enactments regulating largely procedural matters concerning the treatment of servile persons such as slaves (actual or alleged).[14] Enactments are formulated as casuistic law, which is normal for the code, the *protasis* stating the delict or action as hypothetical facts (if a man does . . .), and the *apodosis* stating the consequence or provision (then he shall suffer . . .). By reviewing some examples and some seeming exceptions—and perhaps only in that way—we can gain an appreciation for the dominating presence of *marturia* in Archaic Greek life.

Some early enactments govern the seizing of an escaped slave—or a free man, if his status be disputed. Behind one enactment is the following circumstance: A certain man, *A*, had in his possession a slave whom the court has determined belongs to another man, *B*, and *A* was ordered to restore him to *B*. Before this can happen, the slave runs away, taking sanctuary in a temple (seemingly not uncommon), and creating a serious dilemma for *A*. He cannot now obey the court and restore the slave to *B*. The bracketed words are intended to fill out the text for the modern reader.

> But if a slave, with regard to whom a man has been defeated [in a trial] takes sanctuary, let him [the defeated party] show him at the temple, summoning two witnesses, runners [i.e., adults, having access to the public *gumnasia*], free men, let him point him [the slave] out where he has taken sanctuary, himself or another for him; but if he either does not summon or does not point out, let him pay what has been written.[15]

That is, *A* can resolve his dilemma without penalty only by following certain strict procedures. He must, with two witnesses, summon *B* to the temple where the slave has taken refuge, and he must show the slave to *B* in the presence of the witnesses. Should *A* fail either in the summoning or in the showing, and thus be unable to produce his two witnesses in court to prove that he performed both actions as prescribed, *A* must pay the specified penalty. The magistrate in this stage of the case must "judge according to the witnesses and the oaths" and may not exercise any personal discretion, consider whether *A* exercised due caution in preventing the escape, or the like.

A second example from the code involves a man accused of adultery. The law assumes that he was taken prisoner in the act, having been seized in the very house of the husband of the woman (or of her father or brother). Obvious danger to the social peace lurks here. If the adulterer is killed directly, the vengeance of the adulterer's relatives may escalate into a vendetta between families, a problem to this day in Mediterranean countries and elsewhere. The law seeks to do what it can to prevent this from happening.[16]

> Let him [the husband, father, or brother] proclaim before three witnesses to the relatives of him who has been seized, that they may ransom him within five days; in the case of a slave, to his master before two witnesses. If he is not ransomed, he shall belong to the captors to do with him what they will.[17]

The law requires that the captor follow a series of formal procedures involving an oral proclamation (we note again that no documents surface) that, to be valid, must be before witnesses. If after five days no ransom is paid and the captor kills the adulterer or mutilates him, the testimony of the witnesses would protect him from any further legal action and from the revenge of the adulterer's relations, or at least their lawful revenge.

These are weighty matters likely to bring great disturbance to the community and so require established procedures of resolution. Simpler matters also required procedural witnesses, although fewer of them. A has borrowed, let us say, ten staters from B, the amount and the conditions being duly witnessed. If a witness is later produced before a magistrate testifying that the debt was owed and was to be paid before a certain date, and no counterclaims are introduced, then judgment for the claimant is given according to testimony of the witnesses. The judge has no discretion, but must "give judgment *(dikazei)*" as is written. The case is a simple one, unless, of course, *B* produces his witness testifying that, in fact, he paid A. According to the magistrate's instruction, which is observed without exception in the code, the magistrate judges according to the testimony of formal witnesses until an impasse is reached. This would occur if two sets of witnesses cannot both be correct; chronology will not settle the matter, and so someone is mistaken or, more likely, lying (and so probably "bought"). Then the judge can only take the oath and decide as best he can. Isocrates has a client claim (*Trapeziticus* 54) "for you [jurymen of Athens] think it is possible to suborn witnesses even for actions that never occurred." Gortyn was hardly immune from the "bought witness."

Gortynian procedure becomes especially clear in one case where the ownership of a slave is being contested. The judge is instructed to take the fairness oath and decide either if no witness testifies, or if both parties produce witnesses and the testimony is at odds. This provision is necessary, I suggest, because sometimes the ownership of a slave would be the result of a witnessed act, as in a sale. In other cases, such as when a slave was born into a household or was acquired abroad, no formal witnessing took place, at least none that would be admitted as evidence in a Gortynian court. If only one claimant to a slave's ownership can produce a procedural witness, he wins automatically, and the judge need not take the fairness oath. If none testifies or if both litigants produce rival procedural witnesses whose testimony cannot be reconciled, an impasse is reached, and so the judge takes the oath and "he decides." The terse wording is thus (barely) sufficient: "The judge is to give judgment according to the witnesses, if a witness testify, but he is to decide on oath if they testify either for both or for neither."[18] In none of these cases, as close reading reveals, is the witness an accidental witness. All were summoned beforehand to witness some transaction and then summoned later to testify to the previous action.

In the last case, for example, no provision is made for the testimony of an accidental witness, *X* (or "witness" in the modern sense) to the effect that the contested slave had been seen at work over many years in the household of *A*, one of the litigants, when good citizen *X* often visited *A*, or the like. Did early Greek law courts make no provision for such obviously valuable testimony? I find it hard to believe they did not, a point that cannot be argued here, but how—and under what "rules of evidence" before such rules were known—is difficult to say. We simply do not know, and written law at Gortyn nowhere addresses the issue. However, the use of procedural witnesses will have had a long, regularized history in any complex oral society. This testimony *must* be admitted and be accepted on the face unless countered by another procedural witness, or the society in the absence of written documentation cannot function. Written law at Gortyn provides for what had from time out of mind been a part of the community's oral life; its provisions are simply a recognition and continuation of practices that are much older than written law and much more deeply established. The acceptance of the testimony of the accidental witness is perhaps more problematical at this stage in the development of law, less regularized, less formalized and ritualized, and so regarded as inherently less certain, at least to that society. Our best evidence by far, the Gortyn code, provides no unambiguous example of the testimony of the accidental witness and so no example of "witness" used to designate such a person. Examples of procedural witnesses are almost endless.

From these examples, it is clear that the society as yet knows no other form of record for the sorts of transactions discussed, even though alphabetic writing was available to it and had been since at least the late eighth century.[19] Behind the extensive and exclusive use of procedural witnessing found in the code and found presumably throughout Archaic Greece (for this we must rely mainly on literary evidence, or later written law) lies not a deficiency in technology but the force of oral habit and the essentially conservative practices of local courts. As noted by Oliver Wendell Holmes in the famous opening remarks of his great work, *The Common Law* (1881), what has determined the course of the history of the law is less reason and logic than accumulating human experience, "what works" for our species in a place and a time and so has solidified into custom and habit deemed natural. The law has everywhere and in all periods been inherently conservative, for good reason.

Much space in the Gortyn code is devoted to what American lawyers know as family law, and as a result this area of legislation affords abundant examples of procedural witnessing. Many of these provisions concern women and their property. The argument has been plausibly made that at least some of the ancestral rights of women under Dorian tribal custom law are being revised and curtailed in the written code, whose framers were aristocratic men. If so, then this would explain why these matters are addressed in writing in unusual detail.[20]

Column V is totally devoted to inheritances and their inevitable contingencies. Five groups of heirs and their order of succession are specified. If a man or woman dies, and there are children, grandchildren, or great grandchildren, they shall have the property. If there are none of these, the code orders the possible heirs through brothers (and their children), then sisters (and their children), and so on. The code also distinguishes between real estate or immovable property, and movable property such as livestock, clothing, or personal items. It considers that perhaps heirs may not agree on dividing such movable property. If so, the law directs that it be sold for the highest price possible and the proceeds divided. The considerable detail found here is a reminder, if any were needed, that no form of social life, especially one involving many thousands of people, is really simple, and that sophisticated oral means existed long before written law to manage them.

When inherited property is divided, the law requires that three or more witnesses must be present; these are, of course, procedural witnesses. Their presence legalizes the division, but they are also its only record should a later dispute arise. If, in a later trial, it emerges that *B* has seized what was given to *A*, and the witnesses testify in the *anakrisis* stage that such and such was, indeed, given to *A* in the division, the magistrate decides exclusively on what is written (the law governing division) and the testimony of the eyewitnesses. He may not exercise discretion in the matter, even if he felt the original division was grossly unfair or somehow rigged. The items must be restored to *A*, and the restoration would be witnessed. The judge need not take the fairness oath, for he exercised no discretion in the matter. It was narrowly decided based on written law and the testimony of the procedural witnesses.

The absence of the use of witnesses is notable in one place, and it is an exception that goes to prove the rule. A section of Column VI concerns the ransoming, presumably by a kinsman (some sort of necessity for action is suggested in a difficult text), of a Gortyn prisoner held in a foreign city. If this has occurred, but the freed man and his ransomer fail to agree on (1) whether the man asked to be ransomed, (2) what in compensation the liberated man owes to the one who freed him, or (3) how long a period of servitude would be equal to what is owed, then the magistrate takes the fairness oath and summarily decides on the pleadings. No provision is made for the *anakrisis* stage and securing the testimony of witnesses. Willetts translates the difficult section, a complete enactment (the text breaks after the start of the next enactment), as follows:

> If anyone bound by necessity should get a man gone away to a strange place free from a foreign city at his own request, he shall be in the power of the one who ransomed him until he pay what is due; but if they do not agree about the amount or on the ground that he did not request to be set free, the judge is to decide on oath with reference to the pleas.[21]

This enactment has puzzled commentators because seemingly it is a glaring exception to the use of procedural witnesses to settle such disputes. The *anakrisis* stage is bypassed altogether, and the magistrate proceeds directly to the *krisis* stage in which he decides on the representations of the litigants. I suggest that, uniquely here for such procedures, there had been no *anakrisis* stage because there could not be. There was no formally witnessed testimony to hear. The events took place away from Gortyn, at a "strange place" and in a "foreign city" as the code specifies, where no free, adult, male Gortynians (or Gortynians of any gender or status) were available to serve in the capacity of procedural witnesses to a contract or agreement, as in law only they could do. The magistrate must therefore, in this special case, bypass the *anakrisis* stage and go immediately to the *krisis* stage, that is, take the fairness oath and decide immediately as best he can, according to the litigants' pleas.

Another seeming exception that, upon examination, again turns out to be no exception at all concerns witnessing an adoption. Adoptions are especially tricky in Greek law because only in this way could a man make as his heir someone not in a predetermined line of familial inheritance. It has sometimes been claimed that certain adoptions are not witnessed at Gortyn and so are an exception to the evidence so convincingly mustered by Headlam, but this fails to appreciate a well-known oral procedure. On the contrary, so important was the act of adoption, especially when a propertied man with legitimate heirs adopts a son not related by blood to him or else adopts his bastard, that the whole community becomes the witnesses; that is, the adoption must be orally and formally made a matter of public knowledge. This procedure has close parallels in Germanic and other law codes. The procedure is also revealing, indicating as it does the strong preference for oral performance as effecting the legal act. At Gortyn, as always, no mention is made of written records. Instead, "the declaration of adoption shall be made from the speaking-place of assembly (*agora*) when the citizens are gathered, from the stone from which proclamations are made."[22] Should the man who adopted another wish to reverse the process, he must reenact the same procedure. This is specified in the next column: "And if the adopting party wishes, he may renounce [the previous adoption] in the speaking place of assembly *(agora),* when the citizens are gathered, from the stone from which proclamations are made."[23]

Two conditions are tacked onto this enactment (Col. XI 14–19), and then a separate, related enactment is added (19–23). Terse and to us not entirely clear, each deserves brief notice. First, ten staters shall be deposited with the rememberer of the magistrate "who sees to matters involving strangers," to be given to the renounced party. We thus learn by chance that such a magistrate existed at Gortyn, corresponding to the Athenian Polemarch. Strangers were especially vulnerable in oral Greece, for self-help often required that family members be available for revenge or its threat. Second, a woman may not adopt, nor a male before puberty; there is no explanation or elaboration. Under some circumstances, could a woman have adopted earlier, before written law? Next it is specified—this in a separate enactment, set off by two *vacats*—that written law shall be followed in the matters of these regulations from the time of inscription, but property held as a result of a different, earlier arrangement shall be held without liability. Written law is, in some regards, presumably modifying older custom law, but the social dislocation of applying written law ex post facto to the ownership of real property is recognized.

It is instructive to note who are permitted to be witnesses at Gortyn, and so (by default) who are not, for the division of property. The code requires: "When they divide the property witnesses shall be present, runners [adults], freemen, three or more."[24] Similar terminology is found elsewhere in the code. The term "runner" *(dromeus)* was given to an adult citizen, indicating that he had a right of access to the public gymnasia. Excluded from being witnesses when dividing property thus would be (1) all women, (2) minors, and (3) male adults from classes that do not enjoy full citizenship, and therefore (4) all foreigners. Those covered by the third category would be the *apetairoi,* who were free persons but lacking the political and civil rights of aristocratic citizens, as well as serfs and slaves and probably free men who are temporarily indentured to another for unpaid debts. Whether *nothoi,* bastard sons who remained part of a father's household, would be excluded is uncertain, because the code, otherwise so detailed in its concern with family law and inheritance, nowhere mentions them.

As even a casual reader of the Gortyn code becomes quickly aware, the presence of procedural witnesses was pervasive in Archaic life. At this point in the development of Cretan literacy—and as far as we know anywhere in Greece—only the oral testimony of an eyewitness, not a document, would be accepted as evidence in a court. This was changing only gradually in Athens in the fourth century, but suspicion of the unsupported document remained strong. By chance, the Gortyn code indirectly informs us that no documents (if any were made) of a magistrate's *mnamōn,* his rememberer or recorder, were accepted into evidence, for he, like any other procedural witness, must testify in person to a past event. At Gortyn, this remained true even if a previous decision were crucial for the resolution of a case and the *mnamōn* had died or was away from the city. Apparently the suit simply fell, or the magistrate took the fairness oath and decided on another basis.[25] Remarkably, this was still the case when the written law itself—and rather elegantly transcribed at that—is evidence that such documentation was within easy technological reach.

I believe, as noted previously, this can be explained only by the tenacity of oral habit, and the somewhat reluctant, or at least gradual, adoption of the rival technology of alphabetic notation and record. The role of oral witnessing, so dominant a feature of the code, is, I conclude, a feature of primary orality that has carried over into a period of restricted literacy. It serves all the functions that, in time, would be served primarily by literate documentation. At every turn, disputes must be decided by the magistrates "according to the witnesses," where *maitures* is properly regarded as a technical term for procedural eyewitnesses.[26]

The legal formula in the code, as Headlam argued so many years ago, that demanded correct understanding was the one requiring a magistrate in the *anakrisis* phase (again following the later Attic terminology) of a trial to rule "according to witnesses and oaths *(kata maiturans hē apōmoton).*" What had led to the failure of early commentators to appreciate the distinction between the *anakrisis* and *krisis* phases of the trial was precisely their failure to understand "witness'' in the oralist or procedural sense, and instead to understand it in what Headlam himself called the later or ''modern'' sense of the accidental witness. If ''witnesses'' had the later meaning of an accidental observer of some disputed fact, and the judge *dikei kata maiturans,* then there could be no *anakrisis* phase at all. The real trial proceeded straightaway with the judge taking testimony from accidental witnesses concerning what had occurred, the reputed events, as they by chance had observed them. The sharp and consistent distinction between *dikazein* and *krinein* in the code's wording would again become unintelligible. Instead, insisted Headlam, at this stage in the development of law at Gortyn:

> The *μαίτυρες* are not witnesses to any fact; they are formal witnesses; they are formal witnesses to the proper performance of procedural acts. Before a man can bring a case into court he has to go through certain formalities, these must be performed before witnesses, the presence of the witness is necessary to the validity of the acts, and their statement is the proof required by law that the acts have been performed.[27]

No Accidental Witnesses at Gortyn? Two Difficult Enactments

Until very recently[28] no scholar known to me seriously challenged Headlam's main conclusions. One text especially has provoked a good deal of comment, and Headlam himself noted it. The law, a separate enactment, is (for us) maddeningly terse, and the wording ambiguous: ''If he attempts to seduce a free woman who is in the charge of a relation (a *kadestēs*) he shall pay ten staters, if a witness testifies.''[29] At first reading, students of law might naturally assume—and some commentators have assumed—that this is an accidental witness (a lurking servant or the like) who testifies to the issue of whether the seduction or attempted seduction (the latter translation of the verb has been defended as more probable) took place. Upon reflection, however, that becomes an awkward understanding of a difficult text. The perpetrator is a free male. Would the accidental witness against him not have to be a free, adult male? If not, could just anyone—slaves, or other servile persons, or women—testify? How can the law be silent on this issue when normally it is so specific on the qualifications of witnesses? Further, is it likely that such an outrageous act would be attempted in front of any other person, let alone one who could testify to a crime in a court? Are we to imagine, from the enactment's wording and assuming an accidental witness is meant, that, if intercourse is attempted but no witness happens to be present, then no prosecution could take place? Is this what the conditional clause ''*if* a witness testifies,'' the standard formula for introducing a procedural witness elsewhere in the code, means in this case?

These are not the only problems that arise if an accidental witness is assumed here; there is a weightier one. The *kadestēs* enactment is part of a series of closely related statutes. All are sexual delicts, some far more serious than the one in question. Column 11 of the code, after a few words that have run over from Column 1 (the mason ran out of space), commences with a mighty register of sexual offenses and their penalties (lines 2–45), organized under four kinds: *rape,* commencing with fines for the rape of free persons, female or male, by males who are free or not, with fines apportioned according to the social status of perpetrator and victim (lines 2–10); *forcible seduction* of a female slave (lines 11–16: it has been argued that the law did not concern itself with the fate of male slaves in this regard); *attempted seduction* of a free woman (lines 16–20), the ''*kadestēs* enactment'' in question; and then fourth, in by far the longest section, *adultery* in its many manifestations and social consequences (lines 20–45). In this detailed body of written law, addressing actions that the community's peaceful survival cannot lightly ignore, the need for a witness arises in one instance only, that of the attempted seduction of a free woman in the short *kadestēs* enactment (16–20). If the happy chance of an accidental witness to the offense is intended by the peculiar wording, why is this? More serious offenses by far have been cataloged, and no witness to them is required or so much as mentioned.

Headlam argued, following sound historical methodology, that this case, because it is exceptional in the code if an accidental witness is meant, should be interpreted in conformity with all the others about which no doubt existed, unless that is impossible. Only then should an exception be claimed and ''witness'' be understood as (somehow) an accidental witness in this case. In what follows I have embellished some details and interpreted others, but essentially follow Headlam, with some help from Gernet and Willetts.

The need for a witness arises uniquely in this case among a series of sexual delicts because the woman's relation, in whose charge she is, is not a father or a brother, but a *kadestēs*. In this context the term clearly designates a more distant relative, a kinsman who functions as her *kurios* (in the Attic terminology, ''lord'') or guardian. He was selected, often from a large number of possible candidates in the clan, because the woman's close male relatives predeceased her. At Athens and elsewhere in Greece, there never was a time when a woman was not under the control of either her husband or a male relative serving as her guardian. This was of special concern when her inherited property was involved and a future marriage. It is one of those many instances in which Greek custom, followed by written law, remained mostly uniform in all parts of Greece. In this case, evidently the transfer of the charge of the woman, an *epiklēros* or heiress, and her property had not been automatic, as it would have been if she had a father or brothers who were living. Were any or all of them alive, then to whom her control and protection passed would have been automatic, a matter long fixed by customary procedures. No deliberation about it would have occurred, and the whole community would have known the outcome in advance, and ever after that. No procedural witnesses would have been required to effect the transfer, or to record it. When a kinsman had to be selected from a large number of possibilities, however, this was not so, and witnesses had to be summoned both to formalize the transfer of control of her property and her person to this *kadestēs* and to serve as later record of it.

The relative who was given the control of the woman is now due damages because of the offense to her clan. This arrangement, in which not the injured women herself but her husband or father—standing for the family or clan, which is viewed as suffering the offense—receives the damages is common enough in early law codes, including the Hebrew (Exod.: 21:21–22, where a woman's family receives damages for her miscarriage).

We also should note, as is standard in casuistic legal formulation, that the law cannot address the issue of whether the proscribed action took place; the situation is stated hypothetically. *Protasis* states the offense, "if a man does . . . ," and *apodosis* the penalty now affixed by law. Casuistic law cannot, therefore, address the issue of whether an individual is guilty of the proscribed action. It can, as here, address the issue of the amount to be paid to the male guardian in staters (ten) if the action has occurred, and specify how his claim to be the woman's rightful *kadestēs* is to be established. A procedural witness must testify that he had been present at the formal transfer, had heard what was said, and can now testify to it; thus "if a witness testifies." The law therefore provides that at least one procedural witness to the woman's transfer (which could have occurred many years before, for the woman may have been orphaned at an early age) must have survived and be present in court to testify.

Payment in money, because coinage was recent on Crete, cannot have reached very far back in custom law; therefore written law also addresses the amount, probably fixing it for the first time. The amount appears elsewhere in the code and seems to represent a severe slap on the wrist. That compensation in some form must be given in such cases is immemorially old, and widespread in the Near Eastern law codes. Prior to written law, as we know from the epical sources, compensation might be refused, in which case self-help would be the result, some form of vengeance, with the attendant dangers of a blood feud between families.

The terse wording and the total circumstance now become perfectly intelligible, as no doubt they were to the citizens of Gortyn. If an attempt at intercourse with a free woman by a free man has taken place, then the transgressor shall pay ten staters, "if a witness testifies." The witness testifies not to the act of attempted intercourse, an issue more likely resolved by oaths (where a woman's solemn oath, even if she was a serf, had formidable status in law), but to the fact that this woman had been given in this relationship to this *kadestēs*. The fine is somewhat light, which is noteworthy; the reason is that the *kurios* is not a father or brother, but a more distant relation. Otherwise, the fine would have been far heavier.[30]

Michael Gagarin, in a short article that promises further publication on the subject, has cited a second case that, he suggests, may have been unknown to Headlam. Gagarin's line of argument deserves close attention, although its full analysis must await another occasion. His position is that, except for the *kadestēs* case just mentioned, Headlam was surely correct for all the cases he discussed (that number is many, but Gagarin clearly intends to leave open the reappraisal of Gortyn texts not explicitly discussed by Headlam). Further, in the *kadestēs* case, Headlam *may* be right, but Headlam's is not the only interpretation that the terse wording—taken in isolation from the rest of code—permits. That is true, of course, as any attempt to interpret this enactment, were it a solitary text, would quickly reveal. The power of Headlam's position was that it made good sense of this enactment by bringing it into conformity with what was found uniformly throughout the code. Gagarin grants this. If a case were to be found, however, in which the witness mentioned *must* be an accidental witness and cannot be a procedural one, then the *kadestēs* case is open for reconsideration, leaving an even wider opening to reconsider any other ambiguous wordings in the code.

Gagarin's revisionist opening in future publications will be, I suspect, created in no small measure because the phrasing *ai apopōnioi maiturs,* "if a witness testifies," is formulaic throughout the code, often not telling us specifically to what the witness will testify. Gagarin proposed that the wording in *I. Cret.* IV 41.5.4–11, a text perhaps unknown to Headlam, as parts of the so-called second code may well have been, can refer only to an accidental witness. The enactment seeks to deal with a complex situation. If a man works a field that belongs to another man or carries off another's property when he is under the temporary control of another (i.e., as an indentured person working off a debt that he was unable to pay), he is immune from claims or damages. That claim to immunity can be compromised, however, giving rise to a legal dispute. The enactment, terse in the extreme, has two parts: "If at the command of [or, in the power of?] another he works a field or carries off property, he is immune from all. But if he [the master] testifies that it was not at [or under?] his command, the judge is to take the oath and decide, if no witness testifies." Gagarin claims that the testimony of this witness could not be "anything other than testimony to the fact that the master either did or did not give the wrongdoer an order to act as he did. And this is clearly testimony to a fact, and moreover, a fact learned by chance."[31] I am less sure, but possibly Gagarin is right, as often on these matters he is. In the code the wording assumes that much is understood by the readers, mainly Gortynian magistrates, and so is not being supplied in the text. This feature of the Gortyn code has led to many previous disputes among legal experts. Important for the present discussion, the verb *apopōnioi,* "testifies," is left (for us) suspended, begging for a conclusion to the phrase. A witness if available testifies, that is certain enough, but to what? And what witness? The verb dangles without an object, and so its subject also becomes uncertain, at least to us. Obviously the Gortynians knew the answers and needed no further instruction. We do.

Let us suppose for a moment that a chance witness is meant, as Gagarin believes. Surely, that the master did *not* give the command is not an issue that can be settled by an accidental witness, or a choir of them. For the man who commanded the other man's labor, the "master" as Gagarin usefully calls him, is not going to introduce a witness (the word is singular here) to testify that, having never been absent when master and servant were together, he can verify that at no moment of the night or day was such a command given. No number of accidental witnesses could prove *that,* and no court would entertain the testimony. The master, in a word, cannot prove a negative. So, if the enactment does not entertain the possibility that an accidental witness will testify for the master to the effect that the order was *not* given, the witness could only be testifying that he had, indeed, heard the command being given by the master. He would thus be appearing in support of the indentured servant, not the master—if he is an accidental witness.

This, too, although at least conceivable, has difficulties. Let us be clear about them. It means in this case—by assuming the witness is an accidental witness—the law is providing for a situation in which a master claims not to have given an order to do X, and his impoverished indentured serf, who admits to doing X, claims he did it under orders. The servant, by simply producing one witness—apparently anyone will do—to testify with him, and claim by chance to have overheard the order being given, quits himself of the charge and wins his case. The verdict is automatic, a "directed finding." The magistrate need not take the fairness oath and decide on the basis of pleas, but judges according to the testimony of this witness, finding for the servant. The intent of the enactment, on this construction, is to protect powerless indentured servants from corrupt, aristocratic masters. And that, it seems to me, whereas not impossible, is unlikely.

We may, perhaps, doubt that such an enactment, protecting a servant from trial if but one (accidental) witness—the code here does not specify social class, and the singular is used—comes forth to support him, would be sponsored or permitted by the aristocratic *kosmoi* of Gortyn. If Gagarin is correct, the actual "trial" takes place in the *anakrisis* phase. More precisely, there is no trial at all. Summary judgment, a finding directed by written law, is given for the servant as soon as any witness speaks up for him. On this reading, by the force of the negative wording, the magistrate takes the oath and decides, and so would move to the *krisis* stage, only "if no [accidental] witness testifies." Surely, what we know about established legal procedure at Gortyn argues strongly against an accidental witness being intended here.

Adding to these difficulties, which are formidable enough, if an accidental witness is meant, he would be testifying that by chance he overheard an order, one that an indentured servant is forced to obey, being given to go out and steal or to work another's land. Would such an order, forcing a controlled person to perform actions forbidden in written law, be blatantly given in the presence of witnesses? Also, the formulaic wording, uniform throughout the code, for a judge's taking the fairness oath before deciding on the pleas, and for the testimony of a procedural witness, is reproduced exactly in the Greek text. Would not that linguistic fact alone suggest a more Headlamic interpretation, if one is possible? Perhaps one is.

Could the issue at point, about which a witness might testify and so preclude the need for trial, be the procedural one of whether, at the reported time of the illegal action, the man was serving under the conditions of his indenture? If he were, he would be required to do anything commanded of him, and the master, not he, would be liable for damages. The law itself tells us as much; that is, the wording in the first part of the enactment clearly assumes the servant would have so acted if commanded by his (temporary) master and states that he is immune from all damages: "If when at the direction of another he works a field or carries off property, he is immune. . . . " One way to understand the entire enactment, I propose, is to take the injunction about a witness testifying with the second part of the enactment, where the lawmakers put it. Thus the law says that the automatic immunity of indentured servitude or the presumption of it, which is normal, as recognized in the first clause, can be brought into question. This happens if the man to whom the servant has been indentured denies control; then, if "no witness testifies,'' a judge must decide on the pleas. The issue about which a witness testifies, if one is available, would be the conditions of the contract of indenture itself, for which he had been a procedural witness at the time of the agreement.

If this is correct, then one man, the servant, is claiming that the contract of indenture was still in effect and that he did only as he was told; the law protects him from damages arising from his actions. The other man, the master, is claiming that the servant no longer acted at his command, for example, that the period of indenture had expired. No written records, we recall, are accepted to settle these matters anywhere in the code, only procedural witnesses. If no procedural witness can be produced to settle whether the period of indenture covered the period when the crime was committed (liability, not that the servant committed the crime, is the legal issue), then an impasse is reached, and the judge must take the fairness oath and decide on the pleadings. Either side might still prevail.

A witness, we know, would be called when a debt was repaid, but also when an arrangement was made for the debt to be satisfied by an agreed-upon time of indentured servitude in place of payment. Moreover, as we also know, a witness can meet with an accident, be out of the city, have a falling out with one of the parties, be afraid to testify, be bought off, and so on. The enactment thus *may* intend to specify, elliptically enough (but this is common in the code's wording), that if no witness (note the rarer negative formulation) testifies that the man was, indeed, indentured to this master, or that on the day of the crime the period of indenture had (or had not) expired according to the original terms of the agreement, then the judge takes the oath and decides on the basis of the two parties' respective pleas alone.

I think we must assume that the law envisions that yet a third man, the person whose land was illegally worked or whose movable property, such as tools, was removed, deserves damages; the issue, in a case involving an indentured servant as opposed to a slave, is who shall pay the damages. Who was legally liable at the moment of the tort? Presumably a free man temporarily indentured was not liable for damages arising from work-related actions committed while he was indentured; the master had the legal liability, as in the case of a slave. The law assumes Gortynians fully understood this. The law, thus, does not seek, as it initially appears to us to do, to free an indentured servant from legal responsibility for his work-related acts when commanded to do them, providing only ''a witness testifies.'' On the contrary, it seeks to free the master from paying damages for the servant's actions if he denies—and can prove by a procedural witness—that the man was at the time under his control. For then, as a free man, the former servant must pay the damages himself. If so, then the ambiguous phrasing ''[the master] testifies that it was not at his command'' equates with and appears to be formulaic terminology for ''claims that he was not under his control, not in his power.'' (See the related wording of VI. 48, with the comments of Willetts.) Thus, if no procedural witness can be produced to prove the term of servitude either way, that is, ''if no witness testifies'' (as this enactment negatively reads), the magistrate has no recourse but to take the fairness oath and decide between the two representations as best he can.

This solution, I grant, is not altogether satisfactory and somewhat forces the language of the enactment into addressing a less than obvious issue, but then that is not uncommon for Gortyn. Nevertheless, the argument that an accidental witness is intended is not free of difficulties either. If a more Headlamic interpretation, such as the one tentatively proposed here, is accepted as at least possible, then we are back to the methodological question. Should two difficult cases, the *kadestēs* case and the indentured servant case—both so terse in wording, leaving so much to be supplied by legally informed Gortynians—be interpreted in congruence with all the other cases in the code, or not? Further offerings from Gagarin may provide a more satisfactory resolution than any on the horizon, at least any known to me.

Witnesses and Oaths: Some Comparisons to Societies in Transition

J. W. Headlam, after surveying all the passages in the Gortyn code in which there is a reference to witnessing, concluded that the term *maitures* refers always and without exception to formal witnesses to procedural or contractual acts. There is no case where we should conclude that it refers to a person giving evidence, based on accidental knowledge, in order to resolve some disputed point of fact. In his terminology, the latter is the "modern" meaning of the term "witness" and is, as he notes, a late legal development. As a caveat, we may add that what he calls the modern sense of "witness" was not *totally* unknown in *all* early systems of law, including Greek, but, as Headlam would reply, it went unregulated, and not much confidence was ever attached to it. Additional examples, a few among the legion now possible, help to confirm Headlam's acute observations of so many years ago. He was aware of some of them, and commented on them.

For the early German codes, the word *testis* (or *zeugen*) refers, as in the Gortyn code, to oral witnesses to procedural acts, mainly contracts, agreements, and the like. Significantly, it could also be used to refer to the evidence of the community to matters of public notoriety, that is, situations that had long been a matter of common public knowledge. As "witness" in this sense, the oldest members of the community might often be summoned to give collective voice, for example, to the fact that a particular piece of property with a boundary at such and such a place and with certain water rights had long been the property of one family. This extension of *Zeugenbeweis,* or "proof by witness," to include the "evidence of the community" is still not what is meant by a witness under modern laws of evidence and reflects, rather, the older, oral situation. Further, in early German law disputes over matters of fact are resolved by ordeal or by trial by combat, neither of which is found in the Gortyn code, or generally in Greece. Disputes can also be resolved by the purgatory oath, which is not uncommon. This is, of course, found at Gortyn, and the cases where it purges women of accusations against them by even husbands are noteworthy. Yet it remains true that rarely, if ever, in the German material are disputes decided by the testimony of an accidental witness.

This is true of other early law codes as well, in which "witness" is mainly used in the oralist sense of an eyewitness to some procedure or transaction, a necessary ingredient in the legal process before written documentation. Perhaps the most famous example from antiquity is the beginning of the Law of the Twelve Tables, which Roman schoolchildren (and, until recently, American schoolchildren learning their Latin) were required to memorize:

> *Si in ius uocat, ito;*
> *ni it, antestamino.*
> *Igitur em capito.*
>
> If he [some citizen] calls [a defendant] to trial, let him go;
> If he [the defendant] does not go, let him [the plaintiff] call a witness.
> Then let him arrest him.

The witness is called to make a record of the fact that the defendant was duly summoned by the plaintiff, had refused to go to trial and so had to be arrested by the plaintiff, and that the whole procedure had been properly carried out before the witnesses.

In early Anglo-Saxon law, the same oralist meaning for "witness" prevails without an exception known to me. The postoralist or "modern" meaning (as Headham designated it) seems to have arrived with Norman law. Of many possible examples, the first involves witnessing the transfer of property: "Let no man exchange any property without the witness of the reeve, or the mass-priest, or of the land-lord, or of the hederec or other un-lying men."[32] The reference to the procedural witness, indicating as it does the arrival of Christianity, reflects the fact that a restricted literacy entered Northern Europe with the missionaries and monks who brought the new religion, and who were themselves in varying degrees literate (some highly so). However, the oral habits of indigenous peoples were not immediately, or always willingly, surrendered. Another example:

> And let every man, with their witnesses, buy and sell every of the chattels that he may buy or sell, either in a burh or in a wapentake; and let every of them, when he is first chosen as witness, give the oath that he never, neither for love nor for fear, will deny any of those things of which he was witness, nor declare any other thing in witness, save that alone which he saw and heard; and of such sworn men, let there be at every bargain two or three as witnesses.[33]

These persons, so evidently living in a world of sounds and not documents, are not apt readily to accept a piece of paper in place of the oral procedure they have long known and trusted.

The whole community or county could serve as witness providing that the actions were openly and publicly done; possession of land could, in this way, be "notoriously known" and so belong securely to the holder. Sir Robert Chalmers (1767), commenting on Coke, observes of a contemporary situation that arose from feudal practice:

> He that succeeds to the inheritance [landed estate] must be heir to him who last died *seised,* that is, legally, and notoriously possessed of the estate. Yet entry into part of the land belonging to the deceased is sufficient to vest the possession of all his lands in the same county, because all the freeholders of the county being pares [peers] of the same county court and being supposed in law to meet

> there once a month for the dispatch of business, every solemn act that is openly and publicly done in any part of the county is deemed to be sufficiently notorious to the whole county. . . . [34]

In many respects, the law of contract in early Anglo-Saxon England, such as it was, would not be recognizable to the modern jurist. Rather, I suggest, we find ourselves on familiar, oralist ground and closer to the legal practice of ancient Crete and the Gortyn code than to contemporary legal practice. David Mellinkoff, in his perceptive (from an oralist point of view) *The Language of the Law,* after observing that "Literacy and oral tradition are sides of the same coin," notes the virtual absence of a law of contracts in Anglo-Saxon law, at least as a modern lawyer or barrister might recognize it. He observes that, in its place: "the open sale before a witness, the pledge of faith with oath and surety, the Biblical handshake—these generally sufficed. *Action* more than words."[35]

I would like to suggest a slight caveat. The words *were* actions, of the nature of "performatives" or "performative utterances," in J. L. Austin's terminology,[36] and their syntax betrayed it. The words sought to "do" what they "said." As a result, they had to be mightily impressive and intimidating in the process. And they must be memorable. Hence we discover in them the ancient, oral devices of rhythm, such as alliteration, assonance, rhyme, parallelism, and all the rest. It is why they seduce and impress us yet.

Among many other examples is the famous and still impressive oath of fealty. Like the sayings of Heraclitus, it deserves to be read aloud.

> By the Lord, before whom this relic is holy, I will to [Name] be faithful and true, and love all that he loves and shun all that he shuns, according to God's law, and according to the world's ways, and never, by will nor by force, by word nor by work, do aught of what is loathful to him; on condition that he keep me as I am willing to deserve, and all that fulfill our agreement was, when I to him submitted and chose his will.[37]

The words themselves, as they were pronounced (the slightest deviation nullified the action), accomplished the act; "this was part formula, part ritual." As Mellinkoff observes, the performance of the oath created the immediate relationship, and the words as performed "put in pawn" a man's person and his very self. Referring to the oath, Mellinkoff writes: "Its repetition in this exact form—and in no other—would produce the desired effect. It was this way too in an Anglo-Saxon court."[38]

The actual wording of the various oaths required by the Gortyn code has not, as noted, survived. No doubt they were totally familiar to the populace and the *dikastai* and, having been formulated to reside in oral memory, were permitted to remain there when the law was written down. We may be certain that, in appropriately impressive Greek, parties to a suit swore the equivalent of "to tell the truth, the whole truth and nothing but the truth," which is an Old English legal formula, as ancient as any in the language.

A witness must be truthful, of course, and so also "unbought." Alliteration betrays the oral origins of the ancient oath of the "unbought witness," again from early English law. The wording also reveals that a procedural witness is doing the swearing. "In the name of Almighty God, as I here for [Name] in true witness stand, unbidden and unbought, so I with my eyes oversaw, and with my ears overheard, that which I with him say."[39] In suitably framed sixth-century Doric Greek, addressing Zeus and other deities of that place and time, the citizens of Gortyn solemnly swore in the presence of the court and of each other in much the same manner. What was sworn to, however, was not an event accidently observed but still some procedural act for which a citizen's memory and honesty were the sole record.

What is discovered in a number of cultures of restricted literacy, or whose legal system has only recently or partially adopted writing, confirms what was also discovered on ancient Crete. Direct influence is, of course, out of the question. Rather, the method of storing information and bringing it to bear in an important situation—what may be called the technology of cultural storage—was oral before writing was used. Similar responses were therefore called into existence in widely different places and times.

Also, the performative element, the spoken word as act—doing and performing "justices"—will, in general, dominate over what a later age will prefer to express as an abstract principle as long as the oral way of life has not been seriously eroded by advancing literacy. "Justice" will thus, in Archaic Greece, be largely a matter of acting, doing, saying certain things in certain established ways. Proprieties, the "done things," and "just" actions are the same things; there is, as yet, no conceptual difference between them, and no basis for formulating one. That is in the Platonic future. Before the relentless questioning of the Platonic Socrates, and the written documentation of Plato's *Republic*, it will not occur to Greeks to try to step out of the performance of justice as doing and saying and to define "it" alone "by itself," as the timeless abstraction. It remains a nice question whether the conceptual transition from "justice" as procedure and performance to justice as a defined concept expressing a principle required, as a necessary condition if not the cause, the stabilizing and "fixing" of a society's experience of justice in writing.

Conclusion

In terms of evidence now available for us to examine, literacy and law are allied for the first time in Europe on the island of Crete, perhaps as early as the middle of the seventh century. The enactments from Dreros, if correctly dated, may well be the oldest nonpersonal, civic, official use of the Greek alphabet. The surviving evidence suggests that partial reliance on writing initially went hand in hand with a good deal of residual reliance on oral memories and even on official rememberers, figures whose very existence is first revealed to us by casual references in the earliest written legal records.

The Gortyn code presents initial oddities to the historian of literacy and as well to historians of law. Alphabetic writing has long been available in the city, as the inscribed code makes indisputable, but oral habit is also far from being obliterated by writing's legal presence. The resources of the new technology are not being fully exploited, as is so often the case in the early histories of great technological innovations. No written records are kept, documents are not introduced in evidence, and the oral eyewitness alone is accepted as the record for a procedural act. It is even questionable if "witness" in the later sense of the accidental witness is ever used in the code, so powerful was the association of the procedural, formal, summoned witness with the word *maiturs*. The pervasive presence of the formal witness in the code suggests that *marturia*, or the formal act of witnessing a procedural action, should be added to *xenia* and the *sumposion* as a unique institution of oral life.

Also the code, although demonstrably a complete document—the physical evidence on this issue is beyond dispute—has (to us) curious lacunae. Whereas Gortyn law is often very detailed in dealing with many matters of procedure, only some issues of substantive law are, in fact, covered by written law. Those ignored cannot have fallen outside the province of socially controlled behavior, but the manner of control was still protolegal. One explanation—the one I have come to favor—is that these matters were left to be governed by the community's established and trusted oral procedures and precedents, as for so long they had successfully been. This was the pattern for the rest of Greece as well, at least throughout the Archaic period.

At the very beginning of written law in Europe, there is an almost naive faith that a law, once written, interprets itself without ambiguity and can be applied automatically by a magistrate. That, too, is worth remarking. Before long experience taught framers of written laws and constitutions otherwise, the great pioneering lawmakers of Gortyn were instinctual "strict constructionists," trusting that what they had written would settle all further cases that fell under its formulations and rules. Written law, according to the magistrate's instruction, shall prevail at Gortyn, in such matters as are written, and the magistrate need take no oath, for the law and not the magistrate is determining the outcome.

The magistrate's instruction is a great moment in the history of written law and a major step on the road to the rule exclusively of written law in human societies. Nevertheless, it falls considerably short of that final achievement. The final step in antiquity—and this for the first time in the experience of our species—was taken in the city of Athens, where at the close of the fifth century magistrates were forbidden to enforce *any law* that was not a properly enacted, *written* law. *Nomos*, in the strict sense of an enactment for which one can be formally and publicly charged in a court and, if convicted, punished, now means *written* law. To the Athenian story, the completion of the alliance between literacy and the law in antiquity, we turn next.

Notes

1. In a passing remark, R. W. Willetts, a leading expert on the code and a foremost historian of Crete, designates the code "by far the most comprehensive social document of its time." The Gortyn code is truly valuable beyond the narrow interests of historians of law. See R. Willetts, "Observations on Leg. Gort. II. 16–20," *Kadmos* 3 (1965), p. 170.

See also Willetts, "Cretan Laws and Society," in *CAH* (2d ed. 3.3), pp. 234–248. For the important Heraclitean witness sayings, requiring that one understand for "witness" an oral eyewitness, or procedural witness, for their proper interpretation, see K. Robb, "The Witness in Heraclitus and in Early Greek Law," *Monist* 74 (1991), pp. 638–676. Some sections from this article are printed here with the permission of the *Monist*.

2. R. Willetts, *The Civilization of Ancient Crete* (Berkeley and Los Angeles), p. 164. There are some thoughtful qualifications on what goes to make a "code" in M. Lemosse, "Les lois de Gortyne et la notion de codification, " *RIDA* 3.4 (1957), pp. 131–137.

3. Following Walter Ong's now widely adopted usage in *Orality and Literacy: The Technology of the Word* (London and New York, 1962), a culture of primary orality does not know writing of any kind. Among legal historians, the importance of advancing literacy has been recognized by the distinguished Danish legal historian, Mogens Hansen. In particular, he has emphasized that the first decades of the fourth century are the first period in which there is evidence of a fully developed Athenian literacy, in the administration of justice or in any other activity, as opposed to the mainly oral practices of the fifth century. Independently, I came to the same conclusion and welcomed finding that at least one major legal historian agreed. His comments on literacy are scattered in his many publications, and mainly incidental to other concerns, but always insightful.

4. J. W. Headlam, "The Procedure of the Gortynian Inscription," *JHS* 13 (1892–1893), p. 48.

5. See R. W. Willetts, *The Law Code of Gortyn* (Berlin, 1967) (= *Kadmos* Supplement I). Commenting on Col. II. 20–24, Willetts observes (p. 61): "The gift of the husband has to be witnessed, apparently as an oral act, just as the division of property." I follow the text of Willetts.

6. *Leg. Gort.*, Col. IX. 24. Also see n. 34.

7. Headlam, "Procedure," p. 63.

8. See pp. 86ff. of the commentary in F. Bücheler and E. Zitelmann, *Das Recht von Gortyn* (Berlin, 1885) (= *Reinisches Museum* 40).

9. The suggestion that some laws (or legal rules) may have been transmitted orally in Greece, perhaps even in verse, is controversial, as noted in chapter 3. The suggestion, wearing different dress in each case, has been floated by George Calhoun, Eric Havelock. R. W. Willetts, and Catherine Roth, among others; Michael Gagarin has met the suggestion with strong counters, notably in the cases of Willetts and Roth. Roth's and Gagarin's replies were treated in the earlier chapter; also see Gagarin, "The Organization of the Gortyn Law Code," *GRBS* 23, p. 130, n. 10 (on Willetts). The complex issues of the debate cannot be argued here, but some additional comment may be in order. None of the criteria devised for the recognition of rules that are specifically legal rules in advanced literate societies—such as institutionalized sanctions, the principle *ex auctoritate* (enactment by king or congress, or whomever has the care of the community), formal promulgation (or even *written* promulgation, that a law be "on the books"), and so on—works well for oral cultures. Are these societies, then, devoid of law? Do they make no distinction between moral rules and legal rules, between morality and law, or between law and manners? Despite appearances, the distinctions that may be needed for a modern discussion are not merely semantic or matters of stipulatory definition. Gagarin is more sensitive to them than have been some historians of Greek law. The influence of H.L.A. Hart is also evident in Gagarin's approach, a strong recommendation for some and less so for others. These are, in any case, as Ronald Dworkin remarked, "not puzzles for the cupboard, to be taken down on rainy days for fun . . . they nag at our attention" (*Taking Rights Seriously* [Cambridge, Mass., 1977], p. 14). See also some sensible remarks by the philosopher Richard Taylor, "Law and Morality," *New York University Law Review* 23 (October

1968), pp. 611–647. Whether all of his argument would apply to Greece before written law remains a nice question, however.

10. Headlam, "Procedure," p. 50.

11. XI. 26–31. Good plates, such as those in Willetts *(The Law Code of Gortyn)*, reveal clearly that a *vacat* on the stone both precedes (l. 25) and follows (l. 31) this important enactment (see his Plate 11), a point neglected even by Headlam, who seems to have been forced to work from transcriptions. He was, of course, aware of the *asyndeton*. The physical evidence on the stones supports Headlam's isolation of this passage as both separate and crucially important. Presumably his understanding of how the code accumulated and of its content guided him. Willetts notes the *asyndeton* at the beginning and end of the careful wording, regarding it as a "self-contained special regulation," which serves to make absolutely clear "the two distinct functions" of a Gortynian *dikastēs*. The enactment in a printed text appears to be rather innocuously inserted where it is. (The *vacats* are visually prominent when the stones are viewed in situ).

12. If we ignore the unreliable literary tradition that originated in the propaganda of fourth-century Athenian writers and concentrate on the surviving epigraphical evidence from the Archaic period, then written law did not replace oral custom immediately or all at once, in sweeping and complete law codes such as later Greece (and modern industrialized nations) were to know. The pattern was rather one of a gradual reduction to written enactments (with linguistic reformulations but much continuity of content), rules and admonitions that, in previous oral formulation, had long governed the life of the community. Plausibly, long-established matters that were to be left untouched, such as what to do in the event of deliberate homicide or even impiety or treason, need not be addressed in writing at all, at least at the earliest stages in the development of written law. In a short article (three pages) buried away in a journal published by the Pontifical Law Institute at Rome's Lateran University, C. G. Thomas insightfully suggests that it may be necessary for legal historians to view the evolution of written law codes in ancient Greece from the perspective of "the spread and expansion of literacy." See Thomas, "Literacy and the Codification of Law," *Studia et Documenta Historiae et Juris* 43 (1977), pp. 455–458. The call deserves to be heeded, but seldom is.

13. Headlam, "Procedure," p. 57.

14. After the brief "Altar Law" concerning piling up earth or unwrought stones wherever Yahweh is to be invoked in cult, there follow the "Ordinances," commencing with a section of Slave Law in detailed casuistic formulation (Exod. 21:2–11). See P. Heinish, "Das Slavenrect in Israel und im Alten Orient," *Studia Catholica* 11 (1934–1935), pp. 201–218. R. H. Pfeiffer, among others, has suggested that the similarity between Hebrew law and other Near Eastern codes is not the result of direct literary borrowing from Mesopotamia; a barrier of language, among other obstacles, had to be considered. Instead, Israelites adopted Canaanite law traditions that, in turn, had long reflected Mesopotamian tradition. Israelites needed new enactments for settled, agricultural communities (not much different from those of neighboring Canaanites) when they settled in Canaan; they borrowed Canaanite law (the closely related languages easily permitted even wording to transfer), but infused it with Yahwism, as in the initial Altar Law. See R. Pfeiffer, "The Transmission of the Book of the Covenant," *Harvard Theological Review* 24 (1931), pp. 99–109, for the kernel of such a theory. I suspect that a similar borrowing, one that does not depend on immediate inspection of the legal model, took place on Crete when eighth-century citizens of its many prosperous cities heard from Semitic craftsmen accounts of their own written law codes in the "old country." Semitic craftsmen have left us the evidence of their wares (various Phoenician artifacts, mainly) on Crete, starting in the ninth century; and there must have been many trips "home" at all times, an easy sail in summer. By the

middle of the seventh century, we know from the Dreros inscription that native Cretans were emulating the Semitic legal practice of writing down laws. Some of the terse formulations of the Semitic codes would have been carried in memory (a phenomenon noted by many biblical scholars), preserving the casuistic formulation. Older than any law codes from Crete is an inscription that came to light only in 1969 at Phaistos, the Erpetidamos pithos discussed in a previous chapter. As noted, it is metrical, three Greek words comprising the first four feet of an hexameter. Phoenician uses of writing on Crete now go back to an inscribed bronze bowl (just the sort of artifact Greeks saw in abundance and wished to emulate in inscribing) found in an undisturbed setting near Knossos and dated to ca. 900 B.C. See M. Sznycer, "L'inscription phénicienne de Tekke, près de Cnossos," *Kadmos* 18 (1979), pp. 89–93. I remain convinced that Cyprus, however, was the locus of transfer for letters, not at present a popular candidate. Nothing would surprise me less (or please me more) than if a votive object, bearing a hexameter or two and securely datable to the middle of the eighth century, were to turn up on one of the large, southern islands. I predict that in time one will. Alas, some of the very parts of Cyprus, especially along the southern coast, that it would be most promising to see excavated have occupied cities built over them, or are otherwise inaccessible.

15. I. 39–46.

16. Occasionally an article in a journal will become more influential by far than most books in a field. Headlam affords one example. Another is H. J. Wolff, "The Origin of Judicial Litigation among the Greeks," *Traditio* 4 (1946), pp. 31–87.

17. XI. 28–36.

18. I. 17–24.

19. Crete has always had its defenders as the locus of transfer of letters from Phoenicians to Greeks, starting with Dosiadas in antiquity. Among prominent supporters of Crete has long been Margharita Guarducci, whose four-volume *Inscriptiones Creticae* (Rome, 1935–1950) are indispensable to the study of advancing literacy on the island. See M. Guarducci, *Epigraphia Graeca* I (Rome, 1967), pp. 67ff. For dating the Cretan material see L. H. Jeffery, *LSAG*, pp. 309ff. For her rejection of the claims made for Crete as the place of invention, see pp. 9–10.

20. The suggestion has been made by Willetts in his many publications on Crete, perhaps from the stimulus of the always challenging theories of his Birmingham colleague, George Thompson. See Thompson, *Studies in Ancient Greek Society* (New York, 1965; first published 1949), p. 139: "Though later in date, the Gortynian procedure is more Archaic than the Attic, and both rest on the same principle as the Jewish. This rule of exogamy, and with it the woman's liberty, had been sacrificed to the male interest in private property." Also, see Thompson's index, *s. v.* exogamy. For a critical view of Willetts (and indirectly Thompson) on the general point of possibly an earlier matriarchal period, see H. Meyer-Laurin's review of Willetts (1967) in *Gnomon* 41 (1969), pp. 160–165. Also critical is Raphael Sealey, in chapter 3 of his *Women and Law in Classical Greece* (Chapel Hill and London, 1990), "Women in the Laws of Gortyn," pp. 50–81.

21. VI. 46–55.

22. X. 34–36.

23. XI. 10–14.

24. V. 51–54.

25. XI. 31–33, with Willetts's note.

26. Headlam, "Procedure," p. 63.

27. Ibid., p. 51.

28. See Michael Gagarin, "The Testimony of Witnesses in the Gortyn Laws," *GRBS* 24 (1984), pp. 345–349. Hereafter, Gagarin, "Testimony of Witnesses."

29. II. 16–20. *Epiklēros* is the term in Attic law for an heiress or female orphan. (Here I use the Attic terms for convenience, since they are more familiar to historians.) If father and brothers predeceased an heiress, she was assigned in marriage with her inheritance to her nearest male relative, called at Athens her *kurios,* "lord." The purpose was to secure the birth of heirs to her father's property. At Gortyn the term used is *patrōiōkos* (VIII. 40–42, a rare definition in early Greek law); she is a woman who has no father, and no brothers of the same father. Meyer-Laurin has argued ("Review of Willetts," pp. 163ff.) that *kadestēs (kadestas)* in Gortyn law is used to designate a relative who has the care of another or is required to carry out some obligation for another. However we should understand the troublesome term, the woman in this enactment required a guardian and what is unique in the case, as L. Gernet, Willetts, and first Headlam have seen, is that she did not pass automatically to a *kadestēs.* Instead, a guardian had to be selected from probably a large number of possibilities, for *kadestai* were "les membres d'un groupe familial assez large (Gernet)." See Willetts in "Observations on Leg. Gort.," with his references to Gernet. Willetts has advanced solid reasons to believe that the law assumes that the offender is both a free man and married, and that the offense was one between clans with social ties, which the offender breached.

30. For the practice in early Germanic society, in evidence when a man of one clan slays a man from another, see Grönbech, *Culture of Teutons* (Oxford, 1931), p. 55: "It is the clan of the slayer that promises indemnity, the clan that pays it. It is the clan of the slain man that receives the fine, and the sum is shared out so as to reach every member of the group." Also Willetts, "Observations on Leg. Gort.," p. 174 with note 23.

31. Gagarin, "Testimony of Witnesses," pp. 346ff.

32. Aeth. i 10. King Aethelbert of Kent is credited with the oldest written code of Anglo-Saxon law, published ca. 596 A.D.

33. Quoted in Headlam, "Procedure," p. 62. The example in n. 32 is also used by Headlam.

34. Quoted from T. M. Curley (ed.), *A Course of Lectures on the English Law Delivered at the University of Oxford 1767–1773 by Sir Robert Chalmers*, vol. 2 (Madison, Wisc., 1986), p. 49.

35. D. Mellinkoff, *The Language of the Law* (Boston and Toronto, 1963), p. 41.

36. J. L. Austin, "Performative Utterances," in J. O. Urmson and G. J. Warnock (eds.), *J. L. Austin: Philosophical Papers* (Oxford, 1970), p. 235: "if a person makes an utterance of this sort we should say he is doing rather than merely saying something," for example, "I apologize" or "I baptize you." Austin was addressing the peculiar assumption among certain contemporary philosophers, when verifiability was all the rage, that the sole purpose of human speech was to make utterances of the sort philosophers deal with, namely, "the sole business, or the sole interesting business, of any utterance—that is, of anything we say—is to be true or at least false (p. 231)." Performatives are neither one, but certainly are not meaningless or linguistically negligible. Austin himself happily admitted that "performative" was "a new word, an ugly word . . . but there is one thing in its favor, it is not a profound word."

37. Benjamin Thorpe (ed.), *Ancient Laws and Institutes of England,* vol. 1 (London, 1840), p. 179; Mellinkoff, *Language of the Law,* p. 41.

38. Mellinkoff, *Language of the Law,* p. 41.

39. Thorpe, *Ancient Laws and Institutes of England,* vol. 1, p. 18.

5

The Progress of Literacy and Written Law in Athens

In the fifth century before Christ, the city of Athens became what later generations would recognize, for all its imperfections, as a true democracy, history's first. Power belonged to the *dēmos,*[1] so that the people, ordinary citizens (that is, adult, free, males) participated in nearly every decision of government to a degree unknown in any society before that time—or, arguably, after it. Of even greater importance than the popular Assembly were the courts, for they could, and often did, bring to political and financial ruin even the most powerful political figures in Athens. The courts, too, belonged to the *dēmos,* not a ruling class.

At the very of end the fifth century, Athens produced the most complete code of written laws, secular and religious, that the world of classical Greece—or Europe before Roman law—was to know. In the process of publishing this code, the principle came to be accepted that *nomos* or "law" in the full, legally enforceable sense, and "written law" were synonymous terms. The result was that a legal indictment by any person, high or low, could be made only on the basis of a purported violation of a *written* enactment. Magistrates were forbidden to enforce "laws" of any other kind, such as the powerful oral *nomoi* (e.g., mentioned at *Crito* 50 D) that had not been made matters of written law. This, too, was unprecedented, for not even the Near Eastern societies, famous for their written "codes," knew such a rule. It is a mistake, borrowed from modern legal experience, to assume that their magistrates were similarly restricted, or that their justly famous "codes" (the designation is modern) sought to codify all enforceable law. That was never the inscribers' expectation.

Finally, by the closing decades of the same century, a fair portion of the free males in the city achieved what for antiquity was an impressive degree of literacy, although just how many is a number that will always elude us.[2] These citizens could read, or even write with enough competency to fulfill their political—and especially legal—obligations and opportunities. This, too, was a historical first, for no earlier culture anywhere had been literate to this degree.

Three notable events, then, mark the last quarter of the fifth century in Athens: the world's first democracy in place, the first government to submit itself solely to rule by written laws, and notable progress in a significant segment of the populace (but still a minority) toward popular literacy. Ideas and institutions that would remain at the core of Western civilization were being put into place for the first time, but how do they impinge on each other? Are they somehow closely or even causally related? Intuition tells us that they must be, and one often reads the bold assertion that they are, but demonstrating the causal linkages proves elusive.

Draco and the Beginning of Written Law at Athens

All discussions of the development of both literacy and written law in Attica must begin with the famous sixth-century figures of Draco and Solon. However, the severely restricted literacy of the seventh and sixth centuries and so the limited documentation from them make accounts of these figures precarious. Writing, to the extent that it was known at all in Athens before ca. 625 B.C., was not as yet utilized for political, civic, or legal purposes, let alone for writing local history. Before Solon himself, there is no evidence that it was used for literary purposes. This is a severe handicap for the historian, ancient or modern.

For any history of early Attica, oral tradition was, and was long to remain, the sole source of any information. Orally transmitted tradition from this period did at last get written down by later authors, starting with the foreigner Herodotus (from Halicarnassus), followed by Thucydides, a native Athenian, and Hellenicus (also a foreigner, from Lesbos). Dependence on oral accounts for knowledge of early events is acknowledged more often by these early historians than by many modern ones who depend on them.

Tradition held that it was only in the closing years of the seventh century that the citizens of Athens felt themselves in need of a lawgiver. Tradition also supplied a date, 621 B.C., and a name, Draco. A plausible explanation for what led to the first written laws for the city was the famous Cyclonian conspiracy, a failed attempt by a young aristocrat to set up a tyranny and the subsequent murder (or execution) of his followers. Later generations had no consistent account of it, however. That, too, speaks to the restricted nature of the first stages of Athenian literacy. The earliest surviving versions are in Herodotus (V. 71) and Thucydides (I. 126). By their day the events were part of the remote past, already overlaid in the oral telling with party politics, the complex fortunes of the great Alcmaeonid family, and the deep loyalties and lasting hatreds of clan and class. Variant versions suggest that, by the late fifth century, it was as difficult for Athenians themselves to sort out fact from embellishment as it is for us.

To the accounts in Herodotus and Thucydides, we can now add the *Athēnaiōn Politeia,* or *Constitution of Athens,* a work recovered only late in the last century and often attributed to Aristotle.[3] It commences with an account of the conspiracy, a clear proof of the enduring importance of these early events to later Athenians. By unfortunate accident, what in a printed text would constitute the first few pages of this document are now missing, and only the concluding events of the famous conspiracy survive in this source. They give a somewhat different version from that of the two historians, again indicating that there was no established, early documentation available to fourth-century writers.[4] However versions of the conspiracy are to be reconciled, it is probable that, in the wake of the confusion and unrest that ensued, Draco was called upon to make (some) laws for the city. The concern especially for the proper *procedures* in dealing with persons who have committed homicide is, presumably, the connection between the famous conspiracy and Draco's Law of Homicide, although this, too, is speculative.

We have the beginning of Draco's law, preserved in the reinscription of Nichomachus at the end of the fifth century. After the opening words, "First Axon," it commences with the casuistic formulation, "Even if a man unintentionally kills another. . .". This immediate attention to accidental homicide, and specifically to procedural matters involved with handling the perpetrator, may indicate that Draco got right down to the business at hand. If so, plausibly there is no missing section on intentional homicide. The lawgiver is addressing a present and pressing need. He leaves other matters, such as would be covered in a comprehensive code on homicide, to oral custom procedures, which of course had long dealt with them. Alternatively, a now missing section on deliberate homicide came later in the law than a statute relating to procedural concerns involving unintentional homicide, which is, at the least, odd. This is a much controverted matter, however, and it need not be argued here.[5]

A few modern historians have doubted even the existence of Draco as a historical person.[6] The arguments are not persuasive when weighed against the considerable positive evidence and the unanimous belief of Athenians themselves. On balance, it is reasonably certain that a historical Draco was the author of at least a law on unintentional homicide, thereby commencing the tradition of (some) written laws in Attica. Written law began in Athens, therefore, perhaps a half century later than on Crete. There *may* have been some stimulus from Crete, remembered much later in Athens, as a few historians believe. Behind this belief is the curiously precise mention in the *Constitution of Athens* that a Cretan seer, one Epimenides, purified the city after the pollution created by the massacre of the Cyclonian conspirators (*Ath. Pol.* 1).

What other laws or constitutional legislation can be attributed to Draco is problematical, again reflecting the restricted literacy of the period. Typically of Athens, much legislation was attributed back to him in the fourth and later centuries. One example is particularly outrageous, although the author of the *Athēnaiōn Politeia* accepts it. Chapter 4 of this work, which as often noted is an awkward interruption, makes Draco the author of an elaborate constitution that incorporates innovations that had evolved in the course of the fifth century, including some of the reforms of Cleisthenes. As P. J. Rhodes has observed, the attributions to Draco must be a late-fifth-century, or more likely a fourth-century, fabrication.[7] It is a reminder of how little in the way of written records later Athenians had from earlier, nearly illiterate centuries, even for the most important events in their civic history. The lacuna in information is not created because original documents known to fourth-century writers have not survived for us to read, as is sometimes supposed. Rather, those writers had little more, if any, to read than do we from centuries that made few, if any, records. The problem arises not from what has survived, but from what was made.

The Laws Attributed to Solon

With the exception of the law on homicide, the laws of Draco were superseded by those of Solon, but none of these has survived in the great archon's own wording. In one sense, then, the modern historian is worse off in his case than in Draco's. Under the supervision of Nichomachus, any Solonian laws that may still have been in effect in the late fifth century were reinscribed, along with every statute of a still legally binding nature from the intervening almost 200 years. The controversy surrounding the nature of the labors of the *anagrapheus* and his trial subsequent to it make it certain that he amalgamated and reworded laws on related matters. He was accused at his trial of having been appointed *anagrapheus* ("inscriber"), and then of appointing himself *nomothetēs* ("law-giver"), effectively converting himself into Solon redivivus.

Whatever may have been the creative element in the work of Nichomachus, the end result, the great corpus of Attic law, was as a whole attributed back to "Draco and Solon" (mainly to Solon), in the writings of the fourth-century orators and in all later authors. This was the convention, a well-understood fiction, and had long been so. By the fourth century, this "outrageous anachronism," as it has aptly been termed, was not taken seriously, of course. It had simply become a standard way to commend to Athenians a law, actual or proposed, of which a speaker or author happened to approve. Athenians understood this, but the practice has created havoc with Athenian legal history, beginning with the late, literary sources in antiquity.

The problem is the abundance of riches in those sources.[8] Without doubt, some of the laws mentioned in the literary sources as being Solonian could and probably did at least originate with him, but there is now no way of telling which ones. What is certain is that many laws attributed to him were not his. If we are prepared to believe that every law attributed to Solon, from the turn of the fourth century through Plutarch, was indeed of his making, then there was hardly any aspect of Attic life for which he did not have a written prescription or proscription. The complete list would itself constitute the best argument reductio ad absurdum. To be responsible for the whole collection, the great archon would have concerned himself, inter alia, with regulating the fines for killing various animals, wild and domestic; fixing the rewards for victors at the various athletic games (the figures given are impossibly high); forbidding the speaking of evil against the dead; prohibiting personal abuse in temples or other public buildings, including the courthouses, and at all festivals; interdicting a citizen from remaining neutral in a period of civil strife; also forbidding a citizen from providing his parents with an expensive funeral (and in another version, from making such a provision for himself); regulating the times (three) in a week that an *epiklēros* (female orphan assigned in marriage to a male relative) had a right to sexual intercourse with her husband—to mention a few of the more improbable examples, chosen randomly from later sources. If only a small part of the regulations attributed to him were Solon's, Archaic Attica would have been the Hellenic version of George Orwell's *1984*.

The confusion regarding Solon has two fundamental causes, reinforcing each other, but only one has been widely recognized. The more important cause has been the more neglected. Anything of later legal interest could be attributed back to Solon because of the conditions of severely restricted literacy through the sixth and early fifth centuries and the consequent paucity of documentation. In the absence of hard information, invention ran rampant. The second cause is the practice of later politicians, especially after 410 B.C., and of the fourth-century orators of invoking some supposed *nomos* of Solon whenever they sought to cloak their proposals in archaic dress and authority.

An especially absurd example concerns literacy, yet it has found its way into some standard handbooks on Greek and Roman education. Supposedly great Solon himself, as a matter of written statute, required *all* Athenian fathers to give their male children (and in another version, also female children) an adequate schooling in letters at an early age, making him the first champion of a legislated, popular literacy. A sixth-century source for such a law is out of the question, and is directly contradicted by the testimony of Plato in the *Protagoras*. In a section where he is describing the contemporary Athenian situation, Plato, writing in the fourth century, informs us that, according to then current practice, male children, *if* the father can afford it, do receive varying amounts of instruction in letters, but more or less (or none) solely as a function of the father's whim and the family's financial situation.[9] No law addressed the matter in the late fifth century (the dramatic date of the dialogue) or in the fourth, and certainly none did earlier. In fact, none ever did, although there is some late evidence that Protagoras himself may have been a pioneer in this regard in drawing up laws for Thurii.

F. E. Adcock, writing in 1926 for the old *Cambridge Ancient History*, summarized the situation accurately. Unless new evidence surfaces, his assessment remains valid.

> It is not possible to say exactly how far Attic Law as we know it in the fourth century B.C. is the work of Solon and how far that of the generations which followed him. Attic pleaders did not hesitate to attribute to him any law which suited their case, and later writers had no criterion by which to distinguish earlier from later laws. Nor can any complete and authentic collection of his statutes have survived for ancient scholars to consult.[10]

Unlike Crete, in Athens the oldest laws were published not on stone but on organic material, wood, the famous *axones*—rather like revolving slats—and so perished. When they perished is disputed. What later generations had available to read of Solon's original laws now seems to be a matter of faith among historians, as Rhodes and many others have observed. Any portrait of Solon as the lawgiver who was the Hellenic model for a body of large-scale, comprehensive legislation is debatable, for we do not know how comprehensively he legislated.

In terms of political reforms, Solon's surviving fragments, all from his poetry, confirm that he had in some manner enfranchised the *thetes,* basically the laboring and craftsman class. This is further confirmed by later sources, notably the *Athēnaiōn Politeia*. More important for the future—Aristotle rightly seized on it as crucial—under Solon's laws citizens other than aristocrats were afforded some means to play a greater role in the legal process. Before Solon, the lowest classes, as Aristotle put it, "had no share in anything," including, obviously, the workings of the courts.[11] No doubt magistrates had, as elsewhere in Hellas, been drawn solely from the old aristocratic families, with birth and wealth the criteria for selection. Solon did not abolish this entirely, in that he retained a property qualification. However, he initiated the democratizing of the legal process (somewhat) by abolishing at least the requirement of birth for being a magistrate. Solon also established the *heliaia,* which were courts in some way popularly constituted, as the name ("gatherings") suggests. According to Aristotle, what contributed most to the future rise of the masses was "the right to appeal to the jury-court—for when people are masters of the vote they are masters of the state."[12] This was destined to alter the political future of Athens, and as much as any single thing it would lead to the rise of the democracy. It would, in time, also result in the acceleration of literacy.

Aristotle advances the opinion that three accomplishments attributed to Solon turned out in the long run to be the most favorable to the people *(dēmotikotata).* He prohibited loans for which the person himself is security, he permitted one person to go to law on behalf of another, and he permitted appeal of a magistrate's decision to the *heliaia.* With the establishment of the right of all classes to appeal to the heliastic courts, the future path of Athenian democracy—and of Athenian literacy—was determined. The great archon set in motion events whose consequences no sixth-century Greek could have predicted. It would take the developments of the fifth century, led by the reforms of Cleisthenes, to bring both popular democracy and popular literacy to fruition.

Solon's Poems and a Developmental Theory of Written Law

A difficult question is unavoidable: Just how comprehensive were Solon's laws? The proper answer, as indicated, is that we do not know with any real confidence. Were, perhaps, his written laws an example, as Michael Gagarin suggests, of the "single, large-scale legislation" that, according to Gagarin, was the early pattern for Greece?[13] The evidence may, in fact, point in a different direction.

Before accepting Solon's laws as the early pattern for written law in Greece, two difficulties, it seems to me, should give us pause. First, are we confident that early codes from the Greek cities (always excepting Gortyn) that adopted written law (and not all did) were, in fact, examples of single, large-scale legislation? The pieces of them that have survived from a half dozen or so sites cannot be made the basis of that conclusion.[14] Indeed, in many cases, perhaps all, we seem to be dealing not with a "code," but with only some written enactments on diverse topics, more often procedural than substantive. Second, are we certain that Gortyn—after all, the only city from which has survived an early collection of its laws that is a complete document—should be branded as the wayward Hellenic exception? Any historian feels uneasy when the only hard evidence is dismissed as an aberration in favor of "what must have been." Might not Gortyn's experience with written law be, in fact, an example not of the exception but of the rule?

Only the late and notoriously unreliable[15] literary sources can serve as the basis of the theory of a "single, large-scale legislation" as the initial Greek pattern in the absence of hard epigraphical evidence. In these literary sources, in turn, Athens under Solon is the only credible—and certainly the strongest—candidate. But, as noted, the evidence for Solon is ambiguous.

If the literary accounts for early Greek law making are tainted and the epigraphical evidence is fragmentary, is there any other place to turn? The only *contemporary* evidence, in the absence of Solon's laws, must be sought in his poems, although fewer than 300 lines survive. One of his poems, as many scholars have recognized, reads very much like an *apologia pro vita sua* for the great lawgiver's professional life.[16] Written, significantly, in the past tense, it now comprises twenty-seven verses, the first seven of which respond to the accusation that his work was less than comprehensive or less than what it might have been. In the words of one historian, the issue at stake is that Solon in his laws "had left much business unfinished."[17] Solon himself begins with a rhetorical question: "For myself, why from the purposes for which I assembled the *dēmos* did I desist, before achieving them?" Solon claims that great Earth herself had been his oral eyewitness, or procedural witness, for what he did manage to accomplish, and so she, being ever available, can testify in the future to what his actions had been. That testimony will be in the formidable courtroom of time.

> There will be at my side a witness to testify about this in the justice court of time,
> She, mother best and supreme of Olympian gods,
> even Black Earth, whose marker stones I did
> remove, stuck in the ground everywhere.
> Great Earth, once enslaved, now free.

Solon proceeds to enumerate what he considers to have been his outstanding accomplishments in inscribing laws for the Athenians. He had abolished the mortgage markers and had summoned home to Attica those citizens exiled for debt, including even those "ceasing to utter the Attic tongue."[18] He had also freed those citizens at home who had been enslaved by debt. These things, he boasts,

> I achieved and completed as I had promised, and laws *(thesmoi)* accordingly for lowly men and noble alike
> by fitting justice *(dikē)*, straight for each man, I inscribed.

He concludes by observing that a person of lesser judgment or greater personal ambition would have been unable to restrain the angry *dēmos* on the one hand or to temper the greed and power of the well-born on the other.

> That is why I contrived (to gather) my strength from all sides,
> twisting and turning like a wolf in a pack of dogs.

Notable achievements, to be sure, at any time, but do they describe the agenda of legislation for a comprehensive, all-inclusive law code? On the contrary, does not Solon's own description of his accomplishments sound as though he addressed only, or at least mainly, those matters that were presently troubling and dividing the community?

He put in place some innovations that would, to a modest degree, distribute political power more equally. He did so, his poems reveal, only in response to the pressures being put upon those who held power by those who did not. Social chaos or civil war would have been the alternative. Without pressure from the have-nots, the status quo would have remained in place indefinitely. Solon's laws were thus an ad hoc compromise maneuver, forged in the give-and-take pressures of power politics, however later generations may have idealized them. Some matters long a part of the customary arrangement of things were to be altered, and the new rules must therefore be addressed in writing because they were not established in oral memory.

Solon's reforms made for an immediate lessening of tensions, and his "unalterable" laws speak for the lawgiver during his absence of ten years. But on his own admission it was a political deal, narrowly cut. Where is the evidence for a comprehensive law code?

Solon boasts that he accomplished what *he* set out to do, confident that his witness, Mother Earth, will attest to it, but he is also sensitive to the criticism, no doubt current ten years later when he returns to Athens, that more could have been done in the way of leaving behind additional written laws. This means, plausibly, that he left untouched by newly introduced written law much that was still governed by the ancient and as yet unquestioned control of oral custom. Ten years later—and much can change in a decade—he has grown sensitive to and defensive about the criticism that, in retrospect, he might have legislated more broadly and so left behind more in the way of written laws.

Written law, in this reconstruction, in Athens as on Crete, did not displace oral custom in one fell swoop. A rather more gradual process is the more plausible pattern. Only influence from the outside would have offered an alternative pattern, and for such influences we have no evidence at Athens or elsewhere in Greece. Indeed, the very *idea* of a unitary, comprehensive written code would come only late in the Athenian story, in the great reinscription of "all the laws" supervised by Nichomachus the *anagrapheus* in the last decade of the fifth century. That development would itself be a function of advancing literacy. A law code on a similar scale in the barely literate Athens of the sixth century is to me incomprehensible.

Limited Documentation in the Archaic Age

Restricted literacy and restricted use of written law go together. One is found with the other. That Solon's Athens was a society marked by both can scarcely be doubted. The paucity of evidence from the period does not arise because later Athens, especially its democratic politicians, had no interest in their great founding archon. It arises because little in the way of written documentation for any purpose was produced at the close of the seventh century.

F. E. Adcock, in his contribution to the *Cambridge Ancient History* cited earlier, astutely observed that the poems of Solon, as opposed to his laws, revealed a statesman who wrote in verse because "as yet one did not write in prose." This is correct, but the reason can be made more specific. Verse is memorable and suitable for oral declamation in an age before readers and before the diffusion of literature in manuscripts. Verse alone permitted Solon's thoughts to be memorized and recited in his own day and long after him—as, indeed, they were. His laws, by contrast, which were inscribed on wooden boards that were publicly displayed, did not face the same problems of preservation and dissemination; hence they could safely be put in prose and in the vernacular.

Although some citizens no doubt could read and write in Solon's Athens, an author of a "literary" text could not as yet expect an audience of readers, nor were mechanisms in place for the copying and dissemination of a text. An author's copy, but for use in recitation only, and perhaps a few other copies created under his supervision, are the best, indeed the luxurious best, that an author could hope for. On a famous occasion, according to Plutarch (Solon 8.2), the lawgiver was forced to extreme measures to assure his words a hearing.

> Solon secretly composed a poem in elegiac verse. Then after he had committed it to memory, he rushed out suddenly into the market place, with a small cap on his head, and when a great crowd had gathered he mounted the herald's rostrum and chanted the poem which begins, "As my own herald have I come from beloved Salamis to sing you a poem. . . ."

Bernard Knox has forcefully described this scene in the *agora*—Solon disguised as a herald, reciting his poem, dancing and acting his elegiac exhortation. The island of Salamis *must* be won for Athens no matter the cost. Knox usefully reminds us of the conditions of all publication in the period.

> This episode . . . is a vivid reminder of the fact that in the archaic age poetry was not a written text to be read but a performance to be watched and heard . . . [Solon's performance] is also, with its assumed identity (a herald) and disguise (the cap of the invalid), a fully dramatic performance.[19]

Before the fifth century, we have no evidence that "documents," public or private, played any significant role in daily life in Attica. Thus Michael Gagarin can refer in passing to "the scarcity of inscriptional evidence for early laws or *for any Attic documents* before the fifth century. . . ."[20] Similar cautions, in this case about assuming pre-Herodotean documents for the foundations of Attic history, were sounded by the great Felix Jacoby in 1949, when he published his monumental *Atthis: The Local Chronicles of Ancient Athens.*

Jacoby notes that Aristotle in the *Athēnaiōn Politeia* reveals in several passages that the Atthides (local chronicles or histories of Athens) available ca. 322 B.C. dealt fully with Solon's *life,* "giving what we call the Solon legend, the details of which obviously contradicted the few documentary dates." An example of the manufactured legend surfaced later, in Plutarch. Solon the lawmaker is connected to Peisistratus the tyrant by making them *erastai.* Aristotle observes that the story that the two men were lovers is nonsense because their ages simply will not admit of it (*Ath. Pol.* 17). The authors of the Atthides could hardly leave out even the nonsense in the "Solon legend" because, as Jacoby writes,

> without these [legendary tales] Attic history before Solon would have been empty. They had nothing else. The survey of the documentary history . . . has at least taught us that documentary tradition was almost non-existent for the time before Kleisthenes. . . . Not long after the turn of the fifth century the foreigner Herodotus noted down a fairly long passage of Athenian history from the time about which he "knew something," and later on he incorporated that passage in

> his work. . . . Toward the end of that century another foreigner, Hellenikos [of Lesbos, probably soon after 404/3], published a complete chronicle of Athens from the beginnings down to his time. In entering upon this task there was for both historians one source only on which they could draw, and to which Hekataios, Herodotus, and occasionally Thukydides actually refer, viz. oral tradition, in ancient terms, *μνῆμαι, ἀκοαί, λόγοι*.[21]

Later Jacoby adds that in the oral tradition certain notable accomplishments were given to famed individuals, and these could not be taken away, for example, Solon's legislation had founded *in nuce* the first Attic constitution, or Cleisthenes had fixed the first order of the demes. Motivated additions, however, in a period of living memories but minimal documentation, were always possible, for example, the early constitution adduced under the half-historical name of Draco that is interpolated into the text of the *Athēnaiōn Politeia* (4). Minimal documentation before 400 B.C. invited manipulation, even as increasing documentation after that date made it more difficult, or at the least put a light on the inconsistencies among rival additions. Jacoby writes: "The fixation in writing, once achieved, primarily had a preserving effect on oral tradition, because it put an end to the involuntary shifting of the *μνῆμαι*, and drew limits to the arbitrary creation of new *λό----γοι*."[22] In the course of the fifth century, written documentation and oral memory were forming a new kind of alliance in the city of Athens. Initially, writing was the unequal partner and the less trusted one in the Greek community, as in the courts. The legal experience of Gortyn would be prologue here. However, there is unmistakable evidence for an acceleration in the quantity and quality of literacy in Athens in the second half of the fifth century, especially in the last decades of the century. This development did not occur before Hellenistic times in aristocratic Gortyn, as far as we know. The cause of the Athenian phenomenon, if I am not mistaken, was the peculiar nature of the Athenian democracy. Above all, it can be traced to the daily demands its popular courts made on the adult, free, male populace.

Literacy and the Reforms of Cleisthenes

Cleisthenes is often claimed, with considerable truth, as the real founder of Athenian democracy at the expense of the initiatives of Solon. His legal and political reforms were introduced near the turn of the fifth century, or 508 B.C. They ushered in a period often termed a "moderate" democracy in comparison to that which followed later in the century. Following this nomenclature, a "radical" democracy resulted from the reforms of Epithales which were introduced some forty-six years later, in 462 B.C. At the end of the century, a restored democracy, following a period of brief, traumatic oligarchical rule, voted the decree that resulted in a complete and drastic new codification and reinscription of all Athenian laws. When finished and published, this codification reflected the developments of the whole century, but as amalgamated into a single code of laws, obliterating the steps in the formative process. Before the recovery of a text of the *Athenian Constitution* from the dry sands of Egypt in the last century, our knowledge of

Cleisthenes was meager in the extreme, depending mainly on some obscure references in Aristotle, and a scattering of notices in Herodotus that reveal an outsider's minimal understanding of the Athenian facts.

Based mainly on the account in the *Athenian Constitution,* which in turn shows direct debts to Herodotus, three reforms have been attributed to Cleisthenes. First, perhaps now the most famous but not the most important, Cleisthenes introduced (or perhaps first politically exploited) the institution of ostracism, of which much has been made in the literature concerning popular literacy. It was a short-lived curiosity and never of much political importance. The demands it made on the growing literate skills of free males was minimal and could be easily obviated by having another scratch the required name on the *ostrakon,* a phenomenon for which we have evidence.[23] It is unlikely to be a coincidence that the method of ostracism would be most easily executed by the various *demiourgoi,* or craftsmen, or that this class, always resident in the "town" and available for a vote in the Assembly, was the strong basis of Cleisthenes' support. Often enough, we know from contemporary remains, a partially literate craftsman—a potter or a painter—could write his own name and a bit more, such as "Peikon the potter made me." Spelling and orthography might be erratic, however, and in the extant remains often are. Among this close-knit group, one could readily perform the minimal literate tasks for another. We have no direct evidence that, for the *first* decades of the fifth century, any large percentage of Athenian aristocrats would be literate, although the establishment of schools and the introduction of the figure of the paid *grammatistēs* would change that situation by the last decades of the century.

Second, Cleisthenes reconstituted the council as the Council of Five Hundred, expanding the number and basing membership on his recent reform of the tribes. (*Ath. Pol.* 12) Third, and far and away his most important change, was that reform of the traditional tribes itself. These were now reconstituted as demes ("parishes" or "districts") that radically cut across the old clan lines, in effect wiping them out as a political force. Within a generation the deme had replaced the old, hereditary clan divisions as the central Athenian political unit. Membership in one's deme became where a citizen sought his deepest political roots and where a politician necessarily established his political base. Second (perhaps) only to his patronymic, his deme became the way a citizen of Athens identified himself, and it was attached to his name when he appeared before the courts and at other official occasions.

By complex but effective tiering, the core of each deme was made the city-based middle class, the "town folk" in the old terminology, available and ready to vote in the Assembly and serve on the juries. As a result, political control of Attica effectively fell, with only brief interruption, to whomever this class supported. This would remain true from the first day of Cleisthenes' democratic reforms to the rise of Macedonia and the conquests of Alexander, a period of survival for democratic rule surpassed in history only by the American republic. Uncertain and controversial as the details of this arrangement now are—paradoxically made even more controversial[24] by recent archaeological discoveries—the upshot, evident in the results, is clear enough. Although intended to appear impartial, the result of Cleisthenes' restructuring was that, in practice, the ordinary citizen (or rising "middle class," a term of problematical application to Athens) had the dominating presence in the Assembly, and so controlled the vote. The same persons also provided the bulk of the jurors in the popular courts, as we know from Old Comedy and from Plato. Cleisthenes, master of the game as he was, did not act in indifference to these hard political facts. The outcome, it scarcely can be doubted, was what he had intended.

It has been neglected that the result of these reforms greatly increased the political power of the occupants of the "workshops," or those professional craftsmen whose abilities and skills had taken them into an emerging middle class. Perhaps more accurately, power went to their political leaders and organizers, who were normally of the upper classes. Cleisthenes himself, for example, was an Alcmaeonid, as was Pericles through his mother; Alcibiades was the adopted son of Pericles; Cimon married into the Alcmaeonid family. The list could be extended. Whatever their personal and class biases may have originally been, all knew where power resided and so they cultivated the *dēmos*. Belatedly, the old oligarchs and landed aristocrats realized what was happening. While the most obtuse of them were tending their beloved horses in the country, the emerging democrats, by filling the Assembly and the heliastic courts—all quite legal under the provisions of Cleisthenes' laws and reforms—had stolen control of Athens (and so Attica) from them. Virtually the only road to real power left for the disgruntled landed aristocrats, apart from alliance with the *dēmos,* Alcibiades' solution, would be an armed coup. That, overtly or covertly, also meant looking outside Attica for support, in the direction of Sparta.

For several brief periods, the oligarchs did manage to seize power, but with no lasting effect on Athenian democratic history. The stability, in essentially unbroken continuity, of the Athenian democracy from Cleisthenes to Alexander is one of Greek history's truly remarkable events. It deserves our wonder. Whereas advancing literacy did not create this situation, it went a long way toward making it possible and fostering it. In time, as no one in Athens could have foretold, a working knowledge of letters became indispensable to the daily operation of its greatest institutions, notably the law and the courts. This process, and attendant pressures toward greater literacy, *began* with the turn of the fifth century and the first reforms of Cleisthenes—so, too, I surmise, out of self-defense if nothing else, did an acceleration on the part of wealthy and ambitious Athenians to render, if not themselves, at least their sons competently literate. The first Athenian schools appear just at this time.

In one grand sweep, Cleisthenes had swept away the ancient kinship associations of Attica and replaced or at least drastically realigned them along roughly geographical lines. The reforms were, as far as we know, accepted peacefully. Yet it must have been rather like replacing one's uncles and aunts and cousins by a stranger and his children who happened to be a neighbor of sorts, owning a house four blocks away. By the later decades of the fifth century, the system is firmly entrenched. Its stated purpose, according to the *Athēnaiōn Politeia,* was to "mix up the people" (repeated twice), so that more citizens should share in running things. The successful result—whatever the organizational details—was, as Rhodes remarks, "cutting across old channels of influence and so lessening the dependence of the ordinary citizen on the aristocracy."[25]

Carrying out such a drastic redistribution is, I suggest, unthinkable without a developing literacy. From the day of inception, a degree of popular literacy must have existed in the craftsmen or middle class, always Cleisthenes' power base. He could not expect that a cadre of literates would be created in the "middle class" in every deme overnight. Lists, long and complex, and links based on documentation, not familial and tribal memory or association, became at once the basis of all joint action, legal and governmental. Kinship, which needed no written record, and which Solon perhaps wisely left untouched, is replaced by a somewhat artificially created "locality," each with a component ostensibly drawn from the three tiers of town, country, and coast. This required elaborately maintained written lists, which is obvious enough, and for which we have abundant allusions in the literary sources and in the epigraphical record.

Also, one's deme moved, so to speak, with one, for membership for a citizen was for life and for his descendants in perpetuity, wherever in Hellas they chanced to move. Hence there developed the distinctions between the resident citizens of a deme (or the *dēmotoi*) and the members of a deme not resident in it (or the *enkektemenoi*). These distinctions carried over to their descendants, male and female, who were members of the the deme in perpetuity. Even should a citizen join a colony, as many Athenians did at the city's colony of Thurii, taking up permanent residence with an entire family, that man's status as colonist or a *cleruch* in such distant places did not alter his membership, or rights and privileges, or those of all his descendants, in his Athenian deme, "forever." More lists were needed, and much careful bookkeeping at the local level. Also required were ever more persons from the demes themselves capable of performing the task. From the orators we learn that even in the fourth century some demes were rather better at keeping the deme list up to date than others; and we hear of an occasional disaster. One hapless, absentminded custodian actually misplaced the deme list, an only copy, creating utter havoc. With these changes it would become necessary for increasing numbers of people in the deme to command some literate skills, beyond the mere ability to scratch a name on an *ostrakon*. Just how much more is open to dispute.

The Reforms of Ephialtes and the Rise of the Imperial Democracy

What was, for the democrats, only well begun by Cleisthenes was brought to completion by Ephialtes in 461 B.C., although he was not to live to enjoy the triumph. He was assassinated the following year. Under his further reforms, as far as we can now tell, the Assembly, or Ekklesia, was empowered to settle *all* major matters of the city's public policy by decree, including decisions on making war (or peace), and foreign alliances, with all citizens in good standing who were eligible and who wished to attend being empowered to vote on every important issue. For some matters, a quorum, which amounted to 6,000 people, was required, and debate could range over two full days.[26] All citizens had the right to speak *(isēgoria)*.

To be sure, only more accomplished citizens may have had the confidence or the following to be regular speakers, or *rhetores*.[27] But where were such skills to be acquired? Without, of course, imagining such a result, Ephialtes was opening the way for the sophists and some major changes in the traditional Greek paideia. Before too many decades had passed, the old Homeric paideia would need to be supplemented by instructors who taught one how to perform well in the assembly and the courts, which meant *eu legein,* to "speak well" and effectively, to argue and debate. However they dressed it up, this is what the old sophists taught, for this is what the aristocratic young men or scions of newly wealthy families would pay for. In many cases, this was also the motive that drew young men of Athens to the conversations of Socrates, as he himself observes in Plato's *Apology.* The sophists were both a product of the paideia crisis of the late fifth and fourth centuries, and provokers of it. So too, in his way, was Socrates, as we shall see.

For Athens, increasing evidence for published decrees in the second half of the fifth century implies an ever wider literate class among those who held major offices—or even some lesser ones, such as heralds who must read out a *probouleuma* for a day's debate, or auditors who must review a magistrate's accounts and submit a report. The required *dokismasia,* or examination of all magistrates before they assume office, and the *euthunai,* the required audit or scrutiny as they left office, were under the jurisdiction of the popular courts. Virtually no official of government in any capacity, including the military, was exempt from these exacting procedures, and not a few fell afoul of them. Most citizens who carried them out were, surely, at least craft-literate, if only not to be at the mercy of the secretary appointed to write them up. This is a rather specialized form of literacy, to be sure, and says nothing about the preservation or transmission of literature, or any growing alliance between literacy and paideia, but it is a form of legal literacy nevertheless. This sort of quiet, administrative toil, now so trivial for us to read when we catch glimpses of it in the epigraphical record, increasingly became dependent on an expanding literate class.

The need for administrative and legal literacy was again multiplied significantly by the middle of the century when, especially under Pericles, the administrative pressures of empire were added to the burdens of a developing literate class in Athens. This, too, has been somewhat overlooked in the standard accounts of developing fifth-century Athenian literacy, although Harris in his recent book calls passing attention to it. In some cases, when cities and especially their oligarchs proved recalcitrant, Athens imposed a version of its own complex democracy, including the deme structure and the courts, on the distant city. This happened, for instance, to great Miletus, as well as other cities. The Athenians, who could be heavy-handed, also reserved certain types of trials to the Athenian courts, requiring that the entire proceeding be moved over water to Attica. It dispatched "overseers" *(episkopoi)* with broad powers to supervise local affairs, watching out for Athenian interests and reporting back to the city. The degree of literacy required to run its own democracy and the ever-expanding foreign correspondence grew steadily but accelerated in the second half of the century. It outstripped any demands on literate skills made by the occasional ostracism in the first half, to which so much attention has been paid by historians of literacy.

Accelerating Legal Literacy in Athens

When the fifth-century evidence is weighed, what was decisive in propelling Athens from a restricted literacy of a sort found on Crete to alphabetic dependency was a growing alliance between the alphabet and the law in all its manifestations, including the workings of the Assembly and, especially, the popular courts. *Full* participation in these institutions—the heart of Athenian citizenship—required minimum craft-literacy, that is, some ability to read a repetitive text composed of familiar legal words and to write one's name. Admittedly, both tasks could be performed by a more literate neighbor—as we know often happened—but pressure was clearly mounting on the individual, especially a politically ambitious one, not to depend on others for these tasks. The emergence of the professional teacher of letters (the *grammatistēs*) and even schools in fifth-century Athens may well have been the more affluent classes' reaction to precisely these pressures.

The various degrees of restricted legal literacy that mark the fifth century can, with assurance, be said to have given way to full alphabetic dependency only in the first decades of the fourth century. This is especially true in the area of the daily workings of the courts. The six courtroom or forensic speeches of Isocrates, composed in the first decades following the work of Nichomachus—that is, basically in the first quarter of the fourth century—afford decisive proof of this growing dependency at every turn, including, for example, admitting a document as evidence. In the *Trapeziticus,* a financial memorandum of an agreement that was secret, and so unwitnessed, was read to the court, but its credibility was immediately attacked precisely because written records were so easily altered.

The evidence of Isocrates does not stand alone. Above all, only in the fourth century is it clearly and explicitly understood that a *nomos,* in order to serve as the basis for an action in the courts, must be part of official, written law. Only in the early fourth century can we be certain that the testimony taken in the *anakrisis* phase of a trial was taken down in writing and preserved under seal (in jars) for later use (Dem. XLVI. 6). The clerk of the court would read out the testimony of witnesses at the actual trial; the witness was required to be present and confirm the accuracy of what the clerk read. Whereas many courtroom examples of witnessing are of the old, procedural kind (for example, of marriages and wills; Dem. XXX. 21; XXVIII. 15; Is. IX. 8), accidental witnesses are now also making regular appearances. Written contracts and wills are introduced in evidence in the fourth-century courts, although the degree of credence a jury might put in them, as indicated by the courtroom speeches of both Isocrates and Demosthenes, greatly varied. Demosthenes is again our evidence that a *proklēsis* (i.e., a formal challenge to someone, for example, to produce a slave for interrogation, or produce a reluctant witness) may be presented orally (in front of witnesses), but is not legally binding until, as a kind of contract, the details have been agreed to by both parties and reduced to written form (Dem. XLV. 61).

In general, the line of evolution in legal matters has been from the exclusively oral to the oral *and* written. Even in the fourth century, a written document as evidence normally depended on whether it had been drawn up before witnesses and secured away free from the possibility of tampering, as in a sealed vase (but this was not foolproof or entirely trusted, as the *Trapeziticus* again informs us). Verification by signature was not used for legal purposes and was virtually unknown. Court documents, at least later in the fourth century, were normally drawn up by literate slaves, performing a tedious task; characteristic handwriting *might* rarely be given some weight, but nothing conclusive, in a dispute over authenticity. The same was true even of seals. There were too many ways for the written evidence to be gotten at and manipulated, a fear that was not ungrounded, as later history was to reveal.

In the early fourth century, it becomes commonplace, as revealed in the orators, for sections of the law to be read aloud at trials upon demand of a pleader. Even so, we must not assume "law books" in multiple copies. The pleader himself had to copy, or have copied, from public inscriptions the relevant laws he wished to cite and provide them in advance to the clerk of the court. Thus the laws were treated as a form of evidence that might be presented before the court, and the pleader was himself responsible for presenting them. Granted, if one were illiterate, one might pay another to perform this search, a logographer notably, as Isocrates was initially in his career. If one's life or fortune depended on the outcome—as they well might in increasingly litigious Athens—then one's own ability to read the laws and participate in a defense (or prosecution) was obviously highly desirable.

Of special interest is the requirement, made a matter of law later in the fourth century, that maritime contracts, which were especially detailed and filled with contingencies, must henceforth be in writing for their provisions to be enforceable at law in the courts. Adding to the complex contingencies of maritime agreements was the liability, also a matter of prior agreement: If a ship went down, was it in the harbor or on the high seas? home harbor or foreign? sunk by storm or negligence of captain and crew? captured by pirates or accident of war? The contingencies were almost limitless and financial liability under each circumstance—whether of captain (often the owner) or investors—was entirely negotiable for each voyage. Those who financially lived or died by the precise wording of these contracts, such as commercial traders and ship captains (*emporoi* and *nauklēroi*), may well have depended on a literate banker such as Pasion or his literate slaves to a degree, but the fourth-century motive for such men themselves to become literate enough to watch carefully over the written contracts was a strong one. It may be noted that distinguished economic historians (e.g., R. Bogaert, J. Hasebroek, G. de Ste Croix) have, on the whole, been far more realistic about the restricted nature of Greek commercial literacy in the Archaic period and the minimum commercial use made of letters before the fourth century than have literary historians.

In sum, by the early fourth century, writing and documents manifestly are becoming a presumption of the daily functioning of the courts and of legal procedures, not the marginal exception or the occasional, fitful presence. No doubt all of this was already developing in the fifth century, but we cannot *prove* that it was. We can say only that it could hardly have sprung, like Zeus from the head of Athena, full grown and mature, on that day in 399 B.C. when Nichomachus and his committee halted the laborious cutting of the mason's chisels and declared their great work done. The words of Mogens Hansen, protesting the neglect of such facts in many standard histories, deserve, like those of the *anagrapheus* himself, to be etched in stone:

> Oral tradition was still an essential element in the fifth century democracy whereas literacy dominated in the fourth century. . . . [Histories are written] without sufficient emphasis on the difference between the fifth and fourth century . . . [for] in the administration of justice literacy gained in importance especially in the first decade of the fourth century.[28]

No other statement, especially by so eminent a historian of Greek law, at least none known to me, has so clearly placed the emphasis where it belongs or has gotten the relevant period, the first decades of the fourth century, so right.

The only addendum I would make to Hansen's statement would be to risk a causal assertion. It was accelerating legal literacy—intepreting that phrase broadly—that was the crucial impetus toward converting the restricted literacy of previous centuries in Athens, including the fifth century, into something approaching history's first popular literacy or alphabetic dependency. The accomplishment is a fourth-century phenomenon, but it comes early in that century.

The Restored Place of Nichomachus in the History of Written Law

Until recent archaeological discoveries, the revolutionary work of Nichomachus and the other *anagrapheis*, which took place in the turbulent closing years of the fifth century was underestimated by historians, if noted at all. The reason behind the neglect was that the source of information concerning the *anagrapheis* and their work was a blatantly hostile speech of Lysias.[29] It was written for the prosecution, those disgruntled "wellborn" who, unable to stop Nichomachus while he diligently worked away on his inscription of the laws (he was protected by official decree voted by the democratic Assembly), had hoped to exact some vengeance when he was done. In this they succeeded, for Nichomachus was required to defend himself at a trial conducted according to the laws he had inscribed.

Writing in 1960, Sterling Dow observed that, by virtue of Lysias' monopoly of the literary record before the recovery of the new inscriptional material, he had "caused all posterity *until now* to under-rate Nikomakhos."[30] The depth of resentment to Nichomachus is captured in the wording of Lysias' speech, even if the degree of polemical exaggeration cannot now be assessed: "When he was instructed to inscribe the laws of Solon in four months, instead of Solon he appointed himself as law-maker, and instead of four months he made the office last six years. While getting paid by the day, he inserted some laws and deleted others."[31] The intended sting is, of course, carried in the phrase "he made himself law-maker" in place of Solon. Also, we should recall again that the phrase "laws of Solon" referred to any laws still in force, whatever the origin, with the exception of Draco's law.

Without doubt, the great *anagrapheus* had not been content, as the word might suggest, to be a mere secretary collecting and reinscribing what others had made. Presumably Nichomachus judged that such a passive procedure would only serve to perpetuate the present mess that the body of gradually accumulating written laws and decrees was already in. It seems clear that existing laws and decrees, preserved on separate *stēlai,* had as yet not even been physically collected in one place, and it fell upon the litigant to find the appropriate decree or law, copy it, and have it read to the court. We also do not know if older lapsed or superseded decrees were systematically removed from the Acropolis or from public display, but I know of no fifth-century evidence that they were. The first task would be to sort out such laws and decrees as had not been abrogated or superseded, ranging conceivably from the time of Solon, through the obscure legal activity of the sixth-century tyrants and the twists and turns of the fifth-century democracy. Plausibly, a first step involved a systematic search of the Acropolis and a cataloging of decrees under broad headings.

Reinscription entailed—no doubt, required—amalgamation and a degree of revision (how much we cannot say), in which task Nichomachus exercised considerable initiative. To reword several laws and decrees on related issues, often made many years apart, in order to bring them into conformity—so as to make the "law" consistent—is, in an important sense, to make law, as any jurist knows. To suggest that Nichomachus did anything less is to be overly cautious and to make the later accusations against him hard to explain. Nichomachus, to be sure, could not have made up laws out of whole cloth or he would not have passed his required scrutiny when he gave up office, which he did. Nevertheless, we can be certain that Nichomachus was no mere passive copyist, and that could not have been his brief, or commission, from the Boule.

The process was not without checks and balances, especially in Nichomachus' second term. According to procedures stipulated in the decree of Teisamenos, the work of the *anagrapheis* had to be reviewed by two boards of *nomothetai* and the Boule itself. If we may speculate, it is likely that the first term, interrupted by the fall of the democratic government in 411 B.C., did not have the same checks and balances and that even some citizens who were well disposed to Nichomachus felt that he had gone too far in using his own judgment. Then again, so advantageous was it to have all secular laws in one place, and in one organized text, a single coherent code—presumably he had nearly completed that task in his first term of office—that he was put back to work to finish the task. This entailed, seemingly, some review and revision of what he had done in the first term, perhaps putting final touches on secular law and adding the greatly complex material of religious law or the calendar of religious observances.

By good fortune, we have some contemporary evidence of what Nichomachus accomplished and how the courts, perhaps sometimes grudgingly, interpreted it in the trials that followed the completion of his work. There was an immediate glut of them, starting in 399 B.C. The most famous of these trials was to become the most famous in history, that of Socrates, but more instructive for understanding the changes wrought by the work of Nichomachus is the trial of Andocides.

The Evidence of *On the Mysteries*

Andocides was forced to defend himself in 399 B.C. against an indictment based on the revised code of Nichomachus. His address to the court, *On the Mysteries,* has survived. It tells us that the Athenians were not prepared for the full implication of Nichomachus' work or for what the exclusive rule of written law means. Wealthy and prominent Callias evidently was not prepared, and lost as a result. We should also recall that we are being treated to a biased rehearsal of events, but one in which the legal facts that are recounted could hardly be fudged. Also, the defendant was not a popular figure; he needed all the legalities he could muster to escape with his life.

Andocides' legal troubles go back some fifteen years, to 415 B.C., and to the infamous profaning of the mysteries and the mutilation of the Hermae. By his own confession, made at the time, Andocides had been involved in the affair. He had, however, been protected in the intervening years, both in his person and property, by an *adeia,* a form of immunity, granted by the council in return for his useful testimony concerning other guilty parties. For nearly fifteen years no one had dared violate formal immunity from prosecution on this charge granted by the Boule of the Assembly.

Andocides had a second problem, however, from which immunity did not protect him, which was to haunt him, and which was the immediate source of his legal difficulties in 399 B.C. In the same year Andocides had received immunity, or 415 B.C., a certain Isotimides had successfully carried a decree to the effect that *anyone* who was guilty of impiety and had confessed to it (Andocides' situation exactly: The decree was only technically not *ad hominem* by resorting to the anonymous *tis)* was forbidden access to the temples of Attica and the *agora* of Athens, thus effectively excluding him from the religious and civil life of the city. Life in Athens under such restraints was unthinkable. Voluntary exile, the desired result, was Andocides' only solution for more than a decade, or until 403 B.C., when the democracy was restored and the prominent democrats who had been in exile under the oligarchs returned to the city. The conditions of a general amnesty were hammered out, and mighty oaths were taken by all parties to observe it.

The amnesty was proclaimed on the twelfth day of the month of Boedromion (roughly September) in 403 B.C. From that date, Andocides apparently felt it was safe for him to return to Athens, although he was hardly, like the famous Anytus, a prominent democrat returning from honorable political exile. But the broad mantle of the terms of the amnesty, so he concluded, protected even him. Evidently he also felt free to participate fully in both the civil and religious life of the city, which he did unchallenged until 399 B.C., when the familiar figure (from the works of Plato and Xenophon) Callias—for motives more personal than religious—indicted him for participating in temple worship, no doubt at the trial accusing him of being in violation of the old decree of Isotimides. The speech *On the Mysteries* is Andocides' published version of his defense on that charge.[32]

The strongest part of Andocides' defense to the court was, first, that the covenants of amnesty protected him under a kind of general mantle of "forget the past, and let live.'' Also, of more present interest to us, he was clearly protected, so he argued, by the fact that any older laws, even if once in force, were no longer valid if not reinscribed as part of the revision of the laws begun in 410 B.C. by Nichomachus and completed in 399 B.C. The old decree of Isotimides fell into that category. We must conclude, from Andocides' speech, that Nichomachus had discarded it, as, indeed, he must have discarded the old impiety decree of the seer of Diopeithes, for Socrates was not tried under its wording. Andocides argued that, by law, he could be indicted only under a *written* law that was *currently* in force, that is, reinscribed by the *anagrapheis*. The lapsed decree of Isotimides does not fit that bill. Fortunately, Andocides' defense entailed a rather full recounting for the jury, and so for us, of the legal events that led up to the amnesty, including the revision and reinscription of all laws begun under the supervision of Nichomachus. Most usefully, Andocides had the clerk of the court read into the record (83–84) the crucial Decree of Teisamenos, himself a *hupogrammateus,* or ''assistant secretary'' (MacDowell's rendering), involved in the reinscription.[33]

Initially, we learn, ''the laws of Solon and Draco''[34] were to be in effect on an interim basis following the confusion that was created by the failed oligarchic coup. This vague proposition sought to affirm that the city was returning to ancestral ways, *ta patria,* always a rallying cry. But the plan soon proved unworkable in practice because, Andocides related, too many citizens would fall under indictment. By implication, we may infer that something more restrictive was required or once again the courts would be the arena of choice for exacting personal and political revenge. An assembly was called to address the legal crisis, and it enacted a law to the effect that ''*all* laws'' were to be examined *(dokimasantes pantas tous nomous)* with an eye to any necessary additions. Those that passed scrutiny and were approved were to be inscribed in the *stoa* of the Archon Basileus. The crucial decree begins:

> The people resolved on the motion of Teisamenos that Athens would conduct the affairs of the *polis* according to the ancestral ways *(kata ta patria),* and shall follow the laws (*nomoi*) of Solon, and his weights and measures, and the ordinances (*thesmoi*) of Draco, which we employed in time past.

It goes on to say that such further laws or additions that may be required will be inscribed on boards by the elected *nomothetai* and be offered for public inspection before the statues of the Eponymous Heroes. The laws thus inscribed shall then be handed over to the *nomothetai* elected by the demes, and to the council. In this period any private citizen may appear before the council and suggest further improvements.

The decree ends by specifying what shall be done when the finished result, a code of all law, civil and religious, has been duly enacted.

> When the laws *(hoi nomoi)* have been enacted they shall be put under the care of the Council of the Areopagus, to the end that only such laws as have been approved may be employed by magistrates. Those laws that are ratified are be inscribed on the wall, where they were inscribed in the past, for all to view.

Andocides adds that the laws were revised in accordance with this decree, and those laws that were approved were duly inscribed on the *stoa* of the Basileus.

Then, as a kind of final insurance, another law was passed, which was then, Andocides reminded the court, enforced without exception (85). This law—fortunately for us—he also demanded be read out to the court. It marks the completed transference of the control of behavior by legal means, and the redress of the courts, to what is specified in written law, forbidding *any* exceptions. Brief and unimposing in its wording, it is nevertheless a major milestone in the history of both literacy in Greece and written law in society.

> *Nomos* (Law). Under no circumstances shall magistrates enforce a law that has not been inscribed.

Andocides then demanded dramatically to the jury: Is there any loophole here, any opening for a prosecution save one based on written law? He asserted that the clear intent of the law and the letter of the law as read to court were to prevent precisely what was being attempted in his case, namely, indictment on a basis other than the written law as recently reinscribed, a process begun in 410 B.C. and completed in 399 B.C.

Andocides next asked the clerk to read out several related laws. Two deserve our notice. The first states that no decree *(psēphisma),* whether of council or assembly, shall override a duly enacted and duly inscribed *law (nomos)* of the people.[35] His point was that the restriction of magistrates to enforcing written laws was a *nomos*. It cannot be overridden even by a *psēphisma* voted by the people. The second fixes on "the archonship of Eucleides," or the late summer of 403/2, as the crucial date for the start of amnesty. The legal result, combined with the wording of the covenants of amnesty, which Andocides will go on to discuss next, is clearly twofold, although the full implications may not have been immediately appreciated by all Athenians (e.g., Callias, who attempted a prosecution on the basis of a defunct decree). No unwritten laws *(agraphoi nomoi)* or even written decrees that have been allowed to lapse—which means no laws not inscribed under the direction of Nichomachus—can be valid laws *(keimenoi nomoi).* And no citizen may be prosecuted by anyone for any offense committed before the summer of 403/2, for he falls under the protection of the amnesty.

The amnesty stated, with a simplicity rare in human politics, that no prior action, even if in violation of a then existing law, or even if in violation of a presently existing law, could be made a matter of legal indictment if it was committed earlier than the date the amnesty itself was voted. The intention of the amnesty was to cover primarily political actions but in subsequent trials, such as that of Andocides, was not narrowly interpreted to cover only them. The legal slate was, in effect, to be wiped clean, with rarest exceptions such as those applying to the members of the Thirty themselves. All sides took mighty oaths, as Andocides reminded the jurors—themselves parties to those oaths—not to violate the amnesty, in fact or in spirit. To date, he further reminded the jury, no person, however powerful or however wronged under the tyrants—even an Anytus himself—had done so. The foremost democrat in the city is mentioned by name. His ostentatious support for the amnesty will be important when we consider his participation in the indictment of Socrates. Anytus evidently became *the* outstanding example of a powerful man who has returned from exile and whose party was securely back in power, but who left his old enemies alone and legally absolved out of respect for the amnesty.

Therefore, triumphantly concluded the unpopular Andocides, under the present rule of written law in Athens and under the terms of the amnesty, he *must* be acquitted from the charges brought by Callias. And he was.

Summary of the Events from 411 B.C. to 399 B.C.

In order to grasp the legal importance of what Nichomachus, in the name of the people of Athens, accomplished, it may prove useful to put his work in summary form, in the context of the turbulent events of the final fifteen years of the fifth century. His activity, as best as it can now be dated (some guesses are necessary), emerges as a crucial one for the entire history of written law in Europe.

- 411: Oligarchic coup in Athens followed by the rule of the Four Hundred.
- 410: Democracy restored. Massive recodification and reinscription on stone of the laws of Athens then in force begins under Nichomachus (term I). Concentration is on secular laws; inscription is in the old Attic lettering.
- 409/8: The *anagrapheis* under Nichomachus are also instructed to reinscribe the Law of Draco on Homicide and set it up in front of the stoa of the King Archon.
- 404: Final defeat of Athens by Sparta in the Peloponnesian War. The city's walls are torn down. Occupation is followed by rule of the Thirty. Athens experiences eight months of a lawless reign of terror. The courts are suspended. Socrates resists complicity in the matter of Leon of Salamis, at threat to his own life. Work of Nichomachus (term I), who was six years into his task, abruptly terminated.
- 403/2: Democracy is restored again. Work of Nichomachus (term II) resumes, lasting (in all) another four years. Concentration (apparently) on religious laws and calendar, but the official decree (itself having the force of law) requires a "scrutiny of *all* laws." Presumably this also includes the work of term I, mainly devoted to secular law, especially in light of the traumatic events under the Thirty, and the new situation created by the amnesty. Inscription is now in the newly adopted Ionic lettering. The archonship of Eucleides is regarded as a legal new beginning. No law—even that of Draco on Homicide—would be valid unless included in the reinscription that occurred from 410 to 403. Presumably all secular law was then reinscribed by Nichomachos and the other *anagrapheis*. Covenants of amnesty, backed by oaths from all parties, end the blood bath. No citizen shall be prosecuted for any offense committed before 403/2. The amnesty is honored even by prominent democrats in power, notably Anytus. Decree passed adopting the Ionian alphabet for all official documents.
- 400/399: Nichomachus's great work (term II) is completed approximately ten years (in all) after he had begun. His reinscribed laws are published in columns on two (or perhaps three) impressive walls that stand like great

pages of stone papyri rising up in grandeur from the floor of the stoa of the King Archon. The front of the walls contains "the Laws of Solon," that is, all of the law now valid in the city, and the back contains the sacrificial calendar. Additional *stēlai* of secular laws, led by the reinscription of Law of Draco on Homicide (it alone survives, badly damaged), have been erected opposite the stoa of the Archon Basileus. A central archive, or hall of records, the city's first, has been established in the Metroon. Athens enters a period of democratic rule by written laws only, the first such endeavor in history.

- 399/98: Indictment and trial of Andocides, which ends in acquittal. Andocides fades from history. Indictment on a *graphē asebeias* (that is, for impiety), trial, conviction, and execution of Socrates. Indictment and trial of Nichomachus, the *anagrapheus*. Lysias the orator, son of Cephalus (of Plato's *Republic,* Book I) composes the speech (Lysias 30) for the antidemocratic and disgruntled *gennetai*. The outcome is uncertain, but acquittal is probable. Nichomachus retires from public life, fading from history.

Until the archaeological discoveries commencing in A.D. 1935, the effect of Lysias' speech, which survived in the literary record after the great stone columns bearing Nichomachus' Laws had crumbled and been lost, had been to diminish Nichomachus' place in history to little more than a name.

Nichomachus' work arrived at the end of a process that was occurring in stages throughout the fifth century, but which was not brought to its logical completion until the very end of that century. Literacy and the law are *fully* allied only after 399 B.C. In earlier decades and centuries, legal rules and customary procedures, partially written and partially oral, were in place and both were used in the Athenian courts. Only after 399 B.C. were "law" in the full legal sense, and enacted written law, made synonymous terms. Such at least was the theory, and observed by all magistrates. *Juries* could feel themselves more independent than magistrates, no doubt, as juries do to this day, but even so, the law was followed as far as we know.

It should be clear that Nichomachus also played an important role, one that has been neglected in the history of Greek literacy. His great work, occupying the closing years of the fifth century, served to mark the final decades of the transition in Athens from restricted legal literacy to full alphabetic dependency in the administration of justice. A further step, the final alliance of literacy and paideia, had not been effected as the fifth century ended, but it would be completed in the fourth. That development, as it unfolded in the dialogues of Plato and the characteristic activity of Aristotle's Lyceum is the subject of a later chapter.

Conclusion: N*omos* and Written Law

At some point in the fifth century, a linguistic innovation took place that passed without notice or fanfare, as is generally the case when the spoken language adapts to reflect a new cultural and intellectual situation. A new word was not invented to denominate a new idea. Rather, an old word was given an added burden to carry and stretched to accommodate a new but related usage. The word in question is *nomos* itself, "law." In its new usage, *nomos* designated not only established social custom or ancestral precedent, as it long had, but also written law. This clue alone should be sufficient to convince us that it was in the fifth century that dependence on written law rose significantly in Greece.

Martin Ostwald, who has called valuable attention to the changes in the usage of *nomos* and the earlier *thesmos,* associates this linguistic development with the reforms of Cleisthenes.[36] Whereas that is not provable given the state of documentation when Cleisthenes lived, it is highly probable. The dramatists at any rate, especially Euripides, provide ample evidence that the change was absorbed into the popular vocabulary and consciousness by the end of the fifth century. As early as 450 B.C. or so, the expression *nomon tithenai*, meaning "to enact a law" or a statute, has become sufficiently common for use on the dramatic stage. In the *Prometheus* (*PV* 150) of Aeschylus, the Oceanids complain that "Zeus wields power with new laws *(nomois)* without proper enactment *(athetos).*"

Ostwald observes that a statute differs from the norms for conduct that preceded it first and foremost because it has a precise beginning in time. This is a point of great importance. There is a moment, a fixed point on a calendar, at which the recognized machinery of the state—in Athens and most other Greek cities an assembly—legislates the new *nomoi,* fully binding laws, into existence. After 399 B.C. in Athens, as we have seen, the *nomoi* that can bind in the courts were, without exception, duly enacted, written laws.

Enactment and written law were intimately connected in Greece. As ideas and legal experiments, they developed together. A problem lurks here, however, for moralists and philosophers. It was of the very nature of ancient oral *nomoi* (Hesiod's word was standard by the fourth century) to be immutable and so timeless. For the traditional Athenian, the ancestral *nomoi* never came into existence; they were always there and always would be. What was now raised, at least potentially, was the distinct difficulty that not all *nomoi* would be timeless and immutable. Even so, the new, enacted *nomoi* were intended to have the same binding force as the older, timeless *nomoi* of the community.

The point, of course, is that what men can make can be unmade; where laws are concerned, what once seemed immutable could become very mutable indeed. It was the spirit in the air in the late fifth century. It pervades the early dialogues of Plato. Very competent historians of philosophy have suggested that, as a threat to contemporary morality, it lies behind Plato's adherence, through dialectical thick and thin, to his Forms as timeless, changeless, impassible, and perfect—the ever secure metaphysical *nomoi* (as it were) that are beyond the power of men or even gods to alter or cancel.

There is a lesson about writing and advancing literacy here. To modern literates, writing can be viewed, when they think about it at all, merely as a handy tool, as dispensable as old newspapers flapping in the breeze. Alphabetic literacy makes no *cognitive* difference to our cultural development or to our important social institutions. Law and ethics, metaphysics and logic, *could* all have developed essentially unchanged without it, if less conveniently. Great convenience though alphabetic writing is, the very different written and mnemonic means of preserving cultural information are regarded as cognitively neutral, making no essential difference in the material they preserve, rather in the way different envelopes do not alter the contents of a letter. We would be the same persons, thinking the same thoughts, living not significantly different lives, if we still relied totally on oral and musical methods of preserving the important information our species has accumulated. The essential workings of the human mind remain unchanged, according to this view, by the means used to record and preserve its lofty thoughts.

That assumption deserves to be questioned. The accumulating evidence reviewed thus far points to the opposite conclusion, at least when the material to be preserved puts significant burdens on human memory, and writing had made little or no inroad. It is to the completed alliance of literacy and enculturation, or what Plato and his contemporaries appropriately termed *paideia,* we turn next. Again the change from oral to literate habits results in some significant cognitive and cultural differences. The focus of investigation remains on Athens.

Notes

1. Ambiguity in the Greek meanings of the term are resolved in context, often with an eye to the source. Fundamentally, *dēmos* referred to *hoi Athēnaioi,* "the Athenians," the whole body of the Athenian people. A more restricted sense could refer to their political assembly, the Ekklesia. A social sense, slightly pejorative, could refer to the lower classes, the common folk, and is found in sources not enamored of the democracy, notably some philosophers. The former sense (the "whole of the people") tends to be found in democratic sources, including the official inscriptions.

2. Most historians of Greek literacy recognize that the fifth century saw a significant advance in the use of letters at Athens but debate whether this was realized early in the century or late. The literature has grown so contentious that a new approach may be required, which the present work attempts. A reasonably full bibliography of standard sources could be compiled from the references in W. Harris, *Ancient Literacy* (Cambridge, Mass.,1989), which are conveniently divided into three sections. See the masterly review of Bernard Knox, "Books and Readers in the Greek World," the lead article in vol. 1 of the hardback edition (only) of *The Cambridge History of Classical Literature,* vol. I, part 1 (Cambridge, 1985). Alfred Burns reviewed the older literature of the "when dawned popular literacy (so called) in the fifth century?" debate in "Athenian Literacy in the Fifth Century B.C.," *JHI* 42 (1981), pp. 371–387. Burns's own review and his conclusions provide a good example of how the same pieces of evidence have been chewed on repeatedly by investigators, with very different conclusions being drawn from them. Two pioneering works that focused on the evidence for the fifth and early fourth centuries as the crucial period—previous centuries recognized as representing a decidedly less developed state of Athenian literacy—were F. H. Harvey, "Literacy in the Athenian Democracy," *REG* 79 (1966); and E. G. Turner, "Athenian Books in the Fifth and Fourth Centuries B.C." (London, 1952). Additional works, published a year apart and written independently of each other, were J. A. Davison, "Literature and Literacy in Ancient Greece," *Phoenix* 16 (1962), pp. 147–151; and E. A. Havelock, *Preface to Plato* (Cambridge, Mass., 1963). All historians of Greek literacy are in debt to them. For the often neglected—because

thought to be intractable—question of female literacy, see S. G. Cole, "Could Greek Women Read and Write?" in H. Foley (ed.), *Reflections of Women in Antiquity* (New York, 1981), pp. 219–245. The question of literacy among slaves deserves scholarly attention.

3. The *Corpus Aristotelicum,* as finally determined by the great editor Andonicus of Rhodes and then transmitted to us in the medieval and Renaissance manuscripts, does not contain a collection of constitutions. However, references to the collection from antiquity confirm that Aristotle commissioned such a task for the Lyceum. In 1881, T. Bergk suggested that an *Athēnaiōn Politeia* appeared to be inscribed on the back of some recently recovered fragment remains of financial accounts dated to the first century A.D. But a long quotation from Solon also found in the remains dissuaded him from pursuing his own happy guess. F. G. Kenyon took up the suggestion and in 1891 published the first edition of the text of Aristotle's *Athēnaiōn Politeia,* setting off a controversy that has not yet been resolved. Was the work by the philosopher himself or the commissioned work of an advanced student of the Lyceum? The latter seems to me probable, for the argument is often not up to Aristotelian standards, but this is a subjective conclusion. For the purpose of using the work as evidence of what the late fourth century did or did not know about earlier centuries, it does not matter much. The work must be used by historians. Internal references confirm that the work was composed a decade or so preceding 322 B.C. See F. G. Kenyon (ed.), *Aristotelis Atheniensium Respublica* (Oxford, 1920). The most useful commentary is P. J. Rhodes, *A Commentary on the Aristotelian Athenian Constitution* (Oxford, 1981). A convenient translation, with introduction and notes, is the Penguin edition by P. J. Rhodes, *Aristotle: The Athenian Constitution* (New York, 1984).

4. Plutarch's account of Solon in the *Lives* (Solon 12) conforms to the version found in the *Athēnaiōn Politeia,* suggesting he had access either to it or to a common source. Other sources are given in R. Stroud, *Drakon's Law on Homicide* (Berkeley and Los Angeles, 1968), p. 70, n. 25. See also M. Gagarin, *Drakon and the Early Athenian Homicide Law* (New Haven and London, 1981), who doubts a direct connection between the conspiracy and the law on homicide (p. 21). It should be noted that Herodotus, in his few references to Solon, treats him as a "sage, lawgiver and poet rather than as a constitutional reformer." See P. J. Rhodes, *Aristotle: The Athenian Constitution,* p. 42. Solon is not mentioned by Thucydides.

5. The text of the law begins abruptly with *kai ean,* which Ronald Stroud argued must mean "even if" and not "and." But difficulties did not end there. How can a code, presumed to be logically organized and comprehensive—and therein may lie the problem—commence so abruptly with a discussion of procedural matters concerning what to do in a case of unintentional homicide? Surely a discussion of deliberate homicide preceded this enactment. There is no space for it, however, in that "First Axon" follows immediately after the usual preliminary information. One solution—possibly correct—was proposed by Stroud. While cleaning the stone, which had gone oddly neglected and which is now in the Epigraphical Museum, Stroud recovered, with the aid of precise measurement, a new reading at line 56, a heading about which there is no doubt: "[Sec]ond [Axon]." That requires that the term "First Axon" does not refer to a separate text on voluntary homicide, as some had thought. Traces of four additional lines are also visible before the stele is broken off, supporting the view that there were two *axones* (at least). Because the decree read in part, "[L]et the recorders of the laws pub[l]ish on a marble block th[e] law of Drakon concerning homi[ci]de, after receiving it from the B[a]s[i]le[us" the law of Drakon must have been preserved on more than one *axon.* Stroud concluded that the law on intentional homicide must, however improbably, have followed in the now missing section of the marble stele. But this, in turn, means that the law on intentional homicide was tacked on

after provisions for unintentional homicide (in considerable procedural detail), self-defense, lawful homicide, as well as other provisions of unknown number, all now missing. To some this seemed unlikely. See the objections in M. Gagarin in *Drakon,* pp. 73ff. Gagarin's solution can also be found in this work. A good discussion of the procedural provisions specified on the stele (possibility of pardon, vote of kinship categories, protections for the killer in exile, etc.) is found in D. M. MacDowell, *Athenian Homicide Law in the Age of the Orators* (Manchester, 1963), pp. 117ff. Could it be that the provisions for deliberate homicide, as at Gortyn, were not initially made a matter of written law at all, being sufficiently well known in the oral community that they did not require reformulation as casuistic law and inscription? It would follow that the rise of written law at Athens was gradual, as it was at Gortyn. Did the first stages involve inscription of a series of mainly procedural enactments—possibly quite detailed, being novel—but not a large-scale code of law? This means that the community addressed legal issues as problems about handling them arose under the older pattern of oral usages, basically a response to experience in the courts. The less controversial provisions—but these might involve the most serious offenses, such as impiety or deliberate homicide—were, therefore, not the first to be made matters of written law. As a consequence, I prefer to designate what we have on the stele as part of a "legal text" of unknown total length rather than a part of a comprehensive "code," a designation that creates expectations that go beyond the reliable evidence for Draco. Future finds may, of course, prove me wrong. Stroud (in conversation) has expressed his reservations, which is daunting. But what I doubt, from a somewhat a priori perspective, is that the Athenians at the inception of their legal literacy had any concept of a large scale or complete written legal code, any more than at the inception of literacy Greeks had any concept of a monumental text or a motive to produce one.

6. Karl Beloch (*Griechische Geschichte,* I.[2] I., p. 350) had long ago argued that Draco means "snake" and so likely was in origin the snake god whom the Athenians worshiped as Cecrops. However, it was quickly pointed out that Draco was also used as a man's name, instanced eight times, although all later than the fourth century; see Pauly-Wissowa, *s.v.* Drakon. R. Sealey has revived the sacred serpent theory in *A History of the Greek City States 700-333 B.C.* (Berkeley and Los Angeles, 1976), p. 104. It seems, however, that Draco is not really in the same dubious class as the mythical Minos (who consulted for ten years with Zeus himself, according to Plato's *Laws,* before divulging laws for Cretans) and other fantastic early lawgivers known only from the literary sources. It is sometimes overlooked that Plato's *Laws* (708 Cff.) is probably the original source of the very plausible suggestion that resort to written laws was hastened in the colonies by the fact that their populations drew on more than one mother city (as did, later, Thurii), and so local or transported oral tradition was weak. The tradition concerning the early lawgiver Charondas, to the effect that he not only made laws for Catana but also Cos and the Chacidian colonies to the west, may be based on the knowledge that the colonies, as a group, availed themselves early of written laws. The Greek demand for a *euretēs* and first founder for all things notable—manufacturing names where none existed—took over from there. Ancient cities such as Athens, Gortyn, or Sparta, with deep and well-established oral traditions, may have needed complete codes in their first years of experiment with written law far less than that did new colonies. Finally, some of the wording on the so-called Great Rhetra (= "Pronouncement") ascribed to Lycurgus of Sparta in Plutarch strikes any oralist (or student of Heraclitus) as prose originally designed for memorization and declamation: "having built . . . and having tribed the tribes and obed the obes," and so on. Gagarin's sense of the sound of parts of the preserved *rhetra* (however otherwise mangled in transmission, as he notes) is excellent: "clearly preserves the mnemonic element of rhythmic repetition of sounds." See *Early Greek Law,* p. 53. The case is less strong, perhaps, for the

chiasmus detected in Draco's homicide law; see the discussion of Gagarin in *Drakon,* pp. 155–157. Gagarin has stood almost alone in tuning his ear to the style of the prose. Chiasmus, insofar as it exploits echo, anticipation, and association, is an ancient mnemonic device. Its inspiration need not be "artistic embellishment" or to display structure more clearly to the eye; both assessments make literate assumptions. Was the wording of law so in need of either that it led to a convoluted arrangement of subject and verb patterned SVVS or VSSV? The need that a largely illiterate populace remember the laws is something else. For chiasmus in various sayings of the philosopher Heraclitus, see Robb, "Preliterate Ages and the Linguistic Art of Heraclitus," in Robb (ed.), *Language and Thought,* pp. 188 (B2), 190 (B5), 192 (B10), 196 (B15). Heraclitus wanted his sayings, once heard, to stick in the memories of his fellow citizens in protoliterate Ephesus ca. 500 B.C. Could the same have been true for Draco and his laws among the the protoliterate Athenians ca. 600 B.C.? A few citizens could read, but most would only hear his laws as read aloud.

7. As P. J. Rhodes observes, this must be a late-fifth or more likely, a fourth-century fabrication. See Rhodes, *Aristotle: The Athenian Constitution,* p. 42. A very early voice—raised in the year *Ath. Pol.* was first published by Kenyon—to question chapter 4 and conclude it was an insertion was that of J. W. Headlam in *CR* 5 (1891), pp. 166ff.

8. The most catholic list, with virtually no principle of exclusion (even Latin sources are canvased), is the useful compilation in E. Ruschenbusch, *Solonos Nomoi: Die Fragmente* (Weisbaden, 1986). The title can be misleading. It is improbable that any *nomos* attributed to Solon (let alone all 155 entries in *Solonos Nomoi,* of which only six purport to be earlier than the fourth century) is a "fragment" in the strict sense of the "B" section of Diels-Kranz collection of the Presocratic fragments. In no attribution of a "law" to Solon do we have reliably preserved *ipsissima verba.* In contrast, not even Solon altered the wording of Draco's Law on Homicide (so it is reported, and style confirms), nor did any redactor after him. Thus *Ath. Pol.* 7. 1: "the Athenians ceased to use the ordinances of Draco apart from those concerning homicide." No other Greek law was so treated by later generations. In urging a good dose of skepticism in regard to all attributions to Solon, I am, of course, echoing Adcock, Hignett (*History of the Athenian Constitution* [Oxford, 1952]), and many others. My reservations are in the context of the generally unhistorical (in a modern sense of doing "history") approach to the past on the part of virtually all authors in antiquity, Hebrew as well as Greek.

9. *Prot.* 325 E; 326 C–E; also *Charmides* 159 C. The relevant texts from *Rep.* and *Laws* are discussed in a later chapter.

10. Adcock, *CAH*[1] vol. II, p. 42.

11. *Ath. Pol.* 2.3.

12. Ibid., 9.1.

13. Gagarin writes in *Early Greek Law,* p. 127, that "the Cretan cities do not seem to have followed the pattern of single, large-scale legislation common in the rest of Greece." This is repeated in nearly the same words on p. 138. Then, on p. 139: "the Cretan citizen preferred continual small-scale enactments to the large scale legislation of most other Greek cities. . . . " Gagarin may, of course, be right here. But Gagarin himself has admirably emphasized the heavily *procedural* nature of the early Greek written law (*Early Greek Law,* pp. 12ff. 72ff., and *passim.* He observes rightly of Gortyn, the only complete written code to survive, that "most of the fifth-century Great Code (IC 4.72) concerns family law. . . . " See *Early Greek Law,* p. 139, n. 54. The implication I would draw would be that many nonprocedural matters of legal importance, because not immediately troublesome, were not immediately made matters of written law. Gagarin is, of course, also aware of the estimate of some historians that perhaps as few as 10 percent of the many Greek cities, especially the smaller ones, had *any* experience of written law before the Hellenistic period.

14. If the late Greek literary sources are set aside as an unreliable guide, as they deserve to be, then inscriptions alone remain as evidence. What pattern, if any, is to be found there? Based on the pieces that have survived, in subject matter the earliest written laws seem to concern such matters as the terms of office of magistrates (Dreros) or some of their duties and the penalties for taking bribes (Chios), along with some obscure details of what *may* be a democratic constitution (also Chios), rituals associated with stealing temple utensils (Korope), how soon after a verdict (three days) fines are to be paid in good money (Eretria), or revising certain cult duties (recently found at Tiryns). Or, as at Athens under Draco's provisions, they establish what to do about "killing the killer" even if he is an unintentional killer—including certain procedural matters relating to exiling him or, if compensation is accepted, establishing the relatives (through cousins) who shall have a say in the matter of accepting the blood-price (and also specifying that the decision must be unanimous).

That list, reflecting the practice of seven widely dispersed cities, covers with no important exceptions the sort of inscriptional evidence presently available for determining the subject matter or general tenor of written laws so far found anywhere in Hellas that are earlier than ca. 525 B.C. (Gortyn being perhaps 50 years or so later). The Locrian colony at Naupactus may just barely fall under the chronological line, in which case we can add regulations and penalties concerning the inheritance of rural pasturage and prohibitions against a citizen's alienating himself from the land, unless he claims the gravest emergency for himself and his family. A few other cities afford early scraps of enactments concerning this or that, but nothing that, per se, is even remotely evidence for a missing large-scale or comprehensive code. For example, but not chosen at random, a law from about 460 B.C. from Halicarnassus, the birthplace of Herodotus, requires that jurors take an oath affirming that "what the *mnēmones* (rememberers) *know* [they are *not,* therefore, here mere recorders of written documents] shall be binding." (SIG^2 45; in Meiggs and Lewis, No. 32.) That seems to suggest a kind of balancing act between an older, oral set of customs and regulations (and oral memory of property transfers) and some experience with writing and written law. If so, then it was a "transition code" rather like that of Gortyn, putting some matters of law into writing and leaving other matters of a legal nature to oral custom. Finally, Sparta must be passed over in silence, for obvious reasons. So too must be any empty speculation about comprehensive law codes on perishable materials. That raises the list to nine Greek cities, large and small, from which we have evidence of some written laws before 525 B.C., plus a few from which the evidence may be a bit later. None could be used as a solid foundation of a theory of a comprehensive code. If, indeed, it was in the colonial west that written law gained initial momentum, perhaps on the inspiration of what had long been known on Crete, then the colonial codes may well have been more comprehensive than the early enactments of the mother cities. The laws for Athenian Thurii, reportedly drawn up by the sophist Protagoras, if they had survived, might have been an outstanding example.

15. For assessment of the literary sources for early law writers, debunking in tone but not unfair to what survives in them, see two articles: F. E. Adcock, "Early Greek Code-Makers," *Cambridge Historical Journal* 2 (1927), pp. 95–109; and A. Szegedy-Maszak, "Legends of the Greek Law-Givers," *GRBS* 19 (1978), pp. 199–209. For a polished attempt to salvage as much from the literary sources as credulity will bear, see Gagarin's chapter "Early Written Laws: The Literary Evidence," in *Early Greek Law,* pp. 51–80. Based on the literary sources, what Greek city can be adduced as the basis of the pattern of a sudden, discontinuous leap from no written law to a comprehensive, complete, or at least large-scale, logically organized written code of laws? Setting aside Athens, the favorite candidate at present is Italian Locri, in large measure because Aristotle nominated Za-

leucus of Locri as the first Greek lawgiver, as did Ephorus (also fourth century). But then Aristotle adds that Zaleucus was a shepherd who received his laws from Athena in a dream (Frag. 548 Rose, based on Schol. ad Pind. *Ol.* 11.17). That does not make for much initial confidence, although it is one of the more believable tales in the literary sources. One can wonder with Harris: "It would be interesting to know when widespread legends about law-*writing* activities of the early lawgivers—not only Solon but also Zaleucus of Locri, Charondas of Catana and the others—really began to flourish" (*Ancient Literacy*, p. 75, emphasis mine). Could it have been in the fourth century, when our evidence begins? Gagarin's initial disclaimer, before putting more confidence in the literary sources than I think is warranted, is honest: "The literary evidence concerning the early law-givers is, regrettably, late, relatively meager, sometimes inconsistent, and selective. With few exceptions we have no evidence earlier than the mid-fourth century, two centuries or more after the fact. Many of the earliest lawgivers are scarcely more than names. Where we know more, there are sometimes widely divergent accounts . . . especially in the cases of Zaleucus and Charondas of Catana" (p. 52). All of this is true enough. Yet when Gagarin turns to actual laws (the wording of which he concedes, of course, did not survive), he expresses confidence in establishing their "general tenor," a judgment based on the late literary sources. I find this problematical because Gagarin has himself stated the best case for drawing the opposite conclusion: "Our evidence is fullest for Solon, Zaleucus [the ex-slave and shepherd who got his *nomoi* from Athena in a dream and was freed as a result] and Charondas [of Catana: his *nomoi* were reputedly sung at Athenian, or perhaps Catanian, drinking parties; their content must now be imagined], though some of it, especially in the case of the latter two, is unreliable" *Early Greek Law*, p. 62). If these three afford us our fullest and best evidence, and Solon is the best of the lot, need we bother to turn to figures for whom the evidence is even more meager and less reliable? Probably all students of Greek law would agree that the best case could be made for Solon. I would state it more strongly. The *only* case can be made for Solon, and it is far from being airtight.

16. Solon 24.D. The best text of the fragments, which also offers a brief context from the source, is that of Martin West in *Iambi et elegi Graeci ante Alexandrum cantati 2* (Oxford, 1972).

17. E. Havelock in *The Greek Concept of Justice*, p. 252. My discussion owes debts to this work.

18. Knox reminds his readers that the language of Solon's poems is not Attic but the modified Ionic of the epic tradition. It is thus "less closely tied to the Homeric diction than some of his [seventh-century, non-Attic] predecessors." *The Cambridge History of Classical Literature*, vol. I, part 1 (Cambridge, 1989), p. 110. Only 219 elegiacs, plus some 70 lines divided between iambic trimeter and trochaic tetrameter, now survive from Solon. This does not suggest extensive documentation (even for the literary expressions of the city's great lawgiver) for his time or the period immediately following it. Knox (p. 105) also perceptively observes that Solon is the only Athenian historical figure *before the fifth century* "for whom oral tradition and written documents had preserved material enough for a biography."

19. Knox in the *Cambridge History of Classical Literature*, p. 106.

20. Gagarin in *Drakon*, p. 110, n. 16, emphasis mine. Also now see the useful treatment by R. Stroud, "State Documents in Archaic Athens," in W.P.A. Childs (ed.), *Athens Comes of Age: From Solon to Salamis* (Princeton, 1978), pp. 20–42; also A. L. Boegehold, "The Establishment of a Central Archive at Athens," *AJA* 76 (1972), pp. 23–30. On the general question of archives in antiquity and an instructive comparison with the relatively advanced archival activity in some Near Eastern cultures (Mari, Ugarit, at Bogazkeui, the Hittite capital, and now Ebla, etc.), see E. Posner, *Archives in the Ancient World* (Cambridge, Mass., 1972).

21. Felix Jacoby, *Atthis: The Local Chronicles of Ancient Athens* (Oxford, 1949), p. 215.

22. Ibid., p. 217.

23. Josiah Ober's description is welcome for its caution: "The Athenian people were given the opportunity each year to decide whether or not to hold an ostracism; if a quorum of 6,000 voted to hold one, the Assembly would foregather, and each citizen would scratch on a potsherd—*or have a literate fellow citizen scratch for him*—the name of the man he most wanted to see expelled from the city" (*Mass and Elite in Democratic Athens* [Princeton, 1989], pp. 73–74, emphasis mine). Handwriting analysis of a recently recovered cache of *ostraka* from a single well in the agora have revealed that just this practice of one person producing many *ostraka* was, indeed, the case, and on a large scale. The argument from ostracism to popular literacy is at an impasse; no conclusion can be drawn either way. That, in fact, should have been realized from the start. The ability to scratch a name, perhaps copying an original that is passed around, has never been proof of "literacy" in any degree save, perhaps, the most minimal. Can we deduce that such a person could, for example, read an unpunctuated manuscript of a play of Aeschylus?

24. In less than a decade (the 1980s) publications on Athenian demes and *trittys* have taken on the appearance of a thriving cottage industry, with the most interesting contributions attempting to balance the evolving epigraphical evidence with the older view of city-coast-plain tiering suggested in *Ath. Pol.* 21.4. There the purpose, at least, of Cleisthenes is stated with no ambiguity: "mixing up" (repeated twice) the people so that the *dēmos*, or common people, who supported him against the attempted tyranny of Isagoras, a fact that resulted in his recall from exile, would in the future have greater power. My concern here is with the end result of what Cleisthenes accomplished and its relevance to developing fifth-century literacy, not with the controversial details of how he brought it off. Thus in my text I strive to avoid the involutions of the debate, while also implying some credence for the text of *Ath. Pol.* The basics were (1) The demes, of which 139 were created, were the basis of power; and (2) the demes were grouped in thirds, one third from each region, to form the tribes. Siewert has mustered the evidence for believing the thirds were about equal in size, and each was *based* on one region, but could also include demes from other regions. Herein was the ability to "gerrymander," and it worked out, of course, to the considerable advantage of Cleisthenes politically. Those interested may consult further P. Siewert, *Die Trittyen Attikas und die Herresreform des Kleisthenes* (Munich, 1982); R. Osborne, *Demos: The Discovery of Classical Attika* (Cambridge, 1985); D. Whitehead, *The Demes of Attica 508/7–*ca. *250* B.C. (Princeton, 1986); and J. Traill, *Demos and Trittys: Epigraphical and Topographical Studies in the Organization of Attica* (Toronto, 1986). An earlier, important work of Traill also developed the epigraphical evidence and was widely discussed by epigraphical experts. See J. S. Traill, *The Political Organization of Attica* (Princeton, 1975). Only David Whitehead, as far as I know, has put much emphasis on the ways these changes might in at least some ways relate to literacy (*Demes of Attica,* pp. 139ff.), on literate demarchs.

25. In Rhodes, *Constitution of Athens,* p. 130.

26. Thuc. 1.44.1

27. *Prot.* 319 B–C; Thuc. 2.40.2.

28. Mogens Hansen in a favorable review of R. K. Sinclair, *Democracy and Participation in Athens,* in *Classical Review* 39, n. s. (1989), p. 72.

29. Lysias 30.

30. Sterling Dow, "The Athenian Calendar of Sacrifices: The Chronology of Nikomakhos' Second Term," *Historia* 9 (1960), p. 292 (emphasis mine). The ever-perceptive F. E. Adcock wrote as early as 1927 ("Literary Tradition and Early Greek Code-Makers," [*Cambridge Historical Journal* 2, p. 100]: "Had fate been kinder, Nichomachus, Lysias' *bēte-noire,* might have been a household name. . . . "

31. Lysias 30. 1. The language of the taunt deserves attention. The force of *anagraphein,* with the prefix *ana-*, strongly emphasizes (as stressed by Sandys, Stroud, Gagarin, Havelock, *et al.*) the activity of, specifically, inscription as a form of recording for public view. Further, in Attic Greek, *nomothetēs* could carry, as a secondary meaning, "one who is commissioned to *revise* laws." The thrust of Lysias' accusation is that the commission of Nichomachus was twisted by him to his own ends, personal or political. As *anagrapheus,* he was commissioned to be a *hypogrammateus* (30. 27), or so Lysias claims, but instead he made himself into something he was never commissioned to be, a *nomothetēs*—in the secondary, Attic sense of the word, as a minimum. This is a complex, but very specific and very dangerous accusation. The evidence of the vulgate text (not emended, as by some editors) of Euripides *Frogs* 1084 may be used to confirm that *hupo-grammateōn* can carry the sense of "under-writer"; that is, he is one who explains a written text if necessary, or rewords and amalgamates, but does not elaborate with gratuitous invention. This reconstruction gains support from the decree that gave Nichomachus the charge for his second term. It appears to have been friendly, conferring broad powers beyond merely writing up in one place what already existed, but with checks and balances on the results in terms of a panel for review and approval. The wording of the important Decree of Teisamenos is substantially reproduced in Andocides I (*de Myst.*) 82–7.

32. The most useful text with notes is that of Douglas MacDowell, *Andokides: On the Mysteries* (Oxford, 1962). A useful translation, which I have consulted, is that of K. Maidment in the Loeb series, *Minor Attic Orators,* vol. 1.

33. MacDowell, *Andokides,* p. 122. I risk the speculation that Nichomachus himself had his subordinate introduce the decree to keep the great work going, and that the wording about *ta patria* and Solon and the rest was to assure the democrats in power that he was their man, and "safe."

34. MacDowell (*Andokides,* p. 120), in observing that, apart from Draco's laws, the rest of the Athenian code was by convention attributed to Solon, notes that the law quoted by Andocides at 96–98 as Solonian "is shown by its preamble to have been proposed by Demophantos in 410." For another example, see MacDowell's note on Andocides I. 74. For a conservative treatment of the decree of Teisamenos, with further bibliography, see MacDowell's Appendix H, pp. 194–199.

35. This is more restrictive than it may seem. Granted, Athenian juries, like all juries, could have minds of their own, and we must also grant that Athenian heliastic courts were notably independent. Also, I have no doubt that an Athenian jury could be swayed by an appeal to a hallowed *agraphos nomos.* For all we know, some eloquent latter-day legal Antigone might have appealed on this basis to an Athenian jury and won hands down. All this is granted. But a legal case in 399 B.C., let us say an *asebeia* indictment, in order to be referred to a heliastic court, first had to get past a magistrate. After this decree any indictment that was not based on a written enactment would be stopped cold. An Athenian magistrate under oaths, which were formidable, had no choice, whatever his private opinion may have been. I also do not deny that some Nichomachian laws may have been broadly or ambiguously stated in their final written form, and that it was left to juries to decide just which actions fell under them. The Nichomachian *asebeia* (impiety) statute, under which Socrates had to have been tried in 399 B.C., but whose exact wording has not survived even in the orators, may well have been the outstanding example. Possibly the precise wording of this offense challenged the great *anagrapheus* most and, potentially, as he must have known, could have created for him his greatest political difficulties.

36. Martin Ostwald, *From Popular Sovereignty to the Sovereignty of Law* (Berkeley and Los Angeles, 1986), p. 88.

III

The Alliance between Literacy and Paideia

6

The Epical Basis of Greek Paideia in the Late Fifth Century: *Ion* and *Euthyphro*

Early chapters reviewed the evidence, inscriptional and literary, indicating that Hellenes at all levels of society had heard Homer's language and had absorbed it. As soon as the Greeks emerge from the Dark Ages and begin to make use of an alphabet, what they leave behind on enduring artifacts for us to read proves that they, in the words of Paul Friedländer, "not only understood Homer's language, but *possessed* it."[1] A great epigraphist's assessment of the cultural lesson to be drawn from the inscriptional record will remain an accurate one through the fifth century, although there is some diminishing in metrical virtuosity detectable as literacy advances.

What this meant, in effect, was that ordinary citizens—from all classes, for the epigraphic record is by no means an aristocratic chronicle—assimilated a kind of second language, closely related to their several native dialects (notably Ionic) to be sure, but also distinct from any of them. It was never the spoken dialect of any historical place, but rather an artificial amalgam of dialects forged over centuries by professional singers to perpetuate the national epic. Yet the people listened to it, relished it, assimilated it, and made it their own. That was the lesson of the popular inscriptions from 700 to 500 B.C., confirmed by an ever growing body of written literature from Hesiod and Archilochus, through the early poets and the first prose writers, notably the philosophers when read in their own words. Herodotus' debts to epic have also recently become the object of much scholarly attention, but their full scope cannot be investigated here. Rather, in this chapter we shall discover that the control of Homer over Greek paideia is still firmly in place in the society disclosed to us in Plato's early dialogues. He is not a friendly reporter, making his evidence all the stronger.

An older generation of scholars, led by figures such as Bruno Snell, Kurt von Fritz, Lionel Pearson, Eric Dodds, Werner Jaeger, and John Burnet, demonstrated in a series of brilliant studies that there is a continuity of vocabulary and concepts from Homer through the fifth-century dramatists in conceptualizing two important areas of human experience. In conceptualizing the interior mental life through a psychological vocabulary and in exhorting or praising correct behavior through an ethical vocabulary, there is no fundamental break from "Homer," or epical vocabulary and concepts, until we reach the fourth century, and above all Plato. A few pioneering intellectuals would experiment with this or that term (one thinks especially of Heraclitus on *psychē*, to which Snell called attention), but the hold of Homeric speech and concepts over the popular mind of Greece, as reflected in the literature addressed to it, remained firmly in place well into the fifth century. To be sure, *phrēn-phrenes* go into some decline relative to the other "soul" words, but they are still prominent in tragedy. *Aidōs* loses some ground to the *dik*-words, possibly because of their importance to the law and the courts, but Plato can still employ *aidōs* in its Homeric sense. *Dikaiosunē*, the abstract noun for "justice," is introduced (first in Herodotus) but, before Plato's *Republic*, is rare and has no real prominence in ethical discussions. *Dikaios*, "just" or "right," remains a strong adjective of moral commendation but increasingly is found in a legal as well as a moral or social context. But nothing fundamental is different; the changes have been, intellectually, minor ones. The picture, overall, remains one of continuity with an epical word view.

Intriguing as it has proved since Parry for Hellenists to explore how "Homer," or the great body of Greek epical verse, was composed and transmitted across preliterate generations, it may have been of greater historical importance to ask *why* and to press the issue of motive. It was a stupendous undertaking, one that no power on earth could force on any people. They must themselves embrace it willingly. Some closely related questions are, Why was "Homer" continually performed, extensively memorized, and endlessly quoted, in every century down to Plato's own? Why and how did epic retain its hold over the mind and imagination of Greece? Literacy, after all, makes major strides in this period. Written law is introduced and by the turn of the fourth century has significantly expanded its control over human behavior. By the turn of the fourth century, the alliance between literacy and law is near completion in Athens, as we have seen. But the authority of epic, especially Homer, does not fade away. On this point the testimony of Plato is unassailable.

Historians have observed that, by reason of what is found in such detail in the pages of Plato's dialogues, we know more about daily life—people's thoughts, activities, concerns, conversations, even their humor—for his century, the fourth, than for any other in antiquity, whether in Greece or elsewhere. That is true. No comparable secular portrait comes to us from any other century or culture, nor would one have been possible without a developed alphabetic literacy. Plato's evidence is second to none. In comparison to what he tell us of Hellenic life in the late fifth century and at the turn of the fourth, any earlier century is for us a veritable Dark Age.

Plato's dialogues are set in the second half of the fifth century, and normally late in it, for "Socrates" must be their hero. But they were written in the first half of the fourth century, and the issues that they address and argue are still those of Plato's own day, a point often made by Werner Jaeger, Robert Brumbaugh, Eric Havelock, and many others. Once again we confront the dominating presence of epic, or "Homer." In the late fifth century, as Plato's dialogues incontestably prove, the authority of epic had not yet been displaced or even significantly diminished, a situation that the greatest of Greek prose writers and a philosopher of surpassing genius was about to challenge. "Homer" had met a worthy adversary at long last. In this chapter we examine aspects of his struggle with the "orthodoxy'' of his day as revealed in two dialogues usually considered ''early,'' *Ion* and *Euthyphro*.

A Stubborn Rhapsode from Ephesus

If the question of motive behind the continued popular absorption of epic had been put to a reflective Greek at the turn of the fourth century, the answer doubtless would have been that of Plato himself. The poets in general, and Homer in particular, quite simply had ''*educated* Hellas.''[2] Moreover, the epical figures, but especially Homer, continue to do so, in the persons of their many contemporary reciters. Even those few Greeks, led by Xenophanes and Heraclitus and dominantly philosophers, who had faulted some of the content of epic verse never questioned its role as the Hellenic paideia. Indeed, they constantly affirm it, often making that fact the object of their polemic, sometimes in evident disgust. ''Homer deserves to be thrown out of the contests, and drubbed with his own *rabdos!*'' is Heraclitus' clever assault on contemporary singers who performed while holding proudly forward the official rhapsode's staff (B42). The play on verb and noun are untranslatable, but if we had the verb ''to crozier'' we could say that a bishop should be croizered with his own crozier and thrown out of his diocese.

By describing the activity of long-dead ''Homer'' and other epical figures in the present tense (a Greek commonplace), Heraclitus revealed what we encounter at every turn. The Hellenic paideia was communicated to successive generations of hearers by singers and reciters, or what Xenophanes himself had termed ''the family *(genos)* of Hellenic singers [or song],''[3] orally and traditionally. Some historians can assume if they wish that after 700 B.C. the influential Greek poets were read and came to be popularly known in this way. Greeks themselves always assume that they will be heard, and that what is heard will be instructive as well as pleasurable. E. E. Sikes, in a valuable book devoted to how the Greeks themselves viewed poetry, asserted in his opening paragraph that

> the poet (whatever else he might be) was certainly a teacher. Indeed, the history of Greek criticism is largely occupied, not so much with a denial of [the poetic] art to teach, as with the relation between this teaching and the claim of pleasure to be its immediate end.[4]

Even so, one still finds pockets of tenacious resistance in modern scholarly literature to a serious paideutic role for Homer, or poetry, so alien is it to the literate experience of recent centuries. But the overwhelming evidence in favor of it, to which we now add the voice of Plato, cannot easily be discounted. The pleasure to which Sikes refers, and which is so often the object of Plato's scorn even as he confesses his own susceptibility came, of course, from hearing Homer, not from reading him.

The earliest work by a Greek author who seriously stood outside contemporary experience to examine and reflect on the relationship between the didactic content of the poetic material, or its role as the core of the Hellenic paideia, and the pleasure that its performance gives Greek listeners, is by Plato, in his early short dialogue *Ion*. The dialogue is also generally recognized as the earliest contribution to aesthetics and is often reproduced in important anthologies of aesthetics in first position for that reason. Whereas this correctly reflects the fact that Plato is the first thinker to view the performance of poetry both appreciatively and reflectively, or critically, it may obscure the dialogue's true historical importance by implying that it was a deliberate contribution to theoretical aesthetics.

The dialogue is named for a famous singer-reciter from Ephesus who had just triumphed at an *agōn* of rhapsodes at Epidarus, where his performance had been witnessed by 20,000 persons and where he won the competition. This tells us much. Born an Ionian, widely traveled—for rhapsodes were required to be itinerants—welcomed and understood everywhere, Ion's world is the pan-Hellenic world of epic as Greece knew it in the late fifth century. Being a rhapsode, Ion recites epical hexameters, of course, and, as we learn, restricts himself to performing Homer only.

The *Ion* is of importance to the history of Greek literacy and paideia for several claims that the stubborn rhapsode makes, and will not relinquish, even when he can devise no adequate answer to Socrates' relentless attacks on them. Those claims deserve scholars' attention, for they are really Homer's claims, successfully propounded in the persons of his reciters in every generation down to this one, when at last they must confront the displeasure of Plato's Socrates.

The Hellenic rhapsode, insists Ion, who is himself a consummate performer, by means of a vivid narrative in which he identifies with the various characters he describes, induces the same experience in the audience. It is a powerful experience and a deeply pleasurable one, for which, claims Ion with professional pride, Greeks in every city are willing to pay handsomely, even if the tale be a sorrowful one.

> When I relate a tale of woe my eyes are filled with tears; and when it is of fear or awe, my hair stands on end and my hearts leaps.[5]

His performances, so he also proudly claims, produce, or even "work" (*ergazesthe,* cognate with *ergon,* "work"; Marshall McLuhan would relish the choice of verb), the same effects in the souls of his hearers, so that they are transported "in ecstasy" (so he also claims) to the very site the verses describe, be it Ithaca or Troy or wherever in the epical world that he chooses to take them. Vicariously, the listeners identify with the epical figures, sharing their actions and fortunes for weal or woe. They weep, laugh, feel terror, or give way to joy.[6]

> SOCRATES: Stop now and tell me, Ion, without reserve, what I choose to ask you. When you give a good recitation and especially thrill your audience, either with the lay of Odysseus leaping forth on the threshold, revealing himself to the suitors and pouring out his arrows before his feet, or of Achilles dashing at Hector, or some part of the sad story of Andromache or of Hecuba or of Priam, are you then in your senses [or "in your right mind": *em-phrōn*], or are you carried out of yourself, and does your soul in an ecstasy suppose herself to be among the

> very actions you are describing, whether they are in Ithaca, or in Troy, as the poems may chance to place them?
>
> ION: How vivid to me, Socrates, is this part of your proof. For when I relate. . . .
>
> SOCRATES: And are you aware that you rhapsodes *work* these very same effects in your spectators . . . .
>
> ION: Oh yes, I am fully aware of that. For I look down on them from the platform and see them at such moments. They are crying, and they turn awestruck eyes upon me, and they yield themselves to the amazement of what I relate. . . .

What the rhapsode induces, then, is a vivid, intensely emotional act of visualization on the part of listeners who identify with what they "see" as the reciter skillfully tells the story. This psychological phenomenon is, of course, a familiar one to anthropologists and oralists. It is at the heart of the success of the great professional reciters and storytellers in oral or semiliterate societies in every age. Plato's more professional word for the experience in the *Republic* will be *mimēsis*.

Ion reveals that a donation was solicited after the rhapsode's performance. The rewarding hat was passed around. This is a valuable clue to the motives of the audience and to the economics of an important part of Greek *mousikē*.[7] The immediate experience is valued by listeners in direct proportion to its emotional intensity, or the pleasure it gives; the rhapsode, as a function of his success at emotional manipulation, can be very well paid, and it appears that successful Ion made a rather comfortable living.

The intense pleasure reported from listeners at epical recitals, events that require aural and communal participation for their effectiveness, has been compared to that encountered at a rock concert. This phenomenon, in fact, comes closer to the Greek original experience in all its dimensions, including the emotional "hysteria" (as Plato saw it), than, let us say, a poetry reading at one's local library. But intense pleasure is not the only feature of a rhapsode's performance. Twin claims dominate Plato's dialogue. In addition to the immediate pleasure felt by the audience, the content of epic as orally conveyed instructs the present generation in all sorts of useful matters—technical as well as moral. The claim to give technical instruction Plato can ridicule, dismissing it with satire, as he will do again in *Republic*, Book X. The claim to give moral instruction is another matter, for he intends to take over that function of epic himself. That epic functioned as the Hellenic moral paideia has been widely denied by some critics, even ridiculed; some have been quoted in earlier chapters. Yet it is for this claim that Plato reserves his most scathing attack. His Socrates, as it turns out, is hostile to both claims, attacking both, but on very different grounds.

The first claim, the emotive impact and pleasure rhapsodic recitals held for listeners, is admitted (533 D) but then gradually and masterfully denigrated. The experience, for which Ion's audience was willing to pay, is finally equated with mass hysteria or *enthusiasmos* of a sort induced among Bacchants when they become possessed (*entheoi*), succumb to madness *(mania),* and run raving through the woods at night (534 Aff.). An initially flattered Ion (he is, after all, initially being called "divine" and "god-filled") assents readily enough, then grows wary of what Socrates is imputing to him, and finally rejects it with vehemence.

> I doubt that even you, Socrates, could convince me that I am actually possessed, and stark raving mad, when I . . .

Socrates' attack is based on what Plato perceived to be a similarity in outward behavior and internal psychological pathology between the surrender of the Bacchants to the god Dionysius in their moments of communal "ecstasy" and of the surrender of an epical audience to the singer. Neither experience, for a Plato, is altogether healthy or fully rational. He repeats the attack with the addition of full epistemological and psychological superstructure in the *Republic,* and it is not without echoes in *Laws*.

The didactic claims of contemporary reciters of Homer are treated differently. No initial concessions are made to them. Rather, the older didactic claims of epic are repeatedly reduced by Socrates to the narrower claim that poets and their reciters possess specialized *knowledge (technē* or *epistēmē)* of the subject matters found in the various crafts or sciences, or *technai,* they describe, for example, carpentry, sailing, or doctoring. That claim is then denied absolutely, a denial repeated with ridicule in the *Republic.*[8]

Historically, epical verse did once preserve much useful information of this sort, a feature of oral poetry in all societies of primary orality; literacy and a growing body of technical manuals had largely made that claim an anachronism for Athens. But singers and reciters were once society's repositories of a good deal of technical lore and information, from genealogies and harvesting calendars to sailing instructions. Collectively, they were a kind of tribal encyclopedia, and much specialized information did find its way into their material, a fact still in evidence in sections of Homer and Hesiod. It is interesting that Ion, unaware that his proud profession is itself on the verge of becoming an anachronism, a casualty of advancing literacy, never fully—and always reluctantly—abandons epic's ancient claim to be a source of specialized technical information.

Socrates forces Ion (who is no logician) to admit that the various practitioners of these crafts and sciences, such as doctors, ship captains, carpenters, and seers, would know their particular subject matter better than would he, a rhapsode. For the rhapsode's sole claim to be an expert in the various *technai* is his superior recall for passages describing these specialties in Homer, a memory that Ion proceeds to demonstrate is formidable.[9] In what amounts to a mnemonic tour de force, Socrates matches the rhapsode's extraordinary memory with his own, quoting passage after obscure passage. These concern, for example, such trivial occasions as mixing a medical posset, the line taken by a fisherman's plummet, and how seers examine entrails (538 Bff.). Socrates, who belonged to the craftsman class and who, as far as we know, had no formal schooling, is portrayed as reciting from memory some nineteen obscure epical hexameters drawn from four widely scattered sections of the *Iliad* and *Odyssey.* He offers to recite even more verses, about the professional handling of a chariot by a driver in a race, but Ion insists on reciting those himself. Finally Socrates demands:

> Well, by your own admission the rhapsode's craft *(rhapsodikē)* cannot know all [the specialized crafts], nor the rhapsode either. . . . Well, if he cannot know all [doctoring, ship-building, etc.], what kinds of things can he know?

Ion's reply deserves to be set out in a way that we can grasp at once how sweeping his claim is.

> That, I would say, which it is proper [*prepei:* this important verb implies that which is right, socially approved, warranted by precedent; it corresponds to Homeric *themis, kata kosmon,* etc.]
> for a man to say (speak),
> and those things which it is proper for a woman to say,
> and those for a free man,
> and for a slave,
> and the sort for a ruler,
> and for him who is ruled.[10]

When finally asked what is left of the Homeric reciter's didactic claims, or what content remains for him to be an expert on—or "speak well" about—Ion's answer is highly instructive for the modern reader. Ion asserts triumphantly, despite all of Socrates' badgering, and his quibbling over the difference between speaking well (impressively) and speaking expertly (knowledgeably), that the Homeric reciter is no less than the conveyor of the proper mores of society by informing each individual of his role and how to fulfill it. What the Homeric singer relates are nothing less than the proper actions and attitudes of the entire human social order, its classes and genders, male and female, free and slave, as these had been established by the precedent of ancestors and the long experience of Hellenes. And *that* claim he will not abandon, for he knows that it describes his role in contemporary Greek society. It has been the epical singer's role since Demodocus sang to Alcinous and for uncountable generations before then.

In a word, Homeric speech conveyed the proper mores of class behavior, especially as those classes related to each other. Plato may well be hostile to this contemporary role for "Homer's men," but he is honest in reporting it. The epical characters are models for contemporary behavior, as in Hellas they had always been. Ion knows this full well, and the stubborn rhapsode will not permit Socrates now to badger him out of it. In the arena of popular morality—whatever may have been the advances of literacy and of written law—Homer has not been displaced in the Athens into which Plato was born.

Ion's response, by identifying correct social and class behavior with acts of speech *(eipein),* instruction in proper linguistic behavior, reflects the still essentially oral situation of moral paideia in the late fifth century. To know what to do in an oral society is primarily to know what attitude to take in speech, or what to say to whom and how to say it, and with what degree of deference or abuse. It is, in the language of the *Euthyphro* (14 B), to know how "to speak and to act *(legein te kai prattein)*" in the proper manner in all situations, one pleasing to the gods and to men of worth. Thus an Achilles, a man of oral accomplishment, of superior speech, knows how properly to speak in assembly just as he knows how to address an Agamemnon, ruler of men, a fellow hero, or a slave. In stark contrast, the wretched Thersites, who can be verbally abusive but only in a disordered way, and the brutal Cyclopes, who know no ancestral customs and so were devoid of the instruction of epical singers, are portrayed as being linguistically impoverished and suffer dismally for it.[11]

Earlier in the dialogue Socrates himself had offered an overview of the content of epic verse that could, in fact, stand as an excellent summary of its didactic content. Has not Homer, asks Socrates, in addition to saying much, of course, about war and battles and valor,

> also related the mutual intercourse [*homiliōn,* accustomed ways] of human beings, of good men and bad, of laymen and craftsmen,
> and the accustomed intercourse *(homiliōn)* of the gods, both toward each other and toward men,
> and the happenings in the heavens and in the Underworld,
> and the origins of gods and heroes?[12]

Are these not the very things, concludes Socrates, out of which Homer makes his verses, and so the things that his reciters convey to our contemporary audiences? Ion, of course, readily agrees. Both men accept this didactic role with its strong Hesiodic component as the unquestioned cultural fact at the turn of the fourth century, with one approving of the situation and earning a handsome living by it, and the other decidedly hostile and determined to change it.

The Didactic Function of Epical Verse

It requires effort, now greatly aided by our increasing knowledge of how oral societies function, to view the Greek epical material in this way and to realize that to convey an oral paideia was the fundamental cultural purpose of Homeric speech. Instruction, not pleasure, was its primary purpose, but of necessity a covert or indirect one. Great as the poetry was, it was not poetry as we now know it or as literate Europe has known it for some centuries, and it cannot be understood by literates, even when appreciated in the singer's language and dialect, until its function as an orally performed paideia is also appreciated.

Pleasure, admittedly, was the immediate result, whether in Hesiod's century or Ion's. Thrilled auditors participated in the process of (indirect) enculturation in every generation between the eighth century and the fourth for the pleasure derived in the moment of inspired recitation. But aesthetic gratification alone could never account for the remarkable phenomenon of Homeric speech as an enclave of language removed from the daily vernacular, its longevity in Hellas, or its diffusion and degree of popular absorption.

Plato was the first theoretician of culture who consciously realized that the assimilation of a literate paideia can be socially enforced even when not pleasurable and that to some extent, with the introduction of schools, it has to be. An oral and musical paideia must and will be gratefully embraced. Put in different terms, a musical paideia lies closer to what is basic in us as animals and to what we have been encoded genetically to find pleasurable. To be effective, an oral and musical paideia relies on an appeal to pleasure, utilizing rhythms and sounds that win immediate, unreflective emotional acceptance, a willing embrace by ear and mind that bypasses any mental censor, as Plato first so clearly understood. Plato, of course, then proceeded to rationalize what he observed, concluding that the pleasure that Greeks take in identifying with epical recitals must appeal to some different (and "lower") "faculty" of the human mind or "soul" than that faculty that properly answers the Socratic summons to analyze, define, and reason deductively.[13] We need not accept Plato's rationalization, or his tripartite faculty psychology, in order to accept the contemporary facts that they purport to explain.

The power of poetry, especially epic, to give delight is attested as early as Homer (*Od.* VII. 44–45, and *passim*) and so commonly in the Greek literature of all periods well into Hellenistic times as not to require extensive citation here. In Hesiod, didacticism and pleasure form an untroubled and unquestioned alliance; Muses, which is to say the contemporary *aoido*i who sing what the Muses know, instruct even as they release from cares and assuage human ills.[14] In Gorgias the power of poetry produces in those who hear it "shuddering fright and weeping pity and sorrowful longing,"[15] but it is also a phenomenon to be analyzed and emulated to the degree possible by the practitioners of prose rhetoric. The results were sometimes bizarre—for example, the speech of Agathon in Plato's *Symposium,* a brilliant parody of the style of Gorgias—but seemingly had an appeal to contemporary audiences. Between seventh-century Hesiod and the fifth-century sophists came a chorus of testimony from the poets of Greece; they are the "givers of delight." That is their gift to the Hellenes.

Because for Plato the pleasure that poetry, especially epic, uniquely conferred on Hellenes could not be denied, his hostility forced him to relegate the experience to the irrational. He created, therefore, the enduring figure of the "mad poet," the artist who must be a bit crazed in order to create. On this feature Romantic criticism has seized, failing to detect Plato's hostility and pejorative stance. Poet, reciter, and audience alike, he claims in the *Ion,* are carried out of their minds; *nous* or mind is no longer in them.[16] In the Platonic account, in order to indite his magical verses the poet, deprived utterly of mind, has also been rendered devoid of skill and so skillful knowledge (*technē* and *epistēmē*), a non sequitur that Ion is lulled into accepting. To account, therefore, for the successful composition and performance, the poet or reciter must have been divinely possessed, like mad Bacchants, and so too must be the hearers of those verses.[17] The entire mimetic experience, including reciter and listener—part of the lingering power of oralism in the increasingly literate fifth century—falls under the questionable (for Plato) category of things that come by *theia moira,* an unaccountable, and so not entirely rational or predictable, "gift" or fate or doom of the gods. In Plato, seers and prophets require the same *theia moira* as do singers and poets, a warning that this is a two-edged term for him. For the unconverted rationalist that Plato was (most of the time), the expression can be used, as in the *Ion,* initially to disguise an assessment that becomes increasingly pejorative.[18] *Theia moira* was an "approval word" for pious Greeks in popular speech, and so won Ion's unsuspecting acceptance. Plato could then invest it with whatever meaning(s) he wished, and in several dialogues he does just that, sometimes confounding his interpreters.

Plato's analysis has a clear purpose: exposure and elimination. The (irrational) pleasure conferred by epic was the source of Homer's power as moral suasion and control in Hellenic society—and, indeed, had been its source since the Dark Ages. Plato must therefore attack it and seek its elimination if he wishes to put his rational, critical *philosophos* in Homer's place. His primary target, probably long before he wrote the *Republic,* is shaping up to be no less than the poets of Greece led by Homer, in the persons of their reciters and performers. Ion is an early, hapless target.

The didactic function of epical verse is a thesis that has not always been welcomed in modern Hellenic scholarship, even by some sympathetic to Parry-Lord. The fact that didacticism was no longer a feature of the Balkan poetry studied by Parry and was minimal in the medieval troubadour tradition, where entertainment dominates, contributed to the resistance. But there is a difference. For medieval Europe as well as for early-twentieth-century Balkan mountain villages, the basis of the sustaining culture was urban and literate, and thus the primary modes of cultural preservation had long since been securely transferred to writing. In both cultures, to be educated meant to be literate, and to be very well educated meant to be able to relate to a large body of written texts in established ways. The professions and professional schools depended on extensive documentation, which the professions both hoarded and advanced. Those texts, not laboring memories, had for many generations preserved the information—legal, religious, historical, literary—essential for that culture to maintain its identity and to function on a daily basis. This was true for both the Christian and Muslim communities. As a result, large numbers of individuals and even whole villages may remain illiterate, but the sustaining civilization was highly literate and had long been so. That, manifestly, was not the case as Greece emerged from the Dark Ages, a difference—even if the statistical levels of popular illiteracy could be shown to be equivalent—that cannot be stressed enough when comparing Archaic Greece to the Balkans or to early medieval Europe.

As Greece entered the fourth century, Plato was approaching his thirtieth year. In the preceding fifty years and especially in the preceding quarter century, Athens had seen what was the most rapid acceleration toward cultural alphabetic dependency that any Greek city had heretofore known. Plato had lived through a good part of this development, and he was critically observant. He well understood that, in a generation earlier than his own, a rhapsode like Ion would resist being reduced to the anachronism that rhapsodes would in fact become by the end of the fourth century. Despite Socrates' superior arguments or Plato's satire—Ion finally claims to deserve to be put in charge of the military forces of Athens on the basis of his superior memory for Homer's battle scenes and therefore superior knowledge of military tactics—he reasserts the rhapsode's, and so Homer's, ancient claims to be society's historian, moralist, teacher, social arbiter, and technocrat, as well as its entertainer. Those claims, save for the last, had never been made by Serbian *guslars* or medieval troubadours.

Euthyphro's *Exemplum* from Epic in 399 B.C.: A Bizarre Legal Case

The evidence for epic poetry's continuing didactic role into the fourth century is found in Plato, the contemporary source par excellence and a hostile critic if ever there was one. The clearest case can be made from the *Republic,* as the late Eric Havelock first argued at length.[19] Havelock was taken to task by his reviewers for concentrating on this dialogue, as though Plato later changed his mind, or some other role for epic would be found in other dialogues. An example drawn from an earlier dialogue will prove useful because it reveals how, in practice, members of Greek society resorted to the indirect didacticism all assumed to be contained in epical narratives. The case is a bizarre one, both legally and logically.[20] That Plato's irony and satire are working overtime in this dialogue must be assumed from the start. Even so, Plato is not setting up straw opponents. People who thought and argued as a Euthyphro does were people he grew up with, and he draws on the memories of his youth in depicting them.

In the legally busy year of 399 B.C. a certain Euthyphro, a professional seer, has come to the court of the Archon Basileus where he happens upon Socrates as the philosopher awaits hearing the terms of his own indictment for *asebeia,* impiety. Euthyphro is present not as accused but accuser or, in the Greek legal idiom, the pursuer. Plato has Socrates only gradually draw out the revelation of the identity of the pursued, thereby reserving the shock. Euthyphro, it turns out, is initiating an indictment of his own father for murder, a *dikē phonou*; this was itself regarded as an action of grievous impiety for Athenians. (It seems also to have carried the taint of parricide, a special horror to Greeks.) As a result, the seer's outraged brothers and, as we learn, others in the community have castigated and denounced him.

> SOCRATES: What is your suit, Euthyphro? Are you fleeing or pursuing [prosecuting or defending]?
>
> EUTHYPHRO: Prosecuting.
>
> SOCRATES: Whom?

When Euthyphro reveals it is his own father against whom he is initiating a *dikē,* Socrates reacts, as any Athenian would, with shock.

> SOCRATES: Your *father!* My good man! . . . By Heracles, Euthyphro, surely most men do not know what the right thing is in matters like this, for I surmise that it is not just anybody who can do rightly what you are doing, but only a man who is very far advanced in pursuing wise thoughts.
>
> EUTHYPHRO: Very far indeed, by Zeus![21]

After revealing the complicated circumstances back on the family estate on Naxos that led to the present suit, Euthyphro reveals that he is quite aware of the prevailing *nomos,* or custom, against prosecuting a father.

> EUTHYPHRO: For they [his father and brothers] say . . . it is unholy *(anosion)* for a son to prosecute his father for murder . . .

> SOCRATES . . . for are you not afraid of doing something unholy *(anosion)* yourself in prosecuting your father?[22]

Euthyphro, outraged at his brothers' accusations and the imputation of impiety, proceeds to remonstrate over the whole situation with Socrates as they await their respective appearances before the archon. The exasperated seer offers Socrates a bit of ethical reasoning. Let us attempt to enter into his way of thinking, which is still that of oral Greece.

> Now Socrates, examine the sure proof (tekmērion) I shall give.
> I have offered it to others
> to show that it is the established *nomos* [i.e., the right thing to do, according to proper custom,[23] to do as I do now, prosecute my father] . . .
> These same people [who accuse me] worship Zeus as the best and most righteous of gods.
> And they agree that he put his own father [Kronos] in bonds [for swallowing his children]
> and *that* father [Kronos] had in turn castrated his father [Ouranos].
> Yet they are angry at me for indicting my father.
> So they say opposite(s) [things, i.e., contradict themselves] concerning the gods and concerning me.[24]

The "argument," such as it is, requires even more filling in than I have provided if it is to be fully intelligible to the modern reader. Its structure, as in all paradigmatic ethics, requires that there be an action that serves as precedent, the paradigm case. In this instance the *exemplum* is drawn from epic, specifically Hesiod. Next, those who are to be morally persuaded must accept some significant analogy between the paradigm case and another action whose morality is in dispute. This can require some stretching, and is the source of the imprecision in this form of ethical reasoning that so annoyed Plato. He satirizes it here.

In this passage the implied analogy is one of continuing proper proportionality: as A/B, so C/D, so E/F. In each case, the relationship is one of father to son, which helps things along, that is, Ouranos/Kronos, Kronos/Zeus, Euthyphro's father/Euthyphro. Euthyphro assumes that any Athenian will know the Hesiodic account, and so Ouranos and Kronos can go unnamed. The assumption of the total popular absorption of the epical account is to be noted. Hesiod, like Homer, is a common possession. Moreover, the "logic" of the appeal is to epic as still providing moral *exempla,* a common intellectual maneuver in Plato's Athens, however bizarre the particulars in this instance.

For the argument to be persuasive, several further conditions must be met. All sides must agree to the literal truth of the Hesiodic account, about which, in fact, Socrates later expresses some doubts. But Euthyphro's accusers, so he assures Socrates, worship Zeus and do accept the Hesiodic account as literally true. However, because the argument appeals to an analogy between *actions,* the actions of F, D, and B toward E, C, and A must be the same or significantly alike for the analogies to be persuasive. By exploiting this particular epical *exemplum*—a Platonic favorite for ridicule, as we know from the *Republic*—Plato may be deliberately taking the whole business of appealing to epic, as a way of solving present human problems, to an absurd extreme. His argument is a *reductio*. Yet Euthyphro himself is nothing if not sincere in his indignant logic. The argument from analogy and the castration of Ouranos will present no problems for him, as no doubt they would not for a majority of Athenians either.

The contemporary mind that so readily accepts Euthyphro's reasoning is expected, then, to perceive some relevant analogy (never actually specified) between three actions directed by sons toward fathers: a castration carried out from ambush, brutal exile after fettering in chains, and a legal indictment in an Athenian court. The first two actions involved deities. We need the further premise that, whatever a god does, especially Zeus, cannot be impious, a premise that was in fact stated at the outset by Euthyphro himself. Now we have the nearly completed piece of contemporary, fourth-century ethical and legal reasoning. Because, according to the scripture, or Hesiod, it was not impious for a deity to *castrate* or *banish* his father, it cannot be impious for Euthyphro to *indict* his father. The *exemplum* of epic warrants the ethical conclusion; argument from (dubious) analogy warrants the logical conclusion. The suppressed premise, never articulated, seems to be that the acts of castration, fettering, and legal indictment all belong loosely to the class of actions that involve sons "moving against" fathers and so are sufficiently alike as actions to secure the desired conclusion.

A mind willing to move smoothly forward in this way, so maddening to literates, advancing from step to step by (loose) analogy rather than precise definition and strict logical deductions, is a mind that has been formed in an oral culture. For such an orally conditioned mind, these mental procedures, rooted as they are in analogy and often in concrete metaphor, are the most natural thing in the world and eminently rational. Hence, as Euthyphro laments to Socrates, he is the one who has been reasonable and has been unjustly calumniated; the logic or "proof" *(tekmērion)* he offered was, in Euthyphro's estimation, rock solid.

The reasoning is absurd, of course, as Plato enjoys indirectly exposing. Euthyphro's appeal to the *exemplum* of epic is desperate enough, but seemingly, as a conceptual exercise, totally sincere, and he clearly expects all right-thinking Greeks, Socrates, the Archon Basileus, and a future jury to accept the validity of his arguments. Socrates balks. The response of the the archon is unknown, but it is doubtful that this case would ever have been suited. But Plato's purpose in writing his dialogue about a litigious seer attempting to indict his own father in 399 B.C. was to explore not a contemporary legal case, but current ethical reasoning. The legal outcome was of no interest to him.

Once again, as in many of the early dialogues, Plato is dramatizing the oral mentality as still found embedded in the speech of an interlocutor, only then to sweep it away. Yet Euthyphro himself is portrayed as intellectually sincere, if flawed in his logic. Again, on Jaeger's premise that Plato in his dialogues does not set up straw men who have no relevance to contemporary Athenian life, such epical fundamentalists as a Euthyphro and the cast of mind that he exemplifies must have been familiar enough in Athens in the late fifth and early fourth centuries. Like an Ion, a Polemarchus, or a young Charmides, Euthyphro stands in need of a stiff dose of Socratic chastisement (which he gets), and some fundamental lessons in logical procedure (which he also gets). So, too, I contend, did most

Athenian intellectuals stand in need of them. Literacy may have been making strong advances in the fifth century, but the mentality that oralism sustained, as a complex of mental habits that had for centuries formed part of a way of life, are not altered in a day or even a single generation. As a result, a Euthyphro, when later presented with a most elementary lesson in logic involving which of two terms designates the wider class, can respond with such expressions as "I don't understand you at all, Socrates," and "That is a strange way to speak, Socrates."[25]

The early dialogues are full of such responses from interlocutors, who are otherwise sophisticated men and society's leaders, when they are presented with equally elementary lessons in logical thinking. Unless one resorts to the theory of a gradual transition from oralism to literacy in fifth- and early-fourth-century Greece—each condition embodying different forms of thought and different measures of what is "rational" and so persuasive—they become very difficult to explain. The attempt in some modern scholarship to explain them away by making over Plato's Athenian interlocutors into "the plain man" or "the woman on the Hampton bus" or even "the typical undergraduate" will not work. Typical undergraduates and plain men do not speak as a Euthyphro or an Ion does; they do not fail again and again to grasp the most elementary lessons in logic, and they are not society's intellectuals, moral arbiters, military heroes, professors and dramatists, jurists and statesmen, or its religious and civil leaders. Plato's interlocutors—many of them—were.

The "established right [thing]" catches the contemporary nuances for "the *nomos* we [Athenians] have," which translates literally the Greek text.[26] This phrase is the legal key to the dispute as we look at it more closely, and it, too, has something to tell us about contemporary Athens. Both sides, Euthyphro as well as his brothers and other unnamed accusers, are appealing to oral precedent. Euthyphro's brothers have appealed to a strong Athenian oral *nomos* to the effect that hailing a father into court, especially on a capital charge on behalf of a worthless stranger who had no relatives to come forth on his behalf, is itself impious. Plato's wording clearly indicates that the prohibition against this was a *nomos* and so binding, but not as yet a written one; it was, according to Burnet, later to be incorporated into written law.[27] Euthyphro, of course, feels the force of his brothers' complaint, evidently shared by others, and so must counter with his own rival *nomos,* significantly resorting to the *exemplum* of epic. Euthyphro's appeal to epical authority may be desperate but, as a conceptual exercise, is totally sincere, and he clearly expects the Athenians, their courts, and Socrates to accept the validity of his argument. That Plato is clearly ridiculing this sort of mentality and argument by taking it to a kind of fanatical extreme does not alter the fact that such modes of discourse and ethical reasoning—and no doubt even legal argument—were still powerful forces in his Athens.

The religious feeling driving Euthyphro's action is also real enough. The *miasma* (pollution) created by his father's homicide is, Euthyphro intensely feels, spreading to him by reason of the normal familial contacts that he cannot avoid.[28] Purification is required; that was traditional enough and might involve a period of exile or the like, as in the case of King Theseus in Euripides' *Hippolytus*. But the means that Euthyphro chooses, a procedure of indictment in an Athenian court, is truly bizarre. Euthyphro, if a historical person,[29] clearly took the legal-religious situation to an absurd consequence, a kind of religious quack. Plato's satire, by taking the logical procedure supportive of such an action to the absurd, neatly exposes how indirect didacticism, residing as it must in the specific *actions* of gods and heroes as narrated in the national epic, can be used—and misused—as ethical instruction and guide in each succeeding generation. Plato's relentless attack on such "logic," especially in ethical situations, is inexplicable unless epic still functioned persuasively in this way and the majority of Hellenes still reasoned as Euthyphro does. The protesting seer is certain that they will on his day in court.

The Platonic Socrates cannot accept this level of discourse or "argument" for the resolution of serious moral questions, and it is reasonable to assume that the historical Socrates did not do so not either. In effect, Plato's early ethical dialogues put philosophy and the oral way of life as it still flourished in contemporary Greece into deadly opposition, and he intended that philosophy would prevail. The Platonic dialogues reveal that for most Greeks no serious inroads had been made in the Homeric way of thinking, especially in the area of popular morals or the procedures of formal logic. On this interpretation, then, Plato's attack on Homer and the poets as custodians of the traditional Hellenic paideia and as perpetuators of shoddy forms of thinking that Greeks still find persuasive emerges not as an aberration of the argument of the *Republic* to be explained away,[30] as generations of Plato's admirers have attempted, but as something necessary to Plato's whole philosophical enterprise. Indeed, it may well have been near the heart of that enterprise.

Advanced as it is, Plato's satiric analysis should be compared with Aristotle's far more systematic appreciation of why analogical argument—so fundamental to persuasive or "rational" thinking in all oralist societies—always falls short of strict demonstration. In argument from analogy that required the narrating of specific (but paradigmatic) actions, neither language nor thought ever attains the true universal, and so such argument never deploys a middle term, hence, the severe deficiency of analogical reasoning as compared to deductive reasoning by syllogism.

> So demonstration does not necessarily imply the being of Forms, nor a one over a many, but it does necessarily imply the possibility of truly predicating one of many; since without this possibility we cannot have the universal, and if the universal goes the middle term goes, and so demonstration becomes impossible. We conclude therefore that there must be a single identical term unequivocally predicable of a number of individuals.[31]

The Greek transformation of performative discourse into analytic is here complete, with much gained in terms of precision in argument and understanding of the processes of formal logic, but perhaps also with something lost.

The Function of Epic in Greek Society

For the first time in Hellenic scholarship, Eric Havelock proposed in *Preface to Plato* (1962) to take seriously and make historical sense of the Greeks' own contention, enunciated from Hesiod to Plato, that epic verse instructed as well as entertained. Two facts, therefore, had to be retained, squarely faced, and reconciled. "Homer" as a text and a great monument of human literature presently comprises two long narrative poems, centered in one instance on the wrath of Achilles and in the other on the *nostos,* the return home to Ithaca, of Odysseus. They are, as a form of discourse, poetic narratives and not compendiums of law or ethics. In a word, they tell stories. By contrast, Greeks of every generation did not regard them merely as stories or adventure tales but as the Hellenic paideia, a combination of moral instruction and tribal history. If the Greeks themselves are to be believed, the Homeric poems were, indeed, high poetry and exciting narratives masterfully told, but they also were, for all who heard and cherished them, something like (in Havelock's phrase) the Hellenic "tribal encyclopaedia." As a result, they were memorized, hoarded, cited, quoted, and imitated in every aspect of life, marking all its passages.

For modern readers, then, the Homeric poems, along with those of Hesiod, constitute a challenge to assimilate the Greek epical literature in accordance with the assumptions and conventions of the culture that produced them. Terms such as "Homeric speech" or "epical speech," or "epical discourse," may help to remind us of two important historical facts: Homer was assimilated even in Plato's day not as a text but as a recitation, and Greeks of every generation from Hesiod to Plato received the epical poems as a kind of national paideia.

If one is prepared to read "Homer" in this spirit, with a generous dose of cultural "sympathetic understanding," then one slowly and admiringly comes to realize that the range of what Homeric speech accomplished paideutically in fact covered all the mandatory areas of a great people's paideia. Homeric speech told the Greeks of the accustomed ways of gods and mortals, and of the full range of manners and mores both human and divine, while also (ostensibly) recounting to all Hellenes their own ancestry and complex tribal history. Conveyed in Homeric discourse was a demanding but psychologically satisfying and coherent ethos, presented as the historical experience of a rich ancestral past to which each generation felt itself infinitely in debt. By the antiquity of the words and the power and beauty of those words rhythmically conveyed in inspired performance, it was successfully pretended to each generation that this complex paideia was no less than the very "way of ancestors" and so ultimately was "of Zeus." The father of gods and men himself had bestowed divine assent and so unalterable legitimacy on established ways of the Hellenes. Taken up into Homeric speech and so absorbed by all who heard and learned it were a whole people's deepest values and their most important social procedures. In epical discourse they learned what is *dikaion* or not, *themis* or not, *kalon* or not, *kata kosmon* or not, who were the *agathoi* and who were the *kakoi* of society. All of this was conveyed in the splendid words and deeds—or equally splendid mistakes with their relentless consequences—of the heroes of their race, whose blood, or so they believed, flowed in their own veins too.

This vocabulary, essentially adjectival in Homer as the words were attached to a host of remembered actions, remained the dominant "ethical" vocabulary of Greece until Plato. He twisted it around with liberal deployment of the generic article, for example, *to dikaion,* "justice," *to kalon,* "beauty," and *to agathon* "goodness." He isolateed its meanings as abstractions and as Forms apart from actions with the pronoun *autos,* for example, *auto to kalon,* "beauty *itself,*" and *auto to dikaion,* "justice *itself.*" By putting the epical moral vocabulary on his linguistic anvil in his dialogues, Plato, in effect, invented rational ethics.

In the same narratives in which Greeks imbibed their morals, they also learned the names and lineages of their ancestral heroes, as well as the names, personalities, and lineages of the gods they had dutifully worshiped in their temples from Trojan times to their own, or so they believed. That continuity, tribal and religious, gave the moral content of Homer no small part of its contemporary emotional power in each century.

This orally communicated paideia also afforded all Hellenes with a satisfactory, if vague and fantastic, representation of the great divisions of nature, heaven, earth, and underworld. In their defense, those representations were no more vague and no more fantastic than those of the high cultures that surrounded the Greeks. From these epical representations of the cosmos and its origins, and especially from Hesiod's version, the first philosophers would take their point of departure and begin Western philosophy and science, a Greek journey that their Near Eastern neighbors did not imitate. In learning epical speech, generations of Hellenes also were afforded a complex and descriptively adequate, even if to us psychologically "primitive," vocabulary with which to conceptualize and explain the full range of their cognitive and affective life. To enter it through the medium of the words they used (*noos, thumos, phrēn,* and the rest) is to enter into a world of psychological experience at once somewhat familiar, yet curiously alien and, at times, barely recognizable. From this epical representation of interior mental life, the philosopher Heraclitus would take his departure, and begin the long semantic history of the concept of *psuchē.*[32]

Finally, and not of the least importance, everywhere in this speech were dispersed endless impressive injunctions and cautions, memorably shaped into repeatable aphorisms, devoted to the perennial human concern of how to enjoy such pleasures and consolations as life may offer without offending god or human, how to endure with nobility when they are taken away, and what may be expected at death. Read sympathetically or, perhaps better, heard as Greeks heard it, as a full and rich oral paideia, the primary didactic function of epic verse becomes an increasingly plausible theory and finally an inescapable one. Gradually we comprehend how, in any age before Plato—that is, before his devastating attack on Homer and the poets from which they never revived—Greeks could believe that "Homer" gave to Greece its paideia in the form of the ancient *mousikē.*

Arguably, every culture must in some way afford its members information of the sort long conveyed to all Hellenes in epical speech. Viewed anthropologically, and not as narrowed to the Greek experience, this is the primary function of paideia, however diverse may be its mechanisms (oral or literate) the world over, or how different its specific injunctions. This may lend some support to a well-known definition of "culture" as our species' extrasomatic means of survival. Oralists may now wish to add that the primary means of cultural survival took *linguistic* form, speech as transmitted across generations, putting the experience of oral verse at the heart of the human enculturation process in our long preliterate ages.

Some psychologists and anthropologists have suggested that human beings, deprived of nearly all of the animal signals of scent or sight for correct behavior, seem to require instruction—or paideia in the sense adopted here—in order to flourish and act decisively. Paradoxically, they will languish psychologically and even physically without such cultural direction or when severed from it. The psychologist and anthropologist Durkheim termed this strange malady *anomie*. Individual prescriptions and answers in diverse cultures and periods seem to matter less than that there be *some* prescriptions and *some* answers, and that these be reasonably coherent, psychologically satisfying, and warranted by whatever that society equates with heaven itself. All of this and more, Homer was to Greece.

This role for epic, and especially for Homer, as the Hellenic oral paideia has been stressed in this work because that function for it has not been as widely accepted in contemporary scholarship as has been the theory of the oral origins of the verse itself. What, in part, has stood in the critics' way is their understandable view of the Homeric poems as great art and, moreover as "art" *gratia artis*. Poetry, if good poetry, becomes "art" (the very word defies translation into Archaic Greek) in literate societies, and is pursued for its nonutilitarian reasons. The aesthetics of art criticism makes no room for discussions of the utility of the verse for retaining a body of technical information, such as sailing instructions, a farmer's planting calender, or how to consult a priest. There is even less room for instructing young persons in the proprieties of social behavior, such as exchanging the gifts and vows of guest-friendships. But Ion, the practicing fifth-century rhapsode, has no such aesthetic view of poetry; he thinks that Homer does precisely these things, and so he must do them too.

> While technical procedures such as arming, navigation and diplomacy could be, and were, communicated in the poems, it was ultimately matters of *nomos* and *ethos* that required preservation. Religious customs and beliefs, family relations, questions of legitimacy and inheritance, attitudes toward death, political and social hierarchies and values—all these concerns, which were incapable of incorporation in visible models and could not be conserved by the vernacular, had to be embodied in contrived [i.e., epical] speech.[33]

For oral Greece and for oral cultures generally, poetry or "art" as pleasurable entertainment remains subordinate to the instructional material it contains. Similarly, the words are never subordinated to the music, as was happening with the latest "modern" music of the fourth century (Socrates is disdainful of the development in *Republic*, Book III).

The function of the poems as a complex society's verbal paideia is what called epic into existence and what sustained it over so many preliterate centuries. The introduction of an alphabet permitted poetry to begin to move toward the margins of daily life, but the process was predictably a slow one. If the society becomes fully literate, then great poetry at last has no important social or paideutic roles to play. Literacy will long since have transferred them elsewhere. Understandably, modern scholars and critics—preeminently society's literates, and seldom with direct experience of oral cultures—find it hard to assimilate an oral Homer that does not quite fit their preconceptions of what great poetry is.

An alternative attempt to come to grips with Homer (Hesiod is harder to wrench into this role) is to view the verse as having been for his day merely aristocratic court entertainment. As mere entertainment, the poetry is marginal to life and not at its core. ''Homer'' or the *aoidoi* are thus represented as singing to and flattering the nobles, celebrating their ways, helping them get through those long, cold, Geometric nights. The *Iliad,* sitting before us as a monumental text and an unsurpassed contribution to literature, cannot perhaps be so easily trivialized, but oral epic performances can be. So ''Homer'' or epic becomes *for its time*—as recited and performed and before it became a text in Greek schools—something marginal in Greek life and certainly with no paideutic or encyclopedic role. Both views are untenable, even though both have had numberless adherents since the serious study of Homer was reintroduced into Europe with the advent of printing. They retain many advocates today. One example will suffice. Seeking to deny either a didactic or an encyclopedic role to epic in any period, John Halverson writes:

> Yet it remains true, as Burkert has said (and many others agree) that ''the foundation of all education was Homer.'' There is no paradox here, for the meaning of the statement is simply that the text of Homer was basic required reading for the classical period. As literacy spread and literate education became institutionalized, young readers learned their letters in Homer.

Prior to *that* culturally indispensable role, Homer seemingly had no didactic function whatsoever and no cultural importance either. Only after becoming a school text, part of ''basic required reading,'' could Homer become the Greek Shakespeare and ''comparable too as a literary and artistic influence.'' Halverson continues: ''But no more than Shakespeare does Homer seem to have been taken as an ideological or ethical or religious authority or as a guide for the perplexed or as a storehouse of cultural information.''[34] But then we discover Plato, as perceptive as anyone then living about the mechanisms of Athenian society, portraying an Ion or a Euthyphro as Hellenic ''fundamentalists.'' Theirs is still a world of recitation and memorization, not ''basic required reading.'' And they still accept the old stories, Homeric and Hesiodic—even the castrations of gods and historicity of Trojan battles—as literal truth. They appeal to epic precedent to solve current moral and legal disputes. When Plato shows us ordinary Greeks of his century and of the days of his youth, living their lives according to lessons contained in epical accounts, we may be sure that he was not freely inventing or creating straw men only to subject them to Socratic humiliation. Rather, he was reporting what he had encountered daily on the streets of Athens, in its houses, in the agora or Assembly, and nightly in the *sumposia.* He is not distorting the contemporary practice, but telling us what it is.

Conclusion

Hesiod, the Greek author who observed epic recitals and himself performed in contests of them in the years when the oldest inscriptions were being made, knew that the Muses instruct even as they give pleasure. Lovely daughters of Mnemosyne (Memory), they "delight" the mind of Zeus as they recall the holy precedents, the *ēthē* and *nomoi* that all must know; they "instruct" even as they assuage the grief in people's hearts and banish their sorrows. Perhaps a century after Hesiod composed those lines, an anonymous epical singer, and so Apollo's child, reflects on his role in society in a poem now called the *Homeric Hymn to Apollo.* The god himself speaks, neatly capturing in two hexameters the dual roles of pleasure and instruction that no Greek would for so many centuries have reason to assail. Apollo resoundingly declares for himself and so for all epic singers in Archaic Greece:

> To me ever dear shall be the lyre . . .
> And I shall declare to men the unfailing will of Zeus.

Four hundred years separate Hesiod and Ion. Nevertheless, each singer would have understood what the other was about and appreciated how the singer functions in society. Much had changed, but those things had not.

Epic in the intervening centuries had been supplemented by a great body of lyric and then tragic verse, but epic still reigns supreme. Plato's successive attacks on Homer prove as much. And his reasons for hostility are clear. As grounds for appeal in the sphere of morality, the *exempla* of epic are still very much in place; for Plato the rationalist and the founder of ethics, this is an intolerable situation. The level of contemporary ethical debate must be elevated; indeed, a whole new form of discourse may be required.

In the argument of the *Republic,* Plato puts his polemic with Homer in the arena of rival claims to produce an adequate Hellenic paideia. He positions his two great players, insightfully and shrewdly, under the rival symbols of "music," the entrenched champion now grown old and vulnerable, and "philosophy," the feisty young challenger spoiling for a fight. In so doing, Plato forces the attention of historians to the meaning of the word "music" or *mousikē* as he deploys it in his great argument. To "music" and "paideia" in late fifth-century Athens and to the evidence for residual oralism they reveal in the argument of Plato's *Republic,* we must now turn.

Notes

1. Paul Friedländer, in *Epigrammata,* p. 8.

2. *Rep.* 600 C, where Homer is said to "educate people and make them better men (Cornford tr.)," and *passim.* At 599 D, the greatest and finest thing that Homer conveys to the Hellenes is simply "the education of men *(paideias peri anthropou).*" These texts are discussed more fully in chapter 8.

3. Xenophanes B. 6

4. E. Sikes, *The Greek View of Poetry* (London, 1931), p. 1. Bruno Snell writes that for Greece poetry was "a determinant of social forms, a guide in political experimentation, an innovator in language, a catalyst in the evolution of . . . [Hellenic] society" (*Poetry and Society* [Bloomington, Ind., 1961], p. 1). The influence of Homer on successive forms of Greek social life, political and ethical, is stressed well by T. A. Sinclair in *A History of Greek Political Thought* (London, 1967): "Thought is colored by words and their associa-

tions, and the earliest Greek thinkers made their first acquaintance with political terminology and political history in the poems of Homer'' (p. 14). Also: ''For all its historical inconsistencies and its mingling of discrepant elements Homer's picture of Heroic society, heroic ideals and *heroic speech* remained firmly fixed in men's minds as something philosophical as well as historical'' (p. 18, emphasis mine). And finally: ''They had learned [in all centuries] to look to the *Iliad* and *Odyssey* not merely for historical facts but for ethical principles, to seek in the great men of the [epical] past the standard of good men of the present'' (p. 9). See A. MacIntyre, ''The Virtues in Heroic Societies'' in his influential *After Virtue,* 2nd ed. (Notre Dame, Ind., 1984), pp. 121–130. Until very recently such emphases were more the exception than the rule in Hellenic scholarship. The rediscovery of the oral dimension in Greek life in wake of the gradual acceptance of Parry-Lord (at least in some version) has been a catalyst.

5. *Ion* 535 C. Academic philosophy has mainly ignored the *Ion,* finding its emphasis on performed poetry and the Greeks' response to it baffling and Ion's pedagogical claims eccentric. Historians of aesthetics have taken it more seriously, but mainly to look in it for the earliest philosophical theory of ''art.'' A neglected partial exception was H. Flashar, *Der Dialog ''Ion'' al Zeuginis platonischer Philosophie* [Dt. Akad. d. Wiss.] (Berlin, 1958).

6. *Ion* 535 D-E.

7. *Ion* 535 E. This is a rare reference to the economics of rhapsodic recital. Perhaps Ion here refers to less formal occasions in the *agora* of a sort described in Xenophon than to the great contest before 20,000 that Ion had just won in Epidarus (*Ion* 530 A). According to Xenophon, one can listen to rhapsodes on any day in his Athens (*Sym.* 3. 6).

8. *Epistēmē* is used interchangeably with *technē* in the *Ion,* an early dialogue, a reminder that like *sophia* (Ionic *sophiē*), *epistēmē* along with its cognates initially was felt as a ''skill'' word in the Archaic period, especially in the form *epistasthai* with the infinitive. (A rare, partial exception in Homer that points to the future is found at *Od.* IV. 730.) See in the *Ion* 530 B; 533 D; 536 C *(technē oud' epistēmē);* 541 E *(technē kai epistēmē), passim.* Socrates exploits outrageously the ambiguities in meaning between ''to speak well'' or ''skillfully'' in the sense of accomplished declamation and to speak with knowledge of the subject matter, but Ion does not detect this. Were the students in the Academy meant to catch out ''Socrates'' where more passive interlocutors such as Ion do not? Some logical howlers in the exchange between Socrates and Polemarchus in the *Republic* provide additional examples. Older theories to the effect that such logical blunders as those found in the *Ion* were Plato's own, committed before the logical sophistication of his later dialogues, are untenable. The man who wrote these dialogues (including the *Euthydemus*) is not floundering helplessly on elementary issues.

9. For example, at 539 A Socrates quotes six hexameters spoken by the seer Theoclymenus in the *Odyssey*; he recites three more concerning a simile involving a fisherman's plummet (538 D), and two concerning the contents of Machoan's posset (538 C), and offers to quote six hexameters concerning Nestor's advice about how to negotiate a turning post when racing chariots. Xenophon is at one with Plato is regarding memorized and performed poetry as the core of traditional Hellenic paideia. See Xen. *Sym.* 3. 5–6.

10. *Ion* 540 B.

11. In addition to his ability to skillfully address his equals, or a sceptered king, in council, Achilles also sings hexameters (concerning *kleea andrōn,* the exploits of *his* epic heroes of the past) in his tent for recreation, Patroclus alone being present. For the impropriety of Thersites attacking Agamemnon in council and the contrast with Odysseus, see *Iliad* II. 187ff. Of Odysseus: ''Whenever he encountered some king, or man of influence/ he would stand beside him and with soft words try. . . . '' But Thersites: ''of the endless

speech, still scolded/who knew within his head many words, but disorderly;/vain and without decency, to quarrel with the princes. . . . Beyond all others Achilles hated him, and Odysseus'' (tr. Lattimore).

12. *Ion* 531 C.

13. *Rep.* 411A–412B; 434 D–411 C.

14. See Hesiod's ''Hymn to the Muses'' discussed in chapter 3. What has been called by some anthropologists ''analogical thinking,'' dependent as it is on what is concrete, visualizable, and so capable of narrative incorporation in the saga, is natural to oral societies not because they are ''primitive'' but because the method of storage or preservation for important information is mnemonic. It is mnemonics that determines the ''choice'' of narrative. Action is visualizable and enticing to memory; abstract relationships are not. The alphabet may gradually ease the need for memorization, but not the habit of analogical thought, at least not immediately. Even Plato, who seeks to persuade a contemporary audience, exploits complex analogies far beyond anything found in any later major philosophical writer.

15. Gorgias, *Helen,* 9.

16. See *Ion* 534 B. The successful poet must be *entheos* (god-filled) to compose, but as preparation must be *ekphrōn* (mind-emptied), creating the necessary vacuum, as it were, so that ''the *nous* remains no longer in him.'' Plato's satiric irony, and hostility become increasingly heavy. At last Ion protests: ''Well spoken, I grant . . . but I shall be surprised if you can convince me that I am possessed *(katechomenos)* and raving mad *(mainomenos)* when I praise Homer'' (536 C). Ion finally understood better than many modern aestheticians just what Socrates was imputing to him. He did not like it nearly so much toward the end of the dialogue as in the beginning.

17. *Ion* 535 Eff: ''Are you aware that the spectator . . .''.

18. The phrase *theia moira* is, as noted, two-edged in Plato. The result of a god-sent fate or doom may (or may not) be beneficial, but the process of how it came is out of the bounds of human reason or knowledge. For *theia moira,* see the extensive examples in E. Berry, *The History and Development of the Concept Theia Moira and Theia Tuche Down to and Including Plato* (Chicago, 1940).

19. The initial flurry of hostility has abated as the orality thesis has gained respectability. The book, now translated into many languages, is still vigorously in print after a quarter of a century. The originality of the book and its basic argument are, with few exceptions, normally given the reasoned and careful assessment they deserve, even when the author is in dissent, partial or full. See M. Santirocco, ''Literacy, Orality and Thought'' *Ancient Philosophy* 6 (1986) pp.153–161, for a recent, balanced treatment.

20. There is no way of telling whether this was an actual case. What attracted Plato was that Euthyphro, in order to proceed against his father in face of the contravening Athenian *nomos* about prosecuting fathers, makes an extreme claim to possess knowledge, to know ''very precisely'' (*akribōs,* a strong adverb), just what piety is and what it requires. That is the philosophical opening Plato wanted. The dialogue is only incidentally about legalities, or for that matter competing definitions of piety; its true subject matter is the claim to knowledge.

21. *Euthyphro* 3 E–4 B.

22. *Euthyphro* 4 E.

23. For the Athenians, as for us, context was the guide to which meaning of *nomos* or ''law'' was intended. At some point fairly early in the fifth century, as evidenced first in Aeschylus, *nomos* had come to mean both written law as well as established (oral) custom, a meaning found as early as Hesiod.

24. *Euthyphro* 5 E–6 A. It is significant that because Zeus is *dikaiotatos* (''the most

just") of the gods he can do nothing that is impious, and so in imitating the divine action, neither can Euthyphro be doing anything impious; that is his claim. This dialogue begins the Platonic task of sorting out the various meanings of the adjective *dikaios/dikaion* (and its opposites) that had been accumulating in the Greek experience since Homer: "customary," "established," "proper," "right," "moral," and finally "legal" or what is in conformity with written law (perhaps first in the Gortyn code). In *Republic* Book I, Thasymachus will force Socrates to raise the question of the relationship of morality to law in the context of *enacted* and so written law (specified by Thrasymachus, e.g., *tithetai nomous,* Rep. 338 E; also 339 C). In addition, the fact that some of the meanings of *dikaion* would overlap with what is "pious" begins to create philosophical difficulties, which are also addressed later in the *Euthyphro* when Socrates demands to know which is the wider concept, piety or justice. No other ancient society examined the primary approval words it bestowed on human behavior with this level of sophistication.

25. For example, at *Euthyphro* 6 E: "If you wish me to explain/speak that way, Socrates, I will." At 10 A: "I don't know what you mean, Socrates." At 11 B: "But I don't [now] know how to say what I mean, Socrates. For whatever statement we advance, somehow it won't stay where we put it . . . but they [our statements] would have stayed put, so far as I was concerned." Socrates greatly annoys Euthyphro because, like a linguistic Daedalus, he makes the seer's statements "move," which, left alone, they would not (so the embattled seer thinks). At 12 A: "I simply can't follow what you say, Socrates." Euthyphro was asked which of two related concepts was the wider one and so includes the other, for example, are all holy acts just, but not all just acts holy? Euthyphro does not say that he does not happen to know the right answer; rather, he says that he does not even understand the question. Encounters of this sort abound in the early dialogues. The collision between contemporary discourse, as displayed in the statements of a Euthyphro, and the Socratic demand for alterations and changes both linguistic and conceptual is to be noted.

26. *Nomos* is not a written law here, but a powerful oral custom.

27. Burnet claimed that in Rome written law prohibited indicting one's father, which may have been the case, but I have not been able to verify it. In Athens, as Burnet rightly observes, it "shocked public sentiment" and was "regarded as *anosion* [impious]." See Burnet's note to *Euthyphro* 4 A 7 in the Oxford text (J. Burnet, ed., *Plato's Euthyphro, Apology of Socrates, and Crito* [Oxford, 1924]).

28. The point of Euthyphro's comment is often missed. Euthyphro's concern is not one of equal justice for all, relatives and strangers alike—far from it. Rather, what he feels and dreads is the *miasma,* the pollution, created by a *phonos,* that he believes is spreading to him—more of a physical than a moral contagion. The source happens to be his father, but that makes no difference; the pollution is the issue. The Athenian feeling on this was very strong; *phonikai dikai* were tried in the open air, in order to inhibit the contagion.

29. Euthyphro is mentioned in the *Cratylus,* where he is portrayed as being addicted to finding etymologies (*Crat.* 396 D), but not elsewhere. It seems probable that he was a fairly well-known, if odd, figure of the late fifth century, possibly not born an Athenian citizen.

30. Some scholars, but in diverse ways, still resist taking Plato fully at his word. Older scholarship in this regard was sometimes more faithful to the plain meaning of the text than some recent contributions, which often have been concerned to find an aesthetics in Plato, especially in *Republic,* Book X.

31. *Posterior Analytics* 77A5–10.

32. See K. Robb, "Psyche and Logos in the Fragments of Heraclitus: Origins of the Concept of Soul," *Monist* 69 (1986), pp. 315–351.

33. This paragraph from Matthew Santirocco ("Literacy, Orality and Thought," *An-*

cient Philosophy 6 [1986], p. 155) was not intended as a commentary on the claims of Ion, although it well serves that purpose. Santirocco is insightful in his treatment, and in places seemingly sympathetic, but he, too, doubts that instruction can have been a primary function of epical verse (p. 160). Even so, ''It is safe to say . . . that even if Havelock is only partially right, the majority of classical texts, because of their traditional status, now await substantial revaluation'' (p. 161).

34. J. Halverson, ''Havelock on Greek Orality and Literacy,'' *JHI* 53 (1992), pp. 156–157. In deference to Burkert's influential book, Halverson concedes that Homer was, in a sense, the foundation of Greek education. But he then seeks to explain away his concession by restricting the Homeric influence (as Burkert had not) to the classical period only and by confining Homer's importance in Greek education (also as Burkert conspicuously had not) to texts, that is, to boys' reading Homer in their schools. Burkert's own words are a safer guide to the Greek oral facts. (''The Spell of Homer,'' in *Greek Religion* [Cambridge, Mass., 1985], pp. 119ff). In the context of contrasting Greek anthropomorphism with surrounding cultures, Burkert observes that the Greeks knew no priestly caste with rigid traditions, nor any authoritative revelation in an unalterable sacred text. ''The world of writing is long kept apart; classical drama is still enacted in a single, unique performance, and Plato's philosophy retains the fiction of living dialogue'' (p. 119). Continuing in this vein and noting the great diversity in the Greek tradition, Burkert observes that order must be created from the inherited chaos and that the epical poets played the crucial role. ''The authority to whom the Greek appealed was the poetry of Hesiod, and, above, all Homer. The spritual unity of the Greeks was founded and upheld by poetry—a poetry which could still draw on living oral tradition to produce a felicitous union of freedom and form, spontaneity and discipline. To be a Greek was to be educated, and the foundation of all education was Homer'' (p. 120).

7

Advancing Literacy and Traditional Greek Paideia: *Mousikē* and *Sunousia*

Embedded in the argument of the last chapter was an important lesson for the historian of literacy. Evidence for advancing literacy is one thing. Quite another is specific evidence for how a society, as it goes about replacing long-established oral habits and practices, puts the technology of an alphabet to use. This lesson will prove instructive as we look next at the way in which the traditional mechanisms of Greek oral paideia gradually forged an alliance with the alphabet and then grew dependent on it. We shall attempt to answer Plato's own question in the *Republic:* What then shall our paideia be? Or is it difficult to find one better than that which a long time established?[1]

To answer that question not for a select band of guardians but for Greece itself, the historian's attention must turn increasingly toward Athens, for in fourth-century Athens literacy and formal education were finally allied, a union not to be severed again in Europe. As this alliance was forged, such traditional, oral institutions as the neglected (by modern historians) *sunousia,* as well as the *sumposia* and *choreia*—institutions of *mousikē* that for so many centuries were at the core of the Hellenic paideia—faded into inconsequence.[2] Attempts will be made to revive some of them from time to time in the Hellenistic period, and even at Rome, for nostalgic or even ''cultural'' reasons, but they no longer have important roles to play in the enculturation process. Books and schools have supplanted them.

In Athens, the first evidence for schools is later than for Ionia, where there is literary evidence for some schools in the late sixth century. But as noted earlier, political and legal developments that were spread over the entire fifth century and concentrated in the second half would have provided strong impulse for increasing numbers among the wealthier classes of Athens to insist that their sons, for whom they had political ambitions, receive formal instruction in letters. Schools would be a necessity. In any society, significant progress toward full alphabetic literacy is going to depend on formal instruction in the use of an alphabet, on drills that make its use automatic before adolescence, and so eventually on the development of a school system. Haphazard instruction by private individuals of each other always remains just that and no more. Progress in making reading and then writing automatic skills, if they ever become so, will remain uneven without institutionalized instruction. This is precisely what happened among craftsmen and others whose literacy was self-taught or handed from father to son.

The "letter-master" *(grammatistēs),* who was eventually to become a familiar figure in the city, but who initially appears to have been an itinerant like the foreign sophist, is not attested in the Athenian literature of the fifth century. Direct evidence for permanent *grammatodidaskaleia* (that rare Greek word meaning a school for letters, a clear advancement) and so of a systematic attempt to introduce the early acquisition of letters into the city's life is also lacking for the fifth century or earlier.[3] Even so, the indirect evidence is persuasive for a slow, but steadily increasing advance in the spread of literate skills throughout the fifth century that suggests the presence of such schools. These were private, of course, for free males only, and paid for by the boy's family. Plato himself, who came of age as the century was closing, surely attended such a school, and the references of his interlocutors in various dialogues to their own education, presumably not fictional or anachronistic, imply their existence. The *locus classicus,* as often pointed out, is the famous schooling passage in the *Protagoras.* For the fourth century in Athens we know that these tuition-charging private schools existed, and the presumption is that this was the case elsewhere in Greece also.

Donald Kagan, in describing the formative years of Pericles, who was born six years into the fifth century, has also well described the education of aristocratic youth in that century. We may, perhaps, assume some formal instruction in the rudiments of letters at an early age for most aristocratic boys, although this is highly speculative for the *early* fifth century. Kagan's description of what followed upon it is instructive for the whole century.

> The traditional education of Athenian youth was practical and ethical rather than intellectual. Physical training prepared the boys for the athletic contests that were a regular part of religious festivals in Athens and of Panhellenic competitions. . . . Musical education taught them to sing and play the lyre and an oboelike instrument called the *aulos,* but most of all to learn the traditional body of poetry, chiefly the epics of Homer.[4]

Kagan reminds his readers that this musical instruction also had its practical purposes. Each year thousands of Athenian boys and men were expected to compete in choruses at religious festivals, and nightly the aristocrats among them repaired to the *sumposia* that formed the heart of aristocratic social life. There, as the myrtle branch passed from couch to couch, each participant would be expected at some point to sing. Kagan rightly alludes to the evidence of Plato's *Protagoras,* where the purpose behind Greek boys' being compelled to memorize the poets and especially Homer is set out with unmistakable clarity. The *grammatistēs* has taught the boys the rudiments of letters. Then they undertake to memorize the works of good poets, for, in Plato's words,

> here they meet with many admonitions, and many descriptions and encomia of the great men of times long ago, so that the boy *(pais),* desiring to imitate *(mimētai),* seeks to become like them. . . . Moreover, when they have learned to play the kithera, they are taught the works of a whole other set of good poets. (326 A)

Epic first, and then melic or lyric poets, all to be memorized and recited or sung, and all fundamentally in the interests of moral instruction. The representations of these scenes, dominated by learning to play musical instruments and by boys memorizing poetic texts under the correcting eye of the *grammatistēs* and *kitharistēs,* commence in the pictures on Athenian vase work right at the turn of the fifth century. None is earlier. Probably the best known of these school scenes is found on the famous Douris vase.

To this paideia for the young minds, adds Plato's *Protagoras,* is superimposed training for the young bodies, so that the body may execute the orders of the mind (326 B). Even if the subordination be suspiciously Platonic, what is clearly accepted as contemporary fact is that, taken together, these two forms of training are said to exhaust the traditional Athenian paideia, as they are also said to do in the *Republic:* "music" (sung poetry) and instrumentation for the mind, gymnastic training for the body. Nothing is left, according to the *Protagoras* text, except for the polis then to take over and instruct the young in its laws. Their (fifth-century) education is complete. Again in Plato's words:

> This is what people do who are the most able, and the most able are the richest. Their sons begin with teachers at the earliest age and are freed from them at the latest. (326 C)

But as Kagan has perceptively observed:

> The most important part of the traditional education involved learning the epic poems by heart, for Homer was the fountain of wisdom and the model of Greek behavior. . . . In the early part of the fifth century, this was as much education as a young aristocrat received.[5]

Scrolls, School Scenes, and *Mousikē* on Fifth-Century Vases

In 1964 Henry Immerwahr, putting Greek scholarship in his debt, published an article on scenes on Attic vases that contain book rolls, supplemented by a later article with a few additional examples not discussed in the earlier piece.[6] Neither article claimed to be exhaustive, but together they are the most comprehensive treatment to date, and not much could have been missed. Some of his entries are obscure or in private collections and generally inaccessible; forty-five vases in all are canvased. Significantly, these scenes commence in the fifth century, near the turn of it, but are totally absent from earlier vases. Since this period, 500–490 B.C., also marks the inception of the Athenian democracy, Immerwahr adopts the theory proposed earlier by B. D. Merrit (in 1940, commenting on the stone inscriptions) and Martin Nilsson (in 1955, referring to *ostraka*) that the notable fifth-century Athenian acceleration toward a more widespread literacy is to be associated with that *political* development. This conclusion, I have argued here, seems essentially correct, making the evidence from contemporary Attic vases of considerable importance, for as in the case of the literary evidence, it too points to the fifth century as the period in which literacy and paideia entered into their first Athenian alliance.

Athenian vase painters, as is well known, enjoyed representing all aspects of daily life in the city on their wares, especially novel ones (as Immerwahr notes), for which we now are grateful. The vases take us directly into scenes of *sumposia* in progress, athletic contests underway, praise singers and aulos players at work, even a rhapsode performing, all indicating a keen interest in activities included in the traditional Hellenic paideia. Starting about 500 B.C. or a little after, there is a significant addition. Painters begin introducing scrolls into their scenes that, when their content is also indicated, contain verses that young men memorize and perform (sing or recite). Lyres and flutes are also very much in evidence, and in school scenes generally far more so than book rolls.

The precise relationship of the boy to a text in the scenes where book rolls appear is not always clear to us. Aristocratic boys may well have read selected texts from the teacher's rolls or wax tablets for memorizing purposes, as the *Protagoras* suggests, although in the vase work the young adolescent himself is normally reciting or singing. Whatever the case, these are at most school texts or performance texts, as Immerwahr's exhaustive catalogue demonstrates. Originally no doubt they were prepared by and were a part of the professional equipment of the paid teachers of the rich. In time, copies became the property of individuals in private homes; a boy understandably wanted a book at home in order to "work up" his recitation. In one case, a boy is practicing an impassioned performance before an older woman, presumably his mother (so argues Immerwahr). The mother holds the roll on her lap; dots represents the verses symbolically (from a red-figured cup by the early Sabouroff painter ca. 460 B.C. now in the Allard Pieson Museum in Amsterdam).

On the vases, all texts are in verse when a few words are also shown (about a closed scroll we can say little) and thus poetic. There is one apparent exception, on a fragment of a red-figured cup by the Akestorides painter (from ca. 460 B.C.) from a private collection in Greenwich, Connecticut (formally Walter Bareiss Collection, No. 63), but now in the J. Paul Getty Museum in Malibu, California (Figure 7.1). It is mentioned in Immerwahr's second paper, after it had been called to his attention. In the the first paper he had asserted that *all* the texts were poetic and dominated by epic. But even the Getty Akestorides Painter vase turns out to be no real exception. A seated lad holds a roll before his chest, pointing the writing toward the viewers of the cup; a partially visible male, instructor or admirer, stands before him, waiting to listen. Several readable words appear, four or five letters across, written horizontally across the roll, in the old manner. The opening indicates that the content will deal with "the (men) under Heracles," followed by a blank space and the start of a list of names, of which only part of the first is visible:]*oleo*[. Immerwahr proposed Ioleo(s), which is plausible and fits the spacing (although spacing is deliberately altered from the previous lines). I suggest that the writing refers suggestively or symbolically, in the manner of the vase painters, to an epical recitation in which Heracles led an expedition, as in *Iliad* 653ff. Heracles leads the Rhodian contingent in the mustering of the ships at Aulis; his name on the vase is certain. For the problematic name, the top of one of the preceding letters is visible just above the boy's arm; it is the tip of a straight line and so could be Attic I, but also Attic L. We do not know how

Figure 7.1. A youth prepares for an epical recitation. Fragment from an Attic red-figured cup fragment by the Akestorides painter, ca. 470–450 B.C. Formerly in the Walter Bareiss Collection and presently in the Collection of the J. Paul Getty Museum, Malibu, California (86 AE 324). Courtesy of the J. Paul Getty Museum.

many letters followed the last *o* because the scroll is rolled over the next line, but *ērak/leei,* or Heracles (the *heta* was omitted even though the alphabet is Attic, which is not uncommon) was divided at the *k,* running over two lines. The final readable letter seems to be an almost certain *o* (the first *o* is not certain; only the tip is visible under the boy's arm). The name Tlēpolemos, leader of the Rhodian contingent under Heracles at Aulis would normally be hard to resist, but the physical evidence seems to tell against it. But whoever was the first among Heracles' men, the text is "connected with the study of poetry," as Immerwahr notes. A list of names is what a reciter of the most difficult (mnemonically) passage in all of Homer would want to possess, and memorize—even today, I am told by mnemonists who work at the task.

The lad's recitation, for which he is preparing (he is seated) was epically inspired, as Immerwahr also observed, citing as a model the eleventh book of the *Iliad,* 689ff., where Heracles appears. His recitation will feature the men under Heracles, headed by a man who had the letters *le,* which are certain, or perhaps *oleo,* which are probable, somewhere in the middle of his name, with either L or I preceding them within a short space. The boy's recitation was plausibly but not certainly to be from the Catalog of Ships. This would have been one of the first parts of Homer to be reduced to writing, and it was stabilized early. (It should also be mentioned there have been ingenious attempts to read the Getty Akestorides inscription as epic *verse*—and so not a prose exception to Immerwahr's poetic list at all—by reading the letters as a combination of the Attic and Ionic alphabets, a phenomenon which is not unknown for the period.)

As school excerpts, all of these examples are a single scroll or less in length. We are treated to a few suggestive words at most, always poetic save in the Greenwich vase, which I argue is no real exception, although the words are prose. There is no evidence that the rolls represent the complete works of any Greek poet. As in the *Protagoras,* they are clearly subordinate to the necessity that a Greek boy, a well-bred boy, memorize a vast amount of instructional verse, especially the moralizing portions. Simultaneously, he learns to play the lyre and, normally, the *aulos* too; he learns proper deportment before his elders, and good manners. He becomes *kosmios* and *euatales,* orderly and well-mannered. His special virtue is *sōphrosunē,* that untranslatable word that always connotes a degree of passive acceptance, modesty, and self-control.

This is the picture that emerges as clearly from the vase school scenes as it does from the contemporary literary evidence. Put another way, the priority of *mousikē,* poetry sung to the accompaniment of instruments, has been untouched by the intrusion of performance texts in fifth-century Athens and its recent schools. Indeed, the context in which these poetic texts appear confirms that priority. The texts are extensions of the older practice of memorizing and performing instructive verse, but adding a technology that made the practice more efficient. One activity was oral and the other literate, and so the marriage improbable, but nevertheless it seems to have been a happy, successful one.

It follows that whatever may have been the manner of involvement of Athenian boys with their performance texts, or whether or not they produced their own texts from recitation (but on wax, as on the Douris vase, and so short) to be corrected by the *grammatistēs,* the practice would not argue for a culture of habitual readers of manuscripts popularly diffused—far from it. Rather, it argues for a culture of singers, reciters, and performers into whose *aristocratic* educational practices letters and the schools required to teach them have recently intruded. Some (limited) use is being made of literacy to foster the still more fundamental and older practice of insinuating indelibly into the memories—and in Plato's understanding the very souls—of the young that great body of traditional Hellenic verse that was the core of its verbal paideia. The purpose behind the considerable mnemonic effort undertaken by the young boys of Athens in memorizing this body of verse (epic, as noted, plays the dominant role in the vase scenes with inscriptions) is essentially paideutic and not aesthetic; as the *Protagoras* passage indicated, it always had a heavy moral bias. Moralistic didacticism also emerges as a feature of Greek *mousikē* in the supporting evidence found on vases, as Immerwahr mentions concerning a number of entries. Immerwahr calls these examples the obviously "didactic" and "gnomic" texts. The concluding words of Immerwahr's earlier paper states the situation well for the closing years of the fifth century:

> The popular image of the book was not the prose book, nor the great epic or the tragic text, but the epic tale and the short hymn, the gnomic collection, and the collection of lyric poems. . . . From there the sophists, orators and philosophers (more than the tragedians) took up the cause of the book and spread its popular use further.

Advancing Literacy and the Priority of *Mousikē*

The changing political climate of the fifth century made literacy a desirable achievement for young Athenian aristocrats; the response of the moneyed classes was to imitate the Ionian practice of hiring instructors in letters and, finally, to support schools. The natural result was marriage between the older poetic material, previously learned exclusively by ear, and the new performance texts that added some aid from the eye. Early writing exercises, obviously, were not going to be a matter of eager boys scrambling around the acropolis and copying down decrees, even if "politics" in the wide sense was the motive behind the accelerated interest of the upper classes in literacy. The fifth-century democracy gave its citizens ample reason to desire to know their letters. The sixth-century tyrants had apparently afforded little, and so aristocratic education had remained dominantly oral and musical through that century. As a result, Athens entered the fifth century a society of restricted popular literacy, without even schools that we know of for teaching letters. In the course of the fifth century, possibly around the middle of it, writing schools are introduced in Athens, preceded perhaps by a period of some decades of private instruction in the homes of the wealthy by a *grammatistēs*. Many of these, probably, at least at first, were imported from Ionia. As often noted, some of the scenes on vases, especially those earlier than 450 B.C., in which rolls or instruments appear are as likely to be from a stately private home as in a "school." So accustomed have we become to the great fourth-century Athenian achievement in literature, especially prose literature, and its famous philosophical schools, that it is difficult to imagine that at the turn of the fifth century the city was not, in terms of literacy, the Hellenic leader, but a follower. That would rapidly change.

In light of the incontrovertible contemporary evidence, the fifth-century acceleration in popular Athenian literacy, whereas significant and the object of much scholarly debate, is not the crucial issue for the history of Greek paideia. Indeed, the acrimony of that debate may have obscured the important question. The issue is not whether a certain number of free males, or for that matter their fathers, found it increasingly desirable as the fifth century wore on to learn their letters for *some* purpose or other; all parties to the dispute will, or should, concede that. The relevant issue is, did the degree of literacy acquired replace in the *fifth* century the traditional, oral methods for transmitting the Hellenic paideia to a new generation? A closely related question is at what point is there any evidence that Athenians of any age learn their letters in order to read a body of literature copied in sufficient quantity to make such a practice both feasible and desirable? My point is that an increasing popular literacy in the fifth-century Athenian democracy seems clearly to have been oriented to civil, legal, and diplomatic matters, with some mercantile development, not to producing a revolution in the methods of traditional education. We must resist the automatic assumption of an alliance between literacy and paideia based on a model familiar to us, however natural.

Mention may again be made of the evidence of *ostraka,* for much has been made of it. The fifth century *ostraka,* so often cited as proof for "popular literacy," in fact only indicate pressures toward a degree of literacy that permits scratching a name, although the duplication of handwriting on the extant *ostraka* indicates that one person could perform this service for many others.[7] Such *ostraka* in whatever numbers are silent on the question of changes in the traditional procedures of Greek paideia. They do not so much as touch on the issue of the priority of *mousikē* as centered in the memorization and performance of instructive verse. Persons capable of producing *ostraka* must not be presumed to be reading books of poetry or the tragedies of Aeschylus in their leisure hours.

The same caution must be made concerning the late fifth-century multiplication of official decrees preserved on stone and for the other well-known indicators of advancing civil and legal literacy. They, too, have been claimed as "proof" of popular literacy. First, a more cautious assessment comes from Mogens Hansen:

> even in their case [decrees and laws] there is a distinct balance toward the fourth century. Once again it is not the fortuitousness of survival that is playing us tricks, but the lateness of transition from oral tradition to the written document. As late as 411 the Athenians were in doubt whether the constitutional laws of Kleisthenes existed anywhere in written form.[8]

But even if some fifth-century proliferation of decrees was the case, what relevance is it to issues of popular literacy and the traditional paideia? What alone will significantly alter didactic and cognitive habit is the transference of a previously oral paideia—the manner of its preservation and the way it is brought to bear on the developing and receptive minds of a new generation—from the ear and oral memory to the reading eye. That demonstrably had not occurred in the fifth century, or even early in the fourth. What had for centuries had been traditional oral practices were not simply thrown over, any more than they were in legal matters. The oral paideia of Hellas was in place and was working superbly well. For Greeks themselves, it was part of the glory of Hellas; as an aged Plato in his *Laws* admits, when remembering the Athens of his youth, to be a Greek man was always to be *anēr mousikos,* a "musical man." The most enjoyable and recreational aspects of civic and personal life—*sumposia* and *choreia,* rhapsodic recitations and contests, the performance of the tragedies, joyous hymns in great temples—all were associated with the Hellenic oral paideia and deeply rooted in it. The oral and musical basis of Hellenic paideia, wedded as it was to both cult and recreation, was not going to be overthrown in a day. If the piles of broken *ostraka* and the surviving fifth-century decrees were doubled overnight, we would still need to ask when the memorization of instructional verse designed to be performed and recited was dislodged—or at least significantly supplemented—as the core of the Hellenic paideia.

So important a distinction is at stake here that some elaboration, at the risk of repetition, is called for. A lively scholarly debate over the past thirty years has concerned when in the fifth century Athens had achieved "popular literacy." All parties to the debate reverted to the same pieces of indirect evidence such as the practice of ostracism, some scenes on vases, a few dramatic allusions to spreading literacy, or even a supposed sixth-century "law of Solon." Most contenders had a favorite piece (or pieces) of evidence that, for them, clinched the argument for "widespread popular literacy" in the fifth century, but with no agreement concerning just what evidence it was. In the argument of this work, that controversy, whereas important to the history of Greek *literacy,* says nothing directly about the history of Greek paideia. None of the evidence advanced solves the crucial question of when the traditional oral modes of Greek enculturation gave way to literate practice or became significantly allied with it. When does the priority of *mousikē* in Greek education yield priority to a book-centered education, which is the next step beyond performance texts? With the sort of texts found on the vase work and in literary descriptions (mainly Plato) of the recitation text, we encounter at best a kind of transition stage. The use of the "book" or roll forced the acquisition of the necessary skills of reading and writing before adolescence, but did not itself force the transition to an education centered in the preserving book.

For *that* development, in terms of evidence and not supposition, we move onto firm ground only with the evidence available in the dialogues of Plato and notably the reformed curriculum for primary education found in the *Republic,* Books II and III, the most advanced educational document of the fourth century. That evidence, I shall argue, requires a more radical conclusion. Athenian paideia did not become significantly literate and book centered rather than oral and aural in its practices at any time in the fifth century; indeed, it did not do so earlier than the proposed educational reforms of the *Republic.* Plato's great educational dialogue is the surest proof that the older priority of *mousikē* in its traditional meaning is still very much the practice in Athens as he writes.

A theory suggesting that Greek literacy commenced with economically lower classes—early craftsmen—and that, before the fifth century schools, may have made more early progress, at least on a numerical basis, among Athenian craftsmen than among the aristocratic or wealthier classes of the city runs strongly counter to literate intuition and experience. Resistance to it may be anticipated. But it gains considerable plausibility and confirmation when we face the evidence that letters had no dominating or indispensable role to play in transmitting the Greek paideia to aristocratic young Athenians until some point in the fifth century, with the advent of schools. The late advent of schools is, of course, a direct result of the historical priority of *mousikē,* giving the precise connotations of the term some importance. What the word connotes defies translation by a single English word, in part because its meaning expanded with time, but of one fact we can be sure. *Mousikē* in early-fourth-century prose literature designated that which cultivated the souls or minds of the young, even as athletics *(gumnastikē)* cultivated their bodies. In the conversations found in Plato's dialogues (but Xenophon and even Isocrates could be added), these two are commonly linked and the assertion made that they exhaust contemporary paideia as Athenians knew it. That cultural fact as recorded in the *Protagoras* has already been discussed.

The word *mousikē,* like paideia, is post-Homeric. Both words were brought into use in order to designate cultural procedures and processes far older than the nomenclature finally adopted to describe them.[9] Mousikē, as the name implies, encompassed those skills over which the Muses presided, and in early usages was confined to these. Forming the core of traditional paideia, these were skill in singing and dance, in the memorizing and reciting (or singing) of the traditional poets, and competence in playing musical instruments, notably the lyre. This is what Aristophanes[10] had called "the old education" *(archaia paideia)* and also identified, along with athletic skills, as the singing of memorized poetry combined with instruction on the lyre. In terms of how the mind was formed, paideia was assumed to be an exercise in the ancient "music," that is, in an activity involving the hearing, memorizing, and performing of verse. This understanding of *mousikē* was still firmly in place when Plato wrote his *Republic,* proposing first in Books II and III to reform the traditional *mousikē,* and then, reversing himself in Book X, to banish it flat out. As Plato uses the term in the *Republic, mousikē* does not carry the more general meaning of "culture" or even "philosophy" (or "arithmetic" or "reading and writing") that it carried notably in Hellenistic literature. It could bear all these burdens, depending on context, because, vaguely, the term always had always conjured up "education." In the *Republic,* context always makes the narrower, traditional meaning indisputable, although some notable Platonists (e.g., Paul Shorey in the notes to the Loeb translation) have been misled on the point, and in turn have misled readers of the *Republic.*

The proposals of reform, as such measures always do, tell us much about what is being reformed, especially when the reforms also leave much that is traditional in place, a neglected point in the vast criticism devoted to this dialogue. Plato's proposals for reform thus provide much positive information, not available from earlier sources, about the mechanisms of Athenian education that he was intent upon correcting and supplanting. Werner Jaeger, in his well-known three-volume study, *Paideia,* often returns to the suggestion that Plato never argues with dead men, with historical fossils. Jaeger surely was right. Plato's concern was philosophical, contemporary, often reforming, but never historical per se. Above all, this is true of his polemic with traditional Athenian ways of educating young men, perhaps the subject of greatest concern to the philosopher in his middle years. As he wrote, the matters he proposes to reform were far from being historical fossils. Indeed, it is the degree of his concession to and compromise with traditional Hellenic oralism found in his *Republic* that may surprise us and require explanation.

Residual Oralism in the Educational Reforms of Plato's *Republic*

In the *Republic,* the interlocutors are a group of Athenian aristocrats and intellectuals gathered at the house of Cephalus, an enormously wealthy *metic* who is the father of sons who are, or who are destined to become, politically and intellectually prominent in Athens. Socrates turns to the subject of education by observing that, in the process of conceptually building the perfect society, the New Athens as he (manifestly here Plato) envisions it, they have discovered the qualities that its future rulers must possess innately, by "nature" *(phusis)* or birth. That much accomplished, next they must turn to the manner of their education.

> What then is our paideia? Or is it difficult to find something better than what a long time has discovered? Which is, I suppose, for the body gymnastic *(gumnastikē),* and for the soul "music" *(mousikē).*[11]

In a swift exchange of dialogue, we discover that the contemporary paideia is regarded as consisting of two (and only two) branches: gymnastics and music. *Mousikē* comes earliest in a child's education but initially in a derivative way, in the form of nurses' tales based on Homer and Hesiod and the other poets. Next, still at a tender age, education in *mousikē* is continued by hearing those poets professionally recited, that is, chanted by rhapsodes. This poetic paideia, so the famous polemic goes, is full of lies and distortion; it is addressed to undiscerning ears at an impressionable age and all the more dangerous for that fact; it will require drastic reforms and excisions.

In terms of the specific proposals for reforming *mousikē,* several features emerge that have been neglected in Platonic scholarship. This has been the case in part, I suspect, not only because they are alien to our literate experience but also because they virtually fall through the cracks as the polemic sweeps toward its conclusions. Yet they are unmistakably there and of utmost importance to the documentation of the progress of early Greek literacy and paideia. It will be useful to note briefly the most important of them before turning to their documentation. First, education in *mousikē,* or cultivation of the mind until the age of twenty (this age is specified at 537 B), will remain, in terms of the mechanisms of instruction, *exclusively* oral and will be assimilated in occasions of public performance. A careful reading of the proposed reforms reveals that the new paideia, like the old, will take place in such public and communal forums as the theater, both tragic and comic, in hearing (reformed) rhapsodic recitations, in participating in choirs and in choral dance, and in communal singing of hymns in the temple, as well as in the hearing and singing of lyrics of a sort familiar at *sumposia.* Such a statement, it is readily acknowledged, is not to be found in the standard expositions of this dialogue or in the histories of Greek education (Marrou partially excepted), but I shall argue that it is a fair and accurate summary of Plato's text. In addition, despite many assertions to the contrary in the exegetical literature, the latter often a function of literate bias and assumption, at no point in the reform passages in the *Republic* are provisions made for the teaching of letters, and at no point are those being educated said to *read* anything. They listen, they memorize, and they sing and recite. Moreover, except for a passing allusion best explained as a slip, no mention is made anywhere of *private* instructors or teachers *(didaskaloi)* of any kind; all instruction, in addition to being oral, is communal. In one place only (at 383 C) pupils are said to memorize and sing verses selected by a teacher, a *didaskalos,* but this too remains oral.

The single, passing reference to something like private instruction may be an unconscious slip on Plato's part, adverting as it does to the contemporary Athenian practice whereby sons of aristocrats received instruction in small groups from the *kitharistēs,* the lyre master. But in the reformed *polis* there will, of course, be no aristocratic parent-guardians who, by reason of greater wealth, will pay for their sons' additional education; the whole system is organized to preclude such a practice. Also, the future guardians have not as yet been selected from the children of all classes, so special provision cannot, at least consistently, be arranged for them. It would also violate the principle of equality of access to education before the selection of the future guardians stated in the Allegory of Metals episode and *passim.* Whatever the explanation for this one mention of a *didaskalos,* Plato elsewhere always assumes *public,* not private, performances as being the medium for education in *mousikē,* and the whole *dēmos,* all three classes, are portrayed as being in attendance. *Mousikē* in the New Athens will, therefore, be continued well into young adulthood in an environment controlled by ear, instrumentation, and memory, which is to say, an oral paideia, as was traditional. In the documentation that follows, I especially call attention to what Plato assumes to be commonplace, and so reveals to be the contemporary practice. Also, I shall not be at pains to note that at every point what is assumed by Plato is the essentially *didactic* function of Greek poetry, dominantly epic; the required editorial intrusion would quickly become tedious to the reader.

At 377 Cff., at the outset of the reform of *mousikē,* Socrates claims that the most prominent stories—those of Homer and Hesiod—require the most severe censoring in the interest of properly shaping the souls of the young: "for surely these [Homer and Hesiod] have composed and told false stories to mankind, *and they still tell them (kai legousi).*"[12] Cornford and others have declined to translate the italicized phrase. The verb is in the present tense, a device also used by Heraclitus[13] to refer to contemporary recitals in Ephesus of verses from an earlier generation of epic singers, Homer and Archilochus. The target in 377 C is clearly the content of epic verse as chanted by rhapsodes in contemporary Athens, whose repertoire might include all three poets, Homer, Hesiod, and Archilochus, as confirmed in Plato's *Ion.*[14]

At 386 C, contemporary singers are forbidden "any longer" to supply passages that disparage the condition of souls in Hades, because what these singers *"now relate" (legontas)* is not true or edifying for future warriors to hear. The point is that courage *(andreia),* especially in battle, which is one of the four "cardinal" virtues that it will be the task of singers to inculcate into the souls of future guardians, is not going to be fostered by portraying an utterly cheerless afterlife for those who, like young Elpenor in the *Iliad,* are fated to die young. But Plato's argument clearly assumes that chastised epic recitals will continue in his reformed *polis* as a staple of education in *mousikē* for citizen and future guardian alike. At 389 Dff., a similar case is made for another of the cardinal virtues, *sōphrosunē.* Plato's Socrates will permit continued recitation of poetic passages supportive of its two traditional senses of control of the appetites and recognition of one's place in the social order. Specifically, whereas these will be permitted to be *sung* and *heard* (390 A), those that undermine *sōphrosunē* (in either of its senses) will, in the Platonic future, be strictly forbidden.

At 377 E, epic singers are again the main target in a complex condemnation of the experience of *mimēsis* as exploited by contemporary reciters of epical verses. It operates, as does the image of the magnet in the *Ion,* on three levels, and the failure of Plato's commentators to appreciate the oral basis of the polemic at each level has resulted in much exegetical confusion. First, the epic composer (e.g., Homer or Hesiod) is said to image badly *(kakōs eikaze)*[15] concerning the actions of gods and heroes; that is, his verbal portraits of the several moral virtues, as he narrates them as embodied in the actions of gods and heroes, do not adequately reflect the moral Forms in their role as eternal patterns *(paradeigmata)* of which specific actions are more or less imperfect images and reflections. Once Plato's words are understood in this way, the rest follows by simple logic. So also, perforce, the contemporary singer of Homer images falsely in reciting these same verses; just as inescapably, so do the guardian-hearers image badly in listening to and imitating the singer. As in the famous three-tiered image of the magnetic rings in the *Ion,* the power *(dunamis)* of epic verse as performed passes from Homer, the first composer-singer, to Ion as the present reciter, to the enraptured listeners, and Plato's primary concern once again is focused on the final or third level, that of the corruption that occurs in the psyches of listeners in their daily acts of poetic surrender to *mimēsis.*[16]

At 378 A, Socrates adds for good measure that if, for some unimaginable reason, the uncensored versions of these epic tales must continue to be recited in the New Athens, then the listening audience (*akouein* once more) shall be as curtailed as possible. Economics shall be the stick; the price of admission shall be made something dear and not a mere piglet. The reference is, of course, to what customarily procured the poor man's initiation at Eleusis, and Socrates adds that those initiates who are permitted entrance, that is, who hear the banned verses, shall (as at Eleusis) be sworn by great oaths to secrecy. There is exaggeration and deliberate humor here, but the situation behind the exaggeration is serious enough: only chastised versions of the epic poets will continue to be recited. Once again, the assumption is one of large public audiences composed of citizens and future guardians.

At 387 C, depending on the reading of the text,[17] an annual recitation of Homer may be alluded to, but the more probable reading does not restrict the experience in question to a yearly occurrence. The reference is to a singer of epic verse sending (each year?) a great shudder *(phrikē)* through "all the hearers (*pantas tous akousas*)." Socrates sternly warns that such verses, in this case another reference to the dismal fate ahead for souls in Hades, will no longer be permitted, lest the guardians imitate them and so soften the resolve and courage of their souls. The point is lost unless reformed performances continue as integral to the guardians' education and that of "all the hearers."

At 379 A, in the section on the reform of theology, poets are forbidden to misrepresent the true nature of the gods, whether that poet composes in epic, melic (lyric),[18] or tragic verse. Examples follow, drawn from epic (Homer) and tragedy (Aeschylus). Plato's point is that, in the contemporary situation, all three are what may be called performative educational activities. One is not induced to imitate—that is, vicariously mime, or personally act out in sympathetic imagination the words and actions of another—if the original contains only flat descriptive narration. Lyric has been included because of the intensely dramatic way Greek lyric singers performed (e.g., the famous ecstatic "praise singer" with his lyre portrayed on vase work) and because pupils of the *kitharistēs* were required to sing those verses in the same performative manner. Moreover, from all three—epic, tragic, lyric—apt verses were chosen for memorization and performance largely on the basis of instructional or moral content.

Accordingly, at 392 B, those entrusted with educating the young shall indeed be required to sing *(adein)* and "fableize" *(muthologein)* stories, but henceforth in Platonically censored verses. Earlier, at 390 D, educators were said to chant *(asteon)* an epic verse that in later antiquity was attributed to Hesiod but is not found in our text. It implies that the gods can be bribed: "Gifts persuade the gods, even as they do awesome kings." In the New Athens, educators shall be strictly forbidden such utterances, which are morally harmful to those who *hear* them *(akouousi)* (391 E). In this case, the educator is an epic reciter; in an example now added, he becomes a tragic actor delivering some verses from Aeschylus' *Niobe*. At 383 C, referring to some lines from a lost play of Aeschylus in which Apollo is made intentionally to utter a self-serving false prophesy, Socrates asserts that, in the future, the composer of such lines shall be denied a chorus. What, in the contemporary idiom, is to be denied him is the very production of his play, obviously implying that the production of reformed drama by others will continue. Epical recitation and tragic performances are clearly to continue, or Plato's strictures make no sense.

Socrates adds (383 C) the further negative injunction that neither shall teachers *(didaskaloi)* use such lines (as those that portrayed the god as lying) in the instruction of the young. This appears to be an allusion, as noted, to the Athenian educational practice of aristocratic or upper-class pupils being drilled in memorizing and performing selections of verse under the instruction of a *didaskalos,* a teacher. This is the only unambiguous reference in the reform passages to some instruction that takes place in other than a public forum. The *didaskalos* in this case could be the music master, the *kitharistēs,* which is likely, or the teacher of letters, the *grammatistēs*. By the fourth century the general term *didaskalos* could refer to either figure. The reference, in any case, is not consistent with the utopian and class revisionist proposals of the dialogue and is best explained as a slip. Alternatively, Plato is using *didaskaloi* collectively—it was the general term for any kind of teacher—and he is prohibiting all teachers, which is how he is viewing rhapsodes and tragedians, from making such verses. His grounds are, in any case, moral; poetry instructs, and the young are not to be instructed in how to lie.

Historians of Greek education and philosophy alike have ignored that in the reform passages the primary emphasis is placed on rhapsodic recitation and so on the hearing and memorizing of epic verse. It is treated as though it were absolutely fundamental to contemporary paideia in areas we would term popular theology and normative ethics. Even Havelock, in *Preface to Plato,* in stressing the primary role of Homer in Greek paideia, has not equally stressed the fact that, as late as Plato's *Republic,* the clear assumption is that "Homer" will be exclusively heard in public, rhapsodic recitations. Rhapsodes and their performances, and so listening to epic verse, dominate his polemic to a degree that should reopen the issue of whether this phenomenon had not lingered more prominently into the fourth century than has generally been thought. Xenophon, Plato's contemporary, refers to the possibility of listening to one's choice among rhapsodes performing daily at noon in the Athenian *agora,* if one wished to listen.[19] In light of Plato's strictures, this may be less an exaggeration than is often assumed. Epic recitals and the content of their verse end up receiving Plato's primary attention and supply far and away the greatest number of examples and quotations of what requires reform. Tragedy, by actual count, comes out a distant second, with all other verse forms barely visible on the track. This, of necessity, reminds us again of Havelock's insistence that the role of epic as the primary form of Greek paideia (including Hesiod and then in time the other poets, but the latter always in subordinate partnership) had not been seriously eroded when Plato wrote his *Republic*.

Sufficient evidence has been culled from the reform passages—it is not an exhaustive listing—to assure at least two conclusions. First, well into the fourth century, when Plato's *Republic* was composed, Athenian paideia was still primarily oral and poetic. Participation in the communal life of the city, which was especially rich in the occasions for dramatic and epical performances, was the primary mechanism of this oral paideia. For aristocrats, it was supplemented by private instruction, fundamentally drills that reinforced the public, oral paideia and added some refined skills, especially the playing of musical instruments. Second, Plato expects that in his New Athens this oral and musical education will continue unabated for all citizens well into young adulthood, save for the reforms he has proposed.

This forces a third and important conclusion, one mentioned at the outset of this chapter. Evidence for the spread of literacy in fifth- and fourth-century Athens, clearly a historical fact, is one issue. Quite another is any evidence that Athenians before the second quarter of the fourth century, even a Plato, expected that the great body of poetic literature, which for so long had constituted Hellenic paideia, would be copied in sufficient numbers to be habitually and popularly read, or that, in this *written* form, it would be put at the center of the educational process, where orally and in performance it had so long resided. Here the assessment of Frederic Kenyon, in a dated and in parts flawed book, but a very valuable one nevertheless, may be noted: "it must be admitted that the general picture which we have, both in Plato and Xenophon, is of oral instruction and conversation, not of reading and private study."[20]

The Old Education and *Sunousia*

There is yet another aspect of the oral *archaia paideia* that emerges clearly in fifth- and fourth-century sources, notably in Plato and Xenophon. Its pictorial representation is not absent from vase work but is harder to identify there, without the words. Often verbs are used to describe it in literary sources—and they can get lost in translation—but the noun is well known: *sunousia*, "association." The term, when used quasi-technically, refers to the constant association of a younger generation with the older. Given the male bias of the culture, it also normally referred to younger men associating with older, more accomplished men. The youth listened, they absorbed the accumulated wisdom and skills of elders, and they sought to imitate their virtues. *Sunousia* was an important, cherished feature of oral Greece—and all oral societies—which, as with so much else, was to be violently altered with the advance of literacy. As in the cases of *xenia*, guest-friendship, and the *sumposion* itself, when the advance of literacy has altered an institution of oral life, it can become unrecognizable for what it once was. All too easily we can mistake it for something else.

Eric Havelock, with his usual perception for the workings of oral societies, believed that behind the indictment of Socrates was a perceived offense, mainly in the eyes of conservatives, against the traditional *sunousia*. This means that masked in the formal *asebeia* indictment were deep issues dividing the adherents of a traditional paideia, dominantly oral and poetic—and rooted in memory and performance—and the adherents of a new activity, perceived as a rival paideia and associated in the Athenian public's eyes with men like Socrates and the other *sophistai,* "clever men," the new intellectuals. Regrettably, Havelock never defended that view in any great detail in his published writings, but that it was his conviction was clear from notices in those writings and from his conversations with colleagues. Some of his published words from shortly before he died summarize admirably his conviction.

> The mechanism, if it can be called such, for maintaining this education by guaranteeing its transmission from generation to generation was one typical of an oral society: namely the habit, sedulously cultivated, of close daily association *(sunousia)* between adolescents and their elders who served as "guides, philosophers, friends." The institution favored homosexual bonding for this purpose. In a male dominated society of extended families, the arrangement enjoyed the firm support of male parents. The offense of Socrates was to propose that in effect this education be professionalized, its context no longer set by poetic tradition and practice (*empeiria*) but by dialectical examination of "ideas"—an obvious threat to political and social control hereto wielded by the leaders of the Athenian "first families."[21]

Sunousia as an institution of Greek oralism has received less attention from historians of Greek paideia (Henri Marrou and John Patrick Lynch being excepted) than has *mousikē,* in part because it is more difficult to document than a school scene on a vase. Viewed anthropologically,[22] *sunousia* was, in the preliterate ages of our species, a fundamental and daily exercise, necessary to survival. Before the important knowledge that a group must conserve has been adequately textualized and so made "public," this procedure and the male bonding and relationships it fosters—so strong, so often compared to that of father and son—are indispensable. It is a feature of all oral societies, rendering them inherently conservative and male dominated.

In Athens *sunousia* is a carryover from its oral past. It did not fade away or become a cultural anachronism until the knowledge on which the culture's major institutions depended had found its way into texts that could be read by those who must make daily use of the contents. This, in turn, required schools in sufficient numbers to render fully literate at an early age the sons of at least a ruling elite.

Socrates and *Sunousia*

Some support for Havelock's suggestions concerning the importance of *sunousia,* as we seek to make sense of the indictment of Socrates, may come from a fresh look at the *Meno,* along with some passages in *Laches* and *Apology.* We begin with the short exchange in the *Meno* between Socrates and one of the three formal accusers at his trial, the famous Anytus.

Plato, I suggest, could never introduce Anytus into a dialogue and have the trial of Socrates very far from his mind. We quickly discover that the future indicter of Socrates on a *graphē asebeias* is not in the least interested in any of Socrates' religious beliefs or lack of them, but in his role in the education of young men. The *Meno,* although of mainly epistemological interest to philosophers today, turns out to be another of the "paideia" dialogues, as is evident from its opening question: Can human excellence *(aretē)* be taught? If so, who in Athens are to be its teachers? Anytus arrives late into the conversation, just as Meno, whom we learn is a hereditary guest-friend *(xenos)* to Anytus,[23] has asked Socrates if he thinks there are any teachers of human excellence or virtue. Anytus, we discover, has a keen interest in this question. Socrates hails him as the son of an "industrious" father, a deliberately ambivalent compliment, and "as *very* well educated," which is ironic.

Full understanding of the undertones of the exchange that follows requires that modern readers share what every Athenian knew about Anytus. He was the most important of the democratic politicians who would return from exile after the fall of the Thirty to participate in the restoration of the democracy. Anytus' father was a tanner of hides and he had grown wealthy in the trade through a number of factories, but the grandfather had founded the family fortune. As a result, Anytus received a traditional, "aristocratic" education because his family could afford it, and he was enormously proud of the fact. Anytus was intent on giving his son this same education, that is, one considered appropriate to an Athenian gentleman, which is what, preeminently, Anytus wanted to be considered. The successful democratic politician was, thus, not born to the upper class, but he believed that he had been educated to it and so has "arrived." Understandably, he is defensive concerning traditional education and, above all, wary of any deviations from it (90 Bff.). Plato, who was born into the world to which Anytus aspired and who stood with ease at its pinnacle, has his Socrates treat the conservative ex-tanner with a withering, ironic courtesy.

Socrates immediately greets Anytus, hailing his future nemesis as a man with a reputation for being *kosmios* and *euatales,* very proper and well-mannered. Plato, the ironic master, is at already at work. Moreover, continues Socrates, Anytus' father gave him a good upbringing and a fine education *(eu epaideusen),* or, at least, so the Athenians must believe, for did they not choose him for the highest offices? (Anytus had been made *stratēgos,* an office that was one of the few not determined by the lot, as Plato's readers understood).

> SOCRATES: He [Meno] has been declaring to me at great length, Anytus, that he desires to possess that skill (*sophia*) and virtue (*aretē*) whereby men keep their houses and city in good order, and honor their parents, and know when to welcome, and when to speed on their way, fellow citizens and guest-friends alike, as befits the accomplished (*agathos*) man, a gentleman. (91 A)

These were the things learned by *sunousia,* not from a paid teacher, a letters-teacher *(grammatistēs)* or lyre master *(kitharistēs),* both of whom would have been hired for Anytus by his father. The question is to whom shall they turn to form such a traditional Athenian gentleman, one who can manage his *oikos* or household, know how to honor his parents, and follow such upper-class proprieties as properly maintaining a web of guest-friendships, the requirements of *xenia?* The epical roots of this traditional concept of *aretē,* or excellence, are evident in what Meno reveals he understands this education to effect or accomplish in a young man. The reference to inculcating a deep respect for the parental authority should also be noted.

Shall the instructors be, continues Socrates (who, of course, is deliberately baiting Anytus), the sophists who claim to teach, precisely, excellence, *aretē,* but for a hefty fee? Anytus, as expected, explodes in a torrent of angry words and abuse. It should also be noted that, in concluding his tirade, he uses the word (as a noun) that, as a verb, will be part of Socrates' formal indictment, ''corruption'' *(diaphthora)* of the young.

> ANYTUS: May no member of my household *(oikos),* or that of a friend, either in this city or another, be seized with such madness *(mania)* to let himself be infected with the very presence of those men! For they are a plague and a corruption *(diaphthora)* to those who associate (''having *sunousia*'') with them. (91 C)

When pressed to suggest an alternative, a particular person who can provide this paideutic service if not a Protagoras and others like him, Anytus replies as would a product of any traditional, oral society.

> ANYTUS: Why mention a particular one? Any proper Athenian gentleman he [a young man] comes across will, without exception, do him more good than the sophists, if he will listen and do as he is bid. (92 E)

That is, one generation inducts another into the proprieties of class by oral association with the *agathoi* or *aristoi,* and Anytus believes that he and his family have arrived among that group. Of course, a certain docility in the young is a prerequisite, as Anytus notes. So too are the regular occasions of *sunousia.*

Socrates asks, pointedly, if this present generation of admirable Athenian gentlemen somehow grew up spontaneously into what they are, without guidance, or did they, too, have to learn from an older generation? Anytus, irritated by the question, replies they, too, of course, learned from an older generation, for there have always been good men in the city. By *association* with an older generation of properly educated gentlemen, a younger man becomes one himself. There is no other way. Anytus is sure of it. Professional teachers of *aretē* are not needed or to be tolerated. Their claim to sell gentlemen's accomplishments for a fee cheapens what his family at great effort has achieved over three generations, rising from *demiourgoi,* craftsmen, tanners of skins, to the ruling political elite.

Socrates proceeds, as he did in the earlier *Laches,* to enumerate what seem to have become rather stock examples of notable Athenians who, nevertheless, produced mediocre sons. The examples involve the sons of two famous Athenians of the fifth century and pillars of conservatism, Aristeides and Thucydides. The scene in the *Laches* deserves notice because we can easily slide over aspects of it. The dialogue opens with two older men voicing their concern about the proper education of their sons. Each is, himself, the son of a famous and accomplished father. Lysimachus is the son of Aristeides "the Just," and Melesias is the son of Thucydides, the aristocratic opponent of Pericles. But the sons have accomplished little in comparison to their famous fathers. Even so, says Lysimachus (*Laches* 179 A–B): "We have resolved to give them [their sons] our most constant care and not—as most fathers do when their boys become young men *(meirakia)*—let them run loose as their fancy moves them." The term *meirakion* is applied to a young man between fifteen and twenty-one. The point is that his training in music and gymnastics is over, and in the fifth century nothing in the way of formal education existed to add to it. It was an awkward age and a severe lacuna in the Athenian paideia that the sophists stepped in seeking to fill. Boys were supposed to stay attached to their older male mentors in this period, and that was no problem with the lower and craftsmen classes since the boys were put to work in the shops next to their fathers and uncles. It was proving to be a problem with the upper classes, where in late adolescence the boys had nothing in a formal way to do. Being idle, and now free from the constant supervision of the *paidagogos*, they had altogether too much time on their hands to listen to a sophist or else attend the daring conversations of a Socrates.

Having formed their resolve, the two friends hold daily *sussitia,* that is, share their meals together, have the young men share the table as well, and associate with them *(sussitoumen).* This *sunousia* has, as its purpose, the proper formation or paideia of the boys, as we are explicitly told. The older men will relate to them stories derived from their own fathers—those famous men—of war and peace, proper management of city and household, and the like.

So far so good, and the boys are pliant. Lacking great exploits of their own to relate, however, the two fathers seek out Laches and Nicias, famous generals of the day, concerning how to add to the daily curriculum (related in *Laches* 179 B–D). At one point Laches (179 C) replies: "But to invite *us* to be the advisors on the education *(paideia)* of your boys and not to invite Socrates here, is to me very strange, indeed." Socrates—who conveniently was conversing with the generals when the fathers arrived—is of their own deme, or district. Moreover, Socrates is always (we are told) spending his time wherever can be found any such excellent paideutic pursuits for young men as the ones the fathers now seek for their boys. That this was his reputation in conservative circles, but as yet without hostility, is significant. The dramatic date of the *Laches* is among the earliest in the Platonic corpus, about 425 B.C., and not far from the year of Plato's own birth. The trial of Socrates for corrupting such young aristocratic males in their *meirakion* years is a quarter of a century in the future, and much will happen in the interim years to unsettle the city.

Socrates, we are also told, will be welcome in the household of Lysimachus, for through Socrates' father, Sophphoniscus, the two men had been dear friends before Sophphoniscus died. This is suspiciously Platonic invention, given the class distance between the two families. But the dramatic moment exposes nicely the way households were united in *sunousia,* for that is what is proposed here. Socrates is invited, specifically, to enter upon *sunousia* (181 C) with the households of both Lysimachus and Melesias and to associate and converse with their boys in the interests of their proper paideia. In this way, Lysimachus insists, Socrates will preserve the inherited friendship of their houses—*hosper to dikaion,* as Lysimachus adds with a Homeric flourish, "as is proper," the established way.

In part, no doubt, Plato is seeking to disarm resentment against Socrates by portraying such men as Lysimachus and Melesias as being on intimate and trusting terms with him. So Socrates is invited to help educate their sons through associating *(sunisthi)* and conversing with them in the traditional manner of oral societies. Incidental to this purpose, Plato also describes the traditional mode of paideia by personal *sunousia* between older and younger members of households as it was practiced in his own youth. Modern translations all too easily can obscure the formal and oral importance of what is being proposed here, notably in 180 C–181 D, and some translations trivialize it into what is more familiar to us.

Anytus, to return to the *Meno,* resents fiercely, as may be expected, the suggestion that *aretē* is not passed between generations in this traditional way, by passive *sunousia* of the young with the old. He especially does not like Socrates' recounting the prominent examples where *sunousia* failed to work.

> ANYTUS: Socrates, it seems to me that you are all too ready to speak ill of men. I, for one, if you will take my advice, would warn you to be careful. . . .
>
> SOCRATES: Meno, I think Anytus is angry, and I am not surprised in the least. For, in the first place, he thinks I speak ill of these good men, Athenian gentlemen all, and in the second, he firmly believes himself to be one of them.[24]

When Anytus explodes at the mention of the sophists, it becomes clear that he is prepared to include Socrates in his dangerous ire. He pointedly refers to the citizen, that is, native Athenian, as well as the foreign sophist, who draws a young man away from the *prosēkontes,* the older relatives and tribe members with whom he ought to associate and from whom he would learn *aretē.* Anytus denounces as thoroughly "demented"

> the young men who pay them [sophists] money; and still more demented are the ones who actually *let* the young men have their way, their relations and proper mentors *(prosēkontes).* But most demented of all are the cities that allow them [foreign sophists] to enter, and do not expel them, whether such attempts be made by a stranger *or by a citizen.*[25]

Because all the sophists were visiting foreigners, and so non-Athenians, the angry, unexpected reference to an Athenian citizen could, of course, refer only to Socrates himself. Anytus wanted him expelled from the city, exiled, removed from a position of influence over the young. Probably the intent behind his subsequent participation in the indictment of Socrates in 399 B.C. was only exile. Socrates forced his execution by proposing not exile as the counterpenalty to death, but a far lighter penalty, a fine.

In light of the exchange with Anytus, Socrates' cross-examination in Plato's *Apology* of Meletus, another of his formal accusers at his trial, takes on a new light. Socrates exercises his legal right to demand that his accuser answer his questions in court. The exchange, a long one (*Apology* 24 D–26 B) from an author not given to wasting words, may be summarized in its relevant parts, and paraphrased, as follows.

> SOCRATES: Do you consider it important that the youth become as good as possible?
>
> MELETUS: I do.
>
> SOCRATES: Tell these gentlemen of the jury, then, who makes them better, since you have found out who corrupts them. . . . Answer, for the law requires that you answer.
>
> MELETUS: The Laws *(hoi nomoi).*
>
> SOCRATES: That is not what I asked. If a man corrupts them, then a man makes them better. Who is *he?*
>
> MELETUS: The jurymen *(dikastai)* here.
>
> SOCRATES: All or only some of them [there were many hundreds]?
>
> MELETUS: All.
>
> SOCRATES: How about the many spectators in the court? All of those men too?
>
> MELETUS: Yes, all.
>
> SOCRATES: And the members of the Assembly [some 6,000]. Them too?
>
> MELETUS: Yes. Them too.
>
> SOCRATES: Then *all* the Athenian gentlemen, and good citizens, make our young men into gentlemen, "beautiful and good," as we say. All the citizens of Athens conspire to make young men into fine gentlemen, into one who is who is *kalos k'agathos,* except only one citizen, Socrates. He corrupts the youth. Is that what you say?
>
> MELETUS: Precisely.

Meletus here defends the traditional oral institution of *sunousia* and expects his defense to play well with the jury, as no doubt it did. By associating dutifully with an older generation of good men, tribal elders—fathers, uncles, and an extended family—one becomes good. This is accomplished by listening, admiring, remembering, and emulating.

The association—but not primarily, and not without controversy—could be erotic, and this was permitted by the boy's family. Ostensibly, at least, this was always in the interests of *aretē,* traditional excellence, as the first two speakers of Plato's *Symposium,* Phaedrus and Pausanias, insist.[26] But more fundamentally, Greek *sunousia* was familial, tribal, and civic, not sexual. The essential male virtues are transmitted across generations by constant association of younger men with older, the guiding elders of the group, its Mentors and Nestors; this is what what Greeks in the fifth century understood to be the purpose behind *sunousia.* Dorian communities such as those at Sparta and on Crete were thought to be best at transmitting the civic and social male virtues in the institutions of common meals, or the "male mess," and the men's house *(andreion).* Athenians thought some of the Dorian practices extreme, but admired the resulting *eunomia,* or social "lawfulness," at least in conservative circles.

The final institutionalization of the paideia of young men in their *meirakion* years, a development of the advancing literacy of fourth century and of the Athenian philosophical schools, was greatly to diminish the importance of all levels of *sunousia,* including the erotic, as a part of the Greek educational process. The *sumposion,* too, was to go into decline. It was the older sophists and Socrates who pioneered this move toward institutionalization by first undermining familial and tribal *sunousia.* Plato, Isocrates, and Aristotle brought it to completion in the fourth century, each a founder of a famous school.

Still another passage of the *Apology* takes on a new emphasis in light of the traditional Athenian attitude toward *sunousia.* Socrates says at 19 Eff. that he knows that the young men of Athens swarm around him to listen to his conversations. Some are ambitious for political careers, looking ahead to the give and take of debate in the Assembly and to pleadings in courts. Wealthy young men especially, having leisure as *meirakia* are likely to listen to his exchanges and then try to imitate at home what they have heard. This Socrates is obviously helpless to prevent. However, if any juror has heard that, like a traveling sophist, Socrates takes money for such a service or takes a fee, he is not to believe it.

> For each of these, men of the jury, is able to go into any one of the cities and persuade the young men, who can *associate* for nothing with whomever they wish among their own citizens, to give up the *association (sunousia)* with those good men, and *associate* with them (the sophists) instead, and pay them money for it, and be grateful besides.[27]

The many forms of the word "associate," as noun and verb, sound innocent in translation, but it was a clarion signal to the Athenian jury.

Socrates knows well the source of resentment that the foreign sophist raised in the conservative populace and seeks insofar as he fairly can, to distance himself from it. In the matter of taking fees he is, of course, on solid ground. Notoriously, he did not do that and was perhaps too much a product of an oral society ever to do so. The professional and paid professor was a product of a more literate future, pioneered by great sophists such as Protagoras, who proudly proclaimed their willingness to be paid, and paid well. A Mentor, a Phoenix, or a Nestor was not a paid hireling. That Socrates practiced a rival form of *sunousia* to a different intent and with a radically different sort of conversation, however, he could hardly deny, and he does not. But were his actions impious under the law?

I suggest that if Socrates seriously undermined the traditional institution of *sunousia* between son and father, younger and older generation, then to conservative Athenians he may well have been viewed as being guilty of *asebeia.* If I am not mistaken, it was for his endeavors in the area known as paideia and his attempts to professionalize it away from the traditional *sunousia* that Socrates was tried in 399 B.C., and was found guilty. And it was for this offense that the powerful Anytus joined the prosecution, an event that contributed greatly to securing Socrates' conviction.

Conclusion: *Asebeia* and *Sunousia*

Both Socrates and the resented sophists drew young men away from the traditional *sunousia* with male elders and to themselves; both were the purveyors of a paideia seen as a rival to the traditional one. Socrates was perceived to be an educator, and although he claimed no doctrines, the popular perception was correct. In fifth-century conservative eyes, the differences between Socrates and a sophist, if any, were of little relevance, as the nomenclature used to designate them in Old Comedy reveals. Socrates is never a *philosophos*; he is a *sophistēs*, a figure who was, in the fifth-century literature, often considered too clever by half. The young men of Athens—as the young are wont to do whenever an enterprise smells of rebellion and danger—flocked to the sophists.

The technical legal question is this: Could activities that were an offense against the traditional *sunousia* or that undermined the tight control fathers and immediate families sought to maintain over these paideutic associations constitute the *legal* basis of his trial for impiety? It is a difficult and legally obscure question, but a few suggestions may be ventured here.

Piety in Athens entailed, to be sure, a proper and traditional attitude toward the gods and the civic *cultus*. But, by not so wide an extension (at least for Athenians), it also covered the most sacred customs of tribe and family and city that stood under the gods' special protection. The lines, it is clear from many cases, were not always drawn as sharply as a logician or a modern lawyer might wish. Moreover, *sunousia*, particularly as it submitted sons to the guidance of their fathers, and a younger generation to an older one in an approved and supervised way, was clearly part of that ancestral piety in popular eyes. Feasibly then, any direct assault on it was considered to be impiety. We do not possess the speeches of Socrates' accusers, but there is much indirect evidence, as we have seen, that this was the gravamen of their charges.

Unfortunately, we also do not have the wording of the *asebeia* statute under which Socrates was indicted; it has survived neither on stone nor in the speeches of the orators. But we do know that in 399 B.C. magistrates such as the King Archon could issue indictments only on the basis of the written law. The *asebeia* statute, therefore, had to have existed, perhaps one of the last features of oral custom to be formulated in written law. Also, just what an Athenian legal definition of impiety might have looked like in 399 B.C. is much controverted by legal historians. Greek law—often to our consternation—was not overly given to definitions. Much was left to the common understanding of good citizens, or informed magistrates. More probably than not, a generally worded proscription is what Nichomachus might have drawn up, one that would have included earlier narrower decrees (e.g., of Diopeithes) by permitting the specific actions they proscribed to fall under its broad wording, if a jury so determined. It would leave the crucial term, perhaps wisely, undefined. Impiety, then, would be proscribed in general terms in written law; but Athenian juries were left a good deal of discretion to determine just what actions were impious or fell under its proscription.

One thing, at least, is certain and requires emphasis. Socrates was not indicted for any old political indiscretions, for association with known enemies of the democracy, for being the teacher of Alcibiades, or for anything of the sort. That was legally impossible under the terms of the famous amnesty, of which Anytus himself, as we saw in an earlier chapter, was the most conspicuous upholder among the prominent democrats. The amnesty, as far as we know, was never violated, and the orators remarked on the fact. Under the terms of this extraordinary amnesty, in the year 399 B.C. the philosopher Socrates—who, in any case, was notoriously not a political man—was, necessarily, indicted for something that he refused to stop doing *after* 403 B.C., and which actions therefore did not fall under its protections. That this was the situation with Socrates is suggested by Plato's *Apology,* in which no reference to the amnesty is made. Unlike an Andocides, who came to trial for *asebeia* in the same year and who was saved by direct appeal to it, Socrates makes no such appeal. Whatever we may decide Socrates' real offense was, it is clear that the amnesty could afford him no protections. Moreover, becasue his *graphē* was for *asebeia,* impiety, his offense had to have been for something that Athenians could perceive to be a breach of traditional piety and so fall under a (presumably) broadly written statute.

Unlike a traveling sophist, Socrates was a native son, a free male citizen, and so a person not easily driven from the city. Had he not made it clear that not even dire warnings from powerful men were going to silence him or dissuade him? A *graphē asebeias,* if the indictment could be so worded to get past the Archon Basileus and before a jury, might well have been perceived by desperate men as the only remedy to get at Socrates and so force him to cease and desist from what he was doing that so annoyed them. There was no presiding judge in Athenian heliastic courts and no rules of evidence worth mentioning. The legal obstacles were mainly in the *anakrisis* stage, which took place before a magistrate.

For good measure, and playing to the hoped-for prejudice of a large jury, the accusers of Socrates tacked onto the indictment the standard accusation that he did not acknowledge the customary gods that the city acknowledges. But in Plato's *Apology* Socrates has an easy job of refuting that old saw, and in the *Euthyphro* it is the charge concerning corrupting the youth that he takes far more seriously. He was, he easily proves, no Ionian *sophistēs,* no Anaxagoras or Protagoras, although he acknowledges some lingering prejudice in this regard from Aristophanes' *Clouds.* But, he counters to the jury, for over forty years the Athenians—fathers and sons—have listened to what the philosopher has had to say. He challenges any of them—his legal right—who has personal knowledge that he denied the traditional gods to come forward with it now. Significantly, no one does. It was not for that aspect of the indictment that the conviction was voted.

The charge that he "corrupted the youth"—significantly made part of the wording of an *asebeia* indictment that was approved by the archon—was another matter altogether. Insofar as he had all too successfully "corrupted" the younger generation away from their traditional paideutic associations and from the familial and tribal bonds of *sunousia,* he was clearly guilty. And for this—not his religious beliefs or cult practices—men like Anytus resented him, hated him, and sought to remove him from the city.

Before dismissing this suggestion out of hand, we should recall how deep can run the resentment on the part an older generation against those perceived to be warping the minds of the young or undermining traditional values, especially in times of great national or social upheaval. Generations and families are divided against each other, and even high officers of the law do not always follow the law. Not so very long ago a generation of Americans lived through such a searing experience as the nation pursued a misguided and doomed war in Asia.

Socrates was indicted in the first year that was legally feasible after Athens had lost a war that brought it to its knees, turned it into an occupied city, and destroyed it forever as a military and political power. That was 399 B.C., the year that the reinscription of the religious law (the calendar), as well as the civil sections of the Athenian law code, had at last been completed, and the courts were now cleared for action. There was a flurry of litigation in that year, and no time was lost in bringing Socrates to heel. The pent-up fury against him among Athenians such as Anytus, who saw Socrates and men like him as the ruin of their city, could now be unleashed in the courts.

The best legal weapon that the newly reinscribed laws put in their hands was a *graphē asebeias,* if their intention was to drive Socrates from the city. The threat of one had driven Protagoras out, and in the future would do so for Aristotle as well. Had Socrates countered by volunteering the penalty of exile—as no doubt his accusers expected, and which would have been gratefully voted, given the closeness of the vote for conviction—his enemies would have been quietly rid of him. But, forced by Socrates himself to vote for execution, his accusers and the jury gave the first Athenian philosopher, through Plato, an undying voice.

Notes

1. *Rep.* 376 Eff. This passage is discussed later in the chapter.

2. *Sunousia,* the assiduously cultivated association of the younger men with older mentors, relatives, family, clan members, or *erastai,* is a prominent feature of Greek oralism. It is discussed later in this chapter. Plato in the *Laws* (654 A) can still say of *choreia,* dancing and singing in chorus, *achoreutos, apaideutos.* The neat aphorism, "without chorus, without paideia" requires English paraphrase: He who cannot take his place in chorus, singing and dancing, is uncultured, uneducated, without *paideia.* Also see Theognis I, 239–243, 789–792; H. Marrou, *A History of Education in Antiquity* (Madison, Wisc. 1982), pp. 41ff., "Musical Education," "Education through Poetry," and his references to Greek authors.

3. On the late introduction of teachers of letters and schools in Athens, see L. H. Jeffery in "Writing" in A. Wace and F. Stubbings (eds.), *A Companion to Homer* (London, 1963) pp. 554–555. On the *grammatistēs* see F. Beck's section so titled in F.A.G. Beck, *Greek Education, 450–350 B.C.,* (London, 1964) pp. 111–126. Significantly, his many references are all *fourth* century. In Old Comedy we discover the *paidotribēs,* the gymnastic teacher; and the boys march to the house of the *kitharistēs,* their memories stuffed with fine old songs. But the *grammatistēs* makes no appearance. For the evidence from fifth-century vases, see later in this chapter. For Ionia as the pioneer in the sixth century in establishing schools, we have scattered indirect evidence ranging over many

centuries. Two cautions must be used in dealing with the references. First, not every reference to a school is necessarily a school that teaches letters (e.g., music schools). This assumption infects several of the older handbooks on Greek education. Also, late sources are likely to be projecting their familiar practices into a distant past. That leaves mainly Herodotus as the unassailable contemporary source. The historian reports (VI. 27. 2.) that more than a hundred children were killed in 494 B.C. "while learning their letters" when a roof collapsed, but one cannot generalize from Chios to the rest of Greece, and especially not to Attica. Also, but quoted far less often, the same text refers to the fact that a choir of young men on its way to Delphi contracted the plague and all but two died. Both events were, in retrospect, considered omens. *Mousikē* was also flourishing on Chios. The island was extraordinary even in late Hellenistic times, with contests of reading (or, better, declaiming texts aloud) of Homer, as the inscriptional record reveals (*SIG* 959 8). Moreover, Chios seems to have been a leader among the Ionian cities, a fact perhaps aided by early contact with Euboea by sea. The references to early schools in late Hellenistic sources (e.g., Pausanias 6. 96, but Pausanias also absurdly makes Tyrtaeus an Athenian schoolmaster) cannot be trusted. Immerwahr, in reviewing the evidence for school scenes on vases (see n. 6) refers to the literary evidence for "schools" in the fifth century, but none of the references is to Athens, and only that in Herodotus to Chios is early. The other sources are late, writing centuries after the fact, and in authors often notoriously anachronistic and uncritical: Aelian (Mytilene), Pausanias (Amorgas), and Plutarch (Troezen). Immerwahr also notes that the credibility of these references is weak. Some caution must therefore accompany the use of authors such as Beck, who usefully musters the sources. See F.A.G. Beck, *Album of Greek Education* (Sydney, 1975) and *Greek Education, 450-350 B.C.*

4. Donald Kagan, *Pericles of Athens and the Birth of Democracy* (New York, 1991), pp. 20–21.

5. Ibid., p. 21.

6. H. R. Immerwahr, "Book Rolls on Attic Vases, " in *Classical, Mediaeval, and Renaissance Studies Presented to B. L. Ullman* (Rome, 1964), I, pp. 17–48; and "More Book Rolls on Attic Vases," *Antike Kunst* 16 (1973), pp. 143–147. The eight poetic inscriptions on vases that make sense (there are also symbolic nonsense letters, and dots for letters) were discussed by J. D. Beazley in "Hymn to Hermes," *AJA* 52 (1948), pp. 336–340. In several cases he adduces overtly didactic texts, such as Paris, Louvre G 457 (Immerwahr no. 3); Berlin 2322 (Immerwahr no. 4). On the Louvre cup by the Eretria Painter, ca. 430 B.C., Beazley reads *sophprosunēn*. Immerwahr tentatively supplies what he terms a "didactic text" for the inscription on a cup by the Akestorides Painter in Washington, D.C. (Smithsonian 136,373): "He who heeds me will prosper" (Immerwahr no. 7), but the phrasing is more likely epical. Two earlier works remain useful: T. Birt, *Die Buchrolle in der Kunst* (Leipzig, 1907); and T.B.L. Webster, *Potter and Patron in Classical Athens* (London, 1972). Immerwahr calls useful attention to women on vases with book rolls (not all are Muses or Sappho). The vexed problem of literacy among women (for whom there were no schools) cannot be treated here, but one comment may be ventured. Women, precisely because of their enforced seclusion in Athens, had, like some nineteenth-century literary figures in New England, much motive to be involved with books and to become literate if possible. A brother or a literate slave might have been prevailed upon to help.

7. Basic to any discussion of *ostraka* is E. Vanderpool, *Ostracism in Athens* (Cincinnati, 1970). As early as 1937, O. Broneer had noted that 191 *ostraka* aimed at Themistocles and found (luckily) in a single cache at the bottom of a well were, in fact, the product of only fourteen hands ("Excavations on the North Slope of the Acropolis, 1937,"

Hesperia 7 [1938], pp. 228ff.). The cautious remarks of Harris (*Ancient Literacy*, p. 54), and those earlier of F. D. Harvey, who is always perceptive on matters of literacy ("Literacy in the Athenian Democracy," *REG* 79 [1966], p. 590) concerning sweeping conclusions about popular literacy from *ostraka* or the institution of ostracism, deserve notice. Alfred Burns approaches the fifth-century evidence determined to prove a "convincing case for widespread literacy from the beginning of the fifth century onward" and so popular literacy achieved by the end of the sixth century in Athens. He presses each scrap of evidence, however ambiguous (e.g., Euripides *frag.* 572 N.), as further proof of his premise. ("Athenian Literacy in the Fifth Century B.C.," *JHI* 42 [1981], pp. 375ff., and on ostracism, pp. 382–383). His statement (p. 377) that scribes were unknown anywhere in Greece requires modification. I, of course, doubt that even fourth-century Athens achieved "widespread popular literacy" in anything like the statistical sense, a point on which the late Eric Havelock and I sometimes disagreed in conversation. But more basically, Havelock in his last years felt that he had fought the good fight, with the scars to prove it, in gaining some acceptance for the restricted literacy and aural character of the Archaic period, including the late fifth century, which saw some change. Others could worry about later centuries.

8. Mogens Hansen, *The Athenian Democracy in the Age of Demonsthenes* (Oxford, 1991), p. 20. An early voice moderating the assumption of full legal literacy from the first appearance of written law was the pioneering George Calhoun. He observes that no doubt written complaints handed by the plaintiff to the magistrate were the practice in Demonsthenes' day, but then asks, despite the assumptions of Heffter (1822) and Lipsius (1908), both standard legal historians of his day (especially Lipsius), how far back this practice went or when it replaced *viva voce* pleadings. "It is surprising that the inquiry was not suggested by Bonner's discovery—published in 1905--that the rule requiring evidence to be presented in writing was not enacted until the fourth century" ("Oral and Written Pleadings in Athenian Courts," *TAPA* 1 [1919], p. 177). Calhoun demonstrated that in Athens there was a considerable lag time after the introduction of written law, during which oral habit prevailed in matters of pleading, evidence, and judgment. The first written instrument was the *graphē*, the complaint, initially only in public actions (which later became identified with the name), and then in private *dikai*. Whereas these were no doubt written down *by the magistrate* or his clerk by the late fifth century, there is abundant evidence that only in the fourth century did complaints from plantiffs get handed to the court in writing, "probably not long before the commencement of Demonsthenes' career" (p. 190). This usage itself seems to have become a matter of written enactment not long after 380 B.C. This comports well with Bonner's dates for the requirement that evidence be reduced to writing. Calhoun argued persuasively (p. 193) that it was only in the archonship of Nausinicus, or 378/7 B.C., that Athens saw "the enactment of the prescription that pleadings and evidence must be presented in writing." Early warnings of this sort—few, but not unknown—about a major difference in the degree of legal dependence on writing between the fourth century and any earlier century in Athens were unwanted and so generally went unheeded. Of late, Hansen's many publications on Greek law are making handsome amends.

9. See Pindar (*O*.1.15) and Herodotus 6.129. The phrase "contest of *mousikē*" *(agōn mousikēs)* seems to have been common at least by the fifth century, if not earlier. Ion tells Socrates that Epidarus had sponsored an *agōn* for rhapsodes (which Ion had just won) and for all *mousikē (Ion* 530 A). A fourth-century inscription from Eretria refers to such an *agōn* (*IG* 12(9).189.8; also see Thuc. 3.104). Some additional references are given in Liddell and Scott (s.v. *mousikē*), who incorrectly report, however, a reference to *mousikē, grammata, gumnastikē* at *Rep.* 403 C. Only *mousikē* and *gumnastikē* are mentioned. This

error of a reference to *grammata* in the education of the young guardians has been widely repeated, presumably on the authority of *LSJ*. Finally, Havelock (*Literate Revolution*, p. 14) states well what *mousikē* as *paideia* connoted when he remarks that "the city states of the ninth to the sixth centuries perfected a system of oral instruction in dance, instrumental music and recitation, by which certain works of oral composition were selectively memorized, recited, expanded, but in a disciplined manner imposed by the seniors upon the young as part of their initiation into an oral society which was to command their allegiance." I use *mousikē* in this sense, as, indeed, Plato consistently did in the *Republic*.

10. In the speech of "Right *Logos*" at *Clouds* 961ff. Aristophanes' preference and nostalgia for the "old education" or *archaia paideia*—musical and athletic—and his hostility to the new, for which "Socrates" becomes symbol and scapegoat, is not in question. Marrou believed this passage demonstrated Aristophanic distaste for formal schooling of any kind, preferring the old, aristocratic ways that were based on *sunousia*; that seems to me to go too far, but he catches the mood right. The boys of the same deme, Aristophanes reports, march off to the house of the *kitharistēs*, the music master, winter or summer, observing proper modesty and deportment. Of course, only the deme boys whose fathers could pay would be in this group and so would be mainly, I assume, by the latter part of the fifth century, composed of the old aristocratic class and the sons of the rising *hippeis*. Anytus is an example of the son of prosperous craftsman, a tanner, who was given such an education. Athenian schools were evidently open to whomever could pay. Whether Socrates was educated in one is a nice question.

11. *Rep*. 376 Eff. There is good reason, from dialogues other than the *Republic* (e.g., *Prot*. 325–6) to believe that the formula *mousikē kai gumnastikē* could be replaced by the sequence *grammata, mousikē, gumnastikē* by the *compositional* date of the *Republic*, which is well into the fourth century. The persistence of the older formula reveals that *grammata* is a later addition. The attempt to stretch the meaning of *mousikē as used in the Republic* to include letters, culture, or philosophy is endemic in the commentaries, but no text in the *Republic* will support it. Shorey's note (Loeb ed.) to 376 E is not untypical: "*mousikē* is playing the lyre, music, poetry, *letters, culture, philosophy*, according to context." Shorey can cite no instance from the *Republic* where *mousikē* carries any of the latter three meanings. Because, before later specialization, the *grammatistēs* was initially also instructing in poetry, *mousikē* could be used broadly to include letters (e.g., *Knights* 188–190). But this is very rare early, *Knights* perhaps being a unique instance, and context kept the meanings clear. Aristophanes' sausage seller has had no "musical" training beyond just learning the letters themselves. He seems to be playing on the word. What the sausage seller is saying is that he did not advance to learning to write down traditional verses, memorizing them, putting them to music, or singing them to instrumental accompaniment. Plausibly, his merchant parents would not pay for the continued instruction or perhaps he or they saw no purpose for learning to play instruments. The *grammatistēs* might also teach some rudimentary arithmetic; Plato keeps this feature in the *Republic* by having young boys learn some arithmetic skill while playing games, without force or even a formal teacher. Aristocratic youth acquired all these skills—fundamentally what the acquisition of *mousikē* meant—because their parents paid the fees of the teachers. In the *Republic*, the contrast is between education under the old musical paideia and that under a new philosophical paideia, hence the contest between the traditional poet and the new Platonic *philosophos*. Plato would hardly use *mousikē* as a synonym for philosophy in, above all, this dialogue, nor does he. Rather, as in the *Phaedo*, "the supreme *mousikē* must *become* philosophy," that is, philosophy must now become what *mousikē* had previously been for Greece, the heart of its paideia.

12. *Rep*. 377 D. Some translators do not translate the *kai* clause, presumably because

a modern reader would not readily understand that a professional, contemporary reciter of the epic figures is what is meant. Noting that in every age the city-states were different from towns in heroic times, Professor Sinclair observed that nevertheless "both belonged to him [the Greek]. . . . The essentials of civilization were secured by one no less than the other. Poets, the Greek had been taught to believe, were the great teachers and civilizers and it was from Homer that he had learned the first rudiments" (*A History of Greek Political Thought* [London, 1967], p. 13).

13. Heraclitus B. 42. "Homer deserves to be thrown out of the contests and beaten with his own *rhabdos,* and Archilochus too."

14. *Ion* 531A. Socrates asks Ion: "Are you skilled in Homer only, or in Hesiod and Archilochus as well?" These three—Homer, Hesiod, and Archilochus—were viewed as a kind of epic *troika* by later Greeks of each generation, no doubt in part because all three composed in epic hexameters and diction (Archilochus not exclusively so), and later Greeks knew no names of poets that were older. (Opheus and Museus are rivals only in late sources.)

15. *Rep.* 377 E. The phrasing, which has puzzled commentators, is modeled on the more familiar *kalōs [kakōs] legein.* This verbal phrase must be connected to *eikasia,* the lowest level of the Divided Line, as Plato intended. See chapter 8.

16. *Ion* 533 Dff; 535 B; 536 Aff. In the last century, R. C. Jebb, *The Growth and Influence of Classical Greek Poetry* (Boston, 1893), p. 38, observed: "The first [point to notice] is the rapt attention with which the audience listens—the strong appeal of the minstrel over their emotions." Jebb rightly considers this the outstanding characteristic of epic performances, although of course audience involvement does not record in a text.

17. At 387 C the reading in Paris A and in two other of the best MSS is corrupt, inserting the meaningless *hōs oietai* after *phrittein dē poiei.* Herman emended to the improbable *hosa etē.* This would then be a reference to the yearly recitation of the entire Homer, as (supposedly) ordered by Peisistratus, or at least under the tyrants, but this is forced. The meaningless words are best omitted, which leaves an intelligible sentence with no problems, and no assumptions about the activities of sixth-century tyrants attested only in very late sources. The transmitted Greek text at 387 C, after the prohibition of terrifying scenes—clearly a regular and not a yearly event on the Greek stage—is best rendered: "And the opposite type to these [we shall require] in speech and in verse *(lekteon te kai poiēteon).*"

18. The words *ean te en melesin* are omitted in Paris A, but are found in other MSS and in early quotations (e.g., Eusebius). The inclusion of melic is confirmed by the divisions of poetry at 392ff.

19. *Sym.* III 6. The most natural way to take *oligou an' hekastēn hēmeran* is "almost every day" of one's life when nothing else, for example a festival, is specified. The *Budé* editor, Mazon, for example, takes the passage in this natural way. The point of the passage is that constant hearing permitted the speaker to get the whole of the *Iliad* and *Odyssey* by heart. A single hearing spread over several days once a year at a festival would hardly facilitate such a mnemonic feat. Also see Isocrates (*Paneg.* 74 A, B) who stresses the importance of such constant recitation to reinforce the Hellenic consciousness in face of Barbarian pressures.

20. F. Kenyon, *Books and Readers in Ancient Greece and Rome* (Oxford, 1951), p. 22.

21. E. A. Havelock, *The Muse Learns to Write* (New Haven, 1986), pp. 4–5.

22. Speech arguably was bending humans toward cooperative, not destructive, behavior tens of thousands of years before writing appeared. As Richard Leakey has observed: "Together with learning in a social context, the second major benefit of group living—

group wisdom—represents the beginnings of culture'' (*Origins: The Emergence and Evolution of Our Species* [New York, 1982], pp. 56, 182ff). Leakey observes that what is certain is that primates would not have become social animals unless such behavior gave them an evolutionary advantage: the roots of group experience and shared learning are to be found among the more intelligent primates, notably the chimps, the closest of our animal relatives. See also Jane Goodall, *In the Shadow of Man* (Boston, 1971), pp. 35–37, 109. The shared and transmitted ''group wisdom'' and accumulated experience—preserved and transmitted almost exclusively in speech by humans—is the remote ancestor of a complex paideia. There has been speculation that the evolutionary pressures that selected speech for humans may therefore have been driven by the advantage of our acquiring, preserving, and transmitting the experience that promotes social cooperation, the first step toward culture.

23. *Meno* 90 B.

24. Ibid., 95 E.

25. Ibid., 92 B.

26. The justification—seemingly sincere—claimed for the accommodation of an older male by a youth in the first two speeches of the *Symposium*, those of Phaedrus and Pausanias. By association and emulation the boy acquires *aretē*. In return, the older male gains sexual favors (*Sym*. 180 B, 184 C).

27. *Apology* 19 E–20 A. The words of Protagoras in Plato's dialogue of that name are noteworthy. Socrates leaves it to Protagoras himself to decide whether the conversation to ensue is to be restricted or open to all guests present. Protagoras assumes that he is looking after his *political* welfare. ''You do right by me, Socrates, to be so cautious. For when a man goes as a stranger into great cities, and in them tries to persuade the best of of the young men to cease their associations *(sunousias)* with all others, either with their own households or foreign [his father's guest-friends], both old and young, and instead to join in association *(suneinai)* with oneself alone, with the promise that they will be made better through this association *(sunousian)*, then it is necessary to proceed very cautiously indeed'' (*Prot*. 316 C–D). One draws selectively on the evidence from Xenophon at some risk, but he too takes up the theme of *sunousia* and the resentment that ensued from Socrates' actions. According to Xenophon, Socrates was accused at his trial for inculcating disrespect for the instruction of elders and especially parents. He was reported to have argued that mere goodwill toward offspring is not enough for proper education; knowledge is necessary, requiring an expert. One does not, after all, consult with a relation, however close, who is not an expert when one is in medical or legal difficulty, but seeks out a doctor or lawyer (*Mem*. I. 2, 49, 51, 52). The report may be inaccurate in detail, and may well owe debts to the lost ''Accusation of Socrates'' of Polycrates. But that it represents what people such as Anytus saw Socrates doing, namely, professionalizing *paideia* at the expense of the traditional relationships of *sunousia* and so undermining the family and especially parental (the father's) authority, is no doubt accurate. I suggest that if we had the actual words used by Meletus, backed by the support of Anytus, we might discover that they considered such an action impious and expected a jury to agree. Brickhouse and Smith observe: ''Since the latter law [the impiety statute under the revised code] was vague, its extension would almost certainly be determined in each case *ad hoc*'' (*Socrates On Trial* [Princeton, 1989], p. 33). This book is the best recent treatment of the subject described in its title; also there is a very full bibliography. Finally, also according to Xenophon, Socrates was accused of manipulating the *exempla* of epic by quoting or distorting epical sources to advocate immoral actions. Specifically, Socrates cited what in our texts are Hesiod *Works and Days* 309, *Iliad* II 188–192, 198–202, to the effect that one ought to be a crook, do anything for material gain, and mistreat the lower classes, a very undemocratic sentiment (*Mem*. I. 2. 56, 58, 59). More likely, of course, Socrates often demon-

strated, as does Plato in the *Euthyphro* with the castration of divine fathers, that the analogies from the *exempla* of epic are so stretched by Greeks that the "scripture" can be used to justify any action approved of or desired by the quoter—or its opposite. It is probable that Socrates used a *reductio* argument, was misunderstood, and that this was added to his indictment for corrupting the youth. Whether this explanation is right or not, Xenophon's words reveal again that epic was still a powerful moral *exemplum* for Greeks, used in daily moral argument and debate. That it had been so since the first recorded Greek writing cannot seriously be denied, although a recent article revives once more the fervent wish to deny it. See John Halverson, "Havelock on Greek Orality and Literacy," *JHI* 53 No. 1 (1992), pp. 153ff. The sole purpose of epical poetry, from Homer to Ion, was to entertain: "it would be a good guess, based on Plato's *Ion,* that their performances [rhapsodes] were received primarily or entirely as entertainment, not as one might listen to a reading of the Bible or the Koran" (p. 155). That is not, of course, what Ion himself claims in Plato's dialogue. Nor is it what the *Republic* claims for the role of Homer and the poets, for if it were all a matter of harmless entertainment Plato would hardly have wasted his many books (in the *Republic*) of polemic on them. Halverson's antipathy to the role of verse, and especially Homer, as either encyclopedic or morally instructive is widely shared, however.

8

Mimēsis Banished: The Alliance of Literacy and Paideia in Fourth-Century Athens

The reform passages[1] of Books II and III of Plato's *Republic* have assumed an unusual role in this work. They have become the primary—but far from exclusive—evidence that as late as the composition of this dialogue, which is traditionally placed early in the second quarter of the fourth century, Athenian paideia was still wedded to the practices of an entrenched oral tradition.[2] The core of traditional education, as Plato dissects it and opens it up for scrutiny and ultimate banishment, was *mimēsis,* a word traditionally translated "imitation." Few words in the Platonic lexicon are more important to the philosopher's thought or have produced more dispute among his interpreters.

The word is introduced in Book III as part of the explanation of *lexis,* the manner of presenting the verse as opposed to its content. *What* is said, or the "matter," is one thing; *how* it is said, the "form" or the manner of communication, is another. That such a distinction is required will be inevitable once speech has become a physical object in written language. Plato pioneers it here, appropriating the term *lexis* (later the usual word for "diction") for the form.

The poetic material could be mimetic—and so induce *mimēsis* in the hearers—in varying degrees, suggests Socrates. A composition such as a tragedy that was exclusively dialogue unrelieved by narration would be, as a matter of style, wholly or purely mimetic. But the issue quickly becomes more than one of style or of the presence or absence of dialogue in a composition. In the final analysis, *mimēsis* approximates a Platonic *terminus technicus* with affinities to the usages of *mimēsis, mimeomai,* and their cognates in earlier Greek authors, but not identifiable with them.

Mimēsis, as finally defined in the *Republic,* refers to a rhythmically induced experience and habit of identifying with, and making one's own, the words and actions of another as one hears poetry being emotively narrated or chanted. It is to this psychological usage—not a related stylistic one—that Plato's hostility to *mimēsis* or imitation is directed. In theory, then, a work could be more dangerously mimetical, viewed from the psychological perspective, than is another work that is more mimetic viewed from the stylistic perspective. Concretely, some dithyrambs or dirges composed without dialogue could be more mimetic, and so more dangerous from the psychological perspective than some tragedies, which are entirely dialogue and so wholly mimetic stylistically. This is explicitly said to be the case for some dithyrambs in Book X. Also, the accompanying music or ''harmony,'' as well as the instrumentation, may be relevant to the degree—and danger—of psychological *mimēsis.*

Plato is aware that his usage is innovative for both *lexis* and *mimēsis*—as indeed it will later be in Book VI for *eikasia*—and he is at pains either to explain what he means by these terms as he introduces them, to make their meanings clear from context, or both. If the reader understands the basis for Plato's objection to contemporary poetry and does not assimilate ''poetry'' to experiences more familiar in literate societies, where poetry is normally read (or even read aloud) but is not performed mimetically and carries no paideutic burdens that are not self-imposed, the meaning in a given sentence is always perfectly clear. This will also be true in Book VI when Plato introduces *eikasia,* or ''imaging,'' a word closely related in meaning to *mimēsis.*

The instructors whom we encounter in the reform passages of the *Republic*—dominantly rhapsodes and tragic actors—sing, chant, recite, or act out their roles on the stage while also declaiming the instructing verses. The instructed are being conditioned to pleasurable and unquestioning acceptance of what they hear, memorize, and recite. Theirs will be a mindless but grateful submission. To be sure, the philosopher will reform the grossly objectionable content of the traditional poets where this is necessary, and he will forbid future guardians the extremes of mimetic behavior, such as imitating the calls of animals—all in the interest of what is (Platonically) *kalon,* or ''beautiful.'' But the orally communicated paideia, rooted in music and performed poetry and successful for so many generations in controlling the behavior of the young, will continue to flourish as it now comes under Platonic supervision. Young guardians will listen to the enticing verses; they will memorize, perform, and (selectively) imitate. Where is the evidence for the increasingly literate Athens of the early fourth century in this famous argument?

Texts play no part in this utopian world of Plato's invention.[3] Even the performance texts that had made some headway in the aristocratic schools of the fifth century make no appearance in the reform passages in the *Republic.* Music and performance, verses declaimed and heard, are found at every turn as Plato puts his famous strictures on them. The struggle to deal with texts and what it takes in any society in the way of training from experienced mentors to master them are totally ignored. Indeed, if our knowledge were restricted to the evidence of the reform passages, we would grow suspicious that the society being described was a musical one just emerging from an age of primary orality. The citizens, we would surmise, are illiterate. How are we to explain this?

An Awkward Silence in the Argument of the *Republic*

The puzzle goes deeper. No provision is made in the *Republic* for teaching letters to any class, guardian or craftsman. The citizens are never taught to read or write. At no point is provision made for them to receive instruction in letters, which was already standard practice for sons of Athenian aristocrats when Plato wrote and which he himself describes in detail in the *Protagoras,* a passage that has become the *locus classicus* for modern reconstructions of the late-fifth-century instruction in letters in Athenian aristocratic schools.

More significantly, Plato's future guardians are *always* said in the reform passages to hear (*akouein* and its cognates throughout)[4] the poetic material that they will memorize and recite (or sing); they are *never* said to read it. As for the composers of the instructional material or the poets themselves, Plato seems to go out of his way to avoid verbs meaning "to write" where we might expect them in describing the poets' activity. He strongly prefers verbs meaning to "make," "poetize," "compose," "tell," "speak," "chant," or "sing," such as *poiein, legein, muthologein,* and *adein.* The avoidance of a vocabulary that would suggest literacy is notable. Some circumlocution to accomplish it is occasionally in evidence. Plato's translators often fail to share his preference in this regard and overtranslate, as in the instance of "writer" for *poietēs,* or "*write* wrongly" for *kakōs legousi* rather than "speak" or "tell" wrongly. When this happens again and again, a distorted picture emerges, even though any single instance of transferring the author's idiom into our own would be defensible. The distortion is compounded if a translator in his introduction refers to Plato's reforming activity in Books II and III as editing "school textbooks," or in translation converts Chiron, the talking centaur who instructed Achilles in the *Iliad,* into the hero's "schoolmaster." A world without schools and schoolmasters, books and readers—in a word, the trappings of literacy—may be unimaginable to a Cambridge don, but it is decidedly the world that Plato is describing.[5]

There would be, of course, no anachronistic problem if Plato regularly used "write" in describing the activity of current poets, for surely they were writers. But in the reform passages he prefers to avoid any suggestion of writing and the ambience of literacy. Above all, he avoids absolutely any reference to reading on the part of the instructed rather than their constantly hearing—hardly an accident. Because this is germane to his argument, a matter of substance and not style, translators should respect it.

As a partial explanation for the absence of training in letters, I have suggested that Plato in the early books is content with the resources of oralism in order to impose his social reforms on the entire populace, all three classes, ordinary citizens, *epikouroi* and *phulakes* alike.[6] Thus all classes receive the same education in *mousikē* until at least the age of eighteen (*Rep.* 412 B); only at twenty, after further testing, are the full *phulakes* selected. Only the full guardians then advance to higher education in the specialized sciences outlined in the central books, notably Book VII.[7] But for that promotion and the higher education proposed, literacy that had been acquired in childhood would, of course, be indispensable. Plato in the *Republic* ignores the obvious implications and difficulties that this situation creates, as he does not do in the *Laws.* In the later dialogue, literacy for all classes and both genders must, he realizes, be imposed early, before adolescence, and the provisions are legislated accordingly. Any solution for the *Republic* along the lines of postulated special instruction in letters for children of existing guardians, but not mentioned by Plato, would violate the principle of equal opportunity afforded the children of all classes, which the Allegory of the Metals requires. It would also stand in the way of the promise of promotion or demotion between the classes at *any* time.[8] If, let us say, at age eighteen or twenty the son of a craftsman has proved himself worthy to be promoted to guardian status and so to undertake further training, he can scarcely be said to be put on an equal footing with the the sons (and daughters) of guardians of same age if they are literate and he is not. The playing field has not been kept level. All must become literate at an early age, or no one does.

In the Penguin edition of the *Republic,* Desmond Lee, feeling the problem acutely, asserts that the secondary education in poetry *assumes* that a primary education in reading and writing preceded it. Noting that Plato's "literary education" (as Lee terms it) is the equivalent of modern secondary education, he adds that there *must have been* "the earlier stage of learning to read and write which that *implies,* the equivalent to our primary education."[9] But, of course, Lee is assuming that the poetic or "literary" material that serves as the basis of education will be *read,* as in British public schools, and Plato is assuming throughout that it will be *heard,* as in oral Athens. Also, Lee overlooks the point that his own argument would require not literacy for a few guardians chosen early, but for the whole populace, for all received that same poetic education that, in his view, "assumes literacy." However, Lee's discussion has the distinct merit of seeing there is a serious problem here. No explicit provision is made for learning to read and write in the *Republic* for any class of citizens, including the future full guardians, who obviously would require it before adolescence. Many other commentators have not realized the difficulty or else assert or assume the provision for instruction in letters gratuitously for Plato, so obvious and unavoidable does it now seem.[10] But for Plato himself, the education of the *dēmos* in the New Athens could safely and efficiently be left to the communal oral life of the city, as indeed it had been from remote antiquity in preliterate and protoliterate Athens. The performance texts introduced in the fifth-century schools were a convenience but hardly a necessity, for the traditional poetic education had long functioned without them. Plato can afford to ignore them totally.

By pretending that he is reforming the traditional oral paideia to make it serviceable for future guardians in a utopian Athens—a "far improved place"—it becomes possible for Plato to dissect the education available in his Athens as had never been done before, expose its core, and explain at last the sources of its appeal to the souls of Greeks. It is a literary device for which the comic stage, Old Comedy, of which the plays of Aristophanes alone survive entire, had admirably prepared a sophisticated Athenian audience.

The Role of *Mimēsis* in Archaic Greek Culture

The realization that an entire culture had been preserved and transmitted mimetically in the Archaic period, a feat made possible by a lingering and powerful oralism, has recently been stressed by a number of prominent French scholars. Many of them, like Jean-Pierre Vernant and Marcel Detienne, are associated with the Collegè de France, the École Pratique des Hautes Études, or both. They have usefully argued that the oral situation and the reliance of traditional paideia on the practice of *mimēsis,* viewed as a paideutic activity, must be restored to our modern understanding of Archaic Greek culture. To appreciate Plato in the context of his time requires our seeing him as both the great heir of a still dominantly oral culture—in place by habit or preference, not technological necessity—and simultaneously as its destroyer. What these scholars mean, of course, is not that Plato introduced an alphabet, or championed reading and writing, but that he finally destroyed the cultural situation in which for most people, high and low, important knowledge was transmitted across generations orally, in performances.[11] Moreover, the alternative resources of texts had not been produced in any quantity, and habitual use was not made of them. That is, of course, correct. As Vernant, Detienne, and their colleagues argue, what Plato rejected was a way of communicating knowledge (and so of acquiring it) that also had long been no less than "a way of life" for Hellenes at all levels of society, one to which they were attached with justifiable pride. Indeed, aristocrats had special reasons to be attached to it in the refined version of *mousikē* practiced and performed in their schools. Again, this perspective is correct and rightly puts *mimēsis* and Plato's rejection of it at the core of the late fifth- and early-fourth-century paideia crisis. Plato, I would add, rejects the older mode of preserving and acquiring knowledge *because* it was mimetic and depended on shared acts of *mimēsis* between generations of performers and audiences. Moreover, performer and audience were related as instructor and the gratefully instructed, especially in the area of popular morals, a relationship Plato intended to preempt and transfer elsewhere.

Texts there were, of course, and the great composers of Greek literature were writers. But they wrote not to be read by individuals, but heard by audiences. This has always been accepted for drama and has sometimes been accepted for epic, although many scholars write as though Plato and his contemporaries absorbed their Homer out of books (his own *Ion* notwithstanding). But only recently have scholars widely accepted the view that even lyric was composed to be heard and performed. In a valuable survey of the role of music in Greek culture, Giovanni Comoti of Urbino describes the "intense and complex musical life" of Archaic Greece, which has reached us not as sounds, of course, but in texts.

> All Greek lyrical texts, both archaic and classical, were composed to be sung accompanied by an instrument in front of an audience. In dramatic performances of the classical period, choral and solo singing were at least as important as dialogue and dramatic actions. Music played a role in every moment of Greek communal life—in religious ceremonies, competitions, symposia, festivals, even in political contentions, as the songs of Alcaeus and Timocreon of Rhodes [and Solon] demonstrate.[12]

Plato stood back from the performances he witnessed in his day (had there even been a historical Ion?) and analyzed them in both their psychological and epistemological dimensions. He concluded that the very manner in which poets preserved and presented the content of moral instruction—albeit so effectively and pleasurably—stood in the way, psychologically and epistemologically, of the thinking part of the soul ever attaining to the reality of the Forms. Total banishment was the only fit punishment for the Greek poets—or, more accurately, the only remedy for Greece. The paideia of Greece must be taken out of their hands once and for all and transferred elsewhere. For "the maker/poet of an image *(eidoulou poietēs),* the imitator *(mimētēs),* knows nothing of the reality, but only the appearance" (601 B–C). Plato first perceived that the moral teachers of Greece, always led by Homer, had long mistaken images—by which Plato means their descriptions of the proper behavior of heroes accepted as exemplars for contemporary behavior—for the reality, *ta onta,* his moral Forms. Being deceived themselves, they had deceived a people. In Plato's terms, Homer in the persons of the many generations of epic singers had failed to perceive that there was an even more wondrous reality beyond the verbal images they made, a reality that only Plato had discovered, his Forms.

Mimēsis and *Eikasia*

Eikasia as a noun makes its entrance into the argument of the *Republic* as the state of mental cognition represented by the lowest level of the Divided Line and the furthest removed from the apprehension of reality, or the Forms.[13] The way had been prepared for this term, as noted earlier, in Book II when the poet is said to "image badly *(eikaze kakōs)*" on three levels.[14] Homer, Hesiod, and the poets portray actions that are represented as being good and bad, proper (or "just") and improper. But they offer images only, mistaking them for the reality; that is, they do not realize, and have no suspicion, that behind their descriptions of specific actions—now right and now wrong according to shifting circumstance—stands a whole different order of reality, that of the stable Forms (of the good, *agathou,* of the just, *dikaiou,* etc.).

Eikasia as a level of the Divided Line is said to be an image or *eikōn* of the level of *pistis,* ordinary belief, even as the perceptible is an image of the intelligible. *Pistis* as a cognitive state has as its objects the ordinary things around us, couches or people, including the actions of persons believed by them to be good or bad, that is, conventional moral opinions. The objects of *eikasia* are images, *eikones,* of this ordinary world, including human actions or conventions. *Eikasia* can thus embrace *mimēsis* by being, in Plato's usage, a slightly broader term. *Eikasia* includes the mechanical reflection of images of sensible objects in mirrors or other bright objects (510 A; 596 D–E), *or* the verbal descriptions or images of persons acting virtuously or not (600 E, poets are "imitators of images of virtue," and *passim*).

Viewed from a different perspective, mechanical duplication, as in a mirror, is also an imitation of sorts, and Plato can use *mimēsis* or its verbal cognates in this sense in Book X. When the actions of humans are being described, and the poet is narrating them, *mimēsis* is the more exact term, a kind of subdivision of *eikasia,* although as long as the point at issue is clear (as in context it always is) Plato is not overly fussy about consistency in the technical vocabulary.

This analysis becomes explicit and the basis for Plato's renewed attack on the poets in Book X. *Mimēsis* is also expanded to include such crafts as painting, but only as convenient examples to help his exposition of poetic *mimēsis*. He retains the term *mimēsis* throughout Book X, even for mechanical duplication in a mirror, but drops *eikasia*. Poetry, not epistemology, is the focus. But Plato's contempt for poetic *mimēsis* as a version of *eikasia*, and so firmly located at the lowest rung of the ladder of cognition, remains constant. The term *mimēsis* is retained, I suggest, because Plato's concern in Book X remains performed poetry's deleterious effects on the souls of contemporary Hellenes, and he wants a direct connection with his analysis of mimetic poetry in Books II and III, as well as with the epistemology of the central books and the Divided Line.

Greek *mimēsis* as Plato analyzes it had its origin, then, not as a "theory of art" (the title some editors misleadingly give Book X) in the pages of Plato, but in the ancient demands of oral memory and the manner in which a complex paideia had been communicated to a people. Plato reports, analyzes and catalogs, compromises and condemns, but he does not invent the experience he describes. Instead, he damns *mimēsis* thrice over by incorporating it into his psychology (*mimēsis* appeals to the nonrational parts of the psyche), his epistemology (*mimēsis* is a variety of *eikasia*, at the bottom rung of the Divided Line), and his ontology (the images that are the objects of *mimēsis* are thrice removed from Reality, or the moral Forms). The condemnation could not be, Platonically, more complete. I also suggest that what was fundamental and developed first in Plato's thought was the conviction that epically based popular morality as found in human actions (always *polla*, many) was an imperfect image of the Forms (each always a one, *hen*). Homeric or epical (or poetic) descriptions of these actions were *mimēmata* or, alternatively, *eikones* and thrice removed from the Forms. Typically, for Plato, he then applies this fundamental analysis widely in his thought and to other issues. But Homeric or epical discourse, augmented by tragedy and other forms of verse, is the enemy from first to last in the *Republic* (see 373 B, 382 B–C, 388 C, 402 C, and 382 B–C, *passim*). Plato, to be sure, was a reforming educator, but more fundamentally he was a reforming *moralist*.

From *Mimēsis* to Texts

Mimēsis as Plato describes it can occur only when verses are being heard or performed. For this reason, the performance texts of the fifth century, whose contents were memorized and then mimetically acted out, did not intrude into or significantly alter the fundamental psychology of *mimēsis*. But if the core of education were no longer to be memory and performance but the contents of an expository prose treatise, fostering close analysis and unimpassioned assessment but not imitation, then we have moved into a very different world educationally—and if Plato is right, a different one epistemologically and psychologically as well. A different "part" of the psychic apparatus will now be engaged, and different mental faculties. By contrast, if the Greek learning process is still largely dependent on *mimēsis*, as Plato claims in writing the reform passages of the *Republic*, and mimetic habit had no serious, established rival in Athenian education, then the city's education clearly has not yet grown dependent on the close analysis of texts. If it had, the central argument of the dialogue concerning the role of *mimēsis* in contemporary education would be an anachronism and inexplicable.

Higher education inextricably bound to the study of the contents of texts became, I suggest, a distinguishing feature of the type of education found in Aristotle's Lyceum,[15] insofar as we can now recover its activities, and of Hellenistic philosophical education generally.[16] The whole focus of Greek higher education and many of its characteristic features have shifted drastically from the practices found in Books II and III of the *Republic*. In Hellenistic Greece the evidence for the dependence of higher education on literacy is manifest everywhere; indeed, being educated and being literate fuse in the public's mind, as they do in popular speech. *Agrammatos,* the *alpha* privative with *gramma,* like our term "illiterate," comes to mean not only unlettered but also uneducated, uncultured, or even stupid. Literacy and culture go hand in hand; what started as a temporary marriage of convenience has become a permanent union. The distance from the fifth or any earlier century in Hellas is a marked one. It is as though we have entered a new world—which, in an important sense, we have.

Therefore, it becomes useful to isolate the point in Greek education at which a marked dependence on the nonemotive analysis of texts replaces memorization (whether of a text or not) and mimetic performance, or at least this educational exercise has become a significant supplement to an earlier period in a learner's life perhaps still dominated by memory and performance, and the later activity is regarded as the superior level of learning, or "higher" education. For this development we must look to a date after the composition of the reform passages of the *Republic,* when it is still in the future, or Plato's polemic makes no sense. Then again, probably it had occurred, or was occurring, before the establishment of the Lyceum, whose daily activity seems to have been organized around the *logoi* or treatises of the founder and those of his associates.[17] This would point to the Academy itself, but about its daily workings we are, alas, poorly informed.[18] If this is fundamentally sound in outline, however, then the final alliance between literacy and paideia in Athens, as marked by systematic and supervised study of the contents of texts in the form of expository prose treatises, a certain accomplishment of the Lyceum, did not take place before the second quarter of the fourth century.

My conclusions require that readers agree, as Nettleship, Jaeger, Havelock and others have argued, that what is being reformed educationally in Books II and III describes contemporary Athenian practice as Plato wrote and is neither ancient history nor Platonic invention. He wrote, in Nettleship's phrase, with crying evils in his eyes. Second, the educational practices found in the Lyceum—and perhaps even earlier in the Academy—have grown "text-dependent" in ways that the *Republic* reveals Athenian paideia in the first quarter of the fourth century had not. If these premises are sound, then it is reasonable to conclude that the final alliance between literacy and paideia, creating for the first time a direct and total dependence of paideia—and specifically higher or advanced education—on literacy, was forged before the second quarter of the fourth century, and perhaps was even pioneered in the early years of Academy itself.

Exploring the role of texts in the Lyceum[19] and in Hellenistic education generally is beyond the scope of this book but perhaps is not overly controversial. Exploring the evidence from the *Republic* is another matter altogether, for the analysis of it was begun in the previous chapter. The time has arrived to complete the fascinating picture of a powerful residual oralism that still controlled the mechanisms of Athenian education in the early fourth century, drawing down on it the formidable ire of Plato as he writes his *Republic*.

Residual Oralism in the Reform Passages of the *Republic*

Plato, we recall, in his first assault on the poets in the *Republic,* seeks not to banish poetry so much as to bring it under control and, frankly, make it over for his own uses. The reason is straightforward and initially Plato's Socrates is honest about it, indeed, for Plato's liberal admirers, painfully so. The New Athens needs the mechanisms of oral paideia and its direct appeal to the emotions, or the irrational parts of the psyche, to condition and control the behavior of all three classes in their formative years. *Mousikē* is, therefore, proclaimed to be the very citadel or "guardhouse" of the souls of the guardians, the *phulatērion* of the *phulakes* (424 D).

Then, in Book X, with the final banishment of poetry and the poets, Socrates pulls the rug out from under what had been, for the preceding nine books, his "one big thing" *(hen mega)* that would make the new utopia possible. But what does Plato intend to put in its place? How does he now propose that his utopia is going to work without the resources of *mousikē* to guide and control behavior in the formative years? In the pages of the *Republic* Plato has no answer, although in the founding of his Academy we may surmise that he thought he had found his answer.

To see clearly Plato's reversal (for that is what it is) in Book X and the problems it creates, we need to recall the overall structure of Plato's argument, especially the divisions of the kinds of poetry in Books II and III. It may appear that Socrates follows the argument wherever it may lead, as he claims to do at one point (294 C), but the discussion is, in fact, highly programmatic, affording an early instance of the Platonic method of division. What follows is not exhaustive of Plato's divisions in this section but includes the important ones. The great question, we recall, that launched the reform passages in Book II was what shall our paideia be? Or is it difficult to improve on what long experience has taught?

Current practice, the present paideia in place, consists of two branches, music and gymnastic. *Mousikē* is divided into two aspects, content and "form" or *lexis,* that is, the manner of performance or communication, or how the poetic material is brought to bear on developing young minds.[20] The content, in turn, is divided into two parts, one that which deals with gods and one that deals with heroes. The form is divided into two parts, imitative (involving *mimēsis*) and nonimitative. In Book X we shall be told that mimetic verse is forbidden absolutely and that nonimitative verse has only two allowable categories, hymns (to gods) and encomia (to worthy men), but in the reform passages of Books II and III Plato is concerned with imitative verse and its reform for educational use. (See Figure 8.1.)

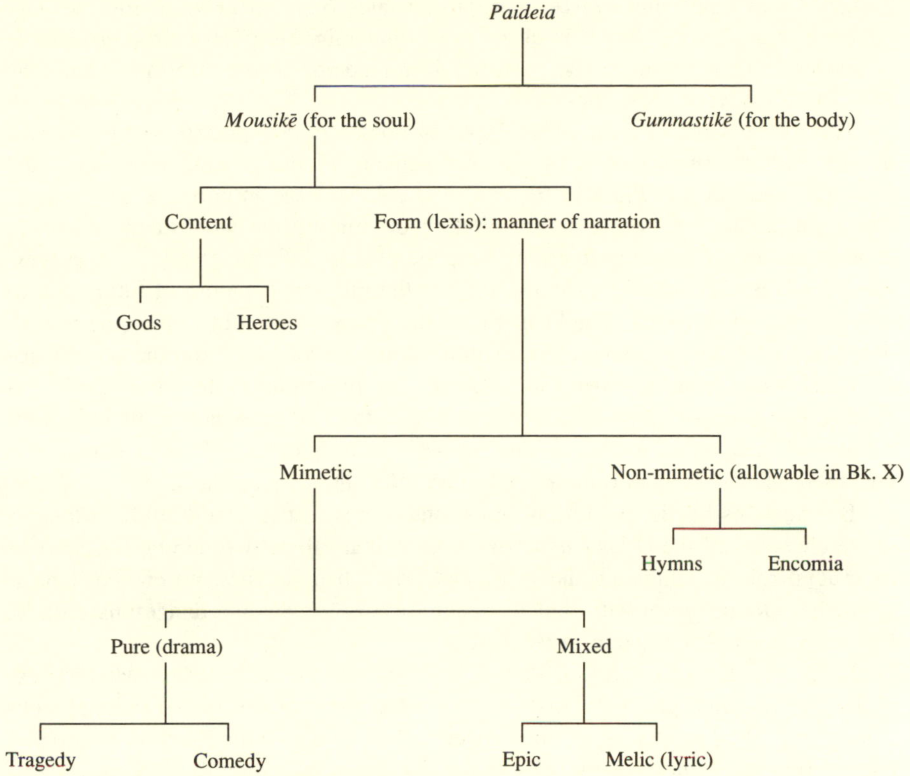

Figure 8.1. The Divisions of paideia and *mimēsis* in Books II–III and X.

Imitative verse, or verse exploiting *mimēsis,* is divided into two parts, that with no narration (e.g., tragedy and comedy) and that which mixes some narration with dialogue (e.g., epic). All forms of mimetic verse—but notably epic, followed by tragic—are discovered to be dangerous in the reform passages because the act of *mimēsis,* or dramatic imitation,[21] by the performer induces the same experience in his hearers. Epic and tragedy become the focus of attack because in contemporary Athens they carry the bulk of didactic information concerning the gods on the one hand and popular morality on the other, which forms the basis of instruction of the young. They are, thus, treated not as entertainment but as authoritative compendiums of popular theology and normative ethics.

The youth, in being induced to imitate what they *hear*—for *mimēsis* is fostered only in the oral situation, not in the quiet study of a text—inescapably become like those whom they imitate, whether the models of behavior are Homeric heroes or, insofar as this is possible, even the gods. In both cases, then, the behavior of the models, or heroes and gods, must be worthy of imitation, "for they [the youth] should from childhood imitate only what is proper to them." The models will, therefore, be persons who are "brave, sober, pious and free, and have all other such [virtues]." Nothing that is shameful *(aischron)* or base may be imitated, lest from the imitation they take in or imbibe the real evil (395 C–D).

Rather, "they shall sing *(adein)* and narrate tales *(muthologein)* saying the very opposite things" (392 B). It is clear, then, that mimetic poetry, in considerable quantities, will continue to be performed and heard, albeit reformed along the lines Plato's Socrates specifies.

This progressive division of the types of contemporary poetry, so obviously a literate author's organization of the mechanisms of the contemporary oral and aural paideia, permits Plato to focus on the role and the importance of *mimēsis,* which he defines as the act of assimilating or miming the words and actions of another and thus becoming in effect someone else, a different "self" or a succession of selves.[22] A trivial reason for limiting the mimetic behavior of future guardians is given in Book III. The Principle of the Specialization of Labor (the restriction of each citizen to a single occupation) would be violated, and the observance of it had been agreed to earlier in Book II. The reasoning is that if a guardian is to have one occupation and practice that alone, then he must not in his imitations become all manner of people. If the rule were strictly observed, as of course it is not, then guardians would imitate only one role, that of guardians.

But Socrates bends, permitting imitations of a sort that would not be offensive to the character of the *kalos k'agathos,* or good man, thereby retaining for *mousikē* its crucial role in educating the guardians. Plato had, in fact, no choice if he is retain his utopian proposals, but the door to *mimēsis* swings dangerously open. He will slam it closed again in Book X.

Later, the deeper reason for Plato's hostility to *mimēsis* emerges. *Mimēsis* exploits the irrational part (or parts) of the soul at the expense of the rational, thus "crippling" it by producing an unbalanced psyche in which the function of one part (rational) is being encroached on by others (irrational or arational).[23] Recurrent acts of *mimēsis* will render the soul Platonically "unjust" and destroy its proper harmony. Therefore, and at last consistently, all mimetic poetry must go. So too, Plato finally adds, must all poetry as heard and performed, save for the trivial exceptions.

Plato emerges a divided man (and educator) in this famous polemic and not altogether consistent. Much of what he proposes for society in the early books (II–IV) will require constant public occasions for the poetic (and mimetic) experience, if all classes are to be induced to accept his controversial and stringent proposals and abide by them. He knows this full well. Plato relentlessly maintains that both citizen and ruler will accept these proposals, however radical (e.g., access to higher education solely on the basis of merit) or even ridiculous and scandalous they now may seem (e.g., women exercising naked alongside men), provided only that the paideia of all classes and genders has been correct.

In Books V and VI Plato proceeds to put in place the epistemology and metaphysics, as well as in Book VII the advanced educational curriculum, which will produce the full guardians or *phulakes* (as opposed to *epikouroi,* auxiliaries). Only these full guardians will be trained to think in the new Platonic way. They will become the philosophic rulers whose primary function—apart from perpetuating their own education—will be to make rules that govern the whole community. This will require that the final phase of guardians' education will be superimposed on the one they shared with the community and will be far superior to it. Book VII tells us that it will commence with the propadeutic benefits of a long course beginning in mathematics and concluding with dialectic.[24] The role of books, treatises, or even Plato's own dialogues in the course of this fifteen-year–long training is not specified, but it is safe to say that mimetic poetry had no place in it. Indeed, with this educational system in place, *mimēsis* can be dismissed.

Plato acknowledges this in the opening words of Book X (595 A) and is able to be consistent at last. The controversial text deserves full citation. Socrates is speaking.

> And, truly, many other considerations convince me that we were entirely right when we organized our polis, and especially, I think, in the matter of poetry.
> How so?
> In refusing to admit *at all* so much of it [poetry] as was mimetic *(hosē mimētikē).*

What Plato was proposing in the central books was nothing less than a fundamental revision in the cognitive habits of Hellenes, requiring a drastic overhaul in their educational practices. Adeimantus had, in fact, first correctly identified the problem and its cause in Book II.[25]

The fundamental cause is, indeed, the traditional paideia, partially the content, but more fundamentally the mode of communication *(lexis),* for it continuously exploits *mimēsis.* In Book X Plato connects this analysis of poetry with the psychology of the soul he had proposed in Book IV. The aural appeal of poetry to the emotions and the seduction of *mimēsis* softens the thinking and rational part of the soul, corrupting it. The deeper reasons behind the appeal of *mimēsis* have been exposed at last. It appeals not to the ruling and best part of the psyche, the reasoning and calculating part, the *logistikon,* but to the inferior emotive and appetitive parts, swelling ("feeding") their role in the personality. *Mimēsis* wears its true face at last. It is a direct threat to the rule of reason, the "justice" or polity of the soul, and so to the integrity of the personality (602 D–603 C; 605 A).[26]

Better than anyone else writing in antiquity, Plato saw what was fundamentally amiss in the Greek paideia and what so urgently needed correcting. If he is to be consistent, surely what is required is that he abolish the performances of poetry altogether. It remains too dangerous, in its aural appeal to Greeks, as long as the ancient verses are still widely received as oral paideia. He must ban them as performed or heard, whether by citizen or guardian, young or old.

With a vengeance, Plato warms to the task in a splendid outpouring of rhetoric in Book X, but only after first claiming that he had already done so in the reform passages of Book III.[27] As a prelude, he first draws on an example from the crafts. The Form of the bed, which is one, no man has made; the many beds we encounter are made by carpenters and craftsmen, in effect many images reflecting the Form. The painter, the imitator, then paints the beds the craftsman makes (507 B), a third removed from the reality of the Form. The comparison was perhaps useful to Plato's contemporaries but has led his interpreters down many a strange path. Always the poets led by Homer were in the forefront of Plato's own mind.

> Shall we then lay it down that all the poets are imitators of images *(mimētas eidōlōn)* of virtue, and of the other [moral forms], in all that they make *(poiousi),* and that they do not lay hold of the truth. Rather, as we were saying a moment ago, just like the painter who knows nothing of working in leather, but makes a

> picture which appears to be a cobbler, both to himself and to others who know nothing [of cobbling and cobblers, the actual makers of reins and bridles] but judge only from the colors and the shape. (600 E)

In like manner the poet, who knows nothing of reality (the Forms), but only how to imitate, gives a certain false reality to his creations by the cosmetics of metered words, rhythms, and harmonies.

In the expanded analysis of *mimēsis,* it will no longer be sufficient to curtail mimetic poetry *somewhat,* such as by censoring some content, limiting some extravagant excesses, restraining certain modes of the music, banning some instruments (e.g., flutes are definitely out, but the more austere kind of lyres are in), controlling the meters, and forbidding guardians unsuitable dramatic and choral roles permitted to ordinary citizens. It all must go. Plato returns to the issue of the *erōs* for poetry, inculcated in Greeks by their most admired institutions, and to the poets who inculcate it, and he now proposes to abolish, once and for all, both it and them.

In unforgettable images and gloriously poetical language, he tells his fellow Hellenes how Greece itself (no talk now of a few emotionally desiccated and intellectually gifted guardians) at long last, like a man forced to relinquish a love that is destroying him, must abandon its love for the ancient verses. Like a man who is no longer a child and so must give up the loves *(erōta)* of a child, Greece must now give up its attachment to poetry. Put those wondrous ancient verses into plain everyday prose, so the philosopher insists, and Hellenes will soon discover that what they said was only deceptively beautiful, like the face of him who was never really handsome after he lost the bloom of youth. To these verses Greeks of this and all future generations will now be required to sing a countercharm to their ancient charms each time they hear them, for one has now been found, Plato's own educational curriculum in Book VII. The enchanting spell of the ancient music has been broken at long last. There will no exceptions, no compromises now. All poetry, save for a few hymns to the gods and *encomia* to men of good character, must be banished from Hellas. More is at stake than Greeks realize: the very polity, the balance and health and "justice," of their souls and of their society.[28]

This is splendid rhetoric, and its images are equal to any found in the poetry Plato banishes. What Plato does not tell us, of course, is what he proposes as the replacement at the primary level of education for guardians and citizens alike if he banishes all memorized, sung, and performed poetry, or how in its absence the populace will be educated into docile obedience. With all this swept away, just how will the souls of the young be bent to accept their assigned roles and to embrace personal and class sacrifices, which it had been the task of "the one big thing," or a properly controlled education in *mousikē,* to produce in all citizens of the New Athens? How, with all but trivial verse banished, will the souls of guardians be insensibly induced in the formative years to accept all the responsibilities, disciplines, burdens, and denials he has proposed for them through their fiftieth year? Plato understood better than anyone else then living the power of a poetically and orally induced *mimēsis* to sway (especially) the young to sympathetic psychological identification and so form their personalities and control their behavior: "Or have you not observed that the practice of these imitations, if begun from boyhood and continued into adult life, settles into the very character and nature of a person, this in *body* and *speech* and *thought?*"[29] How can the revolutionary society Plato proposes in the *Republic* now be made to work without poetic *mimēsis,* in that an acceptance (or *erōs*) of the soul fostered by correct education in *mousikē,* not external compulsion, was its fundamental ingredient?[30]

Plato does not and cannot say. Instead, he turns his attention to the immortality of individual souls and proceeds to spin out the end of the great argument of the *Republic* in a poetic myth of a soul's journey of a thousand years across stars and galaxies where at last—in the dialogue's final two words—*eu prattomen,* "we shall fare well."

Utopian Dreams and Educational Agendas: Interpreting the *Republic*

Once again the rhetoric is without rival, but the inconsistency remains. One line of explanation may, in the end, be unavoidable. The various reforming proposals in the *Republic* must be taken on different levels of seriousness. The utopian political and social reforms—whatever hope Plato may have had for some or all of them on some distant day—emerge as his descriptive or heuristic device, useful for the argument of this dialogue, and in the main are found only here. By proposing to replace the existing order with a utopian one—a "far better" one—Plato affords himself a glorious opportunity to focus on what he finds objectionable in the Athens of his day, and to do so in a medium that invites exaggeration, satire, irony, and humor. It was a technique that had already been made familiar to Athenian audiences on the comic stage.[31]

On an entirely different level of Platonic seriousness are the calls for a new language and a new way of thinking, summarized finally under two banners: the method of the Forms and the theory of a soul divided into rational and irrational faculties, one responding to the dangers of poetry (or pleasure) and the other responding to reason and dialectic. Supremely important to living well is the proper tendance or health of this complex soul. These features, in one guise or another, recur in dialogue after dialogue. They are near the heart of "Platonism" if anything is. The Platonic summons for a new language and a new way of thinking, so important for the health of the soul, can be answered only by providing a whole new basis for the paideia of Greece; the entire argument of the *Republic* is designed to prove as much. Presumably, then, the basics of the curriculum of Book VII were also seriously intended, to be implemented not at the apex of a social utopia but in the new Academy. The subjects were, however, probably pursued in the Academy more informally than suggested in the *Republic* and without the utopian timetable.[32]

On this interpretation, the utopian proposals for the New Athens—abolition of inherited privilege and wealth, wives and children in common, Athenian women naked beside their men in the gymnasia, weddings rigged by crooked lotteries for eugenic purposes, and the rest—as a system and as intended for implementation surely belong to the rhetoric, and perhaps sincere dreams, of only the *Republic.*

By contrast, some of these very suggestions, with all their potential for humor and satire, might play very well to an audience of sophisticated Athenian males gathered in a private home to hear read aloud, over a number of evenings, the great argument of the *Republic,* if that, indeed, is how some of Plato's dialogues were "published."

We do not know which came first, the Academy or the *Republic.*[33] Probably, as many scholars have surmised, they were born together in Plato's mind. If so, some troublesome features of the argument of the *Republic* may fall into place at last. Plato knew that he had no practical means of controlling the early education of Athenian lads, let alone that of the many young men from other parts of Greece who sought out his school.[34] This was out of his hands. Rather, like the sophists and Socrates before him, he sought to step into the lacuna left by the traditional and orally based paideia of Greece. For the *meirakion* years of young males, or roughly between the ages of fifteen and twenty-one, no formal provision was made anywhere in oral Hellas for continuing the mental formation of young men in those critical years, save for regular *sunousia* with male elders. That was no longer adequate, as Socrates had perhaps indirectly demonstrated to a maturing, impressionable Plato many years earlier. It was this lacuna that drew the young men—or most of them—to the sophists and Socrates in the fifth century and to Plato's Academy in the fourth. Aristocratic youths arrived at his door, we must presume, already literate. Plato did not have to begin with an Aristotle, who arrived at age sixteen or seventeen, or with so many other young men—some of whose names we know—by teaching them their ABC's. Rather, they journeyed from every part of Greece to the new Academy to learn lessons never available at the feet of the *grammatistēs* or *kitharistēs.*

Homer's Final Exile

Socrates has not ended his quarrel with *mimēsis.* It must go, of course, ignominiously, with no honor left. But in the interest of consistency so too must its supreme practitioner. There is unfinished business. The final sentence has not been pronounced on Homer. Plato lingers over pronouncing it in the long first half of Book X, a passage that has puzzled his commentators precisely because of its humor, its deep irony, and the depth of Plato's hostility to the lingering moral authority of epic over his fellow Hellenes.

Socrates begins in a low key by referring anonymously to certain persons who have a reputation for knowing the subject matters of the crafts—all crafts, and not one alone—and even "of all things." We must be suspicious of such a person, observes Socrates, if we encounter one. The suspense is allowed to build. Who could this be? Anyone seduced by such claims surely is simple-minded, for he has only met some clever person, a magician and imitator, and has been deceived into believing him to be all-wise. The magician is, in fact, a charlatan, one with a clever mirror. With the twist of his hand he can imitate (duplicate) anything. The problem is that the poor believer himself cannot distinguish among three things: true knowledge, total lack of knowledge, and imitation or *mimēsis* (598

C–D). As a result, the many images the imitator makes are in danger of being taken for realities.

Abruptly, the game is over, and the clever charlatan named; Homer had been the target all along.

> Then must we not examine tragedy next—and its leader, Homer—since we hear people say that these poets know all the crafts *(technai),* and all things human *(anthropoeia)* concerning virtue and vice [that is, moral behavior], and everything there is to know about divine things as well. (598 D–E)

It is a historically fair statement of what was conveyed in epic as oral paideia: paradigms of moral (and immoral) behavior requiring imitation (including avoidance), comprehensive in scope; the family of the gods, reasonably complete and (in Hesiod) systematized; and a good deal of technical lore, but not systematically presented. Moreover, in Athens the epical mantle had partially fallen on tragedians, who were always regarded by Greeks themselves as, properly, poets who were teachers of the people.

The ancient claim of epic verse to be a depository of much practical information in areas covered by the various crafts—from generalship (especially, as in the *Ion*) or navigational rules to medicine—is still to be heard. Some in Hellas still even take it seriously, but Socrates claims he will pass over this preposterous claim as relatively unimportant (although he cannot quite bring himself to do so). Far more dangerous is the claim of epic to be the authoritative source of normative ethics and popular theology. Here the scathing irony of Plato is merciless. Let us watch it unfold.

Homer, remarks Socrates, is certainly presenting himself as a multitalented man. Now would such a man be content with making only imitations while he lived, or would he not wish to produce the real thing? Warming to his subject, Socrates poses a series of rhetorical questions aimed at those who still accept the authority of epic and Homer. Surely such an all-knowing person would want to leave behind endless memorials of his real actions or accomplishments and not, like some petty actor always playing the king, be content to confine himself to a lifetime of imitations. Well, then, where are Homer's real accomplishments? Socrates offers to set aside Homer's claims in the area of the crafts, but not without a jibe. We won't, says Socrates, force Homer to provide us with a list of names of the patients he actually cured, as opposed to imitating cleverly the speech of a physician (599 B–C). Let us, instead, get right down to "greatest and finest" accomplishments attributed to Homer, namely, "the making of wars, generalship, the governance of cities, and the education (*paideia*) of men. For surely it is eminently fair (*dikaion*) to question him about these things, asking . . ." (599 C–D). Socrates suddenly reverts to the vocative, as though he has Homer before him as one of his hapless interlocutors. Socrates directly addresses his great adversary, the *protos didaskalos* as he will soon call him, the "first teacher." In reality, of course, Plato is addressing what Homer had always meant to the Hellenes:

> Oh, friend Homer, if you are not third removed from truth in regards to virtue *(aretē),* and of images a craftsman *(demiourgos),* being what we defined as an

> imitator *(mimētēs),* but instead are even a second place removed, and are capable of knowing what pursuits make men better in private and public life, tell us which city is better governed due to you, as Lacedamon was benefited because of Lycurgus, and as many other cities both great and small have been similarly benefited. What city gives you credit as a good law-giver, and for having benefited it? (599 D–E)

The demand is outrageous, of course, and the humor intentional. Imagined as a historical person, yet living in an age before there was "law," Homer is faulted for not having been a lawgiver for a specific city. But the basic point is serious enough. Homer or epic as the source of morality, initially ancestral custom, has become a total anachronism. His claim to be the guide to how one should live, which now in Athens the laws supremely are, is bogus, and it is time to discard it.

So, continues Socrates, answering his own question, Homer has bequeathed us no law codes and, he adds, no ingenious inventions either. He is no Thales, then. (Thales, one of the seven "wise men," is mentioned by name as being famous in this capacity; Thales the *phusikos* is Aristotle's discovery.) Neither have we heard of any wars won with his help in his day. Because there are no public deeds to credit to his account, what about his greatest claim in the arena of the private affairs of men, namely, that he should be in charge of the paideia of the youth? This, of course, is where Socrates has been heading from the start.

> When you chance upon those who sing the praises of Homer, and claim that this poet educated Hellas *(Hellada pepaideuken),* and that for the management *(diokēsis)* and education *(paideia)* of men he is worthy of our study and devotion, and that we should order the whole of our lives by the guidance of this poet. . . . (606 E–607 A)

The famous—or infamous—expulsion of all poetry follows immediately upon these words.

The sarcasm, humor, and deliberate anachronisms of the first half of Book X, brilliantly addressed to a knowing contemporary audience, have baffled and misled not a few of Plato's interpreters. When the claim of Homer to be the primary source of the Hellenic paideia is first introduced in Book X, it is ridiculed in tones both humorous and satirical. No contemporary reader could miss the associations. The assimilation of Homer's educational activity to that of the sophists makes the irony certain. Sophists (Protagoras, significantly, is mentioned) now make similar claims to Homer's, remarks Socrates. They enter into private "associations" (or *sunousia,* in the plural *idia suggignomenoi*) with young men, convincing their contemporaries that they will not be able to manage *(diokein)* their household or their city unless they put these men in charge of their *paideia* (600 D). And these educators have swarms of followers, as earlier Pythagoras had, who also offered his countrymen a "way of life." All these men have numberless close disciples and devotees who never leave their sides, so eager were they to imbibe the paideia they had to sell. But where is Homer's band of devotees? Has anyone heard of one?

So, if Homer had *really* been able to educate men (*paideuein anthropous,* 600 C), surely *he,* too, would have been honored and loved in the same manner, by a similar group of close disciples who would sooner let go of gold than let go of this poet and his precious paideia (600 D). But do we now hear of any such band of devotees for Homer in his day? No, we do not (of course).

Alas, how can this be explained? Homer must have been but a lonely, wandering rhapsode—and so was Hesiod. Homer's epical partner is suddenly thrown in for good measure and similarly deprecated. Obviously lacking a paideia (Plato's word throughout this section) to dispense, Homer was permitted by those who heard him to move on to the next city, rhapsodizing alone, roaming all over Hellas, a forlorn figure, without any followers attached to him at all (600 C). If Homer had possessed a paideia to teach, surely he would have been engulfed in the warm glow of devoted followers, as is so rightly bestowed on great Protagoras and other sophists today.

The mood initially is humorous, ironic, and, of course, deliberately outrageous in the anachronistic accusations flung at Homer. It exploits the fact that nothing reliable was known of Homer or Hesiod from preliterate Greece beyond the names and the fact of the poems, composed in the meter of rhapsodes' recitations. It also permits a few swipes at the sophists. What binds these men together in Plato's satire is that they have been *accepted* as great educators—a bogus claim in all cases, as Plato sees it—and that their contemporary reputations and importance, while real enough, are undeserved. They are, in a word, the competition. Plato, unmistakably, is exploiting to the full his very considerable literary and especially satirical talents as he seeks to drown their claims in a flood of irony.

Initially, the claim of Homer to possess and dispense a paideia is ridiculed urbanely, by offering outrageous reasons for not believing this claim, that is, Homer is not known to have helped win a war (are we meant to recall General Ion?), written a law code, or had a band of adoring devotees like that great worthy, Protagoras. Just how adoring those followers could be was brilliantly captured in Plato's *Protagoras* (315 B–C), where Protagoras was lecturing as he marched back and forth in Callias' empty cloister, "and behind him two companies were following . . . and it was splendid to see how orderly his train split up into groups on each side, and then wheeling around formed up again in his rear," while those at the far back were straining to catch every precious word. Plato's satire of Homer is no less evident in Book X, although it has been detected less often, largely, I suspect, because scholars do not or will not accept Homer as an educator. In the case of Protagoras, of course, who lectured in a manner familiar to us and demanded a fee, there can be no doubt.

The deeper reason for Plato's hostility to *mimēsis*—namely, its threat to the health and polity of the soul—has been exposed; the tone of the polemic now grows serious and menacing. The reason, says Socrates, is the intense pleasure that *mimēsis* brings can seduce even the best of men. "Listen and examine!" Adeimantus is ordered sharply. The very best *of us*—the pronoun is in the Greek—says Socrates, when we hear Homer or some other imitator among the tragedians (that is, when we hear a rhapsode or tragic actor) imitating one of the heroes who is grieving and stretching out his sad lamentations, or we hear a chorus chanting and beating their breasts in grief, we thoroughly enjoy it and abandon ourselves up to what is represented. We become part of the experience itself, sharing eagerly in the feelings of the characters through the singer's words, as though we were they. Moreover, it is precisely the ability to produce these very emotions in us and to do so powerfully that leads us to praise a poet as a good poet, or not (605 D–E). Adeimantus readily concurs in all of this.

Gone is the tone of condescending humor directed at Homer, the poor, solitary rhapsode without devotees because he has no paideia to bestow on them or on Hellas. Now Homer is again a formidable character in the person of the contemporary rhapsode. Once more the Homeric singer emerges as the master controller of the emotive parts of the human psyche, and he is very much a force in contemporary Athens. To the singer's power to manipulate the psyche has been added the claim that Homer was the educator of Greece and, above all, the arbiter of its morals. What is worse, Socrates laments, large numbers of Hellenes still accept this claim, conducting their entire lives "Homerically." The full and immediate danger has been exposed, requiring drastic action. Socrates does not hesitate to propose it. He will make no further compromises and retracts all those he has made. Moving to the eloquent climax of the great argument, he says we must grant that Homer is "the most poetic of poets and first of tragedians" (607 A) and in that role is the "first teacher," but at the same time we must also know that

> we can admit no poetry into our city save only hymns *(humnoi)* to the gods and praise songs to good men. For if you grant entrance to the Muse of sweet pleasure, whether in lyric or epic, then pleasure and pain will be lords of your city instead of law . . . for from ancient times there is a quarrel between poetry and philosophy. (607 A–B)

In lines that have become famous—or infamous—in the history of philosophy, Homer, which means of course, his reciters, and all the poets are banished from Hellas. Simultaneously, all performed verse—whether mimetic or not, including epic, tragic, or lyric verse—is banished from the Hellenic paideia.[35] The higher education of the Academy is now available to take their place. This radical expulsion of all poetry from the paideia of Greeks and the reasons for it are the climax of the argument of the *Republic,* placed by a great writer where they belong, at the culmination of his book. Book X is indispensable to that argument and hardly, as some critics have felt, a somewhat irrelevant appendix. It would be so only if the power of poetry over the paideia of Greece were a thing of the past and not a contemporary fact of life.

It is generally conceded in Platonic scholarship that writing the *Republic* and establishing the Academy were close together in time. Could the very tensions created in writing that work have provoked in its author a realization that the epistemological and educational reforms it extolled were not attainable in an Athens that he did not and could never politically control? Utopian social reforms must be postponed, if indeed they were ever seriously intended. The only practical solution was to create a new kind of association, a self-perpetuating institution of professional educators to house a radically new kind of paideia, in which succeeding generations of an intellectual elite would be educated in a manner heretofore unavailable in oral Athens. In a word, Plato institutionalized the processes of higher education, taking them once and for all out of the hands of private individuals, whether they were gifted poets, traveling sophists, older male initiators (through "association" or *sunousia*), or even, in the final analysis, a Socrates. In so doing, he invented the idea of the university. As Milman Parry—at the time an obscure young assistant professor who held some bold ideas about Homer—remarked in a now-famous address delivered before the trustees of Harvard University, the European university "is no inglorious thing."[36]

Orality, Literacy, and the Dialogue Form: Some Speculations

Exploring some lacunae in the argument of Plato's *Republic* leads inevitably to difficult questions: Were the dialogues, including the *Republic*, published only in his school while he lived, as some nineteenth-century scholars thought, or did they find even then a wider audience in the city? If published in the school, what precisely was their role in the education of younger members? Were they, perhaps, designed to stimulate further debate and discussion among the senior associates? As possibly in the case of the *Parmenides*, were some of them provoked by contemporary philosophers and mathematicians and replies on Plato's part to positions taken by them, such as Eudoxus on the Forms? If a wider audience was the initial intention, how were all or some of the dialogues popularly published (if they were), or "given to the light" in the contemporary idiom, during Plato's lifetime? Publishers of his dialogues in modern languages find it difficult to keep some of them in print even after Plato has become by universal assent a (if not *the*) seminal figure of Western culture. How are we to imagine that a *Parmenides* found an audience in Plato's lifetime, or the entire *Timaeus*, the dialogue that by sheer accident (and only in partial translation, perhaps a blessing) did the most to secure his reputation in the Middle Ages?

Plausibly, some of Plato's dialogues were read aloud with success to sophisticated groups of Athenians—perhaps gathered in private homes or meeting in the Academy—as Isocrates' envious remarks may indirectly suggest and a few modern commentators have perceptively intuited (Gilbert Ryle, Holger Thesleff, Robert Brumbaugh, Jackson Hershbell). If we are to imagine Plato's dialogues being read aloud, then many passages may have been designed, at least in part, to help engage and retain a potentially restless audience's attention. The syntax would, predictably, be more narrative in these passages; metaphor and analogy would abound. No similar concessions need be made to a solitary reader of a scientific *logos*, however, or even to a few motivated professionals gathered to hear a lecturer reading aloud from a scientific or philosophical *logos*. Indeed, such passages would be an annoying intrusion.

Possibly, then, two audiences were often in Plato's mind: an inner group who at one level appreciated and relished the rich allusions and (often) the humor and irony behind the manipulation of traditional vocabulary or ideas, and a more popular audience, some of whom at least may have accepted the same words pretty much at face value. Once again, a few of Plato's modern commentators, but these among his most sensitive readers, have detected such a deliberate two-level form of discourse in at least some of the dialogues. The distinguished Finnish scholar

Holger Thesleff has defended an interpretation along these lines—or at least one related to it—if I understand him rightly.[37]

In contrast, in the Aristotelian treatise the author gets down to his scientific or philosophical business at once and stays relentlessly at it. Be the author right or wrong, what he defends or believes to be right and what he rejects are never at question or obscure, at least not deliberately so. It is the no-nonsense form of prose exposition that full literacy will always favor for serious topics. No provision need be made for the brain's relaxation, for easy retention, or for future verbatim repetition. If Aristotle's surviving treatises are examples, then the treatises that served as the basis for instruction and lectures in the Lyceum—comprehensive for the topic, constantly updated, serving as the basis of research and discussion, studied carefully by not memorized—reflect an established, comfortable alliance between literacy and education.

For the author of prose works of this sort, widespread diffusion of ideas—and so their popular comprehension—can become unimportant, an intrusive and unwanted encumbrance on an author already sufficiently burdened with a complex and difficult subject matter. Society's important information, as professionally formulated, will thus be increasingly addressed to an intellectual elite who gradually create their own professional language, one that effectively closes out a larger public. This can never happen in an oral culture. The conditions of mnemonically preserving and so of popularly "publishing" the society's important information preclude it. What was so characteristic of the Lyceum's activity and of its greatness was, I suggest, directly related to its heavy dependence on the expository prose treatise as the proper vehicle for philosophy and science. In this regard, the Lyceum, not the Academy, was the European educational innovator.

Allied to the research activity of the Lyceum, concentrated as it was in technical texts and indirectly helping to make it possible, must have been a growing habit of privately reading some literary texts. By the early decades of the fourth century, these texts were being copied in sufficient numbers for private citizens with sufficient interest and means to acquire them. This implies, however initially modest, an ever-expanding trade in books.[38] This stage of literacy was never achieved under the conditions of scribal literacy in the empires of the ancient Near East or in the small kingdoms of Sidon and Byblos. That it was a feature of later Hellenistic Greece is not in serious doubt, but its documentation is beyond the scope of the present work.[39]

The suggestions that follow are based, in the final analysis, on a growing appreciation of the Greek development from orality to literacy. It is not as yet a topic fully recognized in dealing with Plato's text, although it is no longer a waif begging for recognition either. Plato's dialogues, all written in the first half of the fourth century, emerge, in a real sense, as transition documents, making concessions to long habits of Greek oralism and of invented conversations that no later Greek writer or serious philosopher will again feel impelled to make. This is not backwardness or even nostalgia on the author's part. Like every great writer, Plato must conform somewhat to his audience's expectations, and he must look to the conditions of publication.

Plato's Dialogues as Paideutic Textbooks?

The question that deserves to be reopened for discussion has, of late, been somewhat moribund, especially among scholars writing in English. What role did the written word play in this first of European universities? If a major one, then what texts were read and studied, and how? That the core of all education must be written texts is now so obvious to us that the relevant questions are never asked, but they deserve to be. Before standard textbooks such as Copi's on the reasoning process, even before any sustained work in the area we now call logic, what sort of alliance existed in the Academy between written texts and learning how to think? In the *Metaphysics* (1005b2–5), Aristotle complains that those who discuss the condition on which a statement should be regarded as true do so with "a want of training in logic *(tōn analuticōn),* for they should know these things already" and not be learning them when they come to listen to a lecture on an important topic. At the outset of the *Topics (100a25),* Aristotle defines reasoning as an argument in which certain things being laid down, something other than these necessarily follows from them. He goes on (101a25) to explain why a *written treatise* on analytics—or what we, following the medieval philosophers, now call logic—would be useful, giving three purposes. The first is "intellectual training." Aristotle in the *Rhetoric* and elsewhere boasts that he had no predecessors and virtually nothing existed before him in this area (as opposed to other areas such as physics). He is, of course, right. Formal logic, centered in the analysis of rules governing syllogistic deduction, is the product of a late, developed literacy, requiring that language for some time had been a physical object. Oral people are innocent of it; they do not speak that way and they do not think that way.

My point is that no logical treatises or exercise manuals as yet existed for use by the early Academy, and Aristotle is self-consciously (and rightly) proud to be the pioneering innovator in composing them and putting the study of them prior to serious work in philosophy. We have Aristotle's own statement concerning the utility of these treatises as a preliminary *organon* or instrument to be studied first, a practice we may assume was followed in the Lyceum with the logical treatises now known as the Organon. What took their place in the early Academy? Indeed, in the early fourth century what was there in the way of written *prose* of any kind for any educator, especially a Plato, to fall back on for this purpose? The history of Herodotus? The forensic speeches of Isocrates or other logographers?

Oral discussion, especially if a Socrates could be found, could do part of the job, but only part. Can a Socrates redivivus always be found? As Ryle, on the basis of *Letter VII,* reminded us, Plato was away from Athens for at least three extended periods. Did he feel a need for a supplement to oral dialectic in the Academy, and so yet another alliance between the habits of oralism and the resources of literacy?

Some texts relating to the subject matters studied in the curriculum outlined in Book VII were, perhaps, specially prepared, but now lost. Given the subject matters, that seems certain. This must have been true for plane and later for solid geometry, to whose study the Academy was a great impetus.[40] But these too have been lost, although remnants seem to have made their way into Euclid. The apex of the curriculum in Book VII is dialectic and always remained at least partially oral as the moral forms were explored in shared inquirey, plausibly a Socratic inheritance. But was dialectic as found in the Academy entirely oral?

Could it be that Plato's dialogues themselves served some purpose here? Through them one participated, as it were, in a conversation with "Socrates" and detected the outrageous "howlers" of even the master dialectician in dealing with, for example, a Polemarchus or an Ion, as those unfortunate interlocutors themselves could not. Like the Theory of Forms itself, the dialogues are perhaps better viewed, in Plato's own words, as exemplars of a method, a *methodos,* than as doctrinal statements, and even Socrates may be guilty of a well-planted error here and there, or a "Platonic" heresy. Gilbert Ryle's reconstruction may be fanciful and even somewhat donnish in its language, but it is far from implausible. Claiming that we can be sure that Plato not only composed dialectical dramas but also instructed young men in the method of argumentation ("he had tutorially conducted eristic Moots"), Ryle concludes, "Indeed his dialectical dialogues should be read as case-books of recent Moots, dramatized partly to help students to remember and digest the argument-sequences that finally crystallized out of these Moots."[41] Was Plato's intention behind writing the dialogues, at least in part, that they become "paideutic textbooks," the first in European education, "members of a larger species," the fourth-century Socratic *logoi?*[42]

Unless we wish to guess—defensible enough—the *Laws* may afford the only clues for an answer that is based on hard, contemporary evidence. What actually occurred on a daily basis in the Academy while its founder was still alive is an obscure issue, save for one certain fact. He set the pupils, including an Aristotle—the results survive in the fragments—to *writing* philosophical dialogues. Plato, himself the first great philosophic writer, apparently determined while training the first class of graduate students in philosophy that it was not enough that future philosophers read; they must also *write.* From some clues in the *Laws* we also learn that Plato seems to have determined that the best "textbooks" or training manuals then available for doing philosophy were none other than his own dialogues.

It does not matter whether Plato wrote the *Laws,* as most scholars believe, or whether it was a pupil's creation that found its way into the Platonic corpus of dialogues accepted by Thrasyllus.[43] In either case it would reflect the activity of the early Academy, and may be even stronger evidence for my suggestions if indeed *Laws* came from a student who knew all too well the daily drill in Plato's school.

Written Dialogues Put to Use in *Laws*

In *Laws*—and only there among Plato's dialogues usually taken as genuine—Socrates does not appear. The chief interlocutor now becomes a certain "Athenian Stranger," a man who is well informed on affairs in contemporary Athens, as the reader is frequently reminded. The subject under discussion, a transparent fiction, is the devising of a constitution intended for a new colony on Crete, a place of no political or cultural importance in the fourth century but legendary for its lawfulness (*eunomia,* 631 B). In the *Laws,* as in any politically reforming dialogue of Plato, we are not surprised when the conversation turns to education, or in the terminology of the dialogue, paideia.[44] With free adaptation, I follow the spirit of the Loeb translation of R. G. Bury, who tried to reproduce in English prose those stylistic features of the original that imply some distancing on the part of the Athenian Stranger from the procedures he is describing. These educational procedures are, be it noted, treated as still the contemporary practice in Athenian paideia.

> I verily affirm that we have composers of verses innumerable [various meters are enumerated, led by the hexameter] . . . on whom we are told by our tens of thousands of people we ought to rear and soak the young, if we are to give them a correct education *(orthōs paideuomenous),* making them, by means of recitations, lengthy listeners and large learners who learn off whole poets by heart. . . . Would you have me state frankly to these poets wherein they speak acceptably and well, and wherein they do not? (810 D–811 A)

The Athenian Stranger proceeds, in the vein of Socrates in the *Republic,* to assert that much in the vast body of Hellenic poetry is bad educationally, and the young must not be permitted to hear it. What is urgently needed is a criterion or pattern for choosing what is to be retained or rejected. But where is this to be found? Finding it will not be an easy task.

> But I have had it would seem a sudden stroke of luck. For looking back over the discussions *(logoi)* we have been pursuing from dawn to this present hour . . . and all our discourses all marshalled as it were in close array . . . and all the many discourses I have listened to or learned about . . . it struck me that *they* were what is most suitable for the ears of the young. Nowhere, I think, could I find a better pattern than this to put before the Law-guardian who is The Educator, that he may charge the teachers *(didaskaloi)* to teach the youth these discourses of ours and such as resemble and accord with them. (811 D–E)

The Educator[45] has, then, as his standard or pattern, a Platonic dialogue, the *Laws* itself, and may admit to the curriculum what is like it and in accord with it, including some poetry should he happen upon any that meets the requirements and restrictions already established. The latter we may ignore; suffice it to say poetry will have a very diminished role, with its content censored before performance or presentation, by censors not less than fifty years of age (801 C–E), along the severe lines established in Books II–III and X of the *Republic*. The new and important standard is ''discourses such as ours,'' that is, philosophical discussion and analysis in nonemotive prose. However, the emphasis quickly shifts from oral conversation to written prose, for this part of the discussion takes place under the category of the duties of the Educator in respect to writing and letters. If these acceptable philosophical discourses initially are oral, then the Educator has a solemn duty. He is enjoined to

> get them written down. He must first compel the teachers to learn them and praise them, and if any of the teachers fails to approve of them, he must not employ them . . . [or] entrust to them the teaching and training of the youth. Here and herewith let me end my homily concerning writing masters and writings. (811 E)

As Morrow comments,[46] the "reading book" of acceptable discourses for future paideia will be the *Laws* itself and such other literature as is like it or accords with it. That preeminently, if the obvious may be pressed, would be Plato's other dialogues, these *logoi* of ours "marshalled, as it were, in array."[47]

These connected passages in the *Laws* in fact mark the earliest clear reference in Greek literature to the completed process of transferring the primary mechanisms of Greek paideia to the written word. The mechanics of instruction involve direct reliance on the written word and so on a text as the shared medium of instruction by teacher and pupil. Moreover, the *Laws* is consistent, as Plato in the *Republic* was not. All citizens equally, of *every* class and *both* genders, must be rendered literate before the end of adolescence in order to participate in the proper paideia.[48] At last Plato's school has found the true "common education" or *paideia koinē* that in the *Republic* (543 A) Plato could name and even extol, but could not realize. The alliance between literacy and paideia and the dependence of latter on the former are now effected, at least as a matter of social theory.

It would be partially, but very imperfectly realized—especially where the education of women is concerned—in the more literate, Hellenistic period. But the fundamental dependency of education on literacy would not again be broken, however dim grew the lights, in European higher education. The educating "texts" of the society, like the legal, had been safely transferred to written texts, which the educated of the society would be expected to *read.* Prior training and drills in the rudiments of the alphabet would have as a major part of their purpose the ability to *read* those texts, a reason behind acquiring literacy that we cannot presume for any period earlier than the second quarter of the fourth century. I would, therefore, isolate Plato's *Laws* as the work in which this finalized alliance between literacy and paideia can be documented for the first time.

The author of the *Laws* is describing a practice that, it can hardly be doubted, had been initiated in Plato's Academy perhaps as long as forty years earlier. Although minimum room is left for chastised poetic texts if such can be found, they are of no significance. The main emphasis now is placed on a prose text, the "recording" of a conversation. I use quotation marks because discourses such as those found in the *Laws,* or the *Republic,* or the earlier *Euthyphro* or *Ion* are, in fact, nothing of the sort, if the record of an actual conversation is meant. The Platonic dialogues capture something of the spirit and issues of the Socratic encounters, the actual conversations that inspired them, but they are highly orchestrated works of literary art and philosophical thought. If epic verse is to daily speech as the dance is to walking (Wade-Gery's vivid analogy), then, as has been suggested, a Platonic dialogue is to everyday conversation and disputation, with all the false starts and loose ends, what a Gothic cathedral is to a heap of stones.

We are encouraged, in light of the *Laws* passage, to imagine the young students of the Academy reading (or hearing read aloud) the Socratic dialogues of Plato and themselves entering into the dialectic under the guidance of one who was more familiar with them, a trained, professional *didaskalos.* The students were active participants, philosophical combatants in rational argument, not passive memorizers of received truth or reciters of great masses of canonical verse. This was not the sole purpose of the dialogues, of course, but it may have been for the early Academy an important one, affecting how we should now read them. If I am correct, young initiates in the Academy entered into a series of conversations with "Socrates," but only as these had been artfully constructed and beautifully structured in the process of being committed by a highly professional author to writing—and constant, careful rewriting, if the tradition may be believed.

In essence, these discussions in Plato's Academy, guided and molded by the written word under the supervision of a professional *didaskalos,* a "dialectic-master," would have been an exercise in dialectic (in the Platonic sense) of a sort that Plato put at the culmination of the higher paideia for his guardians in Book VII of the *Republic.* The oral and written word have entered into a unique partnership, heretofore unknown to Greece, in the service of a new kind of paideia, also unique for its time. It is with us yet.

Being conversations, an element of oralism always remains in Plato's written dialogues, as we might expect, but it increasingly dims in the later ones. In Aristotle, save for the fragments of his early dialogues—written, it is certain, at the direction of Plato in the Academy—it has disappeared altogether.[49]

Conclusion

It is appropriate that I offer, in support of these suggestions, some final words from Eric Havelock, among the last he wrote and oversaw for publication. At present they reside in an obscure *addendum* to a German republication of an article that Havelock wrote in 1934 on the topic of recoverable evidence for the teachings of Socrates.

> Revolutions in the transitional stage of their development exhibit contradictory forms. The would-be prosaic authors of the new educational texts, in choosing style and format, turned instinctively to the past, to the conventions of that oral composition they were attempting to replace. Useful knowledge (as orally understood) from time immemorial had been communicated through words and acts of personages mythical and historical (with no sharp distinction between them), in epical recital and on the stage, both tragic and comic. In the rhetoric and dialogues of such personages the *ethos* and *nomos* of the Greek community had been encapsulated. The new paideutic *logoi* took over the convention of using rhetoric and dialogue as the format of instruction, and the dramatized personage as the instrument who instructs. For the latter the instructor might substitute his own rhetoric delivered in the first person—a format perfected by Isocrates [as in his exhortation to Philip]—but without discarding the assumed dramatic occasion within which delivery of instruction was rendered. . . . The Platonic and Xenophonic dialogues of the fourth century are paideutic textbooks, members of a larger species, the Socratic *logoi* referred to in Aristotle's *Poetics.* These *logoi* in turn are one particular species of the *genus* paideutic textbook pioneered in the

> fifth century by the Sophists. The "Socrates" of these works represents a mask through which are spoken the sentiments of the writer. This traditional format, borrowed from the previous habits of oral composition, was finally discarded in Aristotle's expository writings. His distance from it enabled him to see it in historical perspective and classify it correctly as a modified form of poetic and dramatic mimesis.[50]

The dramatic prose dialogue devoted to a philosophical topic is a transition piece that will soon give way to the expository prose treatise that became so firmly established in Aristotle's school. The Athenian philosophical dialogue, like the Sicilian mime before it, was a feature, perhaps a necessary one, of the developing alliance between literacy and paideia that marks the fifth and fourth centuries but becomes an anachronism when that alliance has at last been completed.

The late historian Diodorus sums up with a neat aphorism the attitude of the educated elite that will be characteristic of Greece through the Hellenistic period and of Rome at all times. Just how far Greece had come from the world of Homer and oral epic is captured in his phrasing. What has been called a literate revolution has quietly taken place, destined to be more lastingly important to our species than all the wars and kings that came and went in the centuries from Homer to the Caesars.

So it must be considered, Diodorus remarks in concluding an encomium on benefits of literacy, that: "Life is a gift of nature; but the good life is the gift of education that comes from literacy."[51]

Notes

1. The "reform passages" of Books II and III begin at 376 E and are complete insofar as the training for the soul is concerned at 403 E, where the purpose of paideia in *mousikē* is declared to be to inculcate in the young an insensible *erōs* for what is truly *kalon,* beautiful, symmetrical, and harmonious, physically and morally. Reformed musical paideia is the "one big thing" (Socrates here quotes a familiar proverb) and the "sufficient condition" (423 D–E) that will make the utopian state work if it is going to work. Reiterated at 429 E, 487 A, 501 D, 502 E, 522 A, and (almost) ad nauseam.

2. There is general agreement that the *Republic* is a "middle" dialogue, but its compositional date cannot be fixed with certitude. The best contemporary evidence is that the Academy was founded before ca. 367 B.C., when Aristotle joined it at the age of 16 or 17. If we may trust that Theatetus joined the Academy as some sort of mathematical colleague of Plato, then it was founded before 369 B.C., when Theatetus died. C. G. Field guessed (and gave reasons why only a guess was possible) ca. 375 B.C. for a compositional date, give or take a few years either way (*Plato and His Contemporaries* [London, 1948]). The possible clues to a dramatic date have been much chewed on in the older (especially nineteenth-century German) scholarship and were sensibly reviewed again in 1984 by V. Tejera in *Plato's Dialogues One By One: A Structural Interpretation* (New York, 1984), pp. 94–96. The *dramatic* setting is roughly the last quarter of the fifth century and certainly before the death of Polemarchus in the fighting against the Thirty at the Piraeus in 404 B.C. What is important about the *compositional* date, on the rule advanced by Havelock, Jaeger, Nettleship, and others is (in the words of Nettleship): "He [Plato] always writes with

crying evils in his eyes'' (*Lectures on the Republic of Plato* [London, 1964], p. 6). For an account of scholars' attempts, going back to 1792, to arrange Plato's dialogues chronologically and for discussion of individual dialogues, see the review of the Finnish scholar, Holger Thesleff, *Studies in Platonic Chronology* (Helsinki, 1982).

3. In contrast, for the Aristotelian *logoi* or treatises as forming the basis of lectures combined with discussion in a philosophical classroom, see Joseph Owens, *The Doctrine of Being in the Aristotelian Metaphysics* (Toronto, 1951), pp. 27ff. Life in the Lyceum without texts, on which its characteristic activity depended, would be unthinkable, as indeed it would be in a modern university. The words of Tejera (*Plato's Dialogues*, p. 91, emphasis mine) are perceptive: ''Perhaps we should remember that the texts we have of Aristotle were only his so-called 'lecture notes' for use in the live situation of 'classroom' discussion. . . . For Aristotle himself, the texts, his *sharing* and *developing* of them, were a means to the humanly full and good life, *as well as being constitutive of it*.'' Still valuable is the youthful, unfinished essay (a pioneering work) of R. Shute, *On the History of the Process by Which the Aristotelian Writings Arrived at Their Present Form* (Oxford, 1888). Had he not died prematurely (at age 37 in 1886), Shute's investigations into a (then) neglected topic might have led to major discoveries. He was already asking the right questions. Shute's first chapter, ''Problems,'' begins by raising the problem of how *any* of the Greek philosophers down to and including Aristotle were ''published,'' or, in Shute's words, how even the dialogues and *Politeiai* of Aristotle ''received such publication as Athens afforded in his lifetime, for they [at least] must necessarily from the beginning have been intended for publication'' (p. 22). Shute doubted that any of the philosophers enjoyed publication in ways that the word now evokes for us, noting that their works were directed primarily at disciples or a narrow group of interested hearers. ''Many, perhaps the majority of them, never can be said to have published a philosophical work in any sense other than that in which a lecturer publishes his thoughts to his audience'' (p. 1). Drawing on Cicero's testimony (*Acad. Post* 1. 4, 17–18) that from an early period there were regular lectures in both the Academy and the Lyceum, and ''a systematic education given,'' Shute asks: ''In what ways then were Aristotle's works made useful for this education?'' His answer seems correct. ''I think that only one answer is really possible. The notes on Aristotle's lectures, whether his own or those taken by his former pupils—the then lecturers—were read out to the class, who, I believe, could not otherwise easily obtain access to copies of them. Occasional notes and criticisms were interpreted by the lecturer, who probably did not always warn his hearers as to what was interpretation and what text. Only on this supposition can the repetitions of the whole, or nearly whole, of the Aristotelian titles in the works ascribed to Eudemus, Theophrastus, and later, Straton, be explained'' (p. 26). If this is a correct reconstruction of the earliest days of the Lyceum—as I suggest that it is—then the systematic education gained in the Lyceum was clearly alphabetically dependent. The lecture was designed, in part, to make the contents of a great philosopher's ''book'' (or his *logoi*) available to the students, dictating both the lecture format itself and the very long hours each day devoted to it, a situation paralleled in the the teaching of philosophy in the medieval universities. For informed, sober treatments of the Lyceum in its full dimension, from physical location to curriculum and kinds of treatises produced in it, see J. P. Lynch, *Aristotle's School: A Study of a Greek Educational Institution* (Berkeley and Los Angeles, 1972). Lynch's chapter 2, pp. 54–63, is a good short discussion of the early Academy. His forthcoming book on the Academy will be a welcome addition to what can be an elusive topic, especially the Academy under Plato.

4. *Rep.* 380 C, 386 A, 387 B, 387 C, 388 D, 390 A, and *passim*. The verb ''to hear''*(akouein)* appears in all these passages; the verbs for ''read'' never. We note that there is a offhand reference to the interlocutors themselves having learned *their* letters (at

Rep. 402 A). But these are Athenian aristocrats, as in the case of Plato's half-brothers Adeimantus and Glaucon, or sons of wealthy *metics* as in the case of Polemarchus and Lysias. For contemporary Athenian aristocratic practice, see in addition to *Prot.* 325–6 also *Theat.* 206 A, *Polit.* 270 A, and *Crat.* 393 D.

5. My reference is to the distinguished classicist Sir Desmond Lee, whose useful translation of the *Republic* was made for the Penguin series (*Plato: The Republic* [New York, 1955]). Lee (p. 38) talks about the "rigid control" that Plato would apply to "*school textbooks,*" but of course Plato never uses this terminology in the *Republic*. In his introduction Lee also refers to "the citizen of the *Republic* who studied Plato's especially prepared books" (p. 37). And "Chiron the wisest of schoolmasters" is in the translation, at 391 E. See further later in this chapter. In the *Parmenides* Zeno is said to read *(anagignōskein)* from his *logoi,* treatises or discourses, but also from his "writings." The dramatic date of the *Parmenides* is ca. 450 B.C.

6. *Rep.* 414 Bff. Plato's mind is fixed on the future guardians, of course, and he tends at times to pass over the craftsman class and its children rather quickly. F. M. Cornford remarks of the Allegory of the Metals that during the long educational process "children born in any class are to be moved up or down on their merits," as indeed is asserted at several points in the dialogue (*The Republic of Plato* [Oxford, 1945], pp. 102–103). For promotion or demotion at any time in the testing period, whether as child, adolescent, or adult, see 413 E, 415 A, 415 B–C, and *passim.* In some passages, to be sure, Plato speaks as though only the future guardians receive an education in *mousikē* and *gumnastikē* (e.g., 430 A), and no doubt these citizens are in the forefront of his mind. For similar reasons, Socrates often speaks as though only men—youths—receive the guardian's education, then belatedly remembers to remark that women will be included in all this education as well, and in all that has been established (540 C). In Book VII the rule is established that at age ten the children of *all* the inhabitants of the city will be separated from the habits of their parents by physically separating the two groups (540 E–541 A).

7. I ignore the Athenian requirement (when instituted?) of two years of military service between ages eighteen and twenty because, of course, it does not apply to guardians in the *Republic*. Also, although Plato recommends at 536 E that calculation, geometry, and other studies preparatory to dialectic be introduced as far as possible when the guardians are boys in the form of noncompulsory games, *grammata* are *not* mentioned. At *Laws* 819 C Plato claims that such games were the custom in Egyptian schools—a standard way of commending a practice *ex oriente* to Greeks, *not* a record of Plato's historical information concerning the daily activities of early schools on the Nile.

8. The solution of Desmond Lee, David Stockton, and many others who have recognized that there is a problem; this is discussed later in this chapter.

9. *Plato: The Republic,* p. 37, emphasis added.

10. Among many possible examples, one of the most surprising is that of Glenn Morrow, whose work is a model of the struggle for accuracy when contemporary Greek institutions and practices are being described. Yet, in a book on the *Laws,* in a passing remark in a footnote, Morrow refers to the *Republic* that he claims, "treats of *letters* and music first, then gymnastics." See G. Morrow, *Plato's Cretan City* (Princeton, 1961), p. 332, n. 118, emphasis mine. No text in the *Republic* is cited, although the reference is, of course, to the reform passages in Books II and III, where, however, as noted, no reference to teaching letters appears anywhere. By stretching a point, one could claim that the term *mousikē* includes the teaching of letters here, which Plato just happens at no place to mention or describe. But then this would entail, according to the *Republic*'s argument, universal state-supported education by teachers of letters for the children of all classes and both genders, which goes too far beyond what the text says or should be twisted to imply.

11. See J.-P. Vernant, *Mortals and Immortals: Collected Easays* (Princeton, 1991).

12. Giovanni Comotti, *Music in Greek and Roman Culture* (Baltimore and London, 1989), p. 6. This book contains an interesting discussion of the lingering influence of Damon (and Plato) in Hellenistic and later thinkers, notably in Aristides Quintilianus. Comotti also prints the anonymous fourth-century speech (preserved only in a papyrus, *P. Hibeh* 1.13) attacking the view that the three genera—diatonic, enharmonic, and chromatic—affect men's souls, making them more or less courageous, prudent, and the like. Another useful reminder of late-fifth-century controversies in music to which Plato turned his attention in the *Republic* is a fragment from the *Cheiron* by the comic poet Pherecrates (fr. 157; 145 Kock = Ps. Plut. De Mus. 114d–f). The innovations of poets are described in double entendres as acts of sexual violence on Music herself, appearing as a female character. Appreciation of the comedy required a sophisticated audience, one uniquely prepared for the utopian burlesque, and mock-serious reforms, of the *Republic*. Innovation in music away from the older, austere forms is treated again in the *Laws* at 700 Aff. On occasion, Aristotle urbanely wonders at the utility of music (if any) in education, offering various possibilities, for example, at *Pol.* 8.1337b23, and elsewhere. Is music to be pursued as something neither morally good nor bad in itself, but pleasant, like drinking or sleep? Does it conduce to virtue and vice, a clear reference to the *Republic,* and to the whole Damon-Pythagorean tradition? Does it perhaps contribute to the enjoyment of the all-important leisure of the good man, the *phronimos,* as a kind of mental cultivation? What is notable is that all urgency has gone out of the question. There are no longer any ''crying evils'' to be addressed and remedied. *Mimēsis* threatens no souls or polities. Literacy, in the form of prose treatises of the kinds developed in the Lyceum (see Lynch, *Aristotle's School,* pp. 89–90), has become the primary medium of higher education. Lynch suggests that the traditional, intimate *sunousia* as espoused by the historical Socrates had a place in the life of the early Academy, but now as ''institutionalized *sunousia.*'' On *sunousia* Lynch also cites *Epistle VII,* 341 C. See *Aristotle's School,* pp. 63ff. Lynch, however, if I follow him, favors Cherniss's portrayal of the Academy (*The Riddle of the Early Academy* [Berkeley and Los Angeles, 1945], pp. 65ff.) as an association of highly independent senior colleagues, swayed, perhaps, by the strong personality of Plato, but who consider themselves his equal in competence, at least in their several domains of study. That explains a Eudoxus very well, but not the nagging question of *meirakia,* youths as young as fifteen or sixteen, who seem to have arrived at the Academy in numbers, Aristotle among them. A dual type of association within the school must, I think, be supposed, junior and senior. I thus find the Cherniss-inspired portrayal accurate for only a part of the Academy's (admittedly loose) organization. As for Cherniss's further characterization of the Academy as the very opposite of a dogmatic, doctrinal ''sectarian community,'' as so often it has been portrayed, I am in full agreement, as, indeed, is Lynch (*Aristotle's School,* pp. 56ff.). I would also carry Cherniss's portrayal of the spirit of the Academy to the interpretation of the Platonic dialogues, with no exceptions. Here, perhaps, I am more alone. For references to Eudoxus' writings and views, see n. 23.

13. *Rep.* 510 D. For earlier treatments that remain influential, see J. L. Stocks, ''The Divided Line of Plato, *Rep.* VI,'' *CQ* 5 (1911), pp. 73–88; H. J. Paton, ''Plato's Theory of εἰκασία,'' *Proc. Arist. Soc.* 22 (1922), pp. 69–104, and especially pp. 100ff. for a connection with *mimēsis* in Book X; J. A. Notopolous, ''The Meaning of εἰκασία in the Divided Line of Plato's *Republic,*'' *HSCP* 44 (1933), pp. 193–203; and D. W. Hamlyn, *''Eikasia* in Plato's *Republic,'' Phil. Quart.* 8 (1958), pp. 14–23. Also see R. S. Brumbaugh, *Plato's Mathematical Imagination* (Bloomington, Ind. 1954), pp. 104ff. on the difficulties and controversies involved with drawing the physical line that Plato describes. There are useful discussions of aspects of Plato's pervasive image language in David Gal-

lop, "Image and Reality in Plato's *Republic*," *Archiv für Geschichte der Philosophie* 47 (1965), pp. 113–131, especially pp. 130ff., and Richard Patterson, *Image and Reality in Plato's Metaphysics* (Indianapolis, 1985), pp. 27ff. Also see Patterson's Appendix 2 on the important contributions of H. Lee and R. Allen on the image analogy. Often overlooked is S. Ringbom, "Plato on Images," *Theoria* 31 (1965), pp. 86–109. *Pistis* I would translate as "confidence." It has as its objects ordinary things around us, including the actions of persons that are considered right or wrong. For *eikasia*, Nettleship (*Lectures*, p. 241) usefully observed long ago: "The word has a double meaning; it has its regular meaning of conjecture, and an etymological meaning of which Plato avails himself, the perception of images, that state of mind whose objects are of the nature of mere images (εἰκόνες)." Plato clearly exploits the association of *eikasia* with *eikōn, eikones* ("image," "images" as in the case of reflections in a mirror or shiny surface), and the verb *eikazō*, "I conjecture," "I guess" (often slightly pejorative, "merely conjectures") and in Plato "I image." In Thucydides an *eikastēs* is one who conjectures, such as a seer or diviner would do.

14. *Rep.* 377 E, *eikazē kakōs tō logō* ("When anyone [*tis* is the subject of the verb] images badly [falsely] in speech . . .").

15. Aristotle's treatises presumably served as the basis for regular lectures and classroom discussion, mainly but probably not, even while he lived, exclusively by Aristotle. That Aristotle's hand alone had a role in putting together what survives of them for us to read is not likely. The degree to which the *Corpus Aristotelicum* was merged with the *Corpus Theophrasticum* before transmission to Andronicus in Rome is not measurable. The arguments of J. Zürcher and the extensive evidence he reviews, even if his extreme conclusions must be rejected, remain formidable (*Aristotles' Werk und Geist* [Paderborn, 1952]). What we know of both men—Aristotle and Theophrastus—betrays writers whose professional activity depended intimately on the written word and on extensive accumulations of expository texts to which they also added substantially. The activity of the Lyceum reflects that emphasis, a new one in Greek education. I. Düring's estimate in this regard seems correct and is a needed balance to Marrou, who underestimated the originality of the Lyceum—a rare flaw in his great book.

> Aristotle created something new with his school. A systematic collecting of previous literature, which was thoroughly worked up. A wide and likewise systematic amassing of information and material for certain purposes, generally to make possible a survey of a whole field of knowledge. . . . And finally, most important of all, the scientific outlook and the strictly scientific method.

See I. Düring, "Notes on the History of the Transmission of Aristotle's Writing," *Göteborgs Högskolas Arsskrift* 56 (1950), pp. 57–58; see the excellent comments of Lynch, *Aristotle's School*, pp. 84–91. Many of Düring's insightful articles are listed in Lynch's bibliography. Lynch notes that in referring to the association of scholars in his school Aristotle strictly avoids the older, traditional term *sunousia* or any of the cognates of *suneinai*. Could it be their implication of the old, intimate, aristocratic, and essentially oral "association" or *sunousia* that is so alien to the cooperative but dispassionate association of scientists in the Lyceum? See Lynch, *Aristotle's School*, p. 86.

16. For the Hellenistic period, see in general the always informative L. Reynolds and N. Wilson, *Scribes and Scholars* (Oxford, 1991), pp. 5–18. Henri Marrou treats Hellenistic schools, often noting their dependence on literate practices, in his *History of Education in Antiquity*; see especially Part 2, "Classical Education in the Hellenistic Age." Several long sections from *The Harvest of Hellenism* (New York, 1970) by F. E. Peters, a historian with philosophical interests, illuminate the dependency of the Hellenistic age on full literacy and

also its essential bookishness. For the ideal of *enkuklios paideia* and the ubiquitous handbooks, epitomes, and *technai* on which it finally came to depend—a product of literate education that, perhaps, could not be foreseen, although Plato expresses misgivings in the *Phaedrus*—see "A Philosophical Education," pp. 370–379. For the dominant role of the philosophy schools over Greek paideia from, roughly, the accession of Theophrastus as scholarch of the Lyceum, see "Academic Athens," pp. 105–118. Also see Lynch, *Aristotle's School,* pp. 87–105.

17. Aristotle indirectly reveals the interest of the Lyceum in recovering the first stages of science and philosophy when he discusses Thales in *Metaphysics Alpha* and elsewhere. The admission that nothing survived to read from Thales betrays that the effort was made by the school to secure what then was available in the way of the actual *writings* of philosophical predecessors from a less literate age. The characteristic activity of the Lyceum is revealed in the wording of *De Caelo* 294a28: "We have ascertained that the oldest statement of this type [concerning what holds up the earth] is the one attributed to Thales, the Milesian, to the effect that it rests on water. . . ." Note as well the cautious wording in the *De Anima* when Aristotle turns to the oldest views on the soul: "And Thales, according to what is related of him, seems to have regarded the soul. . . ." The caution fades in the doxographical tradition in direct proportion to how much later than Aristotle the doxographer is writing. The status of the library of the early Academy—if there was one—and its contents are unknown. From directors and students of the Lyceum, we first hear of "libraries" as valued personal possessions bequeathed by will to friends and successors, as Theophrastus willed both his own and Aristotle's library to Neleus. (Diogenes Laertius V. 52: "I leave my books to Neleus.") The practice among philosophers began, apparently, with Aristotle or, more likely, his executors, granting the collection to the new scholarch, as Lynch (*Aristotle's School,* p. 101) surmises. There are full discussions of the available evidence for the activity of the early members of Aristotle's school in volumes of W. Wehrli, *Die Schule des Aristoteles. Text und Kommentar* (Basel, 1944–1959), for example, Dikaiarchos (vol. I), Aristoxenos (vol. II), and Eudemos of Rhodes (vol. VIII). A good account of the early activity of Aristotle and the writing of dialogues in the Academy in imitation of those of Plato as a practice of the Academy is found in Werner Jaeger, *Aristotle: Fundamentals of the History of His Development* (Oxford, 1948), pp. 27ff. Cicero and St. Basil report that both Aristotle and Theophrastus wrote dialogues, which they had obviously read in that they comment on the style (Cicero was more impressed than Basil by Aristotle's style). The great Ingemar Düring seems to have first fully understood just how original the philosophical prose treatise was as it took shape in the hands of Aristotle, becoming the core of a new form of education. Greece had seen nothing like it in intent, composition, style, or the use to which it was put. See his *Aristotle in the Ancient Biographical Tradition* (Göteborg, 1957), especially pp. 360ff. There were also pioneering remarks in Jaeger's *Aristotle,* Jacoby's *Atthis,* Pfeiffer's *History of Classical Scholarship* (Oxford, 1958), and Cherniss's *The Riddle of the Early Academy.* To these influential accounts should be added the valuable study of H. Block, "Studies in the Historical Literature of the Fourth Century B.C.," *HSCP,* Suppl. I (1940), pp. 303–376.

18. See the valuable remarks of I. Mueller, "Mathematical Method and Philosophical Truth, " in R. Kraut (ed.), *The Cambridge Companion to Plato* (Cambridge, 1992), pp. 170–199, especially the section on Plato's Academy and the sciences, pp. 170–175. Even the political patrons of the Lyceum were notably bookish. The Peripatos, or Lyceum, was housed in a garden that Demetrius of Phaleron helped Aristotle obtain. Demetrius in turn, when his political troubles ended his rule at Athens and forced him to flee ca. 305 B.C., carried the spirit of the Lyceum to Alexandria. He was influential in establishing the Alexandrian Library, even if his role may have been overstated by some scholars. The immedi-

ate impetus of a comprehensive depository for all learning and literature was, it seems, carried from the Lyceum, where the idea was born independently of any Near Eastern temple collections, to the court of the Ptolemies, whose wealth and power made it a reality. This event marks, perhaps, the final triumph of literacy that the efficiency of the Greek alphabet made possible. Works of importance not in Greek, but famous, such as the the laws of Hebrews, were to be translated into Greek. Thus Strabo can correctly claim (XIII. I. 54) that it was Aristotle who "taught the kings of Egypt how to organize a library." He means, of course, that Aristotle accomplished this through the influence of Strato, royal tutor to Ptolemy and later head of the Lyceum, and Demetrius of Athens. Demetrius even counseled Ptolemy to "read *books* on kingship" if we can trust Plutarch (*Short Sayings of the Kings and Commanders,* 189d).

19. In addition to the first history of philosophy and science and first accumulation of Greek constitutions, the first history of geometry and the foundation documents of botany were parts of Lyceum's ambitious endeavors. While Aristotle lived, the Lyceum even collected *didaskaliai* (the term is a reminder that dramatists were supposed to teach), records of the dramatic performances in the city and lists of victors at the Pythian games (for the last we have inscriptional evidence of the gratitude of the citizens of Delphi). Under the founder, individuals in the Lyceum, perhaps heading teams, such as the notable Eudemus (for geometry) and even the future scholarch Theophrastus (his massive *History of Plants* and *Causes of Plants* are the foundation of the science of botany), seem to have been set the task of acquiring all available information, and thus texts when possible, that existed in the field of their designated research, and then updating and amalgamating their information into encyclopedia types of treatises for use in the school. This remarkable research activity, so manifestly based on accumulating texts—copying, studying, analyzing, and commenting on them—remained central at least through the long period Theophrastus headed the school; he died at the age of eighty-five, having guided the school almost to his final day.

20. On *lexis,* see Havelock, *Preface to Plato,* pp. 21 (with his reference to Adam Parry), 10, 202, and 236. Havelock's chapters "Mimesis" (pp. 20–35), and "Psyche or the Separation of the Knower from the Known" (pp. 197–214) broke major new ground. To Havelock's review of earlier authorities on *mimēsis* (Koller, Else on fifth-century usage, Verdenius, et al.), we can now add G.R.F. Ferrari, "Plato and Poetry" in G. Kennedy (ed.), *The Cambridge History of Literary Criticism* (Cambridge, 1989), pp. 124ff., where more recent treatments are also canvased, and A. Nehamas, "Plato on Imitation and Poetry in *Republic* 10," in J. Moravcsik and P. Temko (eds.), *Plato on Beauty, Wisdom and the Arts* (Totowa, N.J., 1982), pp. 47–78.

21. A valuable treatment of "inspiration" in Greek poetry remains that of Alice Sperduti, "The Divine Nature of Poetry in Antiquity," *TAPA* 85 (1954), pp. 209–240.

22. *Rep.* 394 Eff. Plato's early attacks on poetry, for example, in the *Ion,* would force him to a theory of a divided soul or a "faculty" psychology, if he had not already moved in that direction, perhaps under Pythagorean influences after visits to Tarentum. At a minimum two faculties, or "parts," are required: one emotive and arational responding to oral-poetic conditioning, the other fully cognitive, rational, and responding to training in mathematics and dialectic.

23. *Rep.* 435 Cff. Nicholas White's discussion is especially good on this section of the *Republic*. See N. White, *A Companion to Plato's Republic* (Indianapolis, 1979). On the phrasing of the principle on noncontradiction, see Richard Robinson's earlier discussion (also noted by White), "Plato's Separation of Reason from Desire," *Phronesis* 16 (1971), pp. 38–48. It may be noted that the similar and less than stringent phrasing of "doing and suffering" is also found at *Par.* 127 E: "they would suffer *(paschoi)* the [things] impossi-

ble *(ta adunata).*'' The Eleatics came close enough to an Aristotelian formulation to wield noncontradiction as a weapon, but as in the case of Zeno's pseudoparadox of plurality, fell victim of the as yet underdeveloped state of logic in the fifth century. ''Historically, what Plato confronted was an over-simple understanding of the principle of contradiction'' is William Lynchs's observation in W. Lynch, *An Approach to the Metaphysics of Plato through the Parmenides* (Washington D.C, 1959), p. 52. Literacy and formal logic are intimately connected in the Greek experience, for the development of formal logic depends directly on language having become an object, or *written* language, not a flow of sounds.

24. In general at 521 C–D and 523 A, then at 524 D–525 E for arithmetic; at 527 B for plane geometry, and extended to solid geometry at 527 D, for astronomy at 528 E–529 D, and extended to the ''sister science'' or harmonics at 530 E–531 A. All are undertaken *primarily* as mental preparation or training for dialectic, as Cornford stated (*The Republic of Plato,* p. 241), ''to think abstractly,'' that is, without the crutch of visualizing. Ten years is the utopian time period that will be spent by the guardians in the *Republic* in the mathematical sciences in preparation for dialectic. A more casual but not neglected activity may be presumed, I believe, for the Academy itself. Our best evidence—outside the *Republic*—for the devotion of the Academy under Plato's personal direction to mathematical activity is, of course, Proclus' *A Commentary on the First Book of Euclid's Elements,* 66.8–68.6, where Proclus reviews the history of fourth-century geometry. This section is almost certainly based on Eudemus, as Ian Mueller has sensibly observed (Mueller, ''Mathematical Method and Philosophical Truth,'' p. 196, n. 6). If so, the evidence would be especially good. Mueller also usefully reviews the evidence of the first-century figure Philodemus, in his history of the Platonic school, which is unfortunately preserved only in a badly damaged papyrus roll from Herculaneum. For the great mathematician Eudoxus, whose followers may have merged with the students of the Academy ca. 368 B.C. and who at a minimum was a visitor at the Academy and an influence on it (and on Aristotle), see F. Lasserre, *Die Fragmente des Eudoxos von Knidos* (Berlin, 1966); and Thomas Heath, *History of Greek Mathematics* I (Oxford, 1921), pp. 325ff. There are interesting comments on Eudoxus' many interests, and his influence in the Academy, in R. Brumbaugh, *Plato on the One* (New Haven, 1961), pp. 19–26.

25. Adeimantus opens his supplement to his brother's indictment by claiming that the essential part of the case has not as yet been put. Mentioned by name as the major culprits are Homer (foremost) and Hesiod, and the third epical partner, Archilochus, along with Pindar and others. Repeated twice is the accusation that Greeks summon the traditional poets as their supporting witnesses (*marturas,* 364 C) to testify to the very teachings that his brother Glaucon has reported constitutes the sorry state of Greek morals.

26. Many scholars have wanted to find in Plato a true poetry of self-expression in addition to the damned imitation, often appealing to the ''inspiration'' passages in *Symposium, Phaedrus,* and *Ion.* One recent treatment along this line has the great merit of remaining honest to the strictures on all performed poetry—and the reasons for them based on the appeal of *mimēsis* to the irrational aspects of the tripartite soul—found in Book X. See Elizabeth Asmis, ''Plato on Poetic Creativity,'' in Kraut (ed.), *Cambridge Companion to Plato,* pp. 338–364, along with her references to other studies with an orientation to aesthetics.

27. The commonwealth is considered to be founded on sound principles, ''especially our rule not on any account to admit the poetry of dramatic interpretation'' (595 A, Cornford tranlation). Plato claims that he had already banned all poetry ''insofar as it was mimetic.'' Cornford recognizes that, in fact, this statement and what follows considerably enlarge what is to be excluded, as have many other commentators. Some of Plato's apologists have sought to reconcile Book X with Books II and III, trying to make them, as Plato

claims, say the same thing. Eric Havelock reviewed this issue in *Preface to Plato,* for example, pp. 15 n. 12; 33 n. 37, mustering the authorities. For earlier attempts, instructive in their evasions, add to Havelock's references those in James Adam's commentary, *The Republic of Plato* (2 vols.; Cambridge, 1902), often reprinted. Adam himself is fair to what the text says, although he confesses his dislike of its content. Adam speculates that the earlier attack on Homer, or as he puts it, "his dethronement of the great educator of Greece" (606 E), may have aroused hostility, requiring further defense here. This makes concessions to the "chorizontists" among nineteenth-century scholars who speculated that the *Republic* was delivered to a public in succeeding parts (not itself an unlikely hypothesis, and virtually a necessity if the dialogues were *read* aloud to an audience), and also assumes the first half of Book X is an episode out of place (which it is not). For the evidence from antiquity (e.g, *Attic Nights* XIV. 3.3) that the early books of the *Republic* were issued first, see H. Alline, *Histoire du texte de Platon* (Paris, 1915), pp. 14ff.

28. *Rep.* 595 A–608 B.

29. Ibid., 395 D.

30. Ibid., 403. At *Rep.* 522 A, the earlier education in *mousikē* is recalled by saying that it educated the guardians through habits or constant habituation *(ethesi),* but not through knowledge *(ouk epistēmēn).* There is little appeal to or use made of the highest or reasoning part of the *psuchē*; only the appetitive and spirited elements come into play, and they, especially the appetitive, are trained by habituation. To encourage *epistēmē* as a habitual intellectual activity, a whole new curriculum (and a tripartite *psuchē)* must be introduced into the argument, culminating in training the highest or calculating part of the *psuchē* in the sciences and dialectic (Book VII).

31. Several of Aristophanes' plays come readily to mind, for example, *Archanians* produced in 423 B.C., winning first prize. Dikaiopolis, who claims he understands the causes of the Peloponnesian War, makes a fantastic "private" peace and then proceeds to enjoy wondrous (or utopian) benefits that his wiser "betters" do not. In the *Birds* (411 B.C.), a utopian Cloudcuckooland occupied by birds replicates human life, but the birds make a far better job of it. The obvious candidate would, of course, be *The Women's Assembly* (ca. 392). After my remarks were written I happily discovered a similar suggestion by Terence Irwin in "Plato: The Intellectual Background," in Kraut (ed.), *Cambridge Companion to Plato,* p. 75.

32. As Mueller observes, it seems "highly likely that the Academy would have been still-born if Plato had announced to new enrollees that they would begin their most important studies thirty years later" ("Mathematical Method and Philosophical Truth," p. 171).

33. In addition to authors already cited, see Friedländer, *Plato,* vol. I (New York, 1958), pp. 351–353.

34. Some are known to us from various sources. They include associates of Aristotle from the Troad, Heraclides of Pontus, Xenocrates, probably Theophrastus himself, Dion and those many Academy members who followed him to disaster in Syracuse, at least one ex-slave, and *(mirabile dictu)* two women. Colleagues who joined Plato hardly did so as students, and some came in his old age or theirs: Philip of Opus, Eudoxus with his homeocentric spheres for explaining the cosmos and his physicalist interpretation of Forms (seemingly the view of them attacked in the *Parmenides*), and, of course, Speucippus. The Academy's interest in mathematics and astronomy is evident in most of these names welcomed to its doors, to which should be added Theatetus, who invented the "stereometry" that Plato had wanted. Doctrinal orthodoxy was hardly demanded, or indeed with such a group, possible. One may wonder if academia was ever so sweet again. It probably was in 367/366 B.C., while Plato was in Syracuse, that young Aristotle arrived at the school,

remaining until Plato died in 347/346 B.C. At sixteen or seventeen even an Aristotle is no senior colleague; being in his early *meirakion* years, he was a student.

35. Even in antiquity "Homer" was identified as the unnamed rhapsode who comes soliciting entrance at the gates of Calliopolis in Book III, and there is ceremoniously dismissed. Here in Book X he is named and finally exiled. James Adam's notes to 598 D 28 and 598 E 30 (*The Republic of Plato,* vol. II) are still worth consulting on the role of Homer and the poets as teachers.

36. Printed in Adam Parry (ed.), *The Making of Homeric Verse: The Collected Papers of Milman Parry* (Oxford, 1971), pp. 407–413 (delivered in 1936).

37. See further Holger Thesleff, "Looking for Clues: An Interpretation of Some Literary Aspects of Plato's Two-Level Model," in J. Press (ed.), *Plato's Dialogues: New Studies and Interpretations* (Savage, Md., 1993, pp. 17–45). I recall with pleasure a stimulating conversation on the probable manner of Plato's "publishing" his dialogues, or giving them to the light, with Thesleff on the occasion of our delivering papers at the 1991 meeting of the Society For Ancient Greek Philosophy in New York City. That conversation encouraged me to venture in print some of the opinions found in this chapter.

38. Presumably the first reference is in Eupolis *fr.* 304, if *ou ta bibli' ōnia* refers to a stall where *biblia* (*biblion* could refer to anything from a single sheet of papyrus to a roll) are sold. Frederic Kenyon called attention to this passage in his *Books and Readers in Ancient Greece and Rome* (Oxford, 1951), p. 24, with the caveat of "apparently" concerning a reference to book shops. From the same work I note the insightful observation (p. 25): "It is not too much to say that with Aristotle the Greek world passed from oral instruction to the habit of reading." The evidence is reviewed again and supplemented in a lecture that takes Kenyon's research as a point of departure in E. G. Turner, "Athenian Books in the Fifth and Fourth Centuries B.C.," Inaugural Lecture, University College, London (1952).

39. The contrast with the late fifth century is notable. For example, Euripides in the *Frogs* is satirized for possessing books (1409), which context reveals is regarded as an oddity, and for distilling information from them in his plays, also considered an oddity (937ff.). At 1409, Aeschylus allows Euripides to hold *all* his "books" in his arms as he stands on the scale that will decide who between them was best at his craft—along with his wife and even Cephisophon, the slave maliciously said to have helped Euripides in composing his plays. A society in which an author is ridiculed for possessing some books and using them in his work is not a society in which books are a fully familiar item. In the *parabasis* of *Frogs,* it may be noted, the chorus, sounding rather like upper-class conservative Athenians (and Aristophanes himself), divides the citizen into bad men *(ponēroi)* and good men *(chrēstoi).* The "good men," being well-born *(eugeneis),* well-behaved *(sōphronas),* and "just" *(dikaious)* gentlemen *(kalous te kagathous),* were, of course (729): "educated in the wrestling schools and in choral dance and sung poetry *(chorois kai mousikē).*" They are, in a word, products of the traditional athletic and musical paideia. The teaching role of poetry is, as is to be expected, strongly affirmed, for example, at 636–637: "Proper *(dikaion)* it is that the holy chorus with wise counsels exhort and teach *(didaskein)* the city." In the closing lines of *Frogs* (1528–1531), the poet (but *not* Euripides: a "real" tragedian, like Aeschylus) is again a teacher, and so the chorus prays: "Grant that he find for the city good counsels to guide her aright." Aeschylus is chosen by Dionysius to return to the upper world because of the superior advice he would offer the city. For the important evidence of *Frogs* and the view that such minimal literacy as the *fifth* century knew was recent in Athens, see L. Woodbury, "Aristophanes' *Frogs* and Athenian Literacy, *Ran.* 52–3, 1114," *TAPA* 106 (1976), pp. 349–357. The late tradition that Euripides possessed either a "large" library (a relative term in any case) or the first in Athens is extrapolation

(e.g., the Ravenna Scholiast) from these passages. By the time of Athenaeus (1. 4), an armload of papyrus scrolls *(ta biblia)* has grown into a vast library that was one of the largest in the ancient world. Equally worthless are late reports of the first library for the tyrant Peisistratus, such as Isidore of Seville *Etymologies* VI. 3.3., in the section *De bibliothecis,* "On libraries," where the fashion of sovereigns' collecting books is traced back to the Athenian tyrant. Some modern commentators have been taken in and leapt on these "libraries" as evidence for "widespread literacy in Athens from at least the sixth century." The contemporary picture as discovered in the *Frogs,* which was produced at the Lenaia in 405 B.C., is in sharp contrast to the fully literate practices and bookish paideia found in the philosophical schools in the second and following quarters of the fourth century. I note that F. H. Sandbach traces the relative paucity of books for the average citizen well into the fourth century, in his *Aristotle and the Stoics* (Cambridge, 1985), pp. 1ff.

40. The logical fallacies put into the mouths of Plato's characters have again become a debated issue. For differing opinions, see Richard Kraut's remarks in his introduction to the *Cambridge Companion to Plato* on the views of Griswold *(Platonic Writings, Platonic Readings)* and Tigerstedt *(Interpreting Plato), and on Griswold again (Self-Knowledge in Plato's Phaedrus),* along with Stokes *(Plato's Socratic Conversations),* pp. 49, n. 73; and 50, n. 78. Kraut advances his own views on pp. 25–30. From my text it should be clear that my own views on this issue are closer to those that Kraut faults.

41. Gilbert Ryle, *Plato's Progress* (Cambridge, 1966), p. 18. Ryle oberves that ca. 360 B.C. Aristotle's nickname in the Academy was "the Reader" (and Plato's own designation for him if we can believe the *Vita Marciana*). Ryle's entire second chapter, "The Publication of Dialogues," was bold for its day, the middle 1960s, and remains stimulating. Wilomowitz (*Gnomon* 4, 1928, pp. 362ff.) maintained that all the dialogues were "published" (if that is the right word) in Plato's lifetime in his Academy, which may be an extreme view but at least focuses on the problem. Paul Friedländer believed that the following threefold reconstruction may not be strictly provable, but he remained convinced of its accuracy: "Does this mean that the dialogues reflect life in the Academy? . . . It is hardly likely that there should be no functional relationship between Plato's literary activity and his teaching, and this perhaps in a threefold sense: his dialogues reflected life in the Academy; they, in turn, penetrated its life with their light; and finally, the Academy was the place where Plato's works were 'published' and preserved" (Friedländer, *Plato,* vol. I, p. 87). The second of his suggestions amounts to a theory that the dialogues played a role in the education of the students. Add Friedländer's bold assertion (p. 92): "If any details in the dialogues may be assigned to the Academy, it is the instruction of the guardians in the *Republic* . . . the education [in Book VII] of the guardians cannot differ significantly from that of the students at the Academy." Other scholars have speculated that *only* mathematics was taught in the Academy.

42. The designations are Havelock's, borrowed from a passage quoted more fully at the end of this chapter.

43. The authenticity of the *Laws* is, of course, an old debate, recently revived with his usual verve by Victorino Tejera. His opening paragraph to chapter 10 of *Plato's Dialogues One by One* (p. 139) explodes the appropriate bombshells. Also noteworthy is his treatment (pp. 149ff.) of the probable activity in the early Academy involving discussions of laws and constitutions and notably the influence of the school on an "On Laws" *(Peri Nomoi)* attributed to Archytus of Tarentum. Plato's early travels after the death of Socrates and the influence of Archytus cannot have failed to affect his prescriptions for the Academy.

44. In a formal way at *Laws* 643 E and with a definition that connects paideia both with personal virtue and the citizens' role in bringing about *eunomia*. The connection with *psuchē,* so pronounced in the *Republic,* is also retained in the *Laws* (e.g., 659). For the

mimetic character (of actions, emotions, and characters) of the dance and melodies, see especially *Laws* 655 A–D; G. Morrow, *Plato's Cretan City,* pp. 307ff.

45. The officer in charge of education in the *Laws* is variously denominated as "Superintendent of Paideia," "the Archon of Music," "Law-Guardian" (Bury's translation in the Loeb edition for *nomophulax* is "Law-Warden"), or simply "the Educator" *(ho paideutēs).* In the interest of reducing ambiguity, I use "the Educator" to translate these various terms, all of which refer to the same official.

46. G. Morrow, *Plato's Cretan City,* p. 339.

47. If we grant that Plato's Academy used his own dialogues as educational manuals designed to help produce mentally what they extolled, or what Plato finally designated as *epistēmē,* knowledge, then the fundamental purposes of the dialogues and of the early Academy may have been closely related. The purpose of both may have been more involved in the method *(methodos* is used in the *Republic)* of altering old ways of thinking and speaking and substituting new ones than in inculcating some Platonic doctrine. The difficulties confronting a doctrinal approach to the dialogue form and the history of the many failed attempts to find the "real Plato" in either "the System," or "the Secret Doctrines," has been documented by E. N. Tigerstedt, *Interpreting Plato* (Stockholm, 1977). After rejecting both as the source of Plato's "real teaching," Tigerstedt offers a concluding "modest proposal" (p. 93). He suggests that there is something that must be called Platonic philosophy, it cannot be reduced to nonphilosophic factors, and it is to be found in the dialogues and nowhere else. This, it seems to me, is the not-to-be-relinquished minimum core of common sense.

48. *Laws* 804 Dff. Unlike contemporary Athenian practice, a father shall no longer be free "at his own sweet will" (Bury's translation) to educate his children or not (male and female) in the important branches of paideia. This is one more text, added to the famous discussion in the *Protagoras,* refuting all suggestions—accepted by some modern historians—that an actual "law of Solon" made the teaching of letters mandatory for fathers in Athens in the sixth century. For a sensible assessment of the famous Prosopopeia of the Laws in the *Crito,* see Marrou, *A History of Education in Antiquity,* p. 382.

49. "There were some later nostalgic philosophical dialogues . . . and even an eccentric poet or two, but by and large, philosophy followed Aristotle's example and deserted the dialogue for the systematic and undramatic treatises (*hypomneumata*) that bore some resemblance to the lecture notes from which they derived" (F. E. Peters, *The Harvest of Hellenism,* p. 371).

50. Printed here by the kind permission of Christine Mitchel Havelock.

51. Diodorus Siculus 12.13. J. V. Muir suggests that Protagoras legislated literacy for at least sons at Thurii, which gains some credence from the fact that colonies had greater need for written laws than mother cities, and so greater need for citizens to be able to read them. He also, tentatively, would ascribe the aphorism that closes the encomium to literacy in Diodorus to the great sophist himself. I understand the temptation, but would resist it. Muir seeks, in general, to associate sophistic education with advancing literary, which I would support. See J. Muir, "Protagoras and Education at Thourioi," *Greece and Rome* 29 (1982), pp. 17–24. Literacy per se was not, I think, associated with the distrusted sophists in late-fifth-century Athens, but the prose treatise utilized as part of education (even if memorized, as by Phaedrus in the dialogue that bears his name) probably was. The Lyceum would change that, as it would so many other things.

9

Conclusion: Homer, the Alphabet, and the Progress of Greek Literacy and Paideia

The argument of this book has not wanted for controversial issues. Among them, five may be isolated as being certain to provoke dissent and so further discussion and debate.

First, the motive for the Greek adoption of the Phoenician script and its conversion into the first complete alphabet was to record hexameter verse, but not in the form of literary texts. The first uses of the alphabet were inscriptional and probably votive. It follows that the inscribers and so the first literate Greeks were not aristocrats but rather a small nucleus of craftsmen who made the objects that bore the first inscriptions.

Second, the oldest "long" inscriptions reflect widespread absorption of Homeric or epical verse through the preceding several hundred years of the so-called Dark Ages. The earliest of these inscriptions either are votive or else commemorate and record words spoken by ordinary citizens at important moments of oral life, *sumposia* and *xenia* dominantly. Although competent hexameters indeed, they are "popular." They cannot all have been the work of professional *aoidoi*.

Third, the social or cultural motive behind the remarkable phenomenon of the popular absorption of epical verse was that it served as the Hellenic oral paideia in preliterate centuries. Epical verse was the primary mechanism that a sophisticated, preliterate society utilized to preserve and transmit such verbal information as it required for the humanly necessary processes of "enculturation" or paideia.

Fourth, the Greek alphabet, the first complete or true alphabet, was a recording instrument for human speech of unique precision and simplicity, permitting, in time, the emergence of the first fully literate—by which I mean alphabetically dependent—society. With fewer than thirty symbols to burden the memory of its learners, the Greek alphabet permitted a reader familiar with an underlying language to read with understanding any text, however unfamiliar. It also permitted a reader not familiar with an underlying language to know approximately how any written words ought to be sounded. No earlier script, including Old Phoenician and Old Hebrew, had achieved this. The progress of Greek literacy commences in the eighth century, perhaps but not certainly early in it. It comes to completion, in the form of alphabetic dependency within the operations of a society's major cultural institutions, only in the first half of the fourth century.

Fifth, widespread popular literary—as opposed to the restricted scribe literacy of the Near East—became possible for the first time in history with the invention of the Greek alphabet, but this "Literate Revolution," as it has aptly been called, took some four centuries to come to completion in Greece. The first half of the fourth century marks the final stage of the progress of Greek literacy, cultural alphabetical dependency, especially as literacy takes effective control of the formal institutions of law and education.

Between ca. 700 B.C. and 400 B.C. Greece was, in terms of the way important information was stored and then brought to bear on the consciousness of the populace, a "mixed" culture, relying for this task on methods both oral and written. For the seventh and sixth centuries the reliance on letters and documentation remained meager. For the entire period, Greek institutions seem poised in bizarre ways between entrenched oral habit and the new alphabetic efficiency. This is especially evident in the rise of written law, where despite the availability of writing since the late eighth century, such institutions as *marturia,* or oral witnessing, are not immediately replaced by written records and complete codes of all a city's enforceable laws seem unknown before the Athenian reinscription of all the laws in last decade of the fifth century. It also is evident in education or enculturation, the Greek paideia, where *sunousia,* oral association with elders, and the memorization and recitation of verse in the service of the moral formation of character are not immediately replaced by the textualization of knowledge, although the latter had long been within reach. In both areas, literate practice came to dominate over the older, oral habits and institutions only in the fourth century.

To some historians it will prove shocking—or even final proof of special pleading—to suggest that in the two culturally important institutions of law and education, full alphabetic dependency was not achieved until the *fourth* century. But the evidence points to the conclusion that the law and associated legal procedures became fully alphabetically dependent in Athens just at the turn of the fourth century. It is equally clear that established or institutionalized procedures of education became dependent on literacy several decades later yet, probably first in Plato's Academy in the second quarter of the fourth century. The educational activity of Aristotle's Lyceum was, in any case, indisputably centered around its characteristic texts, preserving books or treatises. The very spirit of the school was devoted to advanced, literacy-supported research. With its ascendancy, oral Greece and the major oral institutions of the Archaic period are clearly finished.

Unless the final decade of the twentieth century has something unforeseen in store for us, the greatest discovery of the century in classical scholarship will turn out to have been the rediscovery of the oral dimension of Greek life in the Geometric and Archaic periods and its strong residual effects in the culture of the High Classical and Classical periods. Milman Parry, by demonstrating the relevance of contemporary oral poetry (which he studied in the Balkans) to his own rigorous analysis of the Homeric formulaic systems, explained how, in the situation of primary orality, poems of the length and complexity of the *Iliad* and *Odyssey* can be orally composed and orally transmitted over centuries. That such transmission, whether verbatim or something rather looser, had taken place had often been asserted in the history of the Homeric question, but its mechanisms had never been satisfactorily explained.

Parry demonstrated that features in the Homeric text itself, mainly the intricate systems of formulas, will yield to no explanation other than that the poems enjoyed a long period of oral transmission before the first alphabetic transcriptions were attempted, whatever may have been their length. In the process of his elegant analysis, Parry effectively replaced the concept of a verbatim "text" (whether of the whole poem or "lays") for an early Homer by the concept of mnemonically stored, traditional elements of composition that are recombined or varied within traditional constraints for each performance. This, clearly, was a form of human creativity of the highest order, but one different from that found in literate societies. We have not fully understood it yet.[1]

Parry, especially in his later papers, showed an occasional passing curiosity about when and how a monumental text of Homer was finally created and some curiosity as well about the early uses of an alphabet. But in his published work (brought to a premature end when he was thirty-three), he never extensively addressed these questions. He believed, quite correctly, that his statistical arguments and the mutually reinforcing pieces of evidence he had advanced required that behind our texts was a long period of purely oral composition and transmission, many generations at a minimum. This argument would hold up independently of how and when the poems as we have them finally found their way to paper. It was enough to have proved that the transmitted text itself contained abundant and undeniable evidence that, in their origins, the poems we know as the *Iliad* and the *Odyssey* were the sort of composition that, independently, oral poetry was known to be, for that, strictly speaking, is what Parry demonstrated.

At present writing, it seems improbable that the period and conditions that produced the remote first ancestor of the text of our Homer, as later copied and preserved in the medieval manuscripts and descended from Alexandria, will ever be known with confidence. In this, Homer bears comparison with other great traditional books, such as the early books of the Old Testament. One can still sympathize with some older scholars—writing long before Parry and before the discovery of pre-Alexandrian papyri—who, on the basis of less evidence than is now available, denied that anything like our vulgate text of Homer existed before the work of the Alexandrians. Those who want to put a monumental, authoritative text near the very introduction of the alphabet into Hellas, whether textualization is imagined as the result of a master singer's autograph or an orally dictated text, cannot be refuted. The impulse to want such a "book" very early and the hope that a Homeric text somewhat close to the one we now know was in existence by, say, 650 B.C., is readily understandable. So is the hope that it was transmitted essentially intact, if not verbatim, and so duly recopied, over centuries (some barely literate) before it arrived at safe harbor in Alexandria. Such is not, to borrow an older philosophical distinction, "metaphysically" impossible. It is a matter of probabilities that must be calculated on the basis of the extant evidence.

From Gilbert Murray's long-influential *Rise of the Greek Epic* I borrow some fighting words on the improbability of an early, authoritative text (not, I stress, *any* texts of any sort, such as short performance texts or rhapsodes' texts, which are probably early). Murray had in mind a work of an influential conservative scholar that was widely read in his day, Ludwich's *Homervulgata*.

> Obviously those who wish to maintain that our present *Iliad* and *Odyssey* were written, approximately as they stand, by one great poet in the eleventh century [Murray wrote in 1907; today he would happily lower the date to "the eighth century," and consider it progress] cannot possibly admit that the text was still in a very fluid state so late as the third century. The position of Ludwich, for instance, is that roughly speaking our present vulgate was in existence as an authoritative text from the very earliest ages, and passed unscathed through the illiterate centuries of early Greece, through the creative ferment of the fifth century, through the chaos of the pre-Zenodotean texts, and lastly through the fires of Alexandrine criticism, always unmentioned but universally recognized, to emerge in triumph in our post-Christian MSS.[2]

Could some of the older scholars have been right after all? Was the stability associated with the vulgate text of Homer in fact created by the efforts of the Alexandrians, and essentially their invention?

If so, what was the state of the national epic relative to writing in the eighth, seventh, sixth, and fifth centuries? What is to be made of Cicero's report, surely on *some* authority (Dicaearchus has been suggested, a fairly reliable source), that Peisistratus was reported to have first brought order to the text of Homer, previously in a state of confusion. Was Cicero merely guessing in the dark about Peisistratus, fabricating out of whole cloth? Could he have ventured such a guess if, in that bookish age of competitive scholarship in which he lived, an early authoritative text was widely known to have existed?

Perhaps we must move toward recognizing that a traditional body of verbal material that serves as a great people's paideia, conserved in a language elevated from the vernacular, can achieve a stability in oral and aural transmission that is different from that of a verbatim text but nevertheless remains an effective conservator and depository of what the society continues to find useful and necessary to preserve. If that is so, then a Homer as finally textualized on a monumental scale only in the sixth century would owe marked debts in the way of consistency, overall organization and patterning, and perhaps certain nuances of character to writing, and to one (or more) great redactor-singer (or rhapsode) who was also a writer. Oral and written creativity enter into an uncommon union, as a traditional oral poem is textualized on a massive scale. Genius was to be found both in the material and in the hand that now reshaped it into a massive, written text. A group of professional rhapsodes under the direction, perhaps, of a master singer, who produced a Panathenaic text to serve as the basis for teams of rhapsodes to perform the great poems for the assembled populace at the festival may somewhat offend present ideas of how creativity is supposed to work. If so, perhaps we need to recall that the great King James translation of the Bible was also the result of a committee effort, and a large committee at that. Also, with a tyrant's purse to support the project in this period, importation of papyrus and the other material conditions required to produce a few copies are all feasible.

At the same time, a monumental text so created may well have remained faithful in the essentials, especially in terms of conservative language and diction, to what would have been performed in the eighth century or earlier. Such a text would still have to be (and, indeed, was) composed with a listening, critical audience very much in mind. It could not deviate far from the familiar, which was what the Athenian audience expected to hear. The very knowledgeable exchange between Socrates and Ion, taking place more than a century later than a postulated Panathenaic text in the middle of the sixth century, reveals just how critical that audience could be and how stuffed with Homeric scenes and verses were their memories. This, too, is an important consideration, contributing to the conservative character of what was produced in written form. The expectant audience knew what Homer should sound like from rhapsodes, great singers, and reciters, who were part of a tradition of performed epical verse that had never been broken.

Be all this as it may, any theory that puts a monumental text of Homer very early, especially in the eighth century, faces a crucial question: What material was it written on? Excluded as materials for a monumental *Iliad* must be stone, painted (whitened) wooden boards, clay whether fired or not, wax, linen, metals, and bone—all used to preserve writing in the ancient Near East, and some of them in Greece as well. Unless papyrus is assumed (as by Barry Powell), only leather or skins specially prepared would be a plausible candidate. Even so, the motive for that effort—no negligible one even for an experienced scribe in a more literate century—as early as 700 B.C. frankly eludes me.

For all practical purposes, a monumental *Iliad* written down in the eighth century requires that papyrus be available on Greek soil in commercial quantities. But importation of manufactured papyrus from Egypt to anywhere in Greece as early as ca. 700 B.C. to produce a longer text seems, if only from economic considerations, out of the question. Accustomed as we are to printed books or the vellum codex, we do not reflect on what it would have taken in the classical period (or earlier) to get a complete work of any length into written form, whether on papyrus or hides. A reasonable guess is that a fairly experienced writer, such as the author *P. Oxy.* 448 (an unremarkable papyrus devoted to the last two books of the *Iliad*; the remains are now in the British Museum), would require something over 300 feet of manufactured papyrus for our *Iliad*. That seems to imply established trade with Egypt and papyrus imported in commercial quantities.

In terms of dates, the reopening of official trade contacts with Egypt during the reign of Psammetichus I (663–610 B.C.), and the establishing of the Greek trade colony at Naucratis would be the favorable period for the start of a small papyrus trade between Egypt and Greece. Probably the importation of papyrus and its use for any modest literary purpose did not precede by much the closing years of the seventh century—at the earliest. Ionia, specifically Miletus, is a good guess as the first major importer of papyrus. In point of fact, however, as these remarks reveal, we know next to nothing about how early papyrus entered Greece, and much guesswork is required. Herodotus (V. 58) claims to know of the temporary use of skins *(diphtherai)*, specifically goatskins and sheepskins, as a writing material in Ionia once when papyrus was scarce, thereby perhaps suggesting that even in Ionia papyrus was not an early import. For a monumental Homer I do not know the number of valuable sheep that would have to be slaughtered to secure the requisite hides—not all parts were usable—but the economics of production seem daunting.[3]

That Homeric diction had evolved into maturity by the turn of the seventh century is guaranteed, of course, primarily by the Homeric and Hesiodic poems themselves. The Hesiodic poems, if not in the exact form we have them at least approximately so, seem to have been written, or written down, not too many decades after 700 B.C. Hesiod composes not in local dialect, Boiotian—although its influence is present—but in the pan-Hellenic *koinē* of epical speech, with its heavy component of Ionic.

Not much if at all later than Hesiod, the first so-called lyric poetry gets recorded or written down but, as in the case of Archilochus, it is still dominated by Homeric speech. It is, of course, absurd to suppose that poetry (songs, really) of diverse kinds suddenly began to be composed in Greece in the early seventh century or that Greeks of that and subsequent centuries deliberately set out to create new ''genres'' of literature to add to the older epic ''genre.'' Such a reconstruction, like theories of a Boiotian ''school'' of theogonic poets (whose membership list significantly has only one name, Hesiod), dominated many older textbooks and is dutifully repeated in many newer ones. But that is to view the poetic words surviving from Archaic Greece with the literate mentality of Alexandria and Byzantium. Work songs, wedding songs, funeral dirges, erotic ditties of hopeful enticement (or disappointed vituperation), the platitudes of initiation from an older generation to the younger one—all are probably as old, or nearly so, as the full acquisition of speech by our species.

What was an innovation on Greek soil from 700 B.C. onward was simply a means of recording the more enduring forms of such song, a new, enabling technology of formidable power and efficiency, the first complete alphabet. It gave us, in time, the great body of Greek literature. The alphabet spread through a Greece long and intimately acquainted with performances of epical verse. This is clearly proven from the texts of Homer, Hesiod, the so-called Homeric Hymns, and the fragment remains of the earliest lyric poets, starting with Callinus and Archilochus, as well as the surviving fragments of the Presocratic philosophers. Less widely appreciated is the fact that the very old inscriptions are also compelling evidence that, in Late Geometric Greece, Homeric speech had not only penetrated to every part of Greece but also been absorbed by all levels of society. Whereas the texts of great poets and philosophers might be claimed as evidence for Homeric dominance of only the literary record (and so involve only a small literary class of authors), the early, popular inscriptions are totally immune from such a claim. As Parry intuited long before he came to the realization that epic verse was specifically oral, Homeric speech was both *traditional* and *popular*, somehow the ''people's poetry'' and not the product of a literary elite. It was always taken in by the ear, not the eye, and as it was popularly absorbed it became the stabilizing core of the oral way of life.

In the past dozen or so years, the fact that Greek ''literature'' of the Archaic period was composed for listeners and not readers has, in one emphasis or another, received important book-length treatments from such diverse scholars as Bruno Gentili, George Nagy, Thomas Cole, Eric Havelock, Charles Beye, Oswyn Murray, and Marcel Detienne, among many others. They had predecessors, some now neglected, among Homeric scholars who lived and wrote long before them and who were, in some ways, the unsung heroes of the recovery of one or another aspect of the oral way of life in the Archaic period.

In the preceding chapters I have deliberately mentioned a number of ''oralist pioneers'' (in the loose sense that their diverse discoveries pointed toward the recovery of Greek oralism) such as Paul Friedländer, Richard Shute, Felix Jacoby, George Calhoun, and, of course, the remarkable J. W. Headlam. I select one more unsung oralist pioneer for notice because some of his ideas and intuitions can prove instructive yet, as well as confirm and help to summarize the argument of this book. In some matters he has been proved wrong, and much that he says is now dated, of course. None of us escapes that. But what he was right about was right indeed, and it deserves our applause and admiration yet. If it offends some colleagues that a ''hopelessly dated'' scholar should today have recognition or attention wasted on him, then I happily make Frank Jevons's words my own and only wish I had said them so well or so long before anyone else. It would be hard, even with all that has been learned since he wrote, to find the case stated better. Jevons is hardly at the cutting edge of today's scholarship, any more than he was in his own day, when he was largely, if politely, dismissed. But in the views that mattered to him, for whatever professional solace it brought, he got it right.

Frank Byron Jevons is known today only to a scattering of the world's classicists and a handful of scholars associated with his home university. Jevons was a classicist at University College, Durham, and in the 1880s was at work on a general history of Greek literature, finally published in 1886. It was, as he said, ''designed mainly for students at our Universities and Public Schools, and for such as are preparing for the Indian Civil Service and other advanced examinations.'' His book, *A History of Greek Literature from the Earliest Period to the Death of Demosthenes,* as Jevons's prefatory notice reveals, is now dated, to say the least. But his perception that, in all periods, the progress of Greek literacy was in close alliance with a tenacious oralism was remarkable for its time.

Jevons, in full knowledge of opposing views, especially among nineteenth-century Semiticists, insisted on placing the introduction of the alphabet into Greece not much, if at all, earlier than 700 B.C. Distinguished historians and epigraphists of the day, both Semiticists and Hellenists, favored dates as early as 1400 B.C. for a variety of reasons, often based on this or that hypothetical circumstance. Jevons stated his grounds for the later date, which he thought no mere theory should be permitted to overturn. There was no inscriptional evidence—or evidence of any other kind—for the alphabet any earlier. Until new evidence emerged, the date ca. 700 B.C. must stand.

By contrast, there was abundant evidence for the gradual and uninterrupted spread of the use of letters after that date. Jevons then went on to argue that epigraphy—that is, a careful study of the extant Greek inscriptions and their dating—not the questionable dates of the literary sources must be our primary evidence for establishing the earliest phase of Greek literacy, and above all for the date of the introduction of the alphabet into Greece. If Rhys Carpenter had a spiritual predecessor among Hellenists, it was Frank Jevons. I know of no earlier scholar, and few later ones, who saw so clearly the necessity of this approach to the evidence for the introduction of Greek literacy. It is, of course, a major thrust of the argument of the present work.

Three reasons for keeping a close eye on the inscriptional record emerge from Jevons's argument, all quite sound. First, normally an artifact can be dated at least to its correct century, if not decade or decades within a century, and it remains free from later tampering, both deliberate and accidental (as can happen in copying a manuscript), of a sort that could alter the evidence. Second, the dates of most literary figures before 500 B.C., let alone a Homer or Hesiod, are generally mere guesswork (however conventional they have become in the handbooks), a point well taken and often overlooked even today. Third, early Greek literary works, even if dated to the right parts of a century, are evidence for little else than the literacy of whoever wrote them, or even wrote them down. The latter person, especially in early centuries, may not always have been the composer himself but rather an amanuensis. In any case, all early composers were poets, and the important fact to keep in mind was that they all composed for *listeners,* not readers.

Jevons observed that written prose held promise for a change in the manner of publication for a writer's work, calling into existence a small literate public of readers perhaps, but he questioned how early that public became a fact. Even the early prose writers, commencing in the sixth century, seem to have gathered together small groups of like minds and read to them from a manuscript that might even be an only copy. Thucydides, in the opening words of his history, would seem to mark the first hint of a change in that practice (quite correct) and to have addressed a future of readers. Therefore, in Jevons's estimate, the survival of a slim body of literature from the seventh, sixth, or even fifth centuries is evidence only for authors' copies, and a few extras. He isolated the last decades of the fifth century as the first period when "books" came into evidence, and then only marginally. Again he has been proved correct. But he always doubted that Greece in antiquity, at least through the Classical period, was ever "literate" as the late nineteenth century understood the term, thus prefiguring some recent contributions.

Jevons also drew a corollary conclusion without flinching. In some ways it is the hallmark of his work. Greek literature remained "classical" (and, we may add, as he constantly at least implies, "great") as long as it remained oral, by which he means not that it was composed without writing, but that it was communicated to audiences orally and aurally. What was distinctive of classical Greek literature, which we now read in silent admiration, was that artist and audience were interacting in a dynamic and creative way through the medium of voice and ear. The artist always composed in anticipation of being performed, and so, on all occasions, of being heard by ears trained to an exacting standard. That was as true for words composed for the great theater of Dionysius, where the tragedies were performed, as it was for a local household's private *sumposion.* Not only was Greek literature aural, therefore; it was, in the best sense, also popular, a fact that saved all early Greek composition from becoming mannered or precious. Literature became so only in Hellenistic and Roman times, when it was addressed to a small, elite public who savored only the written word and who relished the special status this conferred on only them. At the same time, we may note, formal education grew pedantic in the extreme. In Roman times, the poor schoolmaster who did not remember every possible recondite allusion and every minor character in the written text of Homer was disgraced.

All of classical Greek "literature" therefore, although now read in books, in fact was composed under the conditions of what a much later scholar, Eric Havelock, was to call "audience control." Jevons himself used many similar terms. He concluded that this remained dominantly the case down to the fourth-century orators and was the governing principle—as the nature of audiences changed—in the development of Greek literature. The literate classifications, which began in the Hellenistic period and dominated much nineteenth-century scholarship, in terms of a succession of "genres" commencing with epic and terminating in the prose works of the fourth century, obstructed the fact that changes in the forms of composition were a function of changes in the audiences to whom those various compositions were aurally addressed.

Jevons boldly concluded that Homer, the first Greek composer known to us, of necessity sang to an audience of preliterates if he lived earlier than 700 B.C. There was simply no archaeological way around the fact, a point later made by Rhys Carpenter. But Homer's artistic accomplishment also assures us that he stands at the *end* of a great tradition, not at its font. Jevons writes:

> Other poets must have lived before Homer, and must have carried the development of poetry to a considerable height, before such works as the *Iliad* and the *Odyssey* could have been composed. But as there is not a vestige of this pre-Homeric poetry left [because the means to record it—writing—did not yet exist in Greece], we shall proceed at once to Homer.[4]

The perfection of the verse that we can now read means it was not an art form in its infancy, even though the long developmental period must have been conducted without the aid of writing; in a word, it was, of necessity, a period of highly creative oral verse-making. From a far more sophisticated perspective, Parry made the same argument in our century and in so doing revolutionized Homeric studies.

Mnemonics, not aesthetics, also explained, as Jevons correctly perceived, why poetry precedes prose in the history of all peoples emerging from what oralists now, following Ong, describe as the cultures of primary orality. Poetry is not chosen because "simple" peoples and "rude" primitives, being such, like a good, boisterous singsong. There is, as Jevons often remarks, nothing primitive about any early Greek poetry that we now can read, and Homer, arguably, has never been surpassed. Some superior, aesthetic predilection of the Greek people (at bottom a racist premise) cannot be used to account for so much good poetry—and no prose—before the sixth century. Nor can it be a mere accident of survival.

> The fallacy of the [aesthetic] explanation is that it assumes that Hesiod and the other didactic poets had before them the choice whether to compose in verse or prose. But in the seventh century B.C. no Greek author had any such choice. The very idea that it was possible to compose prose was unknown to the latter part of

> the sixth century, and then it was in Ionia the discovery—an important one—was made. If a man had that within him which he felt he must give words to—if his thoughts on the order of things, or his knowledge on the practical matters of life, seemed to him too precious to die within his own breast, he had only one way of giving them extensive publicity, only one way of ensuring they would live after him, and that was to put them into verse. A precept is useless if it cannot be remembered, and cannot be readily learnt by one person from another. Accordingly amongst most peoples, rhyme, meter, or alliteration is used as an aid to memory. [These have] the practical recommendation of enabling the memory to carry a larger amount of fact than it otherwise could retain; and so long as writing is unknown to or little used by a people, verse is not only a means of gratifying man's sense of beauty, but also bears the burdens which paper or parchment are subsequently made to bear.[5]

Initially, argued Jevons, the Greeks wrote down what long had been orally performed, which meant poetry. Literary prose was initially a harder undertaking for them, for which no models existed, an obvious point made much later by Denniston in his brilliant analyses of the style of the earliest Greek prose authors.

If poetry is viewed in this way, that is, as a mechanism for the preservation of what the group finds important in the absence of written records, then it follows that the Hellenes' earliest known poetry, or Homer, long functioned as the Hellenic paideia, as later Greeks always said that it did. Jevons had an arresting image for this role. Such poetry becomes a kind of oral "encyclopedia" for the group's essential information, one not made to be kept on shelves and read but to be hoarded in living memories and passed orally across generations in performance. (Eric Havelock later independently hit upon the same analogy in *Preface to Plato,* and welcomed learning[6] that Jevons had preceded him in viewing Greek epical poetry as a "tribal encyclopaedia.") As a result, this paideia required regular and enjoyable occasions of performance. Greek society conspired at every opportunity to provide them, developing over centuries new means to do so and in the process new forms (or "genres") of literature. Understandably, then, the singer was a *demiourgos* as early as Homer, a craftsman like any other in the town—potter and stonemason—in the service of the *dēmos,* the people. Jevons, like the great F. A. Wolf before him, had a way of keeping a steely eye on the evidence. This view of early Greek poetry is, may I add, the antithesis of a romantic one.

Jevons's book has long been out of print and is now rare. For this reason, below I subjoin some passages from his remarkable (for its time) vision of the development of Greek literature. First, from a chapter on Aeschines, the orator:

> The modern public reads, the ancient public listened. All the citizens of Athens could be gathered together in the theatre to hear a drama; every citizen might be present at the Assembly; great festivals drew a large concourse of people together in whom the essayist or the historian [Herodotus] could find an audience. During the creative periods of Greek literature the normal way of reaching the public was through their ears, not as in modern times their eyes, for even if most Athenians were able to decipher the letters of the alphabet [no certain matter for Jevons], they were not in the habit of reading.[7]

In his summary chapter, Jevons observes that a mastery of the Greek language, which many scholars and even laymen possessed in his day, was a necessary condition for understanding Greek literature, but not a sufficient one. For, he writes,

> we must have some idea of the way in which, in classical times, literature was communicated to the public. It is a matter of doubt whether writing was even known in Greece much before B.C. 700. It is probable that for a century and a half after that date it was only used for purposes of commerce and correspondence [although for this he admits there is no surviving evidence]. For a century after that it seems as though the only use it was to literature was to enable an author to write out a single copy of his works. It is only about 430 or 420 that we find copies of manuscripts multiplied and diffused, and for a century after that it was not to the reading public that authors addressed themselves. In other words, writing seems not to have been known during the period of epic poetry, not to have been used for literary purposes during the age of lyric (except towards the end), and to have been used by the historians, philosophers and dramatists only as an aid to composition, and not to have been needed as a means of publication by the orators, with whom classical literature ends.[8]

What Jevons describes so well, in words that have stood the test of time, oralists have recently called ''audience control'' over Greek composition. It was a literature composed, no doubt, or at least preserved, from Hesiod onward with the aid of writing, but intended not for reading but performing and so to be taken in by the attentive and appreciative ear.[9] What these scholars seek to emphasize is that an author had to anticipate and provide for the way in which his words would reach his audience. This meant he had to please the ear. Greek literature, including Presocratic philosophy, developed under such constraints. Jevons writes:

> Greek literature, then, was communicated to the public orally, not by means of the multiplication and diffusion of manuscripts. But oral communication implies the collection of an audience to whom the author can address his words; and the occasion on which, the purpose for which, the place in which, and frequency with which the audience is collected exercise a considerable influence on the literary form of the works presented to it. Further, the reaction of the audience being more immediate, was more effectual than it is even in these days of the printing press.[10]

No small part of the control of ''Homer'' over Hellas as a way of life, of which Greeks were proud in each generation, was due to the manner in which epical words were brought to bear on the Greek consciousness. Unfailingly, that was oral and aural well into the fourth century.

The last paragraph of Jevons's book summarizes a long, complex, and learned argument of more than 500 printed pages. Yet it is quite short, and I quote all but one sentence of it. To put his closing paragraph in context, I preface it with a few words from an earlier section of his final chapter.

> Bearing in mind that classical Greek literature was designed to be uttered aloud and was necessarily tested by the ears of the audience . . . for taste requires development, and it is the oral communication of literature to which we must

ascribe the cultivation of the Athenians. . . . In fine, Greek literature was classical as long as it was oral. The character and extent of the audience changed as the social and political conditions changed. . . . When the character and extent of the audience changed, fresh means of addressing it were discovered. To the successive changes in the former correspond the successive forms of their literature—epic, lyric, and dramatic poetry, historical, oratorical and philosophical prose. That *is* the history of Greek literature.[11]

Notes

1. The literature on Milman Parry has grown beyond the capacity of one person to assimilate it. The journal *Oral Tradition* will point the interested reader to most of the sources. A recent treatment of Homer is that of Mark Edwards, *Homer: Poet of the Iliad,* (Baltimore and London, 1987), who provides an informed and balanced guide to the diversity of recent opinion. For my own understanding of the oral tradition, I am aware of the influence of the earlier writings of G. S. Kirk, although in arguing for a powerful residual oralism as late as the turn of the fourth century I suspect we go separate ways. Finally, in writing this book and puzzling over how ''Homer'' became a monumental text I returned often to several publications of Adam Parry and in so doing realized again the enormity of the loss that his premature death in 1981 was to classical scholarship.

2. Gilbert Murray, *The Rise of the Greek Epic* (New York, 1960), pp. 284–285. This book, based on a series of lectures delivered at Harvard University, was first published by Oxford University Press in 1907 and went through many editions. In the new prefaces written for the later editions, Murray became the first major figure among English-speaking scholars to welcome the contribution of a then unknown Milman Parry.

3. A useful study is that of N. Lewis, *Papyrus in Classical Antiquity* (Oxford, 1974). Also see R. Reed, *Ancient Skins, Parchments, and Leathers* (London and New York, 1972); and S. West, *The Ptolmaic Papyri of Homer* (Cologne, 1967). The techniques practiced by the great Alexandrian critics come alive in E. G. Turner, *Greek Papyri* (Oxford, 1968), a work followed by that of P. M. Fraser (*Ptolemaic Alexandria* [Oxford, 1972]), who brings the whole period and social context alive. The full triumph of alphabetic literacy in Hellenistic Alexandria is abundantly evident in these pages.

4. F. B. Jevons, *A History of Greek Literature from the Earliest Period to the Death of Demosthenes* (London, 1886), p. 3.

5. Ibid., p. 81.

6. Havelock in a letter to the author, Oct. 18, 1982.

7. Jevons, *A History of Greek Literature from the Earliest Period to the Death of Demosthenes,* p. 463.

8. Ibid., pp. 491–492.

9. Ibid., pp. 41ff. Jevons dismisses the Bellerophon engraved golden tablet (*Iliad* VI. 169) as evidence in the text of Homer for alphabetic writing on sensible grounds: ''There is more than one way of sending a message than by means of an alphabet; so the passage is not conclusive'' (p. 42). His words should have closed the debate but, of course, did not. After noting the questionable dates of Greek authors before 500 B.C., he then writes: ''With inscriptions, however, we are on safer grounds'' (p. 42). Jevons's discussion of the epigraphical material available at the time is hopelessly dated because most of the relevant inscriptional evidence (discussed in my early chapters) had not yet surfaced when he wrote, but his methodology is sound, the general dating correct (remarkably so), and the emphasis

on the fact that there was no early reading public valuable yet. Of the surviving body of lyric poetry from the seventh and sixth centuries, Jevons wrote: "Lyric authors wrote either choral lyrics which were to be performed in public at some festival, or songs of love and wine which were to be sung over wine at dinner. . . . We may safely infer that if he [any lyric poet; Theognis is mentioned by name] caused copies of his MS to be multiplied and distributed, it was not in order that they might be read, but that his friends might learn them and sing them at drinking parties or other social gatherings. . . . The very nature of Theognis' poetry shows that it was not composed for a reading public" (p. 46). The same words could be applied, for example, to the philosopher Xenophanes of Colophon, whose fragments themselves reveal that his method of publication must have been symposiastic. The primary role of the *sumposia* of Archaic Greece—not books—for the popular dissemination of much early poetic composition deserves emphasis again. A stimulating article by Jackson Hershbell extends this suggestion to the publication of Plato's dialogues in his forthcoming paper, "Reflections on the Origins and Literacy of Plato's Dialogues," a version of which was read at the annual meeting of the Society for Ancient Greek Philosophy in New York in 1992. In an age before the manufacture of books, the transition from participants' singing verses at a *sumposion* to reading from their own prose composition was, presumably, a natural one for any author in search of an audience. Noting that Socrates remained an oral teacher, Jevons observed that Plato, too, must have composed not for a reading public but for his own circle. Jevons perceptively wrote that just as "Plato read his *Phaedo* to his friends and pupils, so Protagoras read his treatise on the gods in the house of Euripides or in the Lyceum . . . and Socrates had listened to Zeno reading his works [in Plato's *Parmenides*]. Herodotus read portions of his in Athens and at the festival of the Panathenea, while at Olympia such readings were especially provided for, and not only Herodotus, but Gorgias, Hippias, and Empedocles obtained publicity for their compositions. It seems, then, that the rise of prose literature in the century B.C. 550 to 450 does not necessitate the assumption of the existence of a reading public, but only of an audience to listen to the author reading his manuscripts" (p. 48). All this involved some speculation of the part of Jevons, but describes well the state of Athenian literacy as late as the last decades of the fifth century. It also casts serious doubt on a monumental Homer surviving from the eighth (or ninth) century, continuously copied and faithfully read by large numbers of Greeks in each generation. The assumption of such a text and its loyal readers is drawn from modern, literate experience, not from the facts of Greek oral life.

10. Ibid., p. 492.

11. Ibid., pp. 494 and 501–502.

10

Epilogue: A Linguistic and Historical Analysis of the Invention of the Greek Alphabet

In a series of earlier publications I defended the view that the first complete or true alphabet was the Greek alphabet. I also argued that what called it into existence was the desire to record on durable substances a few hexameters that were felt to be appropriate to occasions of eighth-century oral life. Earlier Wade-Gery had made a related suggestion, and recently Barry Powell has taken up and defended the theory that the alphabet was invented to record poetry, citing Wade-Gery and Robb as his earliest predecessors.

An important difference between us is that I have defended the inscriptional uses of the alphabet as being primary, whereas Wade-Gery and Powell have not. As a result, I suggested that the first ''texts'' ran to a few hexameters at most, not a monumental Homer. I have also argued that ordinary citizens, not professional *aoidoi* or epical singers, must have been the composers of the oldest ''long'' inscriptions, imitating and adapting what they had heard from professional performances. The first inscribers and the first Greek literates were, therefore, in the main local craftsmen.

Powell, borrowing some speculation about orally dictated texts from the school of Albert Lord, has boldly suggested that the motive of the adapter was to write down the entirety of Homer. The adapter, therefore, invented the complete alphabet to create a monumental text. This is possible, but I find it improbable. To me, this reconstruction has problems in the areas of motive—who could or would read such a text even if one could be produced—and of materials. What was it recorded on? But I know of no definitive way to prove the theory wrong. Powell and I are in agreement again on the importance of the work of the Semiticist Ignace Gelb, whom I had called to the attention of Hellenists starting in the 1970s, but with little success that I was aware of (Eric Havelock was an exception). Structurally, according to Gelb, the pre-Greek Semitic scripts remained syllabaries, whatever nomenclature may be used to refer to their unique characteristics (''quasi-alphabets'' has recently been suggested, as has been ''unvocalized syllabaries'').

Behind my theory of the poetic sources of the complete alphabet were two related considerations. Greek poetry has very different characteristics from Semitic poetry in that it puts great emphasis on the meter and very little emphasis on the parallelism of members. These emphases are reversed in the Semitic poetic tradition. Moreover, only a complete alphabet—not an unvocalized syllabary—is adequate to record so much as a single line of Greek poetry or, for that matter, any Greek sentence with much syntax. Aspects of my argument are reviewed in this epilogue for the convenience of interested readers. The bibliography will direct readers to the places where the argument was first published. In what follows, some distinctions borrowed from modern linguistics will be introduced since accurate description requires constant circumlocution without them. They are, at one level, a useful set of shorthand expressions. Since I cannot anticipate that readers from diverse disciplines will necessarily be familiar with this terminology, I offer some working definitions, adequate for present purposes, in my text. (Also, students of linguistics will recognize that I owe debts for nomenclature to the older structural linguistics, which is a matter of convenience in exposition not ideological commitment, an issue on which I remain neutral.) Once the basic distinctions captured by these terms are grasped, it should become clear that only a true alphabet, or one with complete vowel notation, is adequate for recording a language with the morphological characteristics of the Indo-European group and inflected along the lines of Greek.

Signary Follows Morphology

The morphological characteristics of a given language determine the kind of script that can record the sounds of the language; more important, they exclude some scripts or else force their adaptation. That principle is fundamental. Chinese affords a convenient example. The morphological character of the Chinese language permits it to tolerate a logographic writing system, although a vast number of logograms (roughly, a sign for each word or idea) is required. With rarest exception, Chinese words are invariant in form, without suffixes, affixes, or inflections. The word is, as it were, a changeless brick. Its "shape" does not vary to indicate tense or whether the word modifies another (adjective or adverb), is a possessive, or expresses action (verb), names a thing or an attribute (noun), is singular or plural. English has such words (e.g., "must"), but not many, and very few among the basic building blocks of nouns and verbs. What in English and even more so in Greek is largely accomplished by alteration in a word's form is accomplished in Chinese by context, word order (which of two words is placed before the other), tone of pronunciation, or by use of compounds or auxiliary particles. As a result, unless one knows the underlying language, the signs of the script cannot indicate the approximate sounds they represent. The difference from an alphabet in this regard is crucial.

A person who can read English may not know a word of modern Turkish, but with less than twenty minutes of guidance (e.g., *C*addessi or "street" is *Sh*adessi, but almost a *g*) can arrive at the approximate pronunciation of a text. The reason is that under Mustapha Kemal Pasha (Attaturk) a very efficient version of the Western alphabet was adopted for writing Turkish. The Arabic script was abandoned, and the Western script was imposed in the schools and used everywhere for public notices, newspapers, and street signs. Turkish has different morphological characteristics from Chinese in that it is an agglutinating language. A logographic script on the Chinese model would be intolerable for recording it, but an alphabetic one, especially with the simplicity of the Roman version, was ideal for promoting widespread popular literacy. For this reason, after overcoming some initial resistance (often religious, for the Koran was written in the traditional Arabic script), the young Turks imposed its adoption. Turkish students now need to memorize about the same number of signs as English students in order to begin reading their language, and then they must, like their American or British counterparts, work only at more fluent recognition. Chinese students must memorize approximately 4,000 signs before they can start to become moderately efficient as readers and writers. In Turkey, with an adequate school system that imposes the "alphabet trauma" at an early age and drills students in its use, widespread popular literacy became, in theory, attainable. With a system of competent, state-supported secondary schools even in rural areas, considerable progress was made within a generation. Mehmet Ali Agca, who nearly succeeded in assassinating Pope John Paul II, was an avid reader and a product of a good *lisei* in the village of Yesiltepe on the outskirts of rural Malatya. His parents were poor peasants.

Once language has been reduced to written form—becomes, as it were, an object and not a flowing sea of sounds—its components can be analyzed, a process begun by the Greek philosophers and sophists. Eventually one language group can be compared to another on the basis of morphology, phonology, or both, a modern achievement. Both developments are products of societies of advanced literacy. Both endeavors would be incomprehensible to oral peoples, who often fail to distinguish even what a "word" is, let alone a verb from an adverb, and they seem never to study grammar formally, although they use it, of course. By "grammar" in this context, I mean simply the set of rules, or "how the game is played," which in a given language relates sound to meaning. We are genetically encoded to become players, that is, to acquire speech, and in so doing we also unconsciously learn the rules of the language game, or grammar. As a result, we do not prick running with a thistle or gather berries from pleasantly.

Phonology, as the word suggests, is a systematic study, and so a kind of cataloging, of all the sounds used in a given language. Linguists, following the French pioneers (but ultimately Greek: *stoicheia,* "elements") use the term "phoneme" to refer to the smallest unit of sound that can make a functional difference to the meaning of a word. How this is done is best shown by example (my examples will be rather standard ones). In English, kill, mill, pill, bill, fill, sill, till, and so on, differ from each other by a single, but in each case a different, sound. Thus the sounds represented by *k, m, p, b,* and so on are considered separate phonemes. Linguists estimate that English uses about forty-five phonemes. Roughly, on the analogy of Greek atomic philosophy, whose goal was to reduce matter to that which could not be divided further, a phoneme is an "atom" of sound.

Morphology, on the same analogy, is a systematic study of atoms of meaning, or the smallest parts of a language which by themselves are meaningful. Somewhat like the Greek conception of a physical atom, they cannot be split further into parts which are in turn meaningful. Examples are *dog, cat, day, top,* and *be.* In English these are irreducible atoms of meaning and so are morphemes, just as *p* and *k* are irreducible atoms of sound and so phonemes. Many English words form their plurals by adding -s, as in *day, days.* Because this irreducible part of a word also bears meaning, it too can be identified as a morpheme. It is called a "bound" morpheme because it cannot not stand alone, as does a "free" morpheme, such as *day.*

The direction of this sort of linguistic analysis is extremely important for understanding the guiding genius behind the invention of the complete alphabet. It seeks to identify the building blocks, especially irreducible building blocks, of language and then analyzes the way they are patterned into wholes at the various structural levels of a language. Also, this analysis assumes, as first formally recognized by the pioneering de Saussure, that there is a distinction between between *la langue,* or the language system, and *la parole,* the speech of those who use the language. It assumes, importantly, that what linguistics deals with may be *la langue,* but what is fundamental to our species is *la parole.* Only advanced literacy gives rise to a study of, or even formal recognition of, *la langue.* Why such analysis requires that language become a physical object, or a written language, should be evident.

The "morphological characteristics" of a language refer to the characteristic or typical internal patterning of the words used in that language, even as phonology refers to the patterning of sounds. Those features found with great regularity in the internal patterning of words in one group of languages may be rare in another, although perhaps are never absent altogether. To understand why the Greek adoption had to be an adaptation as well, it is necessary to have a general idea of the different morphological structures of Greek, a highly inflected Indo-European language, and Old Phoenician, a member of the Semitic language group. To reiterate the basic principle, the morphological characteristics of a language determine whether, in adopting a script, the language is tolerant of being recorded by a logographic script, or a syllabic script denoting open syllables of the vowel plus consonant type, or whether the adopted script can ignore the vowels altogether in the interest of a restricted number of signs in the signary. The approximate efficiency (none is perfect) of a script for recording a language—and so its adoption, adaptation, or eventual rejection as utterly impossible—is a function of the morphological characteristics of the language spoken by the adopters. It will also be necessary to understand, at the phonological level, just what makes a consonant a consonant and a vowel a vowel. The person who adapted the Semitic script understood the difference and addressed it in an efficient and systematic way.

Morphological Differences between Old Phoenician and Greek

Those familiar with traditional grammar will recognize that what approximates morphology in modern structural linguistics was the older kind of word analysis that sought to identify various stems, roots, prefixes, and suffixes as the building blocks of words. Modern linguists have sought to classify languages into language groups on the basis of their morphological characteristics. Thus agglutinative languages, such as Turkish, or the first written language, Sumerian, form words by stringing together morphemes attached to root words. The affixes are relatively few and fairly regular, rather in the way in English *-ing* can be added to a vast number of verbs—thinking, playing, loving, laughing, and so on. An extreme example of agglutination often cited in linguistics textbooks is a single Eskimo word whose parts mean "I am looking for something suitable for a fish line." Japanese is an agglutinating language whose affixes are simple vowels or open monosyllables consisting of simple consonants plus a vowel. The sentence, "This text will be preserved on a FU-JI floppy disk purchased in YO-KO-HA-MA," affords typical examples in Japanese words. As opposed to this, Indo-European languages abound with consonantal clusters (e.g., "*Str*ai*ght* is the gate") and closed syllables (e.g., "the troublesome laws of God and man"). The old Katakana syllabary, whose characters were borrowed from Chinese, is tolerant of recording spoken Japanese with relatively few signs (only forty-seven basic ones). No such restricted syllabary could handle spoken English or ancient Greek. The phonetic dissolution of words into syllables is not a difficult task, especially for agglutinating languages such as Japanese, and has happened independently several times in the history of writing. The dissolution of the open syllable, such as *ba* or *ka,* into its two components, consonantal and vocalic, proved to be a far more difficult linguistic task. To accomplish this in a systematic way was the notable achievement of the Greeks. It gave us the alphabet we still use.

What is most characteristic of the Semitic language group is that the consonantal root, composed normally of three (but sometimes four) consonants, persists unchanged, for example, the written sequence *ktb* or *ktl.* The root written as *ktl* yields *katil,* "murder," *katala,* "he killed," and so on. A famous example comes from Arabic. The root *slm* means something like "to be peaceful, submissive." Hence, *salama,* "he was peaceful"; *salam,* "peace"; and *islam,* "submission." The vowels placed before and after the consonants $k^X t^X b^X$ can similarly vary, such as *kāteb,* "writing," a participle, with other variations for "he writes" (a perfect) and so on. The root persists as the vowels vary in order to express the grammatical burden, or syntactic function, that the word will have in a sentence. A pointed text could help indicate these differences, for example, by marking with a dot above, indicating a participle, or by marking with a dot below, indicating the perfect. Pointing is, however, a very late development in the Semitic scripts, influenced by the Greek alphabet and of no relevance to the period of transfer.

The chief morphological characteristic of the Semitic languages is often referred to somewhat indifferently as triliteralism, internal vowel variation, or simply vowel change. Because of its morphological features, the radical simplification of the signary for recording a language—reduced from thousands to some twenty-two signs, standing for consonants only—was possible. Some scholars, such as Frank Moore Cross and Albright before him, have argued that the principle of phonetic consonantism was inherent in Semitic writing as early as the Proto-Canaanite "alphabet." The principle, as noted, was rigorously maintained in its direct successor, Old Phoenician.

For the Semitic languages, a reader must first know the language in order to supply the appropriate vowel sounds, of course. Normally one must have a context to do so readily with unfailing success. A familiar text, such as a proverb or a psalm, is ideal. The reader's eye isolates the triconsonantal roots and then, surmising the meaning from the order in which they appear, supplies the requisite vowels in order to pronounce a meaningful text. It was a wonderful solution, for the Semitic languages. In sum, Semitic writing was successful for this language group because the script adequately reflected the basic morphological structure of the languages, namely, root morphemes of three (or four) consonants that can yield a finite number of word patterns readily supplied from context or a familiar text, and an underlying structure of the consonant plus vowel type, that is, with the consonant in the initial position. Neither feature is characteristic of ancient Greek, which is what makes a writing system based on the principle of consonantism intolerable for it.

Let us consider the Greek differences. Nearly all Greek words, excepting particles, connectives, and some adverbs, contain one or more inflectional morphemes, making Greek, like Latin, a highly inflected language, much more so than, for example, English. It is also inflected along lines very different from Semitic languages, involving extensive systems of roots or stems, normally unchanging and ending in a consonant, and of varying endings, normally beginning with a vowel. All students of Latin are familiar with this feature, as in *terr-a, terr-ae, terr-am,* and so on. By "roots" I mean those morphemes that form the nucleus of a word, and by "affixes" I mean those morphemes that are added to roots. A stem is a construction to which affixes can be attached. In highly inflected languages, which both Greek and Old Phoenician are, grammatical differences are expressed by internal phonetic modifications in the words, such as declensions of nouns and conjugations of verbs. It is at once clear how, at the morphological level, Greek differs from a Semitic language. They are inflected along very different lines. At the phonological level there are also major differences, some of which the ear will readily detect; others take practice in listening. But the important difference is morphological.

When we consider the grammatical forms of a Greek noun such as *logos,* we see the morphological difference from the Semitic languages at once. The word is composed of a stem, *log-,* ending in a consonant, and a complex system of endings, each beginning with a vowel. The stem remains constant but the endings vary, altering the meaning or syntactic function of the word, such as *logos* as subject, *logon* as object. Both phonological and syntactic forms of the word vary; in fact, *logos* has nine different phonological forms and ten different syntactic ones. For a highly inflected Indo-European language, almost exclusively composed of root morphemes (one or more) and inflectional morphemes (one or more) combined in this way, recording by means of a string of undivided consonants with no vowel indication would be intolerable and produce chaos.

As Greek developed, words were added by word formation, often in the form of derivational suffixes as in the words ending in *-sis,* especially important for later Greek abstractions. A noted example, important to the history of philosophy and law, involves the root *dik-,* from which more than twenty words are formed.

Some, such as the noun *dikē* (right, decision, justice), the neuter adjective *dikaion* (right, proper, just), and the noun *dikastēs* (judge), are found in early Greek, for example, in Homer and Hesiod, or in the early law code of Gortyn. *Dikaiosunē* (justice) appears first in Herodotus, and figures prominently in the first book of Plato's *Republic*. In the New Testament it is the word for "righteousness," as at Matthew 5:20. In addition, there are, for example, *dikazō, dikasmos, dikasmios, dikaiō,* and *dikaiōs*. Added to these is a whole other group formed with the *alpha-*privative, a vowel. Without vowel notation, the distinctions between these words breaks down, that is, *dkz, dksms, dksms, dik, dik*. Constant guesswork from a context to sort out which word was intended would result in chaos.

In the unadapted script, radical economy—twenty-two signs—would have been purchased at the price of nearly total unintelligibility for recording far too many Greek expressions. For example, without signs for the vowels and using signs for the consonants only, the last two words of the complete hexameter of the Dipylon graffito, *atalotatapaizei,* would be written: *T L T T P Z*. Considerable guesswork would be required to figure out the vocalization, which would be helped not much by word division, even had it also been introduced (which the earliest Greek inscriptions reveal it had not): $t^{x}l^{x}t^{x}t^{x}$ $p^{x}z^{x}$. Granted, the final two words of the Dipylon inscription are especially troublesome because of the initial vowel, the number of vowels relative to consonants, and the diphthongs, but similar breakdowns in intelligible transcription would have been common—very common—in attempting to use an unmodified Semitic script to transcribe spoken Greek. A bilingual Greek living in late-eighth-century Athens who wished to record the dancer's graffito on the Dipylon jug in the unadapted Phoenician script would have faced formidable obstacles to intelligible transcription head on, and without the *idea* of vowel notation, would have abandoned the enterprise.

It is a reasonable inference that the ambiguities and limitations of the Phoenician script would be so troublesome to bilingual Greeks that, before the idea of vowel notation, it would not occur to the Greeks to attempt to use the script for recording their language despite some considerable period of contact (just how long is disputed) between Greeks and Phoenicians. That is why no transitional inscriptions involving the use of consonants alone to record Greek have turned up. Also, the idea was born as a *system* of vowels, a whole, which is why I predicted many years ago that no transitional inscription involving only partial vowel notation would ever turn up (*pace* Gelb).[1]

Before the Greek achievement, at the level of phonology the dissolution of the syllable into its vocalic and consonantal components had not been accomplished, and so any explanation of the abecedarium from the Phoenician side would have been based on syllabic principles. That is what the distinguished Semiticist Ignace Gelb understood so clearly in emphasizing that *structurally* the Semitic scripts remained essentially syllabic in that each sign stood for a consonant *plus any vowel*. The reader supplies the required vowel from context, sometimes readily and sometimes not. In a famous ninth-century Phoenician inscription found on part of a bowl from the great temple of Astarte at Kition, the name of the dedicator appears, ML. Only because the Phoenician name Moula is so common can the guess be hazarded by Semitic scholars that this was the name of the dedicator, and so in translation the necessary vowels are provided. One can stare a long time, notable Semitic scholars assure me, at a transcription of the Ahirim Sarcophagus inscription (early tenth century) in which appears the consonantal sequence *wygl* and, without help from someone knowledgeable in Old Phoenician, have no idea that the vocalization should be *way-yigel,* "and he exposes." In many cases the proper vocalization can now be problematical because no speakers of the language are available for us to consult. Attempts at vocalization must be made on the basis of other Canaanite dialects, especially Hebrew, of course, because no early Phoenician literature has survived, or from later Punic inscriptions found at Carthage or elsewhere. Much dispute has attended the results.

To the consonantal confusion (for intelligible recording of Greek) that would be produced by the Semitic form of writing, some intelligent Greek ("the adapter") introduced the idea of vowel notation by taking over certain consonants that, as the abecedarium was being pronounced to him, had no apparent use for either pronouncing or recording Greek. The consonants were presumably being pronounced as monosyllables, as the vowels *a* in "bay," or *i* in "I am a Roman." Phonetically, he had, presumably, already isolated the vowel component from the consonantal component as he heard the open syllables repeatedly pronounced in Phoenician. He could pick out the least serviceable consonants—the so called "weak" consonants—for Greek and use their signs for the minimum vowels he needed, five. In this manner—in one place and at one time—as some clever Greek, probably a craftsman and probably on Cyprus, was listening to a friendly Phoenician recite the Semitic abecedarium common to Hebrews and Phoenicians, the idea of the Greek alphabet was born. The person, whoever he was, who adapted the script had a good ear, highly refined, I suggest, from hearing the precise pronunciation of the vowels as required by rhythms of the Greek hexameter, especially as it is sung to an accompanying instrument. He recognized a difference in the sounds that involve the obstruction of air by means of tension or slackness of the vocal chords as it passes through the oral cavity, and those sounds that required the shaping of the air's passage.

Having never seen a syllable written with two signs, such as *ba,* he nevertheless realized that this seeming atom (as pronounced) of sound was actually divisible. Its parts were, in fact, phonologically distinct and, as sounds, were made differently, utilizing different parts of the vocal apparatus, although in rapid succession and in speech glided together. Arguably, he was the first human fully to appreciate this *and* appreciate its importance to a recording system for human speech; that is, he distinguished between the sounds of consonants and vowels, whether or not he reflected consciously on the different ways they are made by the vocal apparatus. He then proceeded to create signs for a full system of vowels, five, the minimum necessary. He made no provision for long *ō* or *ē,* which are not critical to a complete system, as would be, say, *a* or *i* or, notably, *u.* But undeniably he set out to create a complete system of vowel notation. It was a deliberate, systematic, highly intelligent act, not a haphazard shot in the dark. It involved a good deal of phonological sophistication and much good sense. And it must have had a strong motive.

Much patience was required on the part of the instructing Phoenician, as no doubt again and again the Greek and his instructor went over the signs in order, first pronouncing the sounds they suggested to the Semitic ear and then finding the closest approximation for the Greek ear. The sibilants were, perhaps, the greatest obstacle, and the fact that the same confusion and mistakes over them are repeated in all local Greek alphabets has long been regarded as an argument that the process occurred only once.

About the place of *aleph, he, yod,* and *ayin* in the abecedarium, and how they became signs for vowels *a, e, i,* and *o,* there is, perhaps, little that is problematical. The *u* is a different story. In the usual reconstruction, one differentiation of the Semitic *waw* became the *digamma* (pronounced somewhat like the English *w*) and, in a secondary differentiation, became the vowel *upsilon* and was placed at the end of the Semitic abecedarium. It is possible that two languages, but three scripts, were involved in the moment of alphabetic transfer. The Cypriot syllabary has signs for the same five vowels as would be noted in the new Greek alphabet and, like it (initially), did not distinguish between long and short *e* and *o*. From this source, then, may have come the inspiration for *u,* for which there was a sign in the syllabary. In addition to the sign *u* alone, signs also existed for *ku, tu, pu, lu, ru, mu, nu,* and *su*. This could have been an important stimulus at the moment of script transfer. Did the handy *u* of the Cypriot syllabary, by way of stimulus diffusion, play a role? Even its shape, at least in the Classical Syllabary, a kind of high Y with floppy arms, bears a resemblance to the Greek *upsilon,* as, for example, the one scratched on the Dipylon vase (but remembering the inherent subjectivity of letter comparisons). For the older period, the *u* in the Paphian and Kourian signaries resembles an inverted V.

The adapter wanted a sign for vocalic *u,* without which his vowel system would be incomplete. He also wanted to retain the Greek consonant *wau* (Ϝ = *digamma*), important for metrical purposes (if that reason played any role). So, he left the consonantal *wau* in its sixth place in the abecedarium, where the Phoenician system had put it but, oddly, altered its shape. He then placed the vocalic *upsilon* at the end of the transmitted abecedarium, after the *tau,* making it the first addition to the Semitic sequence. The *u* has a very important role in the inventor's mind; that much is clear. No other letter is treated in a similar way. In the abecedarium transmitted to Crete, it is the *only* addition after *tau*; the other non-Phoenician letters are missing.[2]

I suspect that syllabic writing on Cyprus, the Classical Cypriot syllabary or its ancestors, may have been known to the Greek learner and played a role in the invention of the Greek alphabet. The coincidence that just these five vowels—and as a complete system from the start—would be noted in the new alphabet, when the Greek ear heard at least seven (excluding the diphthongs), is remarkable. Taken by themselves, neither the Cypriot syllabary nor the Phoenician consonantal script provided what the adequate recording of spoken Greek required. Elements of each, when combined, were all that was needed to yield history's first complete alphabet.

In sum, to take over what structurally ought to be regarded as an unvocalized syllabary and to convert it into the world's first complete alphabet was a major step in the history of writing and of human culture. Considerable phonetic and graphic adaptation was required. It happened once, and only once, and it was a Greek accomplishment. It was made possible, however, by the simplicity and genius of the Semitic consonantal scripts of the Levant, themselves a great advance in the history of writing.

Motive and Place

I have argued elsewhere that the motive behind the invention of the Greek alphabet was to record the hexameter, some few lines of Greek epical poetry. It will be helpful to recall that Greek and Semitic poetry differ in the way that speech is rhythmed by means of different devices in the two poetic traditions. The Greek tradition emphasizes meter, which involves a regular patterning of syllables that are either long or short. It is a quantitative rhythm rather than, as in much English poetry, a rhythm of stresses. The value of a syllable as long or short is a function of the sequence of the *vowels* the syllables contain, taken either in themselves or in relationship to the consonants. A singer and those accustomed to the performances of singers heard the vowel sounds very precisely. A recording device, a script, that ignored them or created ambiguity and chaos in the written version of the verses by failing to specify them would therefore be totally inadequate for recording verse. It simply would not be adopted or used for that purpose, unless, of course, this deficiency could be overcome. Also, Greek has many consonantal clusters with no intervening vowels, vowel clusters with no consonants in between, and a vast number of words with initial vowels. These features, too, presented insuperable obstacles to using a purely consonantal script to record Greek, whether poetry or prose. All appear at every point in a line of poetry, for example, the Dipylon graffito. If the motive in adopting the script were to produce in writing just a few intelligible hexameters, it could not be done. As a rough mnemonic, however, the unadapted script could have been used for short lists, mercantile ledgers, tagging, and marking. If this use were the motive of the first Greek alphabet users, then we would expect some early examples of this kind, but without vowel notation, followed, perhaps, by limited vowel notation. None, to my knowledge, has surfaced.

In the Archaic period the hexameter, the speech of epic, was felt to be the appropriate verbal vehicle for votive dedications. Before the alphabet, the verses were spoken or intoned, but not, of course, written. The adapter saw inscribed Phoenician dedications in fair abundance around him—the product of skilled Phoenician craftsman—which speak to deities, Ishtar or Baal. He desires his dedications to speak to the gods as well, but Apollo or Aphrodite, and in the appropriate epical words. But to do so, and record an intelligible hexameter or two, the complete alphabet was required, as we have seen. Did the inventor's desire to inscribe a dedication—perhaps also identifying it as his gift by incorporating his name, as Mantiklos would do—afford the the motive for the adapter to work patiently at the formidable task of adapting the mother script? This reconstruction is speculation, of course, but its features best fit the evidence and the social conditions of the eighth century.

I propose that the adapter's contact with the Phoenician model was not literary, legal, or governmental—for these he would be required to travel to hostile Sidon to view its archives, a dubious undertaking for any Greek of the period. Rather, it was inscriptional, for to view inscriptions he did not have to travel anywhere. What he viewed around him were repetitive and largely formulaic dedications and short proprietary phrases, somewhere along the trading routes or else at Al Mina or on Cyprus. Of course, accompanying oral instruction (and patience) was also necessary absolutely; no amount of silent staring at a Phoenician inscription could have given him the pronunciation of the words or the order of the signs in the abecedarium. More than casual contact was, it is certain, required. At least one party to the transfer—and almost surely both—had to be bilingual. For this reason and because of its geography, bilingual Cyprus becomes the inviting candidate as the locus of transfer. In the summer, the distant outline of a mountaintop on the great island is visible from the hills of the Lebanon. From the Bronze Age onward, both Phoenician and Greek ships regularly put in at its harbors, always driven by mutual and imperative need for metals. Several of its southern port cities were home to both Greeks and Phoenicians in the period of transfer.

Phonetic consonantism, the principle whereby each sign in the signary represents a consonantal phoneme—especially when four of them may also designate some vowels—can record Semitic speech tolerably well, as we have seen. But the adapter of the Semitic script was forced to abandon entirely the principle of phonetic consonantism, which was so fundamental to Semitic writing and gave it its beautiful simplicity, and to invent something new altogether. As Ignace Gelb argued long ago, in so doing this nameless benefactor of the human race took perhaps the most important—and the final—step in the developmental history of writing as a means for recording speech and thought. The linguistic atom could be divided no further.

The Precursors of the Greek Alphabet: The Proto-Sinaitic and Proto-Canaanite Inscriptions

Until about the middle of the second millennium, cuneiform, with all its cumbersome limitations—some perhaps perpetuated by the scribes whose lifestyle it supported—would be adopted as the method of writing by those peoples of the Near East who knew no writing system and sought one. Texts are heavily economic[3] in the earliest period, but a bit later votives, dedications, and incantations,[4] have an often-neglected role to play, as, of course, later still, do so-called law codes.[5]

About 1530 B.C., a development took place that would prove decisive for the history of alphabetic writing. As so often happens with alphabetic origins, there is no agreement about the historical reconstruction of the event or all aspects of the evidence. From the Sinai, in the area of Serabit el-Khadim and the famous turquoise and copper mines, have come a few inscriptions made presumably by workers who spoke a Semitic language and who sought to emulate the literacy of Egyptian masters by writing down some pieces of their own language. The *idea* of writing passed, therefore, by stimulus diffusion. Also borrowed were the ways some signs were made, based (apparently) on Egyptian hieroglyphs. But the fundamental principles behind Egyptian or earlier writing systems, however, were not adopted. Rather, a major simplification took place, resulting in the principle of consonantism. This may now be more fully defined as the principle whereby each sign in the signary indicates a consonantal phoneme *and nothing else,* although the sign itself represents the consonant *plus any vowel,* the proper vowel to be supplied by a reader. It is a simplification, as noted, uniquely suited to the morphological characteristics of the Semitic language group.

Whereas the basic principle is readily grasped, its interpretation remains controversial. As Ignace Gelb has written:

> The whole formal aspect of the Proto-Semitic and Semitic writings [that is, the formal sign comparison so diligently pursued by older Semiticists] is of secondary importance in comparison with that of the origin of the inner structure of these writings. . . . They all consist of a limited number of signs (22–30) each of which expresses the exact consonant, but does not indicate a vowel.[6]

The inspiration behind what is fundamental to Semitic writing cannot, in Gelb's view, have been either Aegean syllabaries of the Linear B or Cypriot type, or the logographic-syllabic cuneiform systems; it had to have been Egyptian, the third candidate available in the general region, with its principle of some one-letter signs. The idea was derived, specifically, from the approximately twenty-five simple signs, or monoconsonantal graphemes, in Egyptian writing, which correspond in inner structure, as Gelb views it, with the twenty-two to thirty signs found in the various West Semitic scripts. The signs determine only the consonants, but both writings, in Gelb's argument, remain structurally syllabic in that an unspecified vowel is implied. The borrowing Semites also threw out the excess (for them) baggage of word signs and phonetic signs representing consonantal clusters, retaining only what they needed most: signs that represented a single consonant. Hence, graphically, the roots of their words, dominantly three consonants, could be readily and simply displayed. Once again in the history of writing, the nature of the signary is shaped by the morphology of the language.

The new script, relative to the old cuneiform scripts, was far easier to learn and soon traveled from the Sinai to the ''homeland'' of Canaan, where the earliest finds, such as the Gezer calendar (the text is scratched on limestone), reveal a more developed form of the script. The oldest abecedary, dated to about 1200 B.C., has also recently (1974) been found, a pupil's exercise on a potsherd, at Izbet Ṣarṭah, east of Tel Aviv.[7] Four lines are random letters, no doubt practice forms, but the last—and fortunately the clearest—is an abecedary in the standard order of letters, with minor variations, perhaps mistakes. There is some reason to think the pupil learning his ABC's was an Israelite.

These inscriptions, all very short, are now usually termed Proto-Canaanite.[8] From this script Old Phoenician and Old Hebrew evolved. The epigraphical remains indicate that its initial use was not to record literary works, although in time it came to be used to record the earliest portions of the Old Testament, which seem to have been poetic.[9] Just when this occurred is uncertain. Nor were early uses mercantile, which is also, on the basis of any evidence and not assumption, a later development in the Greek case. When the script at last yields epigraphical remains we can read, we discover names, proprietary identifications, and brief dedications, followed by short personal communications.[10] That it was of some early administrative use seems likely, although—as in the Greek case—there is no evidence that any *early* uses were ever specifically administrative or mercantile.

Literate Traders and Ship Captains ca. 800 B.C.?

This may be the place to address again, but briefly, the widespread assumption that mercantile uses were behind both Phoenician and early Greek literacy, leading to the Greek adoption. Trading in Greek waters in the period of transfer, for Greek or Phoenician, seems largely to have been a matter of a few individuals banding together to share risks and rewards; it was confined to a few ships at most. The line between piracy and trade was sometimes fine, on both sides. "The Sidonians" "the Tyranians" and "the Gublites" (i.e., from Byblos) were how these independent coastal towns were known to their immediate neighbors in the eighth century; they were not a political or geographical unity or an empire. Commercially and militarily, the coastal cities were at a very low ebb and constantly threatened from the east.

Barter was the order of the day, at least among individuals, and no contracts seem to have been required. The only Greek evidence, epic, is unambiguous on the point. Even in the Semitic world, oral witnesses, the procedural eyewitness, were summoned where we would expect a written document. The earliest mention of a written contract in the Old Testament is in Jeremiah (32:9–12), acknowledged to be a late book. And preliterate memories were easily capable of any recording of goods, such as any that might be stored in the cargo hold of a ship (the merchantman was never a large ship). Homer himself (*Od.* VIII. 163) tells us that ship captains, as overseers *(episkopoi)* of a cargo, had well-trained *memories.* Euryalos wishes to goad Odysseus into an athletic contest, as befits a Greek hero-traveler, and resorts to insult by comparing him to a seafaring merchant. The stranger is no athlete,

> but like one who plies his way in a many-benched ship
> a master of sailors who are traffikers
> of cargo a rememberer and of freight an overseer
> and very greedy. . . .

The idea that ordinary sailor-merchants and traders, Greek or Phoenician, instructed themselves in the complexities of literacy to facilitate their daily business is, a priori, extremely unlikely so early. It is, really, to transfer our habits and experience back to another time and very different cultures, where there is no evidence for it.

Yet it is from these very persons—or else from craftsmen (as I prefer)—that the transfer of the script must have occurred, not from professional scribes. There is no evidence for scribal literacy or scribal controls at the moment of transfer or anywhere in the earliest Greek inscriptions, and the problem of access to Phoenician archives (we know of none in the colonies) by ordinary Greeks remains acute. Also, it is surely significant, for anyone who would postulate a mercantile motive, that the two Greek number systems are both relatively late, as Alan Johnston has again reminded historians, and were developed perhaps a century and a half after the alphabetic transfer.

But it is pointless to try to prove a negative. Those who hold to a mercantile motive for the Greek adoption of the alphabet have, as an issue of methodology, the burden to come forward with the evidence that supports their theory. Otherwise, surely, the old logical maxim cuts as inexorably as Ockham's razor: What is asserted gratuitously, *negatur gratis*.

A Single Inventor for the Semitic Version of the Alphabet

The recently recovered Izbet Ṣarṭah abecedary gives some confirmation to the theory that there was a single inventor (''the inventor,'' on the model of the phrasing sometimes used for his later Greek counterpart, ''the adapter'') of the Semitic proto-alphabet. It was he who established the order of the signs that, essentially, we still use and who also discovered an efficient mode of instructing in them. Unencumbered by the old cuneiform scribal tradition and with no need to follow the Egyptian practice of his masters, this man—a craftsman probably—sensibly used simple pictures (still recognizable in most of the Proto-Sinaitic signs) as an aid to recognizing and remembering them. Thus Canaanite *alpu, betu,* are the remote ancestors behind *alpha, beta,* the sign representing the initial phoneme of a meaningful word (''ox,'' etc.) in Canaanite. ''Presumably we owe our word 'alphabet' to the order chosen by this man.''[11]

One distinguished Semiticist who believes in a single inventor, as indicated in the quotation, is the well-known Dutch biblical scholar J. C. deMoor. The inventor's greatest discovery, according to deMoor, was that he realized that speech, despite its seemingly endless diversity and variety, in the final analysis is made up of a relatively small number of sounds, endlessly repeated. This is true enough, and a great discovery, but it was not the final step in the analysis of speech necessary to produce a complete or true alphabet. It was, however, the crucial first one. For the Semitic dialect that the inventor spoke, with its peculiar morphological characteristics, a drastic reduction in the number of signs required for a writing system, especially one not initially designed to record a complex literature, was possible: twenty-two consonantal graphemes. The signs do not, as in a complete alphabet, stand for the isolated phoneme, but a syllable with its vowel undetermined until read or pronounced by a reader informed in the language and provided with a context. From the standpoint of structure, what he produced was a radically simplified unvocalized syllabary or, alternatively, a quasi-alphabet.

The Greek Achievement: The Completion of the Developmental History of the Alphabet

The Greek invention thus had its way admirably prepared for it. Standing behind it are millennia of exploration and experiment with writing in the ancient Near

East. The most important of these was the form of quasi-alphabetic writing developed in the coastal cities of Syro-Palestine in the centuries immediately preceding the Greek innovation. Radical economy was, however, purchased at the price of immediate recognition by an unprepared reader. The point is a crucial one for the history of writing and one that frequently is not appreciated by Greek scholars. The ease with which letters were sent and received is, for example, cited as evidence that the Semitic scripts really worked about as well as the Greek alphabet.

A sequence of signs in Semitic writing, especially Old Hebrew and Old Phoenician, did not automatically trigger the memory and consciousness of a reader as to what spoken sound (at least approximately) should be made or what word, if he knew the language, should be supplied. Some guesswork was always necessary for Semitic writing, and without a context absolutely so. As deMoor observes, ambiguity could be rampant, and important letters were always orally delivered by messengers before the text was handed over for verification:

> . . . the ambiguities inherent in a vowelless alphabet could be overcome only if the written text were read by someone who had at least a general knowledge of the content . . . [even when *matres* had been introduced] only the oral tradition of the text could guarantee completely correct interpretation of the text. Especially when great literary works began to be recorded, this became a problem. A correct reading is most important in religious literature. But centuries had to pass before the next logical step was taken. This was done when Greeks added the most frequent occurring vowels to the alphabet.[12]

Only the Greek achievement, the final stage in the developmental history of the alphabet, would add immediate recognition to the desirable economy effected by the Semites in the number of signs in the signary, under thirty. This is what full vowel notation accomplished. For the Greek language it was a necessity; for the Semitic languages it was something closer to a luxury or a welcome convenience, one they later adopted under Greek influences, with diacritics or pointing. Taken together, these two features, economy and ready recognition, are what made widespread popular literacy—as opposed to the always restricted and largely scribal literacy of the Near East—possible for the Greeks and ultimately ourselves.

Alphabetic literacy, as it encountered an entrenched oralism and entered into various complex unions with it, shaped the unique character of Greek culture. Whereas not a *causus omnium* of course, it was a powerful factor in the formation of Greek culture and the evolution of its characteristic institutions. This would remain true from the inception of literacy in the Late Geometric Age, through its gradual development in the Archaic and High Classical periods, to its final triumph in fourth-century Athens in the philosophical schools of Plato and Aristotle. To tell its story has been the goal of this book.

Notes

1. First in 1971 in K. Robb, "The Dipylon Prize Graffito," *Coranto* 7 (1971), p. 17. There was a parallel phenomenon with the *matres lectionis*. Scholars had sought the source of each of them as an outgrowth of historical spelling. But Frank Cross has pointed out

that the *matres,* as used to specify the final vowels, came into existence as a complete scheme as soon as the idea itself was grasped. "Rather, once the idea of vowel representation was grasped, semi-vowels and weak consonants which were homogeneous with certain vowels were readily pressed into into service" (F. Cross and D. Freedman, *Early Hebrew Orthography: A Study of the Epigraphic Evidence* [New Haven, 1952], p. 32).

2. See Jeffery, *The Local Scripts of Archaic Greece* (Oxford, 1961) pp. 24ff; Powell, *Homer and the Origin of the Greek Alphabet,* p. 31; and A. Heubeck, "Die Würzburger Alphabettafel," *Würzburger Jarhbucher fur Altertumswissenschaft* 12 (1986), pp. 7–20. For the long history of *waw* as a *mater lectionis* for a word's final vowel and with the value ū, see Cross and Freedman, *Early Hebrew Orthography,* p. 3, n. 11. For its use in Aramaic orthography, see pp. 32–33 (but not in the Phoenician; see p. 19). This has caused a few historians to look harder in the direction of Aram as an influence in the invention of the Greek alphabet. All Greek alphabets have the *u* after the *tau.* However, two copper tablets claimed to be from Faiyum, and presently in New York and unpublished, contain repetitious abecedaria that lack the *u.* Controversy surrounds these curious tablets. In the past they have been for sale by private parties or through dealers and may still be, as far as I know. This is hardly damning, of course, for the Dead Sea Scrolls, and much else, has surfaced in the same manner. Are the tablets genuine eighth-century abecedaria? If they are early or eighth-century, are they Greek, North Semitic, or perhaps neither one? Or are they perhaps Hellenistic talismans, reflecting a magical use of the alphabet and writing? I have been told on good authority that chemical tests were run on the New York tablets and that the patina is quite similar in chemical structure, as well as appearance, to an ancient Egyptian ceremonial knife now in the Brooklyn Museum (Museum No. 65. 153). *If* the patina has been established as ancient—and I have not seen a published account—then the lettering under it is not a clever modern fake, for even the wiliest of forgers are not able (yet?) to insinuate modern lettering under ancient patina. Heubeck placed confidence in a similar tablet, also claimed to be from Faiyum and including twenty-four abecedaria. He judged it to be eighth-century and Greek. My strong belief is that all the Faiyum tablets must be left out of theories of the origins of the Greek alphabet, at least until further evidence emerges. On the origin of the vowel signs, two older articles are still valuable: F. Blake, "The Development of Symbols for the Vowels Derived from the Phoenicians" *JAOS* 60 (1940), pp. 391–415; and W. Chomsky "The History of Our Vowel-System in Hebrew," *JDR* n.s. 32 (1941–1942), pp. 27–49. Also see J.-G. Février, *Histoire de l'écriture* (Paris, 1948), pp. 208ff. (on the relative unimportance of the vowels, lexigraphically and grammatically, in the Semitic languages, compared to the consonants). The simple fact to be remembered is the high proportion of vowels to consonants in Greek and so their importance in Greek as opposed to Semitic languages. It is the vowel sounds, as precisely enunciated, that gave to Greek a "musical" sound even to outsiders. The contrasting emphasis on aspirates, sibilants, or gutturals were "barbaric" for Greeks, a word *(barbaros)* that has its origin in the unappealing sound of foreign words to the Greek ear.

3. Several long footnotes on the Near Eastern uses of writing and the sometimes neglected place of early dedications are preferable to interrupting my text. See, in addition, notes 4 (votive uses) and 5 (legal uses). Falkenstein, the great excavator of Uruk, argued in 1936 that economics is what called the first writing in Mesopotamia into existence, but it was writing at the service of a vast bureaucracy; all subsequent finds have confirmed his assessment (*Archaische Texte aus Uruk* [Berlin-Leipzig], 1936). The earliest inscribed tablets yet found at Uruk (Level IV) used a script that is both recognizably pictographic and in some of its signs demonstrably the ancestor of the later cuneiform script. The underlying language is uncertain. That of Uruk 3 (Jemdet Nasr) is Sumerian (S. Langdon, *Picto-*

graphic Inscriptions from Jemdet Nasr [Oxford, 1928]). Pictographs clearly seem to develop into stylized ideograms, which, in time, are being used to denote phonetic components of words, mainly syllables. This advance from stylized pictograph to a sign for a syllable is the natural one because the syllable sign represents what the ear hears in pronouncing words, syllables. The Sumerian writing system was initially logographic, comprising more than 2,500 signs. The usual reconstruction involves the gradual development to a logographic-syllabic system of cuneiform writing. A syllabic form of writing, or a sign for each syllable, even with a strong residue of pictographic and logographic elements—as in Sumerian, Akkadian, Hittite, and now Eblaite—greatly reduces the number of signs needed to record a spoken language. After about 2000 B.C. the number was in the hundreds, reduced from thousands. But logographic elements were retained, and many determinative classifiers were used. The full range of human speech could not be recorded in this writing system, and only professionals could recognize and read what had been recorded. At all times and in all languages to which it passed, among which were Sumerian, Babylonian, Hittite, Hurrian, Ugaritic, and later Aramaic and Persian, the mixed syllabic-logographic cuneiform writing (and so reading) remained the preserve of a small, specialized scribal class. Rulers and masses alike remained illiterate. The exception that proves the rule was the "scholar-king" from Nineveh who in a famous inscription boasts of his schooling, and that he can penetrate "the hidden treasure of scribal knowledge." Joan Oates, a noted expert, observes that few persons except scribes could read even minimally, noting that for the scholar-king "the level of his literacy may perhaps be questioned" (*Babylon* [London, 1986], p. 125).

Economic and administrative records dominate in all cuneiform archives of the ancient Near East, although other types of literary documents, or correspondence and lists, make appearances as well. These, too, are scribal documents—sometimes exercise pieces—and not available for popular reading or consultation. Whether some of the material they contain was, on occasion, read out to an assembled populace is debated, but probable. About the archives—if any still existed—of the Phoenician coastal cities in the period of script transfer, we have no direct information. Some precarious extrapolation may be ventured, perhaps, from coastal Ugarit much earlier, and some hints can be found in the eleventh century *tale* (this fact itself a source of difficulty) of Wen-Amon, the Egyptian priest of Amon-Re at Thebes. Wen-Amon, finding himself in reduced circumstances, is at the court of the King of Byblos to purchase lumber by bartering papyrus and other goods (papyrus must have been in *some* demand) and discovers that there is an archive of sorts. A court official or scribe is sent to fetch a document describing an earlier transaction, which the king proclaims will serve as precedent, and the court official, surely an official scribe, reads it aloud. Eleventh century evidence, at a time when the coastal cities were in their glory, is not much to go on for the late eighth century, when they were in serious decline and under constant political threat (and sometimes control) from the east. The papyrus of Wen-Amon's tale is presently in the Moscow Museum. It is translated by J. Wilson in J. Pritchard, *Ancient Near Eastern Texts Relating to the Old Testament* (Princeton, 1955).

Finally, I note the "pebble to wedge" theory for the origins of writing in the Near East, which continues to gain attention and which also finds economic recordkeeping as the initial stimulus. See D. Schmandt-Besserat, *An Archaic Recording System and the Origin of Writing* (Malibu, Calif., 1974); "Tokens and Counting," *Biblical Archaeologist* 46 (1983), pp. 117–120; and "The Envelopes That Bear the First Writing," *Technology and Culture* 21 (1980), pp. 357–385. Her very full evidence cannot be dismissed out of hand, although the theory is still developing. But, overall, the evidence for a first, at least *dominantly* pictographic stage (a pure one may be an illusion), followed by a dominantly syllabic stage—what Gelb called the unidirectional development of writing—is strong.

4. For Phoenicians in the period of script transfer, which is obviously the primary evidence, seven colonial Phoenician inscriptions from the eighth century are now known. Five are dedications, including the important Karatepe inscription (a fact sometimes overlooked). See P. Kyle McCarter, *The Antiquity of the Greek Alphabet and the Early Phoenician Scripts* (Missoula, Mont.,1975), p. 132. In his catalogue, Nos. 1, 3, 4, 5, and 6 are dedicatory; three of these are from Cyprus. McCarter's No. 1, the Kition Bowl from Cyprus, was interpreted by Dupont-Sommer, who was given the responsibility for publication, as dedicatory; McCarter (p. 44) suspects that it may belong to "the long oriental tradition of incantation bowls." For my purposes it makes no difference what kind of dedication it is. The debate is also a reminder of how troublesome the vocalization of the Phoenician script can be, an issue that plagues the interpretation of the important ninth-century Nora fragment. Brian Peckham interprets it as a dedication in "The Nora Inscription," *Orientalia* 41 (1972), pp. 457–468. The oldest Phoenician inscription from Cyprus, the famous Honeyman Inscription (*KAI* 30) from the ninth century, is funereal. At present writing, the Mantiklos Apollo, now in Boston, is the earliest surviving Greek votive statuette that is also inscribed. A Phoenician statuette dedicated to Astarte and recently found in Spain suggests that such inscribed votives could be viewed in all the Phoenician colonies or settlements in the period of alphabetic transfer and so, above all, on Cyprus. See F. M. Cross, "The Old Phoenician Inscription from Spain Dedicated to Hurrian Astarte," *HTS* 64 (1971), pp. 189–195. On epigraphical grounds, Cross dates the inscription to the eighth century (as had Solá-Solé when he published the inscription in 1966) and "probably in the second half of that century." In formulaic phrasing, one Balyatōn makes an offering to Astarte, for she had answered his prayers. Not very many years later, Mantiklos, in epical verse, asks Apollo to answer his. See the discussion and additional references in K. Robb, "Poetic Sources of the Greek Alphabet: Rhythm and Abecedarium from Phoenician to Greek" in E. Havelock and J. Hershbell (eds.), *Communication Arts in the Ancient World* (New York, 1978), pp. 26ff. (In a recent memorable discussion, while we shared the warm hospitality of the École Biblique in Jerusalem under the smiling visage of Lagrange, several specialists in Semitic inscriptions explained to me why the dating of the inscription from Spain *may* have to be lowered. I am not competent to evaluate their reasons.)

The first use of Sumerian writing was to produce lists of persons and commodities, followed by recording religious dedications and the accomplishments of notable persons, usually kings. But the impulse to record religious dedications is present near the onset of writing in the Near East and evident everywhere and in all periods down to and including the moment of transfer from Phoenician to Greek. Of the votive stone effigies characteristic of the Early Dynastic period, Seton Lloyd writes: "Fortunately the dedicatory inscriptions often found carved on them leave little doubt as to their intention. The effigy of an individual worshiper, translated into stone and placed in the sanctuary of a religious building, could be expected to intercede on his behalf with an appropriate deity" (*The Archaeology of Mesopotamia* [London, 1984], p. 111). Lloyd observes that all Sumerian sculpture, whether statues in the round or relief carvings, were religious and played some role in rituals. Votives were the most characteristic art form of the Early Dynastic period, and many were inscribed. See also J. Hansen, "Votive Plaques from Nippur," *Journal of Near Eastern Studies* 22 (1963). A very early votive plaque from Aegina bears one of the oldest Greek inscriptions, as noted in my chapter 2. This impulse, I suggest, is behind all votives that are left in temples, a practice in many cultures, including, of course, the Greek, where dedications become one of the largest categories of inscriptions to survive from the Archaic period. In my view it is also behind the strong desire to inscribe them, if a script makes this possible. Much relevant evidence can be found in E. Reiner, *Šurpu: A Collection of Sumerian and Akkadian Incantations* (Graz, 1958); R. Biggs, *ŠÀ. ZI. GA. Ancient Mesopo-*

tamian Potency Incantations (New York, 1967); A. T. Clay, *Epics, Hymns, Omens and Other Texts* (New Haven, 1923); and J. Seux, *Hymnes et prières aux de Babylonie et d'Assyrie* (Paris, 1976).

It is the ancient practice of offering dedications and incantations to deities, combined with the wish to add the stately epical words in which they were first spoken to the artifacts, which supplied sufficient motive for inventing the Greek alphabet, if I am correct. In this context, Paul Friedländer deserves to be quoted for a final time. His nearly forgotten words are from the introduction to a discussion of the hexametric epigram in a work begun long before the First World War (at the urging, as he often remarked, of old Wilomowitz himself) and finally published three years after the Second World War had ended. To those younger scholars who came to hear him in his last years at the University of California at Los Angeles and who were trained in classics, he urged the study of the oldest inscriptions because they were precious clues—and contemporary evidence, he insisted "beyond price" like the scriptural pearls—for a "way of life." It belonged to an entire people, not an elite, as he so often remarked, and it deserved the name "epical," a deliberately broader term than "Homeric." In what follows, quoted from p. 7 of *Epigrammata,* I omit Friedländer's references to specific examples drawn from that work.

> Imbued with the living epic poetry of their time, these Greeks strove after a stateliness which only such poetry could convey. In the earliest and best specimens [such as the Mantiklos "Apollo" inscription, or the Dipylon or Nestor inscriptions] it was more than a style of speech. The Corinthians and their colonists who wrote on their tombs such short, forcible epigrams [here Friedländer lists several epical sepulchral epigrams from Corinth and Corcya he had discussed] felt themselves and their dead akin to the heroes of Homer and of their own Eumelus. Explanatory verses transposed the primitive, though lively, scenes of early craftsmanship into the representations of a Homeric or Hesiodic event. The verses on the ex-votos [here Friedländer refers his reader to the total of thirty-one representative dedications in one or more hexameters he had discussed in detail] harmonized with the Homeric hymns heard in the same sacred precincts and gave a heroic tinge to that every day occurrence of ancient life: offering a gift to a god.

5. Starting in the Ur III period (2112 B.C.-2004 B.C.), the first law codes or collections of (some) laws began to emerge at the city-state of Ur, in the form of the Code of Ur-Nammu. The degree to which these famous early Near Eastern "codes" were ever used in deciding actual cases is also much in doubt. None, surely, is an attempt to record in writing all the known laws of a place that must guide a magistrate—to the exclusion of any other guide—in rendering a decision, which in this book I argue was achieved first by the Greeks. The most famous of the Near Eastern collections, the so called Code of Hammurabi (now preferably read as Hammurapi) consisting of 282 laws (as divided by modern editors) in casuistic formulation, is, plausibly, a collection of notable judicial decisions, restated in casuistic formulation, that touch on various issues of criminal, civil, commercial, and family law. That its selected laws ever widely served as the mandatory basis of actual court decisions is highly questionable. As is often noted, there is perhaps only one later legal reference to the code (and this one reference is disputed), even though, unlike Greece, where such records were not kept until late, substantial court records or decisions have survived. Then again, some oral promulgation of the laws may have been made by trained scribe-heralds in the larger cities; there are a few hints of some such practice. What is significant is that the "code" of Hammurabi could not have, and clearly never did, totally replace oral custom or common law at the local level.

In discussing the gradual recording of decision-laws in the earlier Eshnunna "code," H.W.F. Saggs describes a situation that I have argued was repeated in the early stages of written law in Greece: "Not only do the laws of Eshnunna not set out to be a comprehensive legal code, but there are major areas of human behavior in which problems must have arisen, which they do not even hint at. . . . Probably the procedure in such matters was so rigidly established by long standing custom that the need to prescribe [in writing] particular solutions never arose" (*Civilization before Greece and Rome* [New Haven and London, 1989], p. 163). Saggs notes that, in substance, large segments of the Eshnunna laws reappear in the Code of Hammurabi. They afford, therefore, strong evidence of how laws accumulated in writing, that is, gradually, not as sweeping comprehensive codes. I have argued the same was true in Archaic Greece. On the intention behind inscribing the laws of the Code of Hammurabi, Oates (*Babylon* p. 75) writes: "Perhaps the true purpose of such a document was justification rather than justice. If, as the prologue suggests, the inscription was addressed largely to the gods as a record of Hammurapi's accomplishments, and was intended to preserve for posterity the deeds of this just king, it could not have been more successful in its purpose." Add the recent cautionary treatment of the distinguished French Assyriologist Jean Bottéro, "The 'Code' of Hammurabi," chapter 10 of his *Mesopotamia: Writing, Reasoning, and the Gods* (Chicago and London, 1992), pp. 156–184. Placing "Code" in questioning quotes is not my addition; it is in Bottéro's text. Bottéro is especially convincing in arguing that these so-called laws were in fact reformulated *verdicts,* and in his qualifications concerning legal historians' uncritical use of the modern term, "code." The relevance of his remarks to the Gortyn "code" will be discussed elsewhere. Finally, some improved readings of the text are found in A. Finet, *Le Code de Hammurapi* (Paris, 1973).

6. Ignace Gelb, *A Study of Writing* (Chicago, 1963), p. 146. Among prominent linguists supporting Gelb's analysis are D. Ambercombie, *Elements of General Phonetics* (Edinburgh, 1967), pp. 38ff.; and E. G. Pulgram, "The Typologies of Writing Systems," in W. Haas, *Writing without Letters* (Manchester, 1976), pp. 23ff. Gelb has had his many critics, of course, including most recently—and from an unusual quarter—Michael Coe in his stimulating "The Word Made Visible," chapter 1 of his *Breaking the Maya Code* (New York, 1992). Coe, a distinguished Americanist and the curator of anthropology in the Peabody Museum at Yale, objects to Gelb's "hyperevolutionist" view that would put a *purely* pictorial stage at the beginning of all writing systems not adopted from the outside. Be that as it may, at the other end of the development, which is relevant to my argument, Coe *does* recognize—as many Hellenists have not—that full vowel notation was indispensable absolutely for the Greek adoption, for "they had to have the vowels to make their writing understandable" (p. 29). This book came into my hands too late to make use of it in my argument. But I do note Coe's valuable report (p. 14) of personally witnessing priests chanting in unison a verbatim oral "text" of the very long Zuni Creation Myth, which is intriguing.

7. A. Demsky and A. Kochavi, "An Alphabet from the Days of Judges," *Biblical Archaeological Review* 4 (1978), pp. 22–30. Izbet Ṣarṭah is thought possibly to be the biblical Ebenezer. See also A. Demsky, "A Proto-Canaanite Abecedary Dating from the Period of the Judges and Its Implications for the History of the Alphabet," *Tel Aviv* 4 (1977), pp. 14–27. The letters are clear on the broken (two pieces) ostracon, commencing with a curiously small *alep,* head pointing to the right, but firmly and deeply incised. Also, the letters are written from left to right. Later conventions obviously have not been established. There is a useful photo in *Biblical Archaeological Review* 4 (1978), p. 22. Five lines of writing, four perhaps letter-doodling, are recognizable; the fifth is the remarkable abecedarium. Archaeologically, the dating could be anywhere between 1200 B.C. and 1000

B.C. Attempts to arrive at a paleographic date by means of letter comparisons so early strikes me, as one outside the field, as futile. The remarks of Saggs on how arbitrary the early users of any script can be in making individual letter forms—and how arbitrary script comparison of individual letters can be, along with the role that pure coincidence plays—are especially valuable: "The variability in the direction of the writing and stance of letters, amongst the earliest examples of Greek script, could well have been the result of these factors; it is not necessary to posit two to three centuries of borrowings for which there is no epigraphic evidence whatever" (*Civilization Before Greece and Rome,* p. 87). I would add that these factors also suggest that the Phoenician models were not literary texts or archival documents, for by the eighth century the standardized Phoenician direction of writing was right to left. Seeing only a few signs or a few strings of them on inscribed artifacts, the direction would seem not to matter much. The Greeks would have no Phoenician models for longer texts. They came to produce longer texts gradually, it seems, as the need arose and literacy advanced. Herodotus' history must have been a phenomenon for its day.

8. The validity of a theory of a single inventor, a Semite working in the mines of the Sinai ca. 1500 B.C., can, of course, depend on dating the oldest Proto-Canaanite inscriptions and on whether the oldest Sinai and the oldest Canaanite scripts are, indeed, related, issues that must be abandoned to Semitic experts. A basic work that will lead to further bibliography is W. F. Albright, *The Proto-Sinaitic Inscriptions and Their Decipherment* (Cambridge, Mass., 1966), who dates the inscriptions to ca. 1500 B.C. Albright interpreted the inscriptions to be a form of the Canaanite alphabetic script. Not all scholars (e.g., Saggs) accept his decipherment and so question translations based on it. See also F. M. Cross, "The Evolution of the Proto-Canaanite Alphabet," *BASOR* 134 (1954), pp. 15–24; "The Origin and Early Evolution of the Alphabet," *Eretz-Israel* 8 (1967), pp. 8–24; and "Early Alphabetic Scripts," *BASOR* 160 (1975), pp. 97–123. By ca. 1000 B.C. or a little earlier, a script that is recognizably Phoenician (or Old Phoenician–Old Hebrew), seemingly a descendent of Proto-Canaanite, begins to appear in inscriptions, beginning (after the new abecedary) with the sarcophagus of Ahiram from Byblos (ca. 1000 B.C.), the Gezer agricultural calender (900 B.C.), and the Moabite Stone (ca. 840 B.C.).

9. At least the lost "Book of the Wars of Yahweh" and "The Book of Yashar," or "Upright," thought to have been the oldest Hebrew literature, were poetic. Some of the poetry is quoted in later prose narratives (e.g., Numbers 21:14; Joshua 10:12; 1 Kings 8:12). See W. F. Albright's isolation of an ancient poem in the biblical text in his "Oracles of Balaam," *JBL* 63 (1944), pp. 207–233. But how the text of the Old Testament was first compiled is shrouded in mysteries and questions similar to those that surround the text of Homer, and every assertion is risky. In both cases we must deal with the end result of a process, the stages of which cannot be recreated with any confidence. The earliest parts of the Old Testament must have first been written down on papyrus in the Old Phoenician-Old Hebrew script in the preexilic period. M. Haran has argued convincingly that the transition from papyrus to leather was associated with the canonization of the contents in "Book Scrolls in Israel in Pre-Exilic Times," *JTS* 33 (1982), pp. 161–173. The manuscripts in which the Old Testament has been transmitted to modern times are written with the postexilic square script that developed out of Aramaic writing. As is often noted, the famous allusion of Jesus (Matthew 5:18) to *yodh,* iota, the smallest letter, can be only to the square script. "I come not to destroy but to fulfill . . . not so much as one *iota* or one dot [*keraia,* i.e., hook as part of a letter] shall pass away from the law until all things are fulfilled." Learned rabbis, so concerned with unaltered transmission of a written text down to every letter and dot, were troubled by what they knew of the facts, finally pleading that the original script had, indeed, been the square one (on perishable materials, of course),

but because of the lapses and sins of the people the script was changed; then, in the time of Ezra (ca. 430 B.C.), the "original" square script was restored. For Homer, where there are problems and resilient legends of a different sort, the best recent, short treatment known to me is that Stephanie West, "The Transmission of the Text," in A. Heubeck, S. West, and J. B. Hainsworth, *A Commentary on Homer's Odyssey I* (Oxford, 1988), pp. 33–48. Her assessment of the early evidence, frail as that evidence is, revives and gives new respectability to the theory of a sixth-century standardization of the text. For some papyri evidence, relative to Hellenistic fluidity (however explained) in the text of Homer, see S. West, *The Ptolemaic Papyri of Homer* (Cologne, 1967).

10. The relevant inscriptions have been conveniently collected by H. Doner and W. Röllig in *Kanaanäishe und aramäische Inschriften* 1–3 (Wiesbaden, 1962–1964). There are valuable comments, intelligible to one who is not an expert, in J.C.L. Gibson, *Textbook of Syrian Semitic Inscriptions I: Hebrew and Moabite Inscriptions* (Oxford, 1971). The use of a version of this script at Ugarit—comparable only to Cyprus in the number of scripts found—affords us the only hints we may ever have of what a Phoenician archive at Sidon at the height of its power may have contained. As at Ugarit, the production and care of the archive would have been under scribal controls. For an overview, see J. C. deMoor, "Ugarit" in *Interpreter's Dictionary of the Bible, Supplementary Volume* (Nashville, 1976), pp. 928–931. Finally, for theories of oral tradition behind the first written biblical texts and of a constant interplay between the oral and written in the ancient Near East, see the masterly review of the literature, from Herder to Gunkel (d. 1932) to the present, in Robert Culley, "Oral Tradition and Biblical Studies," *Oral Tradition* 1 (1986), pp. 30–65.

11. J. C. deMoor, "Systems of Writing and Non-Biblical Languages: Canaan, the Alphabet," in A. S. Van Der Woude (ed.), *The World of the Bible* (Grand Rapids, Mich., 1986), p. 102. This is an English translation of a valuable compendium of contemporary biblical scholarship published in the Dutch in 1981.

12. J. C. deMoor, "Canaan, the Alphabet," pp. 102–103. Modern Semitic texts printed today without diacritics usually include *matres lectionis* for roughly one in four to one in five vowels, greatly aiding the reader, a point sometimes overlooked. The Old Phoenician script made no use of the *matres,* and other ancient scripts used them sporadically, mainly for terminal vowels. For further informed discussion of the serious difficulties this created, see James Barr, who concentrates on the problems confronting the *reader* of Old Phoenician and Old Hebrew, in "On Reading a Script without Vowels," in W. Haas (ed.), *Writing without Letters,* pp. 96ff. and *Comparative Philology and the Text of the Old Testament* (Oxford, 1966), pp. 196ff.

Bibliography

All works that have been cited in more than one chapter are included in the bibliography. Because each citation at first mention in my text contains sufficient information to track it down, I have not listed every work cited, although for my readers' convenience the bibliography contains most of them. I also list some works that influenced my argument or else are in notable disagreement with it, but which were not quoted.

For abbreviations other than the obvious, I have generally conformed to the *American Journal of Archeology* for the relevant journals. Otherwise, I have followed *L'année philologique*.

English spelling of Greek names remains an intractable problem. My goal has been intelligibility and ready recognition for a readership that, it is anticipated, will be drawn from many disciplines. In cases of doubt readers may consult the *Oxford Classical Dictionary* or Liddel-Scott-Jones, *Greek-English Lexicon*. In titles of articles or books, I have followed the spelling of the authors.

I regret that, for reasons of space, I have not been able to acknowledge in each instance the many works—some listed here—that have led me to valuable bibliographical sources, but I assure their authors that they have my warmest gratitude.

Adcock, F. E. 1927. "Literary Tradition and Early Greek Code-Makers." *Cambridge Historical Journal* 2, pp. 95–109.

Adkins, A. 1985. *Poetic Craft in the Early Greek Elegists*. Chicago.

Akurgal, E. 1968. *The Art of Greece*. New York.

Albright, W. F. 1966. *The Proto-Sinaitic Inscriptions and Their Decipherment*. Cambridge, Mass.

Alline, H. 1915. *Histoire du texte de Platon*. Paris.

Ambercombie, D. 1967. *Elements of General Phonetics*. 1967. Edinburgh.

Anderson, O. 1976. "Some Thoughts on the Shield of Achilles." *Symbolae Osloenes* 51, pp. 5–18.

Annas, J. 1981. *An Introduction to Plato's Republic*. Oxford.

Annibaldis, G., and O. Vox. 1979. "La più antica iscrizione greca." *Glotta* 54, pp. 223–228.

Arrowsmith, W. 1973. "Aristophanes' *Birds:* The Fantasy Politics of Eros." *Arion* 1, pp. 119–167.

Asmis, E. 1992. "Plato on Poetic Creativity." In *The Cambridge Companion to Plato,* ed. by R. Kraut, pp. 338–364.

Austin, J. 1970. "Performative Utterances." In *J. L. Austin: Philosophical Papers*, ed. by J. Urmson and G. Warnock, pp. 233–252.

Barnes, J. 1979. *The Presocratic Philosophers*. London.

Barr, J. 1966. *Comparative Philology and the Text of the Old Testament*. Oxford.

———. 1976. "On Reading a Script without Vowels." In *Writing Without Letters*, ed. by W. Haas, pp. 94–107.

Bea, A. 1946, "Die Entstehung des Alphabets." *Misscellanea Giovanni Mercati* 6, pp. 1–35.

Beazley, J. D. 1948. "Hymn to Hermes," *AJA* 52, pp. 336–340.

Beck, F. 1964. *Greek Education, 450-350 B.C.* London.

———. 1975. *Album of Greek Education*. Sydney.

Bekker-Nielsen, H., et al., eds. 1977. *Oral Tradition, Literary Tradition*. Odense.

Beye, C. 1972. "Rhythm of Hesiod's *Works and Days*." *HSCP* 76, pp. 23–43.

———. 1976. *The Iliad, the Odyssey, and the Epic Tradition*. 2nd ed., rev. Staten Island, N.Y.

———. 1987. *Ancient Greek Literature and Society*. 2nd ed., rev. Ithaca and London.

Bianchini, M. 1978. "La suggrafh; ed il problema delle forme contrattuali." In SUMPOSION *1974*, ed. by A. Biscardi et al. Athens.

Biebuyck, D., and K. Mateene. 1971. *The Mwindo Epic*. Berkeley and Los Angeles.

Birt, T. 1907. *Die Buchrolle in der Kunst*. Leipzig.

Biscardi, A., et al., eds. 1978. SUMPOSION *1974*. Athens.

Blake, F. 1940. "The Development of Symbols for the Vowels Derived from the Phoenician." *JAOS* 60, pp. 391–415.

Blegen, C. 1934. "Inscriptions on Geometric Pottery from Hymettos." *AJA* 38, pp. 10–28.

Block, H. 1940. "Studies in the Historical Literature of the Fourth Century B.C." *HSCP* Suppl. I, pp. 303–376.

Boardman, J. 1954. "Painted Votive Plaques and an Inscription from Aegina." *BSA* 49, pp. 183–201.

———. 1980. *The Greeks Overseas*. London.

———. 1982. "An Inscribed Sherd from al Mina." *Oxford Journal of Archaeology* 1, pp. 365–367.

Boegehold, A. L. 1972. "The Establishment of a Central Archive at Athens." *AJA* 75, pp. 23–30.

Bogaert, R. 1968. *Banques et banquiers dans les cités grecques*. Leiden.

Bolgar, R. 1969. "The Training of Elites in Greek Education." In *Governing Elites*, ed. by R. Wilkinson, pp. 23–49.

Bonner, R. J. 1902. *Evidence in Athenian Courts*. Chicago.

Booth, A. 1985. "Douris' Cup and the Stages of Schooling in Classical Athens." *Echos du monde classique* 29, pp. 275–280.

Boring, T. 1979. *Literacy in Ancient Sparta*. Leiden.

Bottéro, J. 1992. *Mesopotamia: Writing, Reasoning and the Gods*. Chicago and London.

Boudouris, K. 1989. *Ionian Philosophy*. Athens.

Bower, A., ed. 1987. *Selected Papers of F. M. Cornford*. New York and London.

Brickhouse, T., and N. Smith. 1989. *Socrates on Trial*. Oxford.

Brumbaugh, R. 1954. *Plato's Mathematical Imagination*. Bloomington, Ind.

Bücheler, F., and E. Zitelmann. 1885. *Das Recht von Gortyn*. Berlin.

Buchner, G., and C. Russo. 1955. "La Coppa di Nestore un inscrizione metrica da Pitecussa dell' VIII secolo avanti cristo." *Rendiconti Lincei* ser. 8, 10, pp. 215–234.

Bundgård, J. 1965. "Why Did the Art of Writing Spread to the West? Reflections on the Alphabet of Marsigliana." *Analecta Romana Instituti Danici* (Copenhagen) 3, pp. 11–72.

Burkert, W. 1985. *Greek Religion*. Cambridge, Mass.

Burns, A. 1981. "Athenian Literacy in the Fifth Century B.C." *JHI* 42, pp. 371–387.

Calhoun, G. 1914. "Documentary Frauds in Litigation at Athens." *CP* 9, pp. 134–144.

———. 1919. "Oral and Written Pleadings in Athenian Courts." *TAPA* 1, pp. 177–193.

———. 1927. *The Growth of Criminal Law in Ancient Greece*. Berkeley and Los Angeles.

Cantarella, E. 1979. *Norma e Sanzione in Omero*. Milan.

Capizzi, A. 1990. *The Cosmic Republic*. Amsterdam.

Carpenter, R. 1933. "The Antiquity of the Greek Alphabet," *AJA* 37, pp. 8–29.

———. 1935. "Early Ionian Writing." *AJP* 56, pp. 291–301.

———. 1938. "The Greek Alphabet Again." *AJA* 42, pp. 58–69.

Cartledge, P. 1978. "Literacy in the Spartan Oligarchy." *JHS* 98, pp. 25–37.

Cerri, G. 1979. *Legislazione orale et tragedia graeca*. Naples.

Chantraine, P. 1950. "Les verbes signifiant 'lire.' " In *Melanges H. Gregoire*, vol. 2, pp. 115–126. Brussels.

Cherniss, H. 1945. *The Riddle of the Early Academy*. Berkeley and Los Angeles.

Childs, W., ed. 1978. *Athens Comes of Age: From Solon to Salamis*. Princeton.

Chroust, A.-H. 1965. "Aristotle Enters the Academy." *Classical Folia* 19, pp. 21–29.

———. 1967. "Aristotle Leaves the Academy." *Greece and Rome* 14, pp. 39–43.

———. 1967. "Plato's Academy: The First Organized School of Political Science on Antiquity." *Review of Politics* 29, pp. 25–40.

Classen, C. 1959. "The Study of Language among Socrates' Contemporaries." *The Proceedings of the African Classical Association* 2, pp. 33–49.

———. 1989. "Xenophanes and the Tradition of Epic Poetry." In *Ionian Philosophy*, ed. by K. Boudouris, pp. 91–103.

Clinton, K. 1982. "The Nature of the Late Fifth-Century Revision of the Athenian Law Code." *Hesperia* 19 Suppl., pp. 27–37.

Coe, M. 1992. *Breaking the Maya Code*. New York.

Cohen. D. 1980. "The Prosecution of Impiety in Athenian Law." *Zeitschrift der Savigny-Stiftung für Rechtgeschichte* 118, pp. 635–701.

Cohen, E. 1973. *Ancient Athenian Maritime Courts*. Princeton.

Coldstream, J. 1968. *Greek Geometric Pottery*. London.

———. 1983. "Gift Exchange in the Eighth Century B.C." In *The Greek Renaissance of the Eighth Century B.C.*: Tradition and Innovation, ed. by R. Hägg, pp. 201–207.

Cole, S. 1981. "Could Greek Women Read and Write?" In *Reflections of Women in Antiquity*, ed. by H. Foley, pp. 219–245.

Cole, T. 1991. *The Origins of Rhetoric in Ancient Greece*. Baltimore and London.

Comotti, G. 1989. *Music in Greek and Roman Culture*. Baltimore and London.

Cornford, F. 1987. "Plato's Euthyphro." In *Selected Papers of F. M. Cornford*, ed. by A. Bower, pp. 221–238.

Cross, F. 1954. "The Evolution of the Proto-Canaanite Alphabet." *BASOR* 134, pp. 15–24.

———. 1967. "The Origin and Early Evolution of the Alphabet." *Eretz-Israel* 8, pp. 8–24.

———. 1975. "Early Alphabetic Scripts." *BASOR* 160, pp. 97–123.

Cross, F., and D. Freedman. 1952. *Early Hebrew Orthography. A Study of the Epigraphic Evidence*. New Haven, Conn.

Culley, R. 1986. "Oral Tradition and Biblical Studies." *Oral Tradition* 1, pp. 30–65.

Curley, T., ed. 1986. *A Course of Lectures on the English Law Delivered at the University of Oxford 1767–1773 by Sir Robert Chalmers*, vol. 11. Madison, Wisc.

D'Arcy, M. 1959. *The Meaning and Matter of History*. New York.

Davison, J. 1962. "Literature and Literacy in Ancient Greece." *Phoenix* 16, pp. 147–151.

———. 1963. "The Homeric Question." In *A Companion to Homer*, ed. by A. Wace and F. Stubbings, pp. 234–265.

Dawkins R., ed. 1929. *The Sanctuary of Artemis Orthia at Sparta*. London.

Dawson, M. 1966. "*Spoudaiogeloion:* Random Thoughts on Occasional Poems." *YCS* 19, pp. 37–76.

Demargne, P., and H. van Effenterre. 1937. "Recherches à Dréros." *BCH* 61, pp. 333–348.

DeMoor, J. 1976. "Ugarit." In *Interpreter's Dictionary of the Bible, Supp. Vol.*, pp. 928–931.

———. 1986. "Systems of Writing and Non-Biblical Languages: Canaan, the Alphabet." In *The World of the Bible*, ed. by A. Van Der Woude, pp. 102–118 (translated from Dutch).

Demsky, A. 1977. "A Proto-Canaanite Abecedary Dating from the Period of the Judges and Its Implications for the History of the Alphabet." *Tel Aviv* 4, pp. 14–27.

Demsky, A., and M. Kochavi. 1978. "An Alphabet from the Days of Judges." *Biblical Archaeological Review* 4, pp. 22–30.

Denniston, J. 1927. "Technical Terms in Aristophanes." *CQ* 21, pp. 113–121.

Detienne, M. 1986. *The Creation of Mythology*. Chicago and London.

Dewald, C. 1987. "Narrative Surface and Authorial Voice." *Arethusa* 20, pp. 147–170.

Diels, H., and W. Kranz, eds. 1956. *Die Fragmente der Vosrsokratiker*. 8th ed. Berlin.

Doner, H., and W. Röllig. 1962–1964. *Kanaanäishe und aramäische Inschriften,* 1–3. Weisbaden.

Dover, K. 1983. "The Portrayal of Moral Evaluation in Greek Poetry." *JHS* 103, pp. 35–48.

———. 1989. *Greek Homosexuality*. Cambridge, Mass.

Dow, S. 1960. "The Athenian Calendar of Sacrifices: The Chronology of Nikomachus' Second Term." *Historia* 9, pp. 270–293.

Düring, I. 1950. "Notes on the History of the Transmission of Aristotle's Writing." *Göteborgs Högskolas Arsskrift* 56, pp. 57–58.

———. 1957. *Aristotle in the Ancient Biographical Tradition*. Göteborg.

Dworkin, R. 1977. *Taking Rights Seriously*. Cambridge, Mass.

Easterling, P., and B. Knox, eds. 1985. *The Cambridge History of Classical Literature*, I. Cambridge.

Edwards, G. 1971. *The Language of Hesiod in Its Traditional Context*. Oxford.

Else, G. 1958. "Imitation in the Fifth Century." *CP* 53, pp. 73–90.

Euben, J., ed. 1986. *Greek Tragedy and Political Theory*. Berkeley and Los Angeles.

Evans, J. 1991. *Herodotus: Explorer of the Past*. Princeton.

Falkner, T. 1983. "Coming of Age in Argos: *Physis* and *Paideia* in Euripides' Orestes." *CJ* 78, pp. 289–300.

Ferrari, G. 1984. "Orality and Literacy in the Origin of Philosophy." *Ancient Philosophy* 4, pp. 194–205.

Fingarette, A. 1971. "A New Look at the Wall of Nikomakos." *Hesperia* 40, pp. 330–335.

Finnegan, R. 1970. *Oral Literature in Africa*. Oxford.

Fitzhardinge, L. 1980. *The Spartans*. London.

Flashar, H. 1958. *Der Dialog "Ion" al Zeuginis platonischer Philosophie*. Berlin.

Flory, S. 1980. "Who Read Herodotus' Histories?" *AJPh* 101, pp. 12–28.

Foley, H., ed. 1981. *Reflections of Women in Antiquity*. New York.

Foley, J., ed. 1985. *Oral-Formulaic Theory and Research: An Introduction and Annotated Bibliography*. New York.

Fontenrose, J. 1978. *The Delphic Oracle*. Berkeley.

Foote, P. 1977. "Oral and Literary Tradition in Early Scandinavian Law: Aspects of a Problem." In *Oral Tradition, Literary Tradition,* ed. by H. Bekker-Nielsen et al., pp. 47–55.

Fornara, C. 1983. *The Nature of History in Ancient Greece and Rome*. Berkeley and Los Angeles.

Fournier, H. 1946. *Les verbs "dire" en grec ancien*. Paris.

Fowler, D. 1987. *The Mathematics of Plato's Academy*. Oxford and New York.

Friedländer, P. 1964–1969. *Plato,* 3 vols. 2nd ed. New York.

Friedländer, P. (with the collaboration of H. B. Hoffleit). 1948. *Epigrammata*. Berkeley and Los Angeles.

Gagarin, M. 1981. *Drakon and the Early Athenian Homicide Law*. New Haven and London.

———. 1981. "The Thesmothetai and the Earlier Athenian Tyranny Law." *TAPA* 111, pp. 71–77.

———. 1982. "The Organization of the Gortyn Law Code." *GRBS* 23, pp. 129–146.

———. 1984. "The Testimony of Witnesses in the Gortyn Laws." *GRBS* 24, pp. 345–349.

———. 1986. *Early Greek Law*. Berkeley and Los Angeles.

Gallop, D. 1965. "Image and Reality in Plato's *Republic*." *Archiv für Geschichte der Philosophie* 47, pp. 113–131.

Garbini, G. 1971. "The Phonetic Shift in Sibilants in Northwestern Semitic in the First Millennium B.C." *Journal of Northwest Semitic Languages* 1, pp. 32–38.

———. 1978. "Un' Iscrizione Aramaica a Ischia." *ParPass* 33, pp. 148–155.

Gauthier, P. 1972. *Symbola: les étrangers et la justice dans les cités grecques*. Nancy.

Gelb, I. 1963. *A Study of Writing*. Chicago.

Gentili, B. 1950. *Metrica greca arcaica*. Messina and Florence.

———. 1988. *Poetry and Its Public in Ancient Greece*. Baltimore and London.

Gentili, B., and C. Prato, eds. 1979. *Poetarum Elegiacorum: Testamonia et Fragmenta*. Leipzig.

Gibson, J. 1971. *Textbook of Syrian Semitic Inscriptions, I: Hebrew and Moabite Inscriptions*. Oxford.

Goold, G. 1960. "Homer and the Alphabet." *TAPA* 91, pp. 272–291.

Grant, M. 1967. *Folktale and Herotale Motifs in the Odes of Pindar*. Lawrence, Kansas.

Griffin, J. 1980. *Homer on Life and Death*. Oxford.

Griswold, C. 1989. *Platonic Writings, Platonic Readings*. New York.

Grube, G. 1935. *Plato's Thought*. London.

Guarducci, M. 1935–1950. *Inscriptiones Creticae,* 4 vols. Rome.

———. 1967. *Epigraphia Graeca* I. Rome.

Haas, W., ed. 1976. *Writing without Letters*. Manchester.

Hägg, R. ed. 1983. *The Greek Renaissance of the Eighth Century B.C.: Tradition and Innovation*. Stockholm.

Hainsworth, J. 1982. "The Epic Dialect." In *A Commentary on Homer's Odyssey* I ed. by A. Heubeck, S. West and J. Hainsworth, pp. 24–32.

Haley, A. 1976. *Roots*. Garden City, N.Y.

Hammond, N. and H. Scullars, eds. 1970. *The Oxford Classical Dictionary*. 2nd ed. Oxford.

Hansen, M. 1975. *Eisangelia: The Sovereignty of the People's Court in Athens in the Fourth Century B.C. and the Impeachment of Generals and Politicians*. Odense.

———. 1976. "*Nomos* and *Psēphisma* in Fourth-Century Athens." *GRBS* 19, pp. 315–330.

———. 1985. T*he Athenian Ecclesia. A Collection of Articles, 1976–1983*. Copenhagen.

———. 1985. "The Athenian *Nomothesia.*" *GRBS*, pp. 345–371.

———. 1991. *The Athenian Democracy in the Age of Demosthenes*. Oxford.

Hansen, P. 1976. "Pithecusan Humor: The Interpretation of 'Nestor Cup' Reconsidered." *Glotta* 54, pp. 25–43.

———. 1983. *Carmina epigraphica graeca saeculorum VIII–V A. Chr. N.*, Text und Kommentare 12. Berlin.

Haran, M. 1982. "Book Scrolls in Israel in Pre-Exilic Times." *JTS* 33, pp. 161–173.

Harris, W. 1989. *Ancient Literacy*. Cambridge, Mass.

Harrison, E. 1960. "Notes on Homeric Psychology." *Phoenix* 14, pp. 63–80.

Hart, H. 1961. *The Concept of Law*. Oxford.

Harvey, F. 1966. "Literacy in the Athenian Democracy." *REG* 79, pp. 585–635.

Hasebroek, J. 1933. *Trade and Politics in Ancient Greece*. London.

Havelock, E. 1963. *Preface to Plato*. Cambridge, Mass.

———. 1981. *The Greek Concept of Justice*. Cambridge, Mass.

———. 1982. *The Literate Revolution in Greece and Its Cultural Consequences*. Princeton.

———. 1983. "The Linguistic Task of the Presocratics." In *Language and Thought in Early Greek Philosophy*, ed. by K. Robb, pp. 7–82.

———. 1986. *The Muse Learns to Write*. New Haven.

Havelock, E. and J. Hershbell, eds. 1978. *Communication Arts in the Ancient World*. New York.

Headlam, J. 1933 (1891). *Election by Lot at Athens*. Cambridge. 2nd edition, rev. by D. MacGregor. Cambridge.

———. 1892–1893. "The Procedure of the Gortynian Inscription," *JHS* 13, pp. 48–69.

Heinish, P. 1934–1935. "Das Slavenrect in Israel und im Alten Orient." *Studia Catholica* 11, pp. 201–218.

Herman, G. 1987. *Ritualized Friendship and the Greek City*. Cambridge.

Hershbell, J. 1970. "Parmenides' Way of Truth and B 16." *Apeiron* 4, pp. 1–23.

———. 1972–1973. "Parmenides and *Outis* in *Odyssey* 9." *Classical Journa*l 68, pp. 178–180.

———. 1983. "The Oral-Poetic Religion of Xenophanes." In *Language and Thought in Early Greek Philosophy*, ed. by K. Robb, pp. 125–131.

———. 1994. "Reflections on the Origins and Literacy of Plato's Dialogues." Forthcoming.

Heubeck, A. 1979. *Schrift*. Göttingen.

———. 1986. "Die Würzburger Alphabettafel." *Würzburger Jahrbucher für Altertumswissenschaft* 12, pp. 7–20.

Heubeck, A., S. West, and J. Hainsworth, eds. 1988. *A Commentary on Homer's Odyssey*, I. Oxford.

Hignett, C. 1952. *History of the Athenian Constitution*. Oxford.

Hommell, H. 1949. "Tanzen und Spielen." *Gymnasium* 56, pp. 201–205.

Hudson-Williams, H. 1949. "Isocrates and Recitations," *CQ* 43, pp. 65–69.

Hurwit, J. 1985. *The Art and Culture of Early Greece, 1100–480 B.C.* Ithaca and London.

Hussey, E. 1972. *The Presocratics.* New York.

Huxley, G. 1969. *Greek Poetry from Eumelos to Panayassis.* London.

Immerwahr, H. 1964. "Book Rolls on Attic Vases. " In *Classical, Medieval, and Renaissance Studies Presented to B. L. Ullman I,* pp. 17–48.

———. 1973. "More Book Rolls on Attic Vases." *Antike Kunst* 16, pp. 143–147.

———. 1990. *Attic Script: A Survey.* Oxford.

Irwin, T. 1979. *Plato's Moral Theory: The Early and Middle Dialogues.* Oxford and New York.

Isager, S., and M. Hansen. 1975. *Aspects of Athenian Society in Fourth Century B.C.* Odense.

Jacoby, F. 1947. "The First Athenian Prose Writer." *Mnemosyne* 13, pp. 13–64.

———. 1949. *Atthis: The Local Chronicles of Ancient Athens.* Oxford.

Jaeger, W. 1939–1945. *Paideia: The Ideals of Greek Culture,* 3 vols. New York.

———. 1948. *Aristotle: Fundamentals of the History of His Development.* Oxford.

———. 1960. *Five Essays.* Montreal.

Janko, R. 1982. *Homer, Hesiod and the Hymns: Diachronic Development in Epic Diction.* Cambridge.

Jebb, R. 1893. *The Growth and Influence of Classical Greek Poetry.* Boston.

Jeffery, L. 1956. "The Courts of Justice in Archaic Chios." *BSA* 51, pp. 157–167.

———. 1961. *The Local Scripts of Archaic Greece.* Oxford.

Jeffery, L., and A. Morpurgo Davies. 1970. "POINIKASTAS and POINIKAZEN: BM 1969.4–2.1, a New Archaic Inscription from Crete." *Kadmos* 9, pp. 118–154.

Jevons, F. 1886. *A History of Greek Literature from the Earliest Period to the Death of Demosthenes.* London.

Jidejian, N. 1968. *Byblos Through the Ages.* Beirut.

Johnston, A. 1979. *Trademarks on Greek Vases.* Warminster.

———. 1983. "The Extent and Use of Literacy: The Archaeological Evidence." In *The Greek Renaissance of the Eighth Century B.C.: Tradition and Innovation,* ed. by R. Hägg, pp. 63–68.

Johnston, A. W. and A. Andreiomenou. 1989. "A Geometric Graffito From Eretria." *BSA* 84, pp. 217–220.

Kagan, D. 1991. *Pericles of Athens and the Birth of Democracy.* New York.

Kearsley, R. A. 1989. *The Pendent Semi-Circle Skyphos: A Study of Its Development and an Examination of It As Evidence For Euboean Activity at Al Mina* (*Bulletin of the Institute of Classical Studies,* Supp. 44). London.

Kenyon, F. 1951. *Books and Readers in Ancient Greece and Rome.* Oxford.

Kirk, G. S. 1962. *The Songs of Homer.* Cambridge.

———. ed. 1964. *Language and Background of Homer.* Cambridge.

———. 1985. *The Iliad: A Commentary,* I. Cambridge.

Klegberg, T. 1962. *Bokhandel och bokförlag i antiken.* Stockholm. (Italian trans., Bari, 1975).

Knox, B. 1968. "Silent Reading in Antiquity." *GRBS* 9, pp. 421–435.

———. 1983. "Greece à la Française." *New York Review of Books* 30 (3), pp. 26–30.

———. 1985. "Books and Readers in the Greek World, I: From the Beginning to Alexandria." In *The Cambridge History of Classical Literature* I, ed. P. Easterling and B. Knox, pp. 1–16.

Koenig, J. 1962. "L'activité herméneutique des scribes dans la transmission du texte de l'Ancien Testament." *Revue de l'histoire des religions* (formally *Bulletin de la Société Ernst Renan*) 2, pp. 141–174.

Kraut, R. 1984. *Socrates and the State*. Princeton.
———. ed. 1992. *The Cambridge Companion to Plato*. Cambridge.
Lafitau, J.-F. 1724. *Moeurs des sauvages amériquains comparées aux premiers temps*, vols. I–II. Paris.
Lagrange, M.-J. 1905. *Études sur les religions semitiques*. Paris.
Lang, M. 1976. *Graffitti and Dipiniti* (= The *Athenian Agora* XXI). Princeton.
———. 1984. *Herodotean Narrative and Discourse*. Cambridge, Mass.
Langdon, M. 1975. "The Dipylon Oinochoe Again." *AJA* 79, pp. 139–140.
Lasserre, F. 1966. *Die Fragmente des Eudoxos von Knidos*. Berlin.
Lattimore, R. 1958. "Composition of the History of Herodotus." *CP* 53, pp. 9–19.
Lawrence, T. 1991. *The Odyssey of Homer*. Oxford and New York.
Leakey, R. *Origins: The Emergence and Evolution of Our Species*. New York.
Lee, D., ed. and trans. 1955. *Plato: The Republic*. New York.
Lesher, J. 1984. "Parmenides' Critique of Thinking: The *poludēris elenchos* of Fr. 7." *Oxford Studies in Ancient Philosophy* 2, pp. 1–30.
———. 1992. *Xenophanes of Colophon: Fragments*. Toronto.
Lesky, A. 1966. *A History of Greek Literature*. New York.
Leuman, M. 1927. "ἀταλός." *Glotta* 15, pp. 153–155.
Levi, D. 1969. "Un pithos inscritto da Festos." *Kritika Khronika* 21, pp. 153–176.
Levin, S. 1983. "The Origin of Grammar in Sophistry." *General Semantics* 23, pp. 41–47.
Lewis, N. 1974. *Papyrus in Classical Antiquity*. Oxford.
Lloyd, S. 1984. *The Archaeology of Mesopotamia*. London.
Lord, A. 1960. *The Singer of Tales*. Cambridge, Mass.
———. 1967. "Homer as an Oral Poet." *HSCP* 72, pp. 1–46.
Lynch, J. 1972. *Aristotle's School: A Study of a Greek Educational Institution*. Berkeley and Los Angeles.
MacDowell, D. 1962. *Andokides: On the Mysteries*. Oxford.
———. 1971. "The Chronology of Athenian Speeches and Legal Innovations in 401–398 B.C." *Revue internationale des droits de l'antiquité*. 3rd ser. 18, pp. 267–273.
———. 1986. *Spartan Law*. Scottish Classical Studies I. Edinburgh.
MacGregor, J. 1912. *Plato: Ion Text, Introduction and Notes*. Cambridge.
MacIntyre, A. 1984. *After Virtue*. 2nd ed. Notre Dame, Ind.
Maine, H. 1861. *Ancient Law*. London.
Marcovich, M. 1969. "On the Earliest Greek Verse Inscriptions." *ParPass* 126, pp. 217–223.
Marrou, H. 1982 (1948, French). *History of Education in Antiquity*. Madison, Wisc.
Martin, M. 1958. *The Scribal Character of the Dead Sea Scrolls*, 2 vols. Louvain.
Masson, O. 1976. "La plus ancienne inscription crétoise." In *Studies in Greek, Italic and IndoEuropean Linguistics, Offered to L. R. Palmer*, ed. by A. Morpurgo Davies and W. Meid, pp. 69–172.
Matthews, V. 1974. *Panyassis of Halikarnasos. Text and Commentary*. Leiden.
McCarter, P. 1975. "A Phoenician *Graffito* from Pithekoussi." *AJA* 79, pp. 40–41.
———. 1975. *The Antiquity of the Greek Alphabet and the Early Phoenician Scripts*. Missoula, Mont.
McIntyre, L. 1991. *Amazonia*. San Francisco.
Meiggs, R., and D. Lewis. 1969. *A Selection of Greek Historical Inscriptions*. Oxford.
Mellinkoff, D. 1963. *The Language of the Law*. Boston and Toronto.
Merlan, P. 1946. "The Successor of Speusippus." *TAPA* 77, pp. 104–111.
Miller, M. 1978. "Parmenides and the Disclosure of Being," *Apeiron* 13, pp. 12–33.

Mitford, T. 1971. *The Inscriptions of Kourion.* Philadelphia.

Momigliano A. 1966. "Historigraphy on Written Tradition and Historigraphy on Oral Tradition." In A. Momigliano, ed., *Studies in Historiography,* pp. 211–220.

———. ed. 1966. *Studies in Historiography.* London.

———. 1978. "The Historians of the Classical World and Their Audiences: Some Suggestions." *Annali della Scuola Normale Superiore di Pisa, Lettere e Filosofia,* ser. 3, 8, pp. 59–75.

Moravcsik, J. 1963. "The Third Man Argument and Plato's Theory of Forms." *Phronesis* 8, pp. 50–62.

Moravcsik, J., and P. Temko, eds. 1982. *Plato on Beauty, Wisdom and the Arts.* Totowa, N.J.

Morpurgo Davies, A., and W. Meid, eds. 1976. *Studies in Greek, Italic and Indoeuropean Linguistics, Offered to L. R. Palmer.* Innsbruck.

Morrow, G. 1961. *Plato's Cretan City.* Princeton.

Mueller, I. 1992. "Mathematical Method and Philosophical Truth." In *The Cambridge Companion to Plato,* ed. by R. Kraut, pp. 170–199.

Muhly, J. 1970. "Homer and the Phoenicians." *Berytus* 19, pp. 19–64.

———. 1985. "Phoenicia and the Phoenicians." In *Biblical Archaeology Today. Proceedings of the International Congress on Biblical Archaeology,* pp. 177–191.

Muir, J. 1982. "Protagoras and Education at Thourioi." *Greece and Rome* 29, pp. 17–24.

Murray, O. 1983. *Early Greece.* Stanford, Calif.

———. 1983. "The *Sumposion* as Social Organization." In *The Greek Renaissance of the Eighth Century B.C.*: Tradition and Innovation, ed. by R. Hägg, pp. 195–199.

———. ed. 1990. *Sympotica. A Symposium on the Symposium.* Oxford.

Murray, O, and S. Price, eds. 1990. *The Greek City from Homer to Aristotle.* Oxford.

Nagai, M. 1971. "Westernization and Japanization: The Early Meiji Transformation of Education." In *Tradition and Modernization in Japanese Culture,* ed. by D. Shively, pp. 35–76.

Nagy, G. 1984. "Oral Poetry and the Homeric Poems: Broadening and Narrowing of Terms." *Critical Exchange* 16, pp. 32–54.

———. 1990. *Pindar's Homer: The Lyric Possession of an Epic Past.* Baltimore and London.

Naveh, J. 1973. "Some Semitic Epigraphical Considerations on the Antiquity of the Greek Alphabet." *AJA* 77, pp. 1–8.

———. 1982. *Early History of the Alphabet.* Jerusalem and Leiden.

Nehamas, A. 1982. "Plato on Imitation and Poetry in *Republic* 10." In *Plato on Beauty, Wisdom and the Arts,* ed. by J. Moravcsik and P. Temko, pp. 47–78.

Nettleship, R. 1964. *Lectures on the Republic of Plato.* London.

Nilsson, M. 1955. *Die hellenistische Schule.* Munich.

North, H. 1952. "The Use of Poetry in the Training of Ancient Orators." *Traditio* 8, pp. 1–33.

Notopoulous, J. 1969. "Archilochus, the *Aoidos.*" *TAPA* 97, pp. 311–315.

Ober, J. 1989. *Mass and Elite in Democratic Athens.* Princeton.

Okepwho, I. 1976. *The Epic in Africa.* New York.

Oliver, J. 1959. "Text of the So-Called Constitution of Athens from the First Half of the Sixth Century B.C." *AJA* 80, pp. 296–301.

Ong, W. 1970. *The Presence of the Word.* New York.

———. 1982. *Orality and Literacy: The Technologizing of the Word.* London and New York.

Osborne, R. 1985. *Demos: The Discovery of Classical Attika.* Cambridge.

Ostwald, M. 1986. *From Popular Sovereignty to the Sovereignty of Law*. Berkeley and Los Angeles.

Owens, J. 1951. *The Doctrine of Being in the Aristotelian Metaphysics*. Toronto.

Page, D. 1964. "Archilochus and the Oral Tradition." In *Entretiens sur l'antiquité (Fondation Hardt)* 10, pp. 117–179.

———. ed. 1951. *The Partheneion*. Oxford.

———. ed. 1962. *Poetae Melici Graeci*. Oxford.

Parry, A., ed. 1971. *The Making of Homeric Verse: The Collected Papers of Milman Parry*. Oxford.

Patterson, C. 1981. *Pericles' Citizenship Law of 451–450 B.C.* Salem, N. H.

Patterson, R. 1985. *Image and Reality in Plato's Metaphysics*. Indianapolis, Ind.

Payne, H. 1951. *Archaic Marble Sculpture from the Acropolis*. 2nd ed. New York.

Peckham, B. 1972. "The Nora Inscription." *Orientalia* 41, pp. 457–468.

Peters, F. 1970. *The Harvest of Hellenism*. New York.

Pfeiffer, R. 1931. "The Transmission of the Book of the Covenant." *Harvard Theological Review* 24, pp. 99–109.

Platthy, J. 1968. *Sources on the Earliest Greek Libraries*. Amsterdam.

Popham, M., L. Sackett, and P. Themelis, eds. 1979–1980. *Lefkandi I: The Iron Age*. London.

Posner, E. 1972. *Archives in the Ancient World*. Cambridge, Mass.

Powell, B. 1988. "The Dipylon Oinochoe Inscription and the Spread of Literacy in 8th Century Athens." *Kadmos* 27, pp. 65–86.

———. 1991. *Homer and the Origin of the Greek Alphabet*. Cambridge.

Press, G. 1977. "History and the Development of the Idea of History in Antiquity." *History and Theory* 16, pp. 280–296.

———. 1982. *The Development of the Idea of History in Antiquity*. Montreal.

———. ed. 1993. *Plato's Dialogues: New Studies and Interpretations*. Lanham, Md.

Pringsheim, F. 1955. "The Transition from Witnessed to Written Transactions in Athens." In *Aequitas und Bona Fides. Festgabe für A. Simonius,* ed. by F. Pringsheim, pp. 287–297.

Reed, R. 1972. *Ancient Skins, Parchments and Leathers*. London and New York.

Reynolds, L., and N. Wilson. 1991. *Scribes and Scholars*. Oxford.

Rhoads, P. 1981. *A Commentary on the Aristotelian Athenian Constitution*. Oxford.

———. ed. 1984. *Aristotle: The Athenian Constitution*. New York.

Ridgway, D. 1992. *The First Western Greeks*. Cambridge.

Ringbom, S. 1965. "Plato on Images." *Theoria* 31, pp. 86–109.

Robb, K. 1970. "Greek Oral Memory and the Origins of Philosophy." *The Personalist* 51, pp. 5–45.

———. 1971. "The Dipylon Prize Graffito." *Coranto* 7, pp. 11–19.

———. 1978. "Poetic Sources of the Greek Alphabet: Rhythm and Abecedarium from Phoenician to Greek." In *Communication Arts in the Ancient World,* ed. by E. Havelock and J. Hershbell, pp. 23–36.

———. 1983. "Preliterate Ages and the Linguistic Art of Heraclitus." In *Language and Thought in Early Greek Philosophy,* ed. by K. Robb, pp. 153–206.

———. 1986. "Psyche and Logos in the Fragments of Heraclitus: Origins of the Concept of Soul." *Monist* 69, pp. 315–351.

———. 1991. "The Witness in Heraclitus and in Early Greek Law." *Monist* 74, pp. 638–676.

———. 1993. "*Asebeia* and *Sunousia*." In *Plato's Dialogues: New Studies and Interpretations,* ed. by J. Press, pp. 85–114.

———. 1994. "Orality, Literacy and the Dialogue Form." In *Plato's Dialogues: The Dialogical Approach,* ed. by V. Tejera and R. Hart. Forthcoming.

———. 1994. Review of J. Lesher, *Xenophanes of Colophon: Fragments. Journal of the History of Philosophy.* Forthcoming. (journal title)

Robb, K. ed. 1983. *Language and Thought in Early Greek Philosophy.* La Salle, Ill.

Robertson, M. 1948. "Excavations in Ithaca V. The Geometric and Later Finds from Aetos." *BSA* 43, pp. 9–124.

Robinson, T. 1974. *Plato's Psychology.* Toronto.

———. 1987. *Heraclitus: Fragments.* Toronto.

Rosenmeyer, T. 1965. "The Formula in Early Greek Poetry." *Arion* 4, pp. 295–311.

Roth, C. 1976. "The Kings and Muses in Hesiod's *Theogony.*" *TAPA* 106, pp. 331–338.

Ruschenbusch, E. 1986. *Solonos Nomoi: Die Fragmente.* Wiesbaden.

Ryle, G. 1966. *Plato's Progress.* Cambridge.

Saggs, H. 1989. *Civilization before Greece and Rome.* New Haven and London.

Salkever, S. 1986. "Tragedy and the Education of the *Dēmos:* Aristotle's Response to Plato." In *Greek Tragedy and Political Theory,* ed. by J. Euben, pp. 274–303.

Sandbach, F. 1977. *The Comic Theatre of Greece and Rome.* New York.

Sandys, J. 1912. *Aristotle's Constitution of Athens.* 2nd ed. London.

Santirocco, M. 1986. "Literacy, Orality and Thought." *Ancient Philosophy* 6, pp. 153–161.

Schapera, I. 1938. *A Handbook of Tswana Law and Custom.* London.

Schiappa, E. 1991. *Protagoras and Logos.* Columbia, S. C.

Schmandt-Besserat, D. 1974. *An Archaic Recording System and the Origin of Writing.* Malibu, Calif.

———. 1980. "The Envelopes That Bear the First Writing." *Technology and Culture* 21, pp. 357–385.

———. 1983. "Tokens and Counting." *Biblical Archaeologist* 46, pp. 117–120.

Schnapp-Gourbeillon, A. 1982. "Naissance de l' écriture et fonction poétique en Grèce archaïque: Quelques points de repère." *Annales (Economies, Sociétés, Civilisations)* 37, pp. 714–723.

Sealey, R. 1957. "From Phemius to Ion." *REG* 70, pp. 312–355.

———. 1976. *A History of the Greek City States 700-333 B.C.* Berkeley and Los Angeles.

———. 1990. *Women and Law in Classical Greece.* Chapel Hill and London.

Segal, C. 1962. "The Phaeacians and the Symbolism of Odysseus." *Arion* 1, pp. 17–74.

———. 1970. "Protagoras' *Orthoepeia* in Aristophanes' 'Battle of the Prologues' (*Frogs* 119–97)." *Rhein. Mus.* 113, pp. 158–162.

———. 1974. "Eros and Incantation: Sappho and Oral Poetry." *Arethusa* 7, pp. 139–160.

Shively, D., ed. 1971. *Tradition and Modernization in Japanese Culture.* Princeton, N.J.

Shute, R. 1888. *On the History of the Process by Which the Aristotelian Writings Arrived at Their Present Form.* Oxford.

Siewert, P. 1982. *Die Trittyen Attikas und die Herresreform des Kleisthenes.* Munich.

Sikes, E. 1931. *The Greek View of Poetry.* London.

Sinclair, T. 1932. *Hesiod: Works and Days.* London.

———. 1967. *A History of Greek Political Thought.* London.

Skafte Jensen, M. 1980. *The Homeric Question and the Oral-Formulaic Theory.* Copenhagen.

Snell, B. 1961. *Poetry and Society.* Bloomington, Ind.

———. 1969. *Tyrtaios und die Sprache des Epos.* Göttingen.

Snodgrass, A. 1974. "An Historical Homeric Society?" *JHS* 94, pp. 114–125.
———. 1980. *Archaic Greece*. Berkeley and Los Angeles.
Sperduti, A. 1954. "The Divine Nature of Poetry in Antiquity," *TAPA* 85, pp. 209–240.
Stock, S. 1909. *Plato's Ion: Text, Introduction and Notes*. Oxford.
Stolz, B., and R. Shannan, eds. 1976. *Oral Literature and the Formula*. Ann Arbor, Mich.
Stroud, R. 1968. *Drakon's Law on Homicide*. Berkeley and Los Angeles.
———. 1978. "State Documents in Archaic Athens," in *Athens Comes of Age: From Solon to Salamis*, ed. by W. Childs, pp. 20–42.
———. 1979. *The Axones and Kyrbeis of Drakon and Solon*. Berkeley and Los Angeles.
Svenbro, J. 1976. *La Parole et le marbre: Aux origines de la poetique grecque*. Lund.
Szegedy-Maszak, A. 1978. "Legends of the Greek Law-Givers," *GRBS* 19, pp. 199–209.
Sznycer, M. 1979. "L'inscription phénicienne de Tekke, près de Cnossos." *Kadmos* 18, pp. 89–93.
Taylor, R. 1968. "Law and Morality." *New York University Law Review* 23, pp. 611–647.
Tejera, V. 1971. *Modes of Greek Thought*. New York.
———. 1984. *Plato's Dialogues One by One: A Structural Interpretation*. New York.
———. 1993. *The City-State Foundations of Western Political Thought*. Lanham, Md.
Tejera, V., and R. Hart, eds. 1994. *Plato's Dialogues: The Dialogical Approach*. Forthcoming.
Thalmann, W. 1984. *Conventions of Form and Thought in Early Greek Epic Poetry*. Baltimore and London.
Thayer, H. S. 1993. "Meaning and Dramatic Interpretation." In *Plato's Dialogues: New Studies and Interpretations*, ed. by J. Press, pp. 47–59.
Thesleff, H. 1957. *On Dating Xenophanes*. Helsingfors.
———. 1966. "Scientific and Technical Style in Early Prose." *Arctos* n.s. 4, pp. 89–113.
———. 1967. *Studies in the Styles of Plato*. Helsinki.
———. 1982. *Studies in Platonic Chronology*. Helsinki.
———. 1993. "Looking for Clues: An Interpretation of Some Literary Aspects of Plato's Two-Level Model." In *Plato's Dialogues: New Studies and Interpretations*, ed. by J. Press, pp. 17–45.
Thomas, C. 1977. "Literacy and the Codification of Law." *Studia et Documenta Historiae et Juris* 43, pp. 455–458.
Thomas, R. 1989. *Oral Tradition and Written Record in Classical Athens*. Cambridge.
Thompson, G. 1965. *Studies in Ancient Greek Society*. New York.
Thorpe, B., ed. 1840. *Ancient Laws and Institutes of England*, vol. 1. London.
Tigerstedt, E. 1965. *The Legend of Sparta in Classical Antiquity*. Stockholm.
———. 1977. *Interpreting Plato*. Stockholm.
Traill, J. S. 1975. *The Political Organization of Attica*. Princeton.
———. 1986. *Demos and Trittys: Epigraphical and Topographical Studies in the Organization of Attica*. Toronto.
Trumpf, J. 1973. "Uber das Trinken in der Poesie des Alkaios." *ZPE* 12, pp. 139–160.
Turner, E. 1936. "A Writing Exercise from Oxyrhynchus." *Museum Helveticum* 13, pp. 236–238.
———. 1952. "Athenian Books in the Fifth and Fourth Centuries B.C." Inaugural Lecture University College, London. (Italian translation with significant expansion in *Libri editori e pubblico nel mondo antico: Guida storica e Critica*, Bari, 1975).
———. 1965. "Athenians Learn to Write." *BICS* 12, pp. 67–69.
Urmson, J., and G. Warnock, eds. 1970. *J. L. Austin: Philosophical Papers*. Oxford.

Van Compernolle, R. 1981. "La legislation aristocratique de Locres epizephyrienne, dite legislation de Zaleukos." *L'Antiquité Classique* 50, pp. 759–769.

Vanderpool, E. 1970. *Ostracism in Athens*. Cincinnati.

Vanderpool, E., and W. Wallace. 1964. "The Sixth Century Laws from Eretria." *Hesperia* 33, pp. 381–391.

Van Der Woude, A., ed. 1986. (1981 in Dutch). *The World of the Bible*. Grand Rapids, Mich.

Van Effenterre, H., and M. van Effenterre. 1985. "Nouvelles lois archaïques de Lyttos." *BCH* 109, pp. 157–188.

Vansina, J. 1961. *De la tradition orale: Essai de méthode historique*. Tervuren.

Verdelis, N., M. Jameson, and J. Papachristodoulou. 1975. "Archaic Inscriptions from Tiryns." *Archaiologike Ephemeris*, pp. 150–205.

Vernant, J.-P. 1975. "Image et apparence dans la théorie platonicienne de la mimésis." *Journal de psychologie* 2, pp. 133–160.

———. 1980. *Myth and Society in Ancient Greece*. Atlantic Highlands, N.J.

Vlastos, G. 1983. "The Historical Socrates and Athenian Democracy." *Political Theory* 11, pp. 495–515.

———. 1991. *Socrates*. Ithaca and New York.

Wace, A., and F. Stubbings, eds. 1962. *A Companion to Homer*. London.

Wade-Gery, H. 1952. *The Poet of the Iliad*. Cambridge.

Walsh, G. 1984. *Varieties of Enchantment: Early Greek Views of the Nature and Function of Poetry*. Chapel Hill, N. C.

Watkins, C. 1976. "Syntax and Metrics in the Dipylon Vase Inscription." In *Studies in Greek, Italic and IndoEuropean Linguistics, Offered to L. R. Palmer*, ed. by A. Morpurgo Davies and W. Meid, pp. 435–441.

Webster, T., 1959. *Greek Art and Literature: 700–530 B.C.* Dunedin.

———. 1972. *Potter and Patron in Classical Athens*. London.

Wehrli, W. 1944–1959. *Die Schule des Aristoteles. Text und Kommentar*, 10 vols. Basel.

West, M., ed. 1966. *Hesiod: Theogony*. Oxford.

———. ed. 1972. *Iambi et elegi Graeci ante Alexandrum cantati 2*. Oxford.

———. ed. 1978. *Hesiod: Works and Days*. Oxford.

West, S. 1967. *The Ptolemaic Papyri of Homer*. Cologne and Opladen.

———. 1988. "The Transmission of the Text." In *A Commentary on Homer's Odyssey* I, ed. by A. Heubeck, S. West, and J. Hainsworth, pp. 33–48.

White, N. 1979. *A Companion to Plato's Republic*. Indianapolis.

Whitehead, D. 1986. *The Demes of Attica 508/7–ca. 250 B.C.* Princeton.

Wilkinson, R., ed. 1969. *Governing Elites*. New York.

Willcock, M. 1964. "Mythological Paradeigma in the *Iliad*." *CQ* 14(n.s.), pp. 141–154.

Willetts, R. 1967. *The Law Code of Gortyn*. Berlin.

———. 1982. "Cretan Laws and Society," in *CAH*, ed. 2, 3.3, pp. 234–248.

Wilson, J. 1990. *Lawrence of Arabia*. New York.

Wolff, H. 1946. "The Origin of Judicial Litigation among the Greeks." *Traditio* 4, pp. 31–87.

Woodbury, L. 1976. "Aristophanes' *Frogs* and Athenian Literacy, *Ran*. 52–3, 1114." *TAPA* 106, pp. 349–357.

Youtie, H. 1971. "Βραδέως γράφων: Between Literacy and Illiteracy." *GRBS* 12, pp. 239–261.

Index